# ADOLESCENTS AT RISK

# ADOLESCENTS AT RISK

*Prevalence and Prevention*

JOY G. DRYFOOS

New York    Oxford
OXFORD UNIVERSITY PRESS

Oxford University Press

Oxford   New York   Toronto
Delhi   Bombay   Calcutta   Madras   Karachi
Petaling Jaya   Singapore   Hong Kong   Tokyo
Nairobi   Dar es Salaam   Cape Town
Melbourne   Auckland

and associated companies in
Berlin   Ibadan

Copyright © 1990 by Joy G. Dryfoos

First published in 1990 by Oxford University Press, Inc.,
200 Madison Avenue, New York, New York 10016

First issued as an Oxford University Press paperback, 1991.

Oxford is a registered trademark of Oxford University Press

Library of Congress Cataloging-in-Publication Data
Dryfoos, Joy G.
Adolescents at risk : prevalence and prevention / Joy G. Dryfoos.
p.   cm.
ISBN 0-19-505771-6
ISBN 0-19-507268-5 (pbk)
1. Socially handicapped teenagers—United States.   2. Teenagers—
Counseling of—United States.   3. Juvenile delinquency—United
States—Prevention.   4. Drug abuse—United States—Prevention.
5. Teenage pregnancy—United States.   6. High school dropouts—
United States.   I. Title.
HV1431.D79   1990
362.7'96'0973—dc20          89-70974   CIP

9 8 7 6 5 4 3 2 1

Printed in the United States of America

# Preface

This book is about young people aged 10 to 17 growing up in the United States today. Most of these children have a high probability of maturing into responsible adults. A certain group, however, have only limited potential for becoming productive adults because they are at high risk of encountering problems in school, at home, or in their communities. This is an exploration of four problem areas that have received a great amount of resources, public interest, and social concern: delinquency, substance abuse, teen pregnancy, and school failure. For the first time, we can see how risky behaviors interrelate and gain an understanding of the size and the scope of the prevention interventions needed.

If the problems are connected, then the solutions may require a more cohesive, less fragmented, approach than is currently in practice. This book moves toward a synthesis of solutions. The framework is made up of prevention programs that "work" to change specific behaviors in the four separate areas. Many similar and replicable elements are present in successful programs but should be integrated into a more effective strategy for assisting high-risk children.

Part I presents data about each of the four problem areas, showing who is at risk of each problem and with what consequences. Quantification of the overlap in these risky behaviors produces estimates of target populations for different levels of interventions. Part II examines prevention programs in each of the four fields, extracting workable concepts about program development on which there is consensus among experts. Part III incorporates the ideas generated from the categorical program reviews and presents a set of common concepts to guide the formulation of comprehensive strategies. The book concludes with examples of the application of these principles at the local, state, and federal levels.

The goal of this book is to provide evidence that the knowledge base exists on which successful programs can be initiated. The state-of-the-art of prevention of high-risk behavior, while incomplete and fragmented, is adequate for developing interventions that "work." Much has been written separately about each of these problem behaviors: each of these fields has its own literature and "gurus," independent categorical funding sources and agencies, advocates and detractors. This volume builds on that rich foundation and presents a unique synthesis of what is known.

This book is addressed to a wide range of audiences. It is a general resource guide for those interested in youth development, providing an overview of the issues of delinquency, substance abuse, teen pregnancy, and school failure and dropout. For practitioners in a specific field such as teachers, case workers, health educators, physicians, and program administrators, it offers descriptions of the components of successful programs. For researchers, it presents the major findings of youth surveys and program evaluations, with emphasis on the strengths and weaknesses of the many data sources utilized. And finally, for decision-makers, this work suggests policies that should be implemented at the local, state, and federal levels to further a more cohesive, more successful approach to preventing high-risk behavior.

The research for this work was undertaken for a project, *Adolescents-at-Risk: A Strategy for Intervention,* supported by the Carnegie Corporation of New York. I am deeply indebted to the foundation for giving me this unique opportunity to explore the complex subjects of adolescent behavior and programs aimed at changing that behavior. Vivien Stewart, Program Chair, Healthy Child Development, has been both a mentor and a friend, enriching my work with important observations and questions as well as providing me with consistent assurances that this project was worth pursuing. The interpretations of the findings are, of course, my own and do not necessarily represent the views of the Carnegie Corporation.

Many individuals and organizations contributed to this work by providing information and responding to requests for materials. I am particularly indebted to several intrepid friends who read and critiqued the entire manuscript: Ruby Takanishi, Elizabeth McGee, George Dryfoos, and Alice Radosh. In addition, Rebecca Kenard and Cynthia Rogers commented on specific chapters and Shana Millstein and Richard Jessor commented on earlier drafts of reports that led to this book.

I must also acknowledge the strong support I have received from Joan Bossert, Editor at Oxford University Press, who encouraged me to "tell it like it is" and who arranged for critical reviews by Scott Menard and Perry London. All of these people contributed enormously to clarifying and validating the findings presented in this volume.

In a sense, this book is a "status" report on an unfinished piece of work. What happens to American youth in the future will be partially shaped by the programs put forth in this book. But programs alone cannot change the social environment in which children live. Our society is being tested in a way that is different from all that has gone before. It has to face up to that potential loss of fully one-fourth of its youth who will never become productive citizens unless they receive immediate attention. I hope I have contributed to an increased awareness of just how critical this situation is and offered some new perceptions about what to do.

This book is dedicated to Paul Dryfoos who demonstrated that seemingly obstreperous children can mature into strong and responsible adults and to George Dryfoos who made it all possible.

*September 1989*                                                                                                 J. G. D.
*Hastings-on-Hudson, N.Y.*

# Contents

# ADOLESCENTS
# AT RISK

# 1

# Introduction:
# Hypotheses and Theories

Many children are growing up in the United States today without a hope of enjoying the benefits that come with adulthood. They are not learning the skills necessary to participate in the educational system or to make the transition into the labor force. They cannot become responsible parents because they have limited experience in family life and lack the resources to raise their own children. The gap between achievers and nonachievers is expanding. A new class of "untouchables" is emerging in our inner cities, on the social fringes of suburbia, and in some rural areas: young people who are functionally illiterate, disconnected from school, depressed, prone to drug abuse and early criminal activity, and eventually, parents of unplanned and unwanted babies. These are the children who are at high risk of never becoming responsible adults.[1]

There is growing concern in this nation about the future status and work potential of these high-risk youth. This concern has been heightened in direct proportion to the awareness that at least one-quarter of future labor force requirements will not be met unless these ill-equipped young people are helped. We cannot say that their problems are being ignored. The press and television are full of stories dramatizing the difficulties of young people, and hundreds of local, state, and national conferences address these issues and make recommendations about amelioration. There are literally thousands of programs addressed to preventing or ameliorating various problem behaviors. In fact, each problem area (e.g., school achievement, drugs, pregnancy, delinquency, suicide, mental health) has its own specialized constitutency, meetings, publications, and "gurus." One might well ask, if all of these resources are being used to combat the separate problems, why is the status of high-risk youth deteriorating?

An array of explanations can be offered in response to this critical question. Success is elusive because the programs as interventions are too fragmented and weak to have enough impact. They do not create change either in the individuals who exhibit the behavior or in the institutions responsible for the environment in which the behavior is learned. The programs are not targeted on the children who most need them, and many resources are wasted. The programs are not addressed to changing the quality of life of the child, but only to some symptom of disadvantage. The programs do not deal with the antecedents or the predisposing factors that lead to the behavior, but only with the outcome.

Yet, in each of the problem areas mentioned, there are successful programs. Some interventions do work. Children who start out with certain disadvantages do achieve in school, do not abuse drugs, are not delinquent, do not experience early unprotected intercourse. The hypothesis of this volume is that it is possible to document what works to prevent negative outcomes, to know which interventions produce what results under what conditions. It is possible to synthesize the diverse experience from myriads of categorical programs and extract the common concepts from successful models. And it is necessary to utilize these common concepts, interventions from all disciplines, that change individual or institutional behavior as the building blocks for designing more integrated and stronger programs that address high-risk children's needs.

In the same vein, it is possible to design programs that impact directly on the antecedents of problem behavior. It is possible to determine who within each community needs what kind of help and to launch prevention efforts *before* the damaging behavior occurs rather than after the fact. This is a program-oriented book. The challenge here is to extract and organize knowledge from academic sources to ensure that it will be valid and useful for program planning and implementation.

## Defining High-Risk Behavior

One goal of this study is to identify and quantify a broadly defined segment of the population: young people who are at risk of not maturing into responsible adults. In the United States, we expound the credo that all children are born with "equal opportunity," meaning that being born an American endows each individual with the same options: to live in a community, go to a public school, and to gain access to the economic system. It is not necessary to document that the American ideal has not been reached, and that many children are born with little chance of success.[2] But not all children born in poor social environments fail, nor do all children born into privileged circumstances succeed.

To define our target population, it is necessary to understand what problems create barriers to maturing into responsible adulthood. What are the markers of high risk? In this work, the concept of *antecedents,* events or conditions that occur prior to problem behaviors, is used to identify those markers. Included in this definition are *characteristics,* demographic descriptors such as age, sex, and race, and *predisposing factors,* such as social status and community quality which create a state of susceptibility. Some researchers refer to *determinants* of behavior, meaning *causal factors,* but this definition is too narrow for our purposes here. We often do not fully understand the causal links (the chicken or the egg) even when an antecedent and a behavior are clearly associated.

Social science and behavioral research have produced a large pool of information into which we can dip to find out who is at risk of what. In each different problem area, it is possible to construct an aggregate life history, to see what the antecedents are for specific behaviors. This literature can also be used to study what the consequences of the behaviors have been.

Four areas have been selected for this investigation: delinquency, substance abuse, early childbearing, and school failure. These are the four major problems that today's youth experience and that impact on their chances of growing up into healthy functioning adults. These problems interrelate in complex ways, and as will be documented, they have many common antecedents.

Before risk behavior can be quantified, it is necessary to define what constitutes this behavior in each field. In some cases, a behavior (smoking cigarettes) carries little or no immediate risk of damage, but the long-term consequences can be fatal (lung cancer). In other cases, a behavior (sexual intercourse) can have immediate negative consequences (unintended pregnancy), but when sufficient protection is used, negative consequences may be avoided. Risk behavior may have minor or major, short- or long-term consequences. In defining risk, those youngsters for whom there is a high probability (risk) that the negative consequences will occur would make up the primary target population for interventions. This means that some young people may not have initiated the behavior yet, but their demographic, personal, or social characteristics predict that they are vulnerable. Thus risk is used here in the actuarial sense (as insurance companies predict risk). Given certain characteristics, the probabilities that these behaviors will occur can be calculated and applied to current population estimates, assuming conditions are unchanged.

In the separate chapters about these problems (Chapters 3 to 6), risk status will be defined according to variables of interest (for example, early initiation of any substance, truancy, intercourse without contraception, poor grades). These variables will be presented in terms of "prevalence rates"—the total number of "cases" existing in a given area (the United States) at a particular time related to the total number of individuals exposed.[3] To gain a further understanding of who is at risk of what, prevalence rates will be presented by sex, age, race/ethnicity, and other relevant variables.

Prevalence rates by sex are important for determining whether gender-specific interventions are required. Age of initiation of some of the behaviors is necessary for understanding trends as well as needs. The tables in this book generally present prevalence data for 10- to 17-year-olds (broken into smaller cohorts, if available). Many studies of adolescents concentrate on ages 15 to 19, but the focus of prevention must take place earlier, and 18- to 19-year-olds are often already out of school and out of the range of interventions. Race/ethnicity rates are often used as surrogates for indicators of the effects of poverty and segregation. It would be preferable to present data by social class, since when these controls are added, racial differences are minimized. However, in most social research, rates for minority groups are presented because few investigators include social class indicators.

The analyses of prevalence are drawn from scores of different sources. Most studies of behavior are cross-sectional; they describe a certain population at one point in time. A few studies are longitudinal; a population is followed for a period of years to document changes in individuals. A few major studies include carefully selected national samples. Others select samples from a state or a community. Many studies are limited to a classroom or a school, or treatment groups, or clinic users. Each study uses its own definitions (for example, heavy use of alcohol may be measured by frequency of drinking or amount consumed at one time), age groups, descriptive variables, and methodologies. Most behavioral surveys are based on self-reports. As a result of this wide array of conditions, the data on which the prevalence rates are based are less than perfect. But they are the best data that could be located for the purposes of this study. Each chapter includes a discussion of sources and the limitations of present data.

## Estimating the Overlap in Problem Behaviors

While the separate prevalence rates for each problem behavior are of considerable interest, what we really want to know is the co-occurrence of these behaviors. How many young people are at risk of all or most of the negative outcomes from risk behavior? Are there a small number of children who are most likely to end up in each of these sets of statistics? No one data set has been identified that meets all the necessary criteria (age, sex, antecedent characteristics, the full range of behaviors) to produce an estimate of what proportion of the youth population is at risk of all, some, and none of the negative outcomes from high-risk behavior. However, several data sets contain enough evidence to allow the construct of "synthetic estimates" of the number of high, medium, and low-risk children between the ages of 10 and 17. This process is elucidated in Chapter 7, which shows how various data sets can be combined to develop rough approximations of the proportion of young people who probably fall into the various risk groups. These proportions are then applied to the population to develop estimates of the numbers of children potentially in the target population for various interventions. These numbers are important tools for helping decision-makers and the general public understand the magnitude of the task of assisting high-risk youth.

## Looking for Successful Programs

Having dealt with the quantification of the problems, we can then turn to the question of solutions. What works to prevent which kind of behaviors? The search for categorical programs designed to change specific behaviors leads beyond the library and into the field. The literature in the different areas (delinquency, substance use, adolescent pregnancy, and educational remediation) serves mainly to document that not very many human service programs have been scientifically evaluated.[4] However, we are greatly indebted to those programs that have been evaluated and are found to be effective; they prove that carefully planned and implemented social interventions do work. A number of evaluation efforts have never been published, but it is possible through the process of networking with researchers, foundations, and organizations to identify research reports that contribute to our knowledge base. Some programs can only be documented through site visits. Personal contact does not generate data; observations, however, can often refine and even alter conclusions drawn from "harder" data. Chapters 8 to 12 describe the processes undertaken to identify well-evaluated programs and enumerate the evidence on which the determination was made that a program is a "successful model."

Certain programs emerge nationally as "the" models of prevention, despite the lack of scientifically acceptable evaluation data. In some instances, the reputation of a charismatic program director has led to discovery. In other instances, a public relations campaign has put the program in the news for the purposes of marketing curricula.

## Demands of Program Evaluation

It is extremely difficult to prove that a program "causes" a change in behavior. If behavioral change can be measured, not an easy procedure, how can one prove that the change is attributable to the program? The following conditions are required: random assignment of a population to treatment and control groups and the capacity to track individual behavioral changes over time. If measurement is limited to pre- and post-surveys (do you drink, smoke marijuana, get in trouble with the police, have sexual intercourse, play "hookey"), there is no evidence generated of either long-term effects or diminished consequences. Survey responses may merely reflect a desire to please a teacher. It is possible to mount a program with an evaluation design that uses official statistics as a measurement tool—for example, school grades, arrest rates, or birth rates. In a sense, these are behavioral outcomes. But these kinds of data are difficult to collect, often inaccurate, and generally aggregated beyond applicability to a specific program.

It is not the purpose here to write a treatise on evaluation but merely to remind the reader that the state-of-the-art is far from perfect.[5] Nevertheless, where science may falter, common sense can be a great asset. Enough is known to proceed. It is not the lack of evaluation data that keeps this society from moving ahead to develop strong interventions to help disadvantaged children. Such qualities as leadership and commitment may be in shorter supply than research.

## Theories of Prevention

The theoretical construct on which this book is based is relatively simple. Prevention interventions should be directed toward the common *antecedents* of the categorical problem behaviors rather than at the separate manifest behaviors. Thus, if it is concluded that children who act out through drugs, truancy, or early unprotected intercourse generally lack parental support and guidance, than the strategy for prevention should focus on making up for that lack in parental support. Inter-

TABLE 1.1. Framework for Developing Strategies for Prevention of High-Risk Behavior

PREVENTION
INTERVENTIONS

$\downarrow$

| ANTECEDENTS $\longrightarrow$ | HIGH-RISK BEHAVIORS |
|---|---|
| *Demographic* | Delinquency and acting out |
| Age | Substance abuse |
| Sex | Early unprotected intercourse |
| Race and ethnicity | School failure and dropping out |
| *Personal* | |
| Expectations for education | |
| Perception of life options | |
| School grades | |
| Conduct, general behavior | |
| Religiosity | |
| Peer influence | |
| Peer use | |
| Conformity–rebelliousness | |
| Involvement in other high-risk behaviors | |
| Psychological factors | |
| Self-esteem | |
| *Family* | |
| Household composition | |
| Income, poverty status | |
| Parental education | |
| Parental role, bonding | |
| Parental practice of high-risk behaviors | |
| Culture in home | |
| *Community* | |
| Neighborhood quality | |
| Segregation | |
| School quality | |
| Employment situation | |

ventions that focus only on the specific behaviors such as substance use and sexual activity might be less effective because they are not addressing the antecedents of the behaviors. Table 1.1 presents a graphic representation of this model of prevention. Antecedents are grouped by four general categories: demographic, personal, family, and community. In this construct, prevention strategies would be designed to influence and affect these different categories of antecedents simultaneously. Programs would be shaped to be appropriate for different demographic age/sex groups (since these variables are immutable).

This work builds on that of Richard Jessor and his colleagues who advanced the concept "problem behavior syndrome."[6] Using sample survey data, they showed the clustering of adolescent high-risk behaviors (e.g., drinking, smoking marijuana, precocious sexual intercourse) and claimed that this constituted a kind of adolescent life-style, "an organized constellation of behaviors rather than a collection of independent activities."[7] According to Jessor, these behaviors had to be simultaneously addressed in order to change the life trajectory of these young people. He proposed that in each of the areas of life experience (personal, psychological, and social) negative "health compromising" behaviors had to be discouraged and positive "health enhancing" behaviors rewarded.

Most current prevention theories recognize the need for multidimensional approaches centering on family, school, and community. They build on our growing understanding of the interrelatedness of problem behaviors. Hawkins and his colleagues have promulgated the "social development model" to prevent a range of deviant behaviors.[8] Their research has led them to believe that the existence of strong social bonds to others exhibiting prosocial behaviors is an essential component of healthy childhood experience. Their model of prevention calls for three kinds of interventions to help high-risk children: the creation of opportunities for positive involvement with families, in schools, in communities, and among peers; the acquisition of social, cognitive, and behavioral skills to participate successfully in those social units; and the availability of reinforcements through consistent rewards for prosocial behavior.

Mueller and Higgins in their discussion of prevention models favor an "ecological framework" encompassing four different levels: individual or psychological, family, community or school, and societal.[9] They think of these environments as concentric circles surrounding an individual, and problems are defined as increasingly complex as they fall into more rings.

The emerging body of theories addressing prevention of substance abuse supports the multidimensional view (see Chapter 9). Gilbert Botvin, along with many others in his generation of researchers, believes that adolescent high-risk behaviors stem from a complex interplay of factors: social influences from parents, peers, and the media; personality characteristics; and values.[10] Thus, interventions must be designed to address these multiple antecedent factors by dealing with social influences and by teaching coping skills.

As we will see in the discussion of successful intervention programs, the Perry Preschool early childhood education program has received more attention than all others because of its documented success in altering the life course of participants.[11] This successful intervention was based on a very simple cause-effect model. The program designers focused on only two factors: setting and performance. By their definition, *setting* is the physical and social environment in which a child lives. *Performance* is behavior within the context of that specific setting. For their intervention, they characterized the setting as family poverty (unfavorable levels of parental education, occupation, and housing). The intervention was designed to offset the deleterious effects of poverty on school performance. A special curriculum was organized around the "key experiences" important for child development.[12]

While broad theories of prevention may be generally untested, some social and political scientists believe that enough is known to pursue specific strategies. Schorr bases a strategy on the facts linking high-risk behavior to poverty.[13] In her view, interventions must go beyond individual and personal aspects of children's lives and involve a large-scale social response. Her major theme is that sufficient knowledge exists to match effective interventions with problem behaviors (e.g., she believes that unintended pregnancy can be reduced through better access to family planning services). Within this framework, the problem behaviors would be addressed directly (rather than the antecedents), but the interventions would be more targeted, more intense, and more effective.

Ginzberg et al. review the individual, family, institutional, and societal forces that may negatively impact on the development of young people. In their prevention strategy, racism, poverty, and single parenthood are the three powerful deterrents to the establishment of the protective and supportive environment that children need to help them develop and mature.[14]

Prevention strategies range from simple cause-effect models that identify one or two powerful antecedents of problem behavior for a program's focus to complex multivariable risk assessments that call for an array of interventions. Some analysts believe that since high-risk behavior derives largely from social disadvantage, major social changes in the economic system are required. They see the behaviors as symptoms of larger social issues. Other analysts believe that interventions must be targeted on individuals and families, to modify behavior rather than to change institutions.

## Building a Prevention Strategy

Despite shortcomings in program evaluation, many common themes run through the research from all prevention fields. As we will see, a review of the "what works" literature (Chapters 9 to 12) will reveal a number of common components (Chapter 13). But the programs in each field are typically aimed at only one behavior, supporting the hypothesis that program planners think that each behavior emanates from a different part of the child. There are good and sufficient reasons why programs such as pregnancy prevention, substance abuse, school remediation, and delinquency prevention developed along categorical lines. Most problem-oriented approaches emerged from crises: the epidemic of teen pregnancy, crime in the streets, plummeting SAT scores, and, most recently, the "crack" disaster. The AIDS catastrophe has only recently emerged as a potential problem for inner city youngsters. Public funding, the support base for all large-scale efforts, responds to crises; money is generated by pressure groups who have to fit their demands into the exigencies of line-item budgets. Consider the crises just mentioned here and the structure of the U.S. government—each problem is the responsibility of a different bureaucratic jurisdiction, and this fragmentation carries down to the state and local levels (see Chapter 8). And the private sector mirrors the public sector with endless programs following along categorical lines, furthering the particular interests of the volunteer board that makes the policies and raises the money.

This structure for the delivery of services is not immutable. All over the country, programs are emerging that address the multiple needs of disadvantaged youngsters in a more comprehensive fashion. Chapter 14 describes programs that jointly address school failure, teen pregnancy, substance abuse, and delinquency. This holistic approach is being encouraged by state and local initiatives and foundations, which are moving intervention in the direction of collaborative, multi-agency efforts. The research leads to a strategy for developing a broad-based program at the community, state, and national levels, what we have called a Youth Development Initiative. The components that make up the package are drawn from documented evidence of what works.

In sum, this book reviews and abstracts state-of-the-art prevention strategies that have focused on problem behaviors. The prevention model directs interventions toward the common antecedents of these behaviors rather than toward the specific acts. This is an attempt to offer a workable, commonsense strategy for assisting disadvantaged children aged 10 to 17 to move ahead in school by lowering their risk of early childbearing, substance abuse, and delinquency. An assumption of this strategy is that existing institutions are amenable to change. And the knowledge base required for designing more effective programs, though fragmented, is sufficient to move ahead.

## Notes

1. Ginzberg et al. used the term "ineffective performers" to describe adolescents at risk—i.e., young people who would not be able to support themselves or their dependents, would get in trouble with the law, would not be able to sustain a long-term marital relationship, or serve in the armed forces. See E. Ginzberg, H. Berliner, and M. Ostow, *Young People at Risk: Is Prevention Possible?* (Boulder, Colo.: Westview Press, 1988).
2. See L. Schorr, *Within Our Reach: Breaking the Cycle of Disadvantage* (New York: Doubleday, 1988), pp. 1–22.
3. *Prevalence* is defined as the total number of cases at a given time. *Incidence* is the number of new cases occurring within a time frame, usually a year.
4. For a useful summary of the status of prevention program research, see D. Mueller and P. Higgins, *Funders' Guide Manual: A Guide to Prevention Programs in Human Services* (St. Paul, Minn.: Wilder Foundation, April 1988).
5. See P. Rossi and H. Freeman, *Evaluation* (Newbury Park, Calif.: Sage, 1985); S. Shortell and W. Richardson, *Health Program Evaluation* (St. Louis: Mosby, 1978).
6. R. Jessor and S. Jessor, *Problem Behavior and Psychosocial Development: A Longitudinal Study of Youth* (New York: Academic Press, 1977).
7. MacArthur Foundation, *At Issue* (Spring 1988).
8. J. Hawkins and J. Weis, "The Social Development Model: An Integrated Approach to Delinquency Prevention," *Journal of Primary Prevention* 6 (1985): 73–97.
9. Mueller and Higgins, *Funders' Guide Manual*, p. 7.
10. G. Botvin, "The Life Skills Training Program as a Health Promotion Strategy: Theoretical Issues and Empirical Findings," in J. Zins, ed., *Health Promotion in the Schools* (New York: Haworth Press, 1985).
11. J. Berrueta-Clement, L. Schweinhart, W. Barnett, A. Epstein, and D. Weikart, *Changed Lives: The Effects of the Perry Preschool Program on Youths Through Age 19* (Ypsilanti, Mich.: High/Scope Press, 1984).
12. D. Wiekart, *Quality Preschool Programs: A Long-Term Social Investment* (New York: Ford Foundation, 1989).
13. Schorr, *Within Our Reach*, pp. 30–32.
14. Ginzberg et al., *Young People at Risk*, pp. 122–31.

# PART I

# HIGH-RISK BEHAVIOR

# 2

# The Setting: A Description of Adolescents in the United States

Before problem behaviors are examined in detail, it is important to understand the current status of American youth and what comprises so-called "normative" behaviors. It is not sufficient to describe the situation only in aggregate terms; there are such vastly different life scripts that are being experienced by the subgroups in this complex and diverse society. Many books on adolescents solve this problem by presenting an array of vignettes from children's lives with detailed accounts of individuals and quotations from them.[1] This makes more interesting reading than statistics, but vignettes are not necessarily generalizable to the whole society. For an overview of the "setting," describing the youth population and the social and economic characteristics of various subpopulations, we turn largely to census data.[2] For a look at health status, we rely on national health statistics. However, to gain an understanding of adolescent developmental issues, different kinds of information are required. For these insights, the works of social and behavioral scientists based on small samples of subjects and personal observations will be explored.

## Demography of Adolescents

In 1987, there were about 28 million 10- to 17-year-olds in the United States, with half a million more boys than girls (Table 2.1).[3,4] More males are born than females, but the sex ratio reverses as populations grow older. This becomes an important factor when individuals reach the age of marriage (about 23 for females and 25 for males) because it controls the pool of partners, a particular problem for marriage-age black females, who outnumber marriage-age black males. The number of young people will increase over the next decade by about 10 percent because the number of births has increased every year since 1973, when the current 15-year-olds were born. One way to understand the expected change is to

TABLE 2.1. Population Aged 10 to 17 Years Old by Sex and
Race/Ethnicity, 1986 (in thousands)

| Sex and Race | 10–14 | 15–17 | Total |
|---|---|---|---|
| TOTAL | 16,687 | 11,110 | 27,797 |
| *Males* | 8,541 | 5,647 | 14,188 |
| White | 6,891 | 4,629 | 11,520 |
| Black | 1,315 | 808 | 2,123 |
| Spanish | 897 | 478 | 1,375 |
| *Females* | 8,146 | 5,463 | 14,009 |
| White | 6,541 | 4,446 | 10,987 |
| Black | 1,284 | 822 | 2,106 |
| Spanish | 816 | 520 | 1,336 |

*Note:* Total includes white, black, and others. Spanish origin may be white or black.

*Source:* Bureau of the Census, "Marital Status and Living Arrangements," *Current Population Reports,* Series P-20, No. 418, 1987.

compare the number of births in 1986, almost 3.76 million, with the number in 1973, 3.13 million. By the year 2000, babies born in 1986 will be 14 years old, right in the center of our population of interest. This group will be enlarged by immigrants as well as by increased numbers of births.

We are interested in the racial and ethnic distribution of the youth population for several reasons. Many of the problems discussed here are experienced differently by children from different social classes and cultures. However, the only descriptive data available come in "colors," typically black and white. Most social indicators and research studies are limited to cross-tabulations by race. These data provide valuable insights into the differences between races in regard to social and economic characteristics. In the absence of better data, race as a variable is perceived as a "surrogate" for economic and social disadvantage. Yet prevalence rates by race do not tell the whole story about the status of children and their families. In actual fact, the numbers of disadvantaged children who are white exceed the numbers in minority groups.

The vast majority of young people age 10 to 17 (81%) in the United States are white, with 15 percent black and 4 percent other races. According to census reports, 10 percent are of "Spanish origin" and are described as either white or black; however, almost all are probably counted as white. The national aggregate obscures significant differences in states and local areas. In California and Texas, more than half of the public school children are Hispanic or other nonwhites, and in many cities, almost the entire youth population is made up of "minorities." The minority population is growing both from higher birth rates among nonwhites and from immigration. The Census Bureau projects that, by the year 2000, 20 percent of the youth population will be black and 18 percent Hispanic . . . and that a decade later, the Hispanic portion of the youth population will have increased to 23 percent, while blacks will make up 21 percent.

## Social and Economic Characteristics

One in four of our nation's youth live with only one parent, typically the child's mother. However, among black families, more than half of the young people do not have a father in the home. The significant increase in the number of female-headed households represents a dramatic shift away from what Americans think of as the ideal family—mom at home, dad on the job, and the children in school. In many homes, dad is absent and mom is out working (and many of the children are not in school). Almost 70 percent of women with children aged 14 to 17 are currently in the labor force.

The indicator typically used to describe the economic status of the American family is the "poverty rate." This is the proportion of families that fall below a threshold, an index based on family size and amount of income in a year, adjusted annually according to changes in the Consumer Price Index and food consumption patterns. In 1987, the index was $11,611 for a family of four, assuming that families spend approximately one-third of their income on food. (The median family income in the same year was $30,863.) Poverty rates have fluctuated over the past decade from a relative low point in 1978 to a peak in 1983, with continuing high rates through the 1980s.

Currently, 21 percent of young people aged 10 to 14 are in families with incomes below the poverty level as are 17 percent of 15- to 17-year-olds (Table 2.2). The younger the child, the more likely the family is to be poor. In 1986, about 5.5 million 10- to 17-year-olds were in these very disadvantaged families. Black and Hispanic children are much more likely to be poor than white children: 45 percent of black and 41 percent of Hispanic youngsters were in poverty families compared with 13 percent of white young people. The prevalence of poverty among Hispanics is related to their point of origin. Puerto Rican families have the lowest incomes, followed by Mexican-Americans; Cuban families have higher incomes than other Hispanic families (but still lower than non-Hispanic families).[5]

TABLE 2.2. Youth in Poverty by Age and Race/Ethnicity, 1986 (in thousands)

| Sex and Race | Percentage in Poverty by Age | | | Number in Poverty by Age | | |
|---|---|---|---|---|---|---|
| | 10–14 | 15–17 | 18–19 | 10–14 | 15–17 | 18–19 |
| TOTAL | 21 | 17 | 17 | 3,586 | 1,889 | 1,219 |
| *Males* | 21 | 17 | 15 | 1,794 | 960 | 530 |
| White | 17 | 13 | 12 | 1,171 | 602 | 354 |
| Black | 44 | 38 | 30 | 579 | 307 | 148 |
| Spanish | 42 | 38 | 29 | 377 | 182 | 94 |
| *Females* | 22 | 17 | 19 | 1,792 | 929 | 689 |
| White | 17 | 13 | 17 | 1,112 | 578 | 504 |
| Black | 46 | 36 | 34 | 591 | 296 | 186 |
| Spanish | 39 | 40 | 32 | 318 | 208 | 101 |

*Note:* Spanish origin may be white or black.

*Source:* Bureau of the Census, "Poverty in the U.S.," *Current Population Reports*, Series P-60, No. 158, 1987.

One tends to associate the problem of poverty with the problem of racism, and clearly the two are related. However, because the white population is so dominant, 64 percent of all poor youth aged 10 to 17 are white. There are 3.5 million poor white youth in this country as well as 1.8 million poor black youth. About 1.2 million of the youth in poverty families are Hispanic youth (and are included among the white and black totals).

Living in a female-headed household increases the probability of poverty. While 11 percent of all families are in poverty, 46 percent of the female-headed households that include children are in poverty. As we have seen, the median income for all U.S. families is more than $30,000, but for a female householder with children and no husband present, the median is around $9,000. And the more children, the greater the chances of being poor. Many of these families rely on public assistance for support. The 3.7 million families currently receiving Aid to Families with Dependent Children (AFDC) include approximately 3 million children aged 10 to 17. Thus, roughly two-thirds of the nation's youth who are in poverty families are currently welfare recipients.

Poverty status and race are powerful determinants of where children live. Almost half of American children now reside in suburbs of metropolitan areas, 30 percent live in central cities, and 23 percent live in nonmetropolitan areas. About 2 percent of all children under the age of 18 still live on farms. The distribution of children under the age of 18 living in each kind of area according to race and poverty status shows important differences (Table 2.3).

Black children are much more likely to live in central cities and much less likely to be suburbanites no matter what their income status is. White children who are poor are also less likely to live in the suburbs than nonpoor children. In aggregate, about 8.5 million 10- to 17-year-olds live in central cities, 2.5 million of them in poverty families. About 13 million youth live in suburban areas, outside of central cities, and 1.5 million are poor. The remaining 6.5 million live outside of metropolitan areas; of these, 1.5 million are poor. These huge numbers and their distribution reflect the diversity and vastness of this country and give evidence that interventions to assist disadvantaged families and their children cannot be limited to minority populations in inner cities.

Moreover, Americans move a lot. During the past five years, two out of five

TABLE 2.3. Percentage of Children under Age 18 by Residence, Race, and Poverty Status, 1986

| | White | | Black | |
|---|---|---|---|---|
| | Not Poor | Poor | Not Poor | Poor |
| TOTAL | 100% | 100% | 100% | 100% |
| Live in central city | 23 | 35 | 54 | 57 |
| Live in suburbs | 54 | 34 | 30 | 18 |
| Live in nonurban area | 23 | 31 | 16 | 25 |

*Source:* Bureau of the Census, "Poverty in the U.S.," *Current Population Reports,* Series P-60, No. 158, 1987.

10- to 14-year-olds moved, almost half to a different county. This indicates the degree to which children live in shifting environments, with frequent changes in schools and adjustments to new family conformations and new communities. Homelessness is a relatively recent phenomenon that shapes the lives of young people. It has been estimated that as many as 2.5 million children in the United States are in homeless families.[6] One study of children living in temporary housing estimated that 36 percent of the middle-school-age children did not regularly attend school.[7] No data are available on the age of the homeless children, but judging from news media and anecdotal accounts, many are in the 10- to 17-year-old age group. They are, of course, living in very dangerous settings with high prevalences of substance abuse, promiscuous sex, crime, and depression. In addition, there are runaway youth who live on the streets and are probably not counted among the homeless.

As should be evident from the data about residence, poverty, and race, social class in the United States is a major predictor of where people live. Suburbia is the creation of an upwardly mobile middle class that considers getting out of congested urban areas the symbol of "making it." While we have access to an array of census statistics about the social and economic status of American families, virtually no attention is paid to the question of social class. That is one reason why society perceives that the problem of disadvantage is associated with being black or Hispanic rather than understanding that social class is also a determinant. In other countries (for example, England), families are typed by one of five social classes, according to the occupation, education, and income of the householders. Thus, it is possible to examine various social and health indicators by social class (for example, the prevalence of tuberculosis). In this short summary of available data, it is clear that a sizable number of young people—black, white, and Hispanic—are growing up in families with low social-economic status. One simple example of social class effects comes from a census survey of access to home computers by students; 15 percent of families with school-age children reported owning a computer. However, computers were owned by only 8 percent of families in which the parents were high school graduates compared with 80 percent for college graduates. Just 3 percent of families with incomes below $10,000 had computers compared with 85 percent with incomes of $50,000 or more. As we review the findings from specialized surveys in Chapters 3 to 6, the impact of social class on each of the problem behaviors will be examined.

## Youth in the Labor Force

Although we are primarily interested in younger adolescents, the issue of work is important. Many young people have jobs today, mostly part time, and mostly in what is considered marginal employment. There are no labor force statistics for children aged 14 or under. Among 15- to 17-year-olds, 41 percent had some kind of job in 1987; 7 percent reported that they worked full time and 34 percent part time. Poor youth were much less likely to report any kind of employment; only

26 percent had jobs—8 percent full time and 18 percent part time. Most of these young workers are students. Black and Hispanic youth at this age who are still in school are much less likely to be working than white students.

Youth unemployment rates have been high in recent years, particularly among black 16- to 19-year-olds. (Unemployment rates do not exist for younger teens.) Studies have shown a drastic deterioration in the employment picture among black teens, associated with school dropout, living in central cities, being a member of a long-term welfare family, and having never acquired any work experience.

Increasing attention is being paid to the growing gap between those who will be able to find a place in the labor force and those who will not. The emerging economic picture in the United States is shaped by what is described as "two-tier" job growth. In the future, the only new jobs will be for those who are equipped to work in high-pay, "high-tech" industries or for those who have no skills and are forced to work in low-pay, deadend service jobs.

## Health Status of Youth

Adolescence should be the healthiest time of life, and for most young people it is. Only a few teenagers report fair or poor health status; they make fewer physician visits and occupy fewer hospital beds than any other age group.[8] Teenagers have low levels of disability, illness, and mortality. However, a small number of young people have very serious health problems, and often they result in lifetime impairment.

The death rate is very low in this age group (Table 2.4). The 1986 rates— 32.6 per 100,000 12- to 14-year-olds and 72.7 per 100,000 15- to 17-year-olds— were lower than in 1980 by 5 to 8 percent. Yet the rate in 1986 indicates an upturn in recent years; the 1983 and 1984 rates were the lowest in the decade. Rates for males were more than twice the female rate. While the racial differences among females were insignificant, the rates for black males in both age groups was 30 percent higher than for white males.

TABLE 2.4. Death Rates by Gender, Race, and Age, 1986 (rates per 100,000)

|  | Age 12–14 | Age 15–17 |
|---|---|---|
| TOTAL | 32.6 | 72.7 |
| *Males* | 42.5 | 100.0 |
| White | 40.8 | 100.4 |
| Black | 52.8 | 131.8 |
| *Females* | 22.3 | 43.9 |
| White | 22.1 | 45.4 |
| Black | 23.7 | 48.6 |

*Source:* Unpublished data from National Center for Health Statistics, Mortality Statistics Branch, Division of Vital Statistics, Washington, D.C., 1986.

Many of the deaths in this age group can be attributed to social causes (which we assume are therefore preventable). The leading causes of death among young adolescents are accidents, suicide and homicide, followed by cancer, heart conditions, and chronic conditions. In 1986, about half of all deaths in these age groups were attributable to motor vehicle and other accidents (the older group were more likely to die in auto and motorcycle accidents). Of 3,264 deaths in the 12 to 14 age group, 7 percent died by suicide and 6 percent by homicide. Of 8,203 deaths in the 15 to 17 age group, 11 percent died from suicide and 9 percent from homicide.

The problem of suicide has received a great deal of attention in recent years because of what has been described as an ''epidemic.'' As can be observed from the data presented in Table 2.5, white males are much more likely to commit suicide than any other group; however, between 1980 and 1986, rates increased in each of the four race-gender groups and the largest percentage increases were among black 12- to 14-year-olds. Still, the overall rates are very low. Nevertheless, this rate represents 1,164 very dramatic and tragic deaths from suicide among 12- to 17-year-olds in a year (plus 958 reported suicides among 18- to 19-year-olds). While not shown in the table, it is reported that Native American youth have significantly higher suicide rates than the U.S. average.[9]

The sex-race differences in homicide rates are even more striking. Black male teens are 5 to 6 times more likely to die from homicide than white male teens, and black female teens have 2 to 3 times the rates of white female teens. Homicide rates among black and white 12- to 14-year-old males have increased slightly since 1980, while the rates for all 15- to 17-year-olds, except black females, have dropped a little. In actual numbers, there are almost as many adolescent deaths from homicide annually as suicide (982 deaths from homicide among 12- to 17-year olds plus 1,085 among 18- to 19-year olds), but the occurrence of this form of violent death receives much less attention than suicide. As can be seen in Table 2.5, the 1986 homicide rate for black males 15 to 17 years old (35.9) was more than twice the suicide rate for white males 15 to 17 years old (14.3).

TABLE 2.5. Suicide and Homicide Rates for Youth 12 to 17 by Gender, Age, and Race, 1980 and 1986 (rates per 100,000)

|  | 1980 | | | | 1986 | | | |
|---|---|---|---|---|---|---|---|---|
|  | 12–14 | | 15–17 | | 12–14 | | 15–17 | |
|  | White | Black | White | Black | White | Black | White | Black |
| *Suicide* | | | | | | | | |
| Male | 2.1 | 0.9 | 10.4 | 4.5 | 3.5 | 2.3 | 14.3 | 6.5 |
| Female | 0.5 | 0.2 | 2.3 | 1.5 | 1.1 | 0.6 | 3.7 | 1.6 |
| *Homicide* | | | | | | | | |
| Male | 1.2 | 6.0 | 7.3 | 36.4 | 1.8 | 6.8 | 5.5 | 35.9 |
| Female | 1.3 | 3.0 | 3.0 | 7.4 | 1.4 | 2.6 | 2.6 | 8.1 |

*Source:* Unpublished data from National Center for Health Statistics, Mortality Statistics Branch, Division of Vital Statistics, Washington, D.C., 1986.

The fact that most adolescent mortality stems from a mix of social, environmental, and behavioral causes is supported by recent data on depression, stress, violence, and abuse among teenagers. Most practitioners believe that the suicide rate is just the "tip of the iceberg" and that, for every completed suicide, there are many more young people who suffer from "suicidal ideation." A recent AMA White Paper issued by the American Medical Association estimated that 16 percent of males and 19 percent of females aged 13 to 18 are depressed.[10] A Minnesota survey of youth found that over one-quarter of females and 15 percent of males felt some form of suicide ideation in the month prior to the survey.[11] A survey of 14- and 15-year-olds in New Mexico found that more than 30 percent had recent feelings that life wasn't worth living,[12] while a similar survey of Delaware high school youth found that 22 percent felt highly stressed.[13]

In 1987, a National Adolescent Health Survey was administered to 11,000 eighth and tenth graders nationwide with support from the Office of Disease Prevention and Health Promotion, part of the Public Health Service.[14] At the time, 42 percent of the girls and one-fourth of the boys reported that they had "seriously thought" about committing suicide at some time in their lives, and 18 percent of girls and 11 percent of boys reported that they had actually tried to commit suicide. More than half of the girls and one-third of the boys reported that it was hard for them to deal with stressful situations at home and at school. A third of the girls and 15 percent of the boys felt sad and hopeless. Csikszentmihalyi et al. observed that "Adolescent daily life is a mine field of things that go wrong" . . . with family, teachers, friends, and strangers.[15] Newcomb described adolescence as representing a lifetime peak for the experience of stress.[16] Events such as death in the family, divorce, or remarriage have been shown to create great stress in young people.

As we have seen, motor vehicle and other injuries constitute the leading cause of death among teenagers. In the National Adolescent Health Survey, more than half of the students reported that they did not wear seat belts the last time they rode in a car. More than half rode a motorcycle or minibike, but 42 percent rarely or never wore a helmet. Guns are very accessible to American teenagers: 41 percent of boys and 24 percent of girls report that they could obtain a handgun if they wanted one.[17] A study of homicide rates among young black males revealed that more than half of the victims were killed by persons they knew; over three-fourths were killed by firearms.[18] Most of these homicides occurred during an argument or other nonfelony circumstance (e.g., they weren't involved in a robbery or with the police). Two out of five black children on Chicago's south side reported having witnessed a shooting, and one-fourth had seen a murder—a life experience resulting in what one observer described as similar to the "posttraumatic stress disorders Vietnam veterans have suffered."[19]

The picture that emerges from these statistics is very disturbing: excessively high rates of stress and depression, overexposure to violence, excessively high rates of risk-taking behavior. Many of the young people who feel hopeless have had damaging physical and emotional experiences including neglect as well as physical and sexual abuse. The AMA White Paper reports an estimate that 6 percent of boys and 15 percent of girls have been sexually abused prior to their sixteenth birthdays. It is estimated that one in four fatalities among teens, and 41 percent of serious impairments, resulted from abuse. Half of all rape victims are under the age of 18 as are 40 percent of the perpetrators. Incest is a serious problem among teenagers; 60 to 70 percent of foster children, runaways, and serious drug abusers report experiencing incest in their lives. Anecdotal reports from school-based clinics reveal an alarming occurrence of sexual abuse among students.

Not all the physical and emotional problems of youth are related to the "new morbidities" (drugs, sex, violence). About 7 to 10 percent of all teens suffer from chronic diseases. Asthma and allergies are the most common of these conditions; however, 2 percent are mentally retarded and 8 percent learning disabled. Many teens have speech, hearing, or visual defects. And poor children are much more likely to have disabilities than nonpoor children, not surprising since many emotional disorders and chronic diseases are rooted in poverty conditions.

## AIDS and Teenagers

We can see how today's teenagers live in a world full of threats, from inner feelings of hopelessness to outer fears of violence and disorder. Now they are confronted with a disease for which there is no known cure: Acquired Immune Deficiency Syndrome, or AIDS. High-risk behavior among teenagers both in the areas of intravenous drug use and unprotected sexual intercourse gives them a greater vulnerability than other cohorts. Because the disease has a very long incubation period (close to eight years from contraction of HIV, or human immunodeficiency virus, to clinical manifestation), the current rates do not fully reflect the level of risk.[20] As of August 1988, 283 cases of AIDS had been reported among 13- to 19-year-olds, 1 percent of the total.[21] This number is doubling every year. Also, one in five AIDS cases are aged 20 to 29 (10,434 cases), indicating that they probably contracted the disease while still in their teen years. Hispanic and black youth are highly overrepresented among persons with AIDS; they make up more than half of all teens and three-fourths of all younger children (babies of infected parents) known to have the disease.[22] Repeated surveys have shown that teenagers know a lot about AIDS, at least as much as adults, but that they have not changed their behavior in regard to the use of condoms.

Although media attention has focused heavily on the AIDS epidemic, teenagers have been experiencing escalating rates of other sexually transmitted diseases (STD). It has been estimated that 2.5 million sexually active teens contract a sexually transmitted disease annually.[23] Chlamydia (an infection of the urinary tract or vagina) is the most frequently diagnosed STD among adolescents, followed by gonorrhea, genital warts, herpes, and syphilis.

## "Normal" Development of Adolescents

So far we have looked at the down side of growing up in America. Behavioral scientists do not believe that the teen years are necessarily so difficult or unrewarding; many young people feel optimistic and have high expectations for their futures. What then is "normative" teenage behavior? The study of adolescence has been going on for a long time. Anthropologists have described "rites of passage" from childhood to adulthood that go back to the beginning of history. There have been many theories about the behavior of youth, with little agreement about developmental stages.[24] Current thinking suggests that life for young people as we approach the twenty-first century is very different from earlier epochs, and therefore our perceptions about "normative" behaviors have to change accordingly.[25]

One of the most marked changes in the twentieth century has been the extension of the period of adolescence. Girls reach menarche four years earlier than in the past century. As we will see in later chapters, girls and boys begin to initiate drinking, drugs, sex, delinquency, and truancy at earlier and earlier ages. What we call the "peer culture" appears to dominate the American scene, in terms of clothing, music, films, fast foods, and mall life. Family configurations are markedly different from those of the past, with decreasing likelihood that a child will grow up with the same two parents in residence. Yet, young men and women stay attached to their families (if they have one) often until their late twenties, because of the later age of marriage nowadays and the lack of affordable housing.

For the purposes of this book, we are interested in understanding developmental stages of adolescence in order to design more effective interventions.[26] We are addressing the needs of a wide age span, encompassing at least two very different stages, roughly from 10 to 14 and 15 to 17. The younger group is largely prepubescent and the older group well into puberty, but there are many individual differences in the patterns of development. The first precept in understanding youth, therefore, is individual differences. We must avoid generalizations about teenagers and recognize that the aggregate behavioral patterns are the sum of many differing subgroups.

The second precept is biological change. At no other time in life, except for infancy, is growth so rapid or so dramatic. During these years from about 10 to around 17, children gradually undergo the vital transition that thrusts them into adulthood.[27] During puberty, children grow heavier and taller. They develop secondary sex characteristics. Girls first menstruate, on average, at age 12½ (within the wide range between ages 8 and 16) but in some cases are not fecund for at least a year (i.e., cannot get pregnant). Boys become fecund at about 14, although they can experience sexual intercourse long before they are fecund. Biologically, young people during this period gain the capacity to create children; cognitively, they increase the capacity to reason in the abstract and make moral and ethical decisions; and emotionally, they gain independence from their families and learn how to function on their own. The changes that take place during adolescence do not take place in a vacuum. Contemporary psychologists now acknowledge that the social environment has as much impact on development as individual genetic endowments.[28] A girl who experiences menarche at the age of 12 in a highly structured, protective environment is at much less risk of pregnancy than one who has little support or supervision (see Chapter 5 on the antecedents of adolescent pregnancy).

With all these bodily changes, it should not be surprising that young adolescents are egocentric. They are looking inward, probably for the first time, to form a consciousness of self, to confirm their individuality. At the same time, there are emerging self-doubts and a growing need for reinforcement from the social group. On one hand, they search for autonomy and, on the other, they are very dependent on support from their friends and families. Much attention has been given to the theory that adolescence is the time during which abstract thinking develops. Psychologists do not agree on this point. Either cognitive capacity increases during the teen years, or the environment is presenting young people with more challenges about which they have to make decisions. In either case, they learn to make decisions based on a greater understanding of the consequences.

Boys and girls follow different patterns of change, shaped both by the biological imperatives and the social conditioning. Boys appear to be more driven to achievement and aggression, while girls are more influenced by interpersonal relationships and the need for support and approval. Boys seem to get into more trouble with authorities, both in school and in their communities.

Theories about changes are used as the framework for delineating what "adolescent experts" call the *developmental tasks* of adolescence.[29] This term fits in well with the notion that adolescence is the time when children equip themselves for a responsible adulthood, as workers, parents, and members of a community. One psychologist calls adolescence the "training ground" for adulthood.[30]

Here are some of the tasks most psychologists would agree are necessary for achieving a responsible adulthood:

- The search for self-definition.
- The search for a personal set of values.
- The acquisition of competencies necessary for adult roles, such as problem solving and decision making.
- The acquisition of skills for social interaction with parents, peers, and others.
- The achievement of emotional independence from parents.
- The ability to negotiate between the pressure to achieve and the acceptance of peers.
- Experimentation with a wide array of behaviors, attitudes, and activities.

While much attention has been made of the tempestuous quality of teenage life, the stereotype of the moody, surly, aggressively challenging teenager is currently being questioned by developmental psychologists and psychiatrists. Recent research has suggested that most adolescents go through the transition from child to adult with less trauma than previously assumed. A recent *New York Times* article states that the "mainstream of psychological research dismisses this emphasis on turmoil as balderdash."[31] The chief proponent of this new view is psychiatrist Daniel Offer. His studies show that 80 percent of (middle-class) adolescents see themselves as having no major problems.[32] The most healthy adolescents have strong egos, are able to cope well with internal and external stimuli, and have "excellent genetic and environmental backgrounds." They accept general cultural and societal norms and feel comfortable within this context. However, according to Offer, a subset of adolescents experience more problems in their genetic and environmental backgrounds; 20 percent of adolescents fall into what he calls the "tumultous growth group," with unstable family backgrounds, histories of mental illness in the family, parents with marital conflicts and economic difficulties. These troubled youth are prone to depression and other traumas.

What Offer and others appear to confirm is the significant differentiation between children who are "making it" and those who are not.[33] It is interesting to note that Offer and others find that one in five of all adolescents are deeply troubled (about the same level as appear in the national surveys), and that troubled adolescents are much more likely to come from disadvantaged families. As already stated, one in five children are growing up in poverty and one in four are currently being reared in a single-parent household. However, not all troubled adolescents are disadvantaged and not all disadvantaged adolescents are troubled. The quality of the parenting and the ability of the child to cope are crucial in allowing early adolescents to go about their challenging and critically important developmental imperatives; equally important are the climate of the school and the environment in the community.

## Summary

The 28 million children aged 10 to 17 in the United States are a diverse lot. Almost half live in the suburbs, 30 percent in central cities, and 23 percent in nonmetropolitan areas. They are primarily white, although the proportion of the population that is black or Hispanic is growing. About one-fourth of the children live with only one parent. Their mothers are most likely in the labor force. About one in five of these young people are in poverty families. Increasing numbers are homeless. There are significant differences between subgroups in this society: black and Hispanic families are much more likely to be disadvantaged than white families. However, because of the dominance of whites in the population, the majority of needy children are white.

Adolescence is primarily a time of physical and emotional health; mortality rates are low and disability infrequent. However, a sizable portion of young people suffer from socially induced problems of violence, stress, depression, and neglect.

The literature on adolescent development provides a useful framework for designing interventions. Adolescence is clearly a time of change—biologically, emotionally, and cognitively. Children present unique patterns of growth and development shaped by their genetic backgrounds, their family conformations, and the social environment in which they live.

## Notes

1. See, for example, B. Lefkowitz, *Tough Change: Growing up on Your Own in America* (New York: Free Press, 1987), for portraits of disadvantaged youth; S. Littwin, *The Postponed Generation: Why American Youth Are Growing up Later* (New York: Wil-

liam Morrow, 1986), for personalized accounts from interviews with youth; M. Csikszentmihalyi and R. Larson, *Being Adolescent: Conflict and Growth in the Teenage Years* (New York: Basic Books, 1984), for a detailed portrait of the daily lives of 75 adolescents.

2. Most of the figures cited here come from the U.S. Bureau of the Census, *Statistical Abstract of the United States, 1988* (Washington, D.C.: U.S. Government Printing Office, 1988). More detailed cross-tabulations on most of these indices can be found in the Current Population Survey Reports issued periodically by the Census Bureau, on marital and family status, income and poverty status, and educational attainment. It is almost impossible to find census tabulations that meet the exact requirements of this book—that is, indicators by age groups 10–14 and 15–17.

3. The first half of this book contains many basic tables. To the degree possible, presentation of statistical data has been simplified and summarized. Most percentages have been rounded eliminating decimal points. Numbers are usually presented in thousands (in 000s) or millions (in millions). Where source documents show rates per 1000 population, the text reinterprets the rates as percentages (e.g., per 100 population). Therefore, the figures presented may differ somewhat from source documents.

4. The birth ratio always favors males. However, since males have a higher early mortality rate, by the mid-twenties, the numbers of males and females in each age group are similar. Later in life, since males die younger, there are more females. Among blacks, the sex ratio shifts dramatically during the teen years. By age 20 to 25, there are only 93 males per 100 females. At ages 35 to 39, the ratio is down to 84 for blacks, and just below 100 for whites. (U.S. Bureau of the Census, *Statistical Abstract, 1988,* Table 20, p. 16).

5. U.S. Bureau of the Census, "The Hispanic Population in the U.S.: 1986 and 1987," *Current Population Reports,* Series P-20, 434, 1988.

6. Select Committee on Children, Youth and Families, "The Crisis in Homelessness: Effects on Children and Families," Factsheet, February 24, 1987.

7. "Report Documents Effects of Homelessness on Education, *Education Week,* May 3, 1989, p. 10.

8. National Center for Health Statistics, *Health United States: 1987* (Washington, D.C.: U.S. Government Printing Office (PHS) 88–1232, 1988).

9. D. Shaffer, K. Bacon, P. Fisher, and A. Garland, "Review of Youth Suicide Prevention Programs," Prepared for the Governor of New York State's Task Force on Youth Suicide Prevention, January 1987.

10. M. Schwarz, W. Hendel et al., *AMA White Paper on Adolescent Health* (Chicago: American Medical Association, 1988).

11. R. Blum, L. Geer, L. Hutton, C. McKay, M. Resnick, K. Rosenwinkel, and Y. Song, "The Minnesota Adolescent Health Survey," *Minnesota Medicine* 71 (1988): 143–49.

12. New Mexico Health and Environment Department, *New Mexico Adolescent Risks Survey,* November 1985.

13. Delaware Department of Health and Social Services, *Statewide Adolescent Health Study,* 1987.

14. National Adolescent Student Health Survey, *National Survey Reveals Teen Behavior, Knowledge and Attitudes on Health, Sex Topics,* Press Release, August 9, 1988.

15. Csikszentmihalyi and Larson, *Being Adolescent,* p. 8.

16. M. Newcomb and P. Bentler, *Consequences of Adolescent Drug Use* (Newbury Park, Calif.: Sage, 1988).

17. National Adolescent Student Health Survey, Violence Factsheet.

18. P. O'Carroll, "Homicides Among Black Males 15–24 Years of Age, 1970–1984," *Morbidity and Mortality Weekly Report* 37 (February 1988): 53–60.
19. Select Committee on Children, Youth and Families, "Hearing Summary, Down These Mean Streets: Violence By and Against America's Children," Factsheet, May 16, 1989.
20. National Center for Health Services Research, *HIV-Related Illnesses: Topics for Health Services Research,* Program Note, October 1988.
21. Council of Chief State School Officers Resource Center on Educational Equity, *Concerns,* Issue 23 (July 1988).
22. E. Steel, "Special Needs Populations: Implications for AIDS Prevention" (Paper presented at the Annual Meeting of the American Public Health Association, Boston, November 1988).
23. Office of Population Affairs, *Family Life Information Exchange,* USDHHS Public Health Service, Resource Memo, November 1988.
24. See L. Kaplan, *Adolescence: The Farewell to Childhood* (New York: Simon and Schuster, 1984), for a review of the psychological and psychoanalytic literature on adolescent development.
25. For a synthesis of the research on adolescent development, see S. Feldman and G. Elliott, *At the Threshold: The Developing Adolescent* (Cambridge: Harvard University Press, 1990).
26. Unfortunately, much of our information about adolescent development comes from studies of middle-class youngsters or small samples of either very deprived or dysfunctional youth.
27. See C. Chilman, *Adolescent Sexuality in a Changing American Society,* 2nd ed. (New York: John Wiley & Sons, 1983), and Csikszentmihalyi and Larson, *Being Adolescent,* pp. 3–29.
28. A Pederson, "Biological, Socio-Emotional and Cognitive Development in Adolescence" (Paper presented at Workshop on Adolescence and Adolescent Development, Committee on Child Development Research and Public Policy, National Academy of Sciences, Summer Study Center, Woods Hole, Mass., July 1985).
29. J. Lipsitz, "Understanding Early Adolescence" (Unpublished paper from Center for Early Adolescence, November 1983).
30. Newcomb and Bentler, *Consequences of Adolescent Drug Use,* p. 11.
31. R. Flaste, "The Myth about Teen-agers," *New York Times Magazine,* October 9, 1988, pp. 19, 76–82.
32. D. Offer, "Adolescent Development: A Normative Perspective," in A. Frances and R. Hales, eds., *Annual Review, Vol. 5* (Washington, D.C.: American Psychiatric Association, 1986), pp. 404–19.
33. See Kaplan, *Adolescence,* pp. 40–42, for a rebuttal of Offer's theories.

# 3

# Prevalence of Delinquency

The term *delinquency* suggests a wide range of behaviors from socially unacceptable acts performed early in childhood that parents describe as "naughty" and psychologists call "acting out" to violent and destructive illegal behaviors. The seriousness of the act and the age of the perpetrator further sharpens the definition. Acts such as robbery, aggravated assault, rape, and homicide are not age-related offenses. They are criminal acts whether committed by juveniles or adults and are categorized by the Federal Bureau of Investigation as *index offenses*. Other less serious offenses, such as running away, truancy, drinking under age, sexual promiscuity, and uncontrollability are categorized as *status offenses*, because they are performed by youth under a specified age which classifies them as juvenile offenses. States differ in their penal codes in regard to the age at which an individual moves from juvenile to adult jurisdiction. About three-fourths of the states have set age 18 as a maximum for defining juveniles, two states have set age 19 as a cutoff, seven states use 17, and four states (including New York) 16.[1] Thus, running away from home at age 17 may be an offense in one state but not another.

Almost every child at one time or another acts out, defies parents or teachers, tells lies, or commits minor acts of vandalism. Clearly, they are not all current or potential juvenile delinquents. Many of the behaviors that are considered delinquent are included in a psychiatric diagnosis called *conduct disorder*.[2] The symptoms of this diagnosis include multiple behaviors extended over a six-month period; 17 behaviors are listed including truancy, stealing, cheating, running away, firesetting, cruelty to animals or persons, "unusually early" sexual intercourse, substance abuse, breaking and entering, and excessive fighting, among others. When three or more of these behaviors co-occur before age 15, and a child is considered unmanageable or out of control, then the clinical diagnosis is *conduct disorder*.[3] Kazdin defines this disorder as a "pattern of antisocial behavior, when there is significant impairment in everyday functioning . . . and the behaviors are regarded as unmanageable by significant others."[4] No one knows how many children are at risk of this diagnosis, although it is possible to make estimates based on self-reported behavior.

For the purpose of defining target populations for prevention interventions, we need to determine the number and characteristics of young people age 10 to 17 who have a high probability of becoming delinquent. Without intervention, they will commit illegal acts that will impair them (and/or their victims) and limit their potential to grow into responsible adults. For this purpose, the concept of conduct disorder is too abstract. At the opposite pole, the juvenile delinquency field is shaped by official definitions and statistics. These statistics report the annual number of arrests of persons under the age of 18. Yet we know from surveys of individuals that children report committing many more antisocial acts than appear in the official statistics.

In this and subsequent chapters about defining target populations for interventions, a general strategy will be followed, picking up on the concepts discussed in Chapter 1 and focusing on the antecedents of high-risk behavior. First, there will be a short review of sources of data used for this analysis. Then, we will examine the short- and long-term consequences of the specific behaviors, in this case conduct disorders and delinquency. Clearly, if there are no negative consequences of a behavior, it is not necessary to prevent it. Those behaviors with negative outcomes are used as the framework for defining high-risk status. Based on these definitions of high risk, target populations are quantified, first by estimates of prevalence (rates of occurrence in the 10- to 17-year-old population) and second by estimates of numbers at risk. Finally, the antecedents or predictors of the specific behaviors are discussed to identify the characteristics of those who will fall into the risk groups.

## Sources of Data

Information about juvenile delinquency in the United States derives from public documents and population surveys (Table 3.1). Official statistics on crime are published annually by the Federal Bureau of Investigation, based on information collected from local police departments.[5] Two categories of crimes are included: serious or "index" crimes (e.g., murder, rape, robbery, assault, etc.) and nonserious or "nonindex" offenses (disorderly conduct, substance abuse, vandalism, loitering, running away, etc.). As previously mentioned, the second group of offenses are considered crimes because they are committed by youth under a certain age, crimes such as purchasing liquor or being out on the streets in places where there are curfews. From these annual reports, it is possible to track trends in the numbers of adolescents who are arrested each year according to the type of offense.

Not all arrests become "cases." The U.S. Department of Justice compiles statistics on the cases that reach juvenile courts. The report *Juvenile Court Statistics* describes the number and characteristics of delinquency and status offense cases disposed by courts with juvenile jurisdiction.[6] These statistics are gathered from state-automated reporting systems by the National Center for Juvenile Jus-

TABLE 3.1. Sources of Data on Delinquency

| Source and Subject | Year | Sample Size | Citation |
|---|---|---|---|
| Federal Bureau of Investigation: arrests reported by age | Annual | Count | Flanagan et al. 1988 |
| National Center for Juvenile Justice: cases in juvenile courts | Annual | Count | Snyder et al. 1987 |
| Bureau of Justice Statistics: residents in juvenile facilities | 1985 | Count | U.S. Department of Justice 1986 |
| National Youth Survey: longitudinal, national data | 1976– 1983 | 1,725 | Elliott et al. 1983 |
| *Samples* | | | |
| Adolescent Health Behavior Study: grades 7–12 in 11 Colorado schools | 1985 | 1,667 | Donovan et al. 1988 |
| New York State: grades 10–11 in public high schools | 1971– 1980 | 1,325 | Kandel et al. 1986 |

tice, with support from the Office of Juvenile Justice and Delinquency Prevention.

A very small number of youth who are arrested are actually held in custody. A biennial survey of public and private residential facilities holding juveniles in custody provides useful information on the characteristics of juveniles who are held in confinement.[7]

There are few additional sources for current information on risk behavior that relates to delinquency. The most complete study ever conducted on the subject was the National Youth Survey, initiated in 1975 by Delbert Elliott with funds from the National Institute of Mental Health.[8] A large national sample of 11- to 17-year-olds was selected in 1976, and most of them were followed until 1983, when they were between 18 and 24. A special survey instrument was designed to capture the full range of "official" delinquent offenses so that the results would be comparable to crime statistics. Respondents were asked not only whether they ever participated in a wide range of behaviors, but how often. Thus, the study produced incidence rates as well as prevalence rates, by age, gender, and race.

Other more recent surveys include measures of self-reported delinquent acts. The Adolescent Health Behavior Survey, conducted among a sample of Colorado junior and senior high school students, used a 10-item scale to measure antisocial behaviors.[9] A sample of high school students in New York State was followed up nine years later, tracking their drug use and delinquency experience.[10]

A number of "classic" studies are important points of reference, although the data are not descriptive of current U.S. populations. The works of Farrington and Rutter in England and Wolfgang in Philadelphia are examples of detailed surveys and analyses of special populations that produced significant insights into our understanding of delinquent behavior.[11]

## Consequences of Delinquent Behavior

To understand the consequences of acting out and committing delinquent offenses, it is necessary to follow a population over a long period of time to see what happens to them when they grow up. Longitudinal data are hard to find.[12] One pioneer study conducted by Robins and Ratcliff tracked a sample of black males in St. Louis over a 30-year period, ending in 1966.[13] The researchers analyzed the effects of truancy during the elementary school years on later outcomes. They showed that elementary school truancy (often beginning in first grade) predicted high school truancy and dropout. At the same time, the truant boys were much more likely to get involved in other kinds of deviant behavior, such as drugs and drinking. As adults they earned less, continued to be more deviant, and had many more psychological problems (anxiety and depression) than those boys who were rarely or never truant. Early truancy was clearly related to adult criminality, violence, marital problems, and job problems.

While the classical St. Louis study was conducted twenty years ago, its findings are probably valid today. More recent surveys suggest that conduct disorders may lead to delinquent behaviors, and that delinquency may lead to criminal careers.[14] The more frequent and intense the deviant behaviors conducted during the early years, the more likely that serious negative consequences will ensue. Being convicted as a juvenile very often leads to subsequent convictions as an adult. However, as Menard has pointed out, "Most convicted criminals have a history of juvenile delinquency, but most individuals with a history of juvenile delinquency do not go on to become convicted criminals."[15] It has been well documented that a very small number of individuals are responsible for a very high proportion of all the crimes committed in a community. Many young people commit delinquent acts when they are in their early teens but "grow out" of this kind of behavior as they mature.

Table 3.2 summarizes the negative short-term and long-term consequences of early aggressive and antisocial behavior as well as later delinquency. Children with conduct disorders more often get into trouble in school and are initiated into other problem behaviors early on. In the long term, they may have poor health and experience difficulties at home, in school, and on the job. Once young people commit serious illegal acts, they more often encounter trouble in school or simply drop out, have some further entanglement with the judicial system, get involved with illegal substances, and when they are older, are at higher risk of criminality leading to prison, drug abuse, marital instability, and severe employment problems.

## Prevalence of Delinquency

To develop estimates of target populations for prevention interventions, it is necessary to make some assumptions about the number and characteristics of 10- to 17-year-olds who are at risk of not growing into responsible adults because of their delinquent behavior. In attempting to define who is at high risk for negative

TABLE 3.2. Consequences of Delinquent Behavior

| Behavior | Consequences | |
|---|---|---|
| | Short Term | Long Term |
| Conduct disorders, such as aggression and truancy | Antisocial behavior<br>School problems<br>Psychiatric problems<br>Heavy drinking<br>Smoking<br>More delinquent acts<br>Suspension from school | Delinquency arrests<br>School failure<br>Poor mental health<br>Alcoholism/drug abuse<br>Poor health<br>Low occupational status<br>Poor marital adjustment<br>Impaired offspring<br>Violence |
| Delinquency, such as index offenses (burglary, theft) | Early substance use<br>Violence<br>School dropout<br>Involvement with judicial system<br>Detention | Drug abuse<br>Adult criminality<br>Prison<br>Marital instability<br>Out-of-wedlock parenting<br>Unemployment<br>Low-status jobs, low income<br>Reliance on welfare |

*Sources:* A. Kazdin, *Conduct Disorders in Childhood and Adolescence* (Newbury Park, Calif.: Sage, 1986), pp. 63–66; E. Werner, ''Vulnerability and Resiliency in Children at Risk for Delinquency: A Longitudinal Study from Birth to Young Adulthood,'' in J. Burchard and S. Burchard, eds., *Prevention of Delinquent Behavior* (Newbury Park, Calif.: Sage, 1986), pp. 16–43; L. Robins, ''Changes in Conduct Disorder over Time,'' in D. Farran and J. McKinney, eds., *Risk in Intellectual and Psychosocial Development* (New York: Academic Press, 1986), pp. 227–57.

consequences of delinquent behavior, we are dealing with various levels of risk behavior. The most concrete level is legally defined: the risk of being arrested for an illegal act. However, there are many frequently practiced behaviors that may have negative consequences that do not lead to the court system. An analogy from another problem behavior field, substance abuse, would be the difference between drinking occasionally (a very large group) and drinking excessively (a much smaller group; see Chapter 4). For the purposes of this exercise, three measures will be used to define high-risk groups:

Arrests
Self-reported serious offenses
Self-reported truancy (as a proxy for conduct disorders)

There is no way to estimate the prevalence in any given population of conduct disorders as defined by psychiatrists. Kazdin's review of the literature on this subject found estimates of the syndrome ranging from 4 to 10 percent of all children.[16] However, as mentioned above, prevalence of any one of the specific behaviors, such as theft, assault, or vandalism, is very high.

The National Youth Survey (NYS) has produced the most thorough analysis of self-reported delinquent behavior available. However, the data for youth aged 11 to 17 are more than a decade old (the survey was first conducted in 1976).

Table 3.3. Prevalence of Self-Reported Delinquent Behavior Among 10- to 17-Year-Olds by Age, Gender, and Race

| Type | By Age | | By Gender | | By Race | |
|---|---|---|---|---|---|---|
| | 10–14 | 15–17 | Male | Female | White | Black |
| *Index offenses* | | | | | | |
| Total | 20% | 22% | 29% | 11% | 19% | 29% |
| *Lesser offenses* | | | | | | |
| Truancy | 18 | 53 | 34 | 29 | 32 | 27 |
| Suspension | 7 | 15 | 13 | 7 | 8 | 22 |

*Source:* Estimates based on data in D. Elliott et al., *The Prevalence and Incidence of Delinquent Behavior: 1976–1980* (Boulder, Colo.: Behavioral Research Institute, 1983).

Nevertheless, the patterns that emerge from the NYS appear to be consistent with more recent local area or small sample studies.[17] When asked in surveys about their behavior during the past year, most young people report that they have participated in various forms of delinquent behavior. In fact, four out of five 11- to 17-year-olds in the NYS reported that at some time or another they had been delinquent. One in three admitted truancy and disorderly conduct (not necessarily the same youth). A total of 21 percent had committed index offenses (criminal acts), with physical assaults and thefts leading the lists.

Table 3.3 presents the prevalence of self-reported delinquent behavior during the past 12 months prior to the interview in the NYS, according to age groups, gender, and race for index offenses and truancy.[18] Boys have much higher rates than girls for most forms of self-reported delinquency, and as we will see, for arrests as well. Boys are almost three times as likely to report index offenses, but there is much less difference in regard to status offenses such as truancy. There are no significant differences between races in the prevalence of self-reported general delinquency, but when the rates are examined for specific kinds of offenses, some differences emerge. The 1976 survey (on which Table 3.3 is based) showed much higher rates for index offenses for black young people; however, truancy rates were higher among whites.

The rates of self-reported delinquency are much higher than the arrest rates. One early study of delinquency reported that juveniles committed 8 to 11 serious index crimes for each offense that led to an arrest.[19] A review of the literature on self-report surveys concluded that no more than 15 percent of all delinquent acts result in a police contact.[20]

Table 3.4 presents data from the Uniform Crime Reports that compile data on all arrests in the United States every year according to type of crime and age.[21] Crude estimates of prevalence rates can be made by using the number of arrests as the numerator and the population as the denominator, but it should be kept in mind that some youth are arrested more than one time during a year, and therefore rates may be slightly overestimated. The data suggest that about 3 percent of 10- to 14-year-olds and 11 percent of 15- to 17-year-olds were arrested in 1986 for an offense. Roughly one-third of the juvenile arrests were for index offenses and two-

TABLE 3.4. Percentage of 10- to 17-Year-Olds Arrested by
Type of Offense in 1986

|  | Percentage of 10- to 14-Year-Olds | Percentage of 15- to 17-Year-Olds |
|---|---|---|
| *Total arrests* | 2.9 | 10.9 |
| *Serious crimes* | 1.3 | 3.6 |
| Larceny/theft | 0.8 | 2.0 |
| Burglary | 0.3 | 0.8 |
| Motor vehicle theft | -.- | 0.4 |
| Aggravated assault | -.- | 0.3 |
| Robbery | -.- | 0.2 |
| *Other arrests* | 1.6 | 7.3 |
| Liquor law violations | -.- | 1.1 |
| Vandalism | 0.2 | 0.5 |
| Disorderly conduct | 0.1 | 0.5 |
| Other assaults | 0.2 | 0.5 |
| Drug abuse | -.- | 0.5 |
| Runaways | 0.3 | 0.7 |

*Note:* -.-<0.0.
*Source:* T. Flanagan and K. Jamieson, eds., *Sourcebook on Criminal Justice Statistics—1987* (Washington, D.C.: U.S. Government Printing Office, U.S. Department of Justice, Bureau of Justice Statistics, 1988), Table 4.5, p. 372.

thirds for nonindex general delinquency or status offenses. Larceny, theft, and burglary are the most prevalent serious offenses perpetrated by juveniles. Among the lesser offenses, status violations are the most frequent (liquor law violations, running away, violating curfews, etc.).

About 17 percent of all arrests in the United States in 1986 were of people under the age of 18, and more than 5 percent were under 15.[22] Certain crimes have disproportionate numbers of youth; 11 percent of all serious charges are to those under 15, particularly for property crimes such as arson, burglary, and larceny-theft. Older youth (15 to 17) are more likely to be charged with rape, motor vehicle theft, and assault. In 1986, 78 percent of juveniles arrested were males. The only category with more females was runaways (56%). (It has been estimated that one-fourth of all urban males in the United States are arrested at least once by the time they are 18.)[23]

While black-white differences are not striking in the self-reported behavior, arrest rates are much higher for black males than for any other group. Black adolescents are much more likely to have police contact, to be arrested, to be convicted and detained, and to be classified as chronic offenders. While black youngsters make up 15 percent of the juvenile population, 23 percent of juveniles arrested in 1986 were black as were 52 percent of those arrested for violent crimes committed by those under 18. Among nonindex crimes, blacks juveniles are much more likely to be arrested for receiving stolen goods, fraud, and gambling, while white juveniles are overrepresented among charges of vandalism, driving under

TABLE 3.5. Juvenile Court
Statistics: Delinquency and Status
Offense Cases by Age and Sex,
1984

| Age | Percentage of Population Charged as Delinquent | |
| --- | --- | --- |
| | Male | Female |
| 10 | 1.0 | 0.2 |
| 11 | 1.6 | 0.4 |
| 12 | 2.8 | 0.9 |
| 13 | 5.0 | 2.0 |
| 14 | 7.9 | 3.4 |
| 15 | 10.9 | 4.3 |
| 16 | 13.6 | 4.4 |
| 17 | 15.1 | 3.7 |

*Source:* H. Snyder et al., *Juvenile Court Statistics, 1984* (Pittsburgh: National Center for
Juvenile Justice, 1987), p. 21.

the influence of alcohol, drunkenness, violation of liquor laws, vagrancy, and
running away.

Information from the Juvenile Court Statistics is useful for comparing the
prevalence of various crimes by age and gender.[24] The actual rates are based on
the juvenile justice systems' estimates for each state, depending on how juveniles
are defined (e.g., the maximum age limit in the jurisdiction of the juvenile courts).
Table 3.5 demonstrates the significant demographic differences in case rates: the
rate for males is two to five times greater than for females at every age.[25] The
male case rates spike upward so that, by age 17, close to 16 percent of the total
were in juvenile court in one year. For females, the rates peak at 16 and then
begin to recede, never reaching 5 percent.

The available statistics are striking in revealing that the concentration of crime
exists among a very small proportion of the juvenile population. One study in
England showed that 47 to 62 percent of all offenses were committed by children
from 11 to 16 percent of families.[26] Elliott et al.'s estimate from the NYS is that
15 percent of adolescents (who are serious offenders) account for two-thirds of all
offenses, 87 percent of crimes against persons, and 85 percent of all thefts.[27]

**Trends in Prevalence**

While 17 percent of all arrests were of juveniles in 1986, this represents a dramatic decrease since 1975, when 26 percent of arrests were under the age of 18.
The number of arrests of juveniles during this 10-year period dropped by 15 percent.[28] However, the number of teenagers also dropped dramatically during this
period by a similar percent.

The number of delinquency and status offense cases that reached juvenile courts dropped by 7 percent during the decade; however, the case rate (number of cases related to the number of juveniles) increased from 4.5 percent of a defined "youth-at-risk" population in 1975 to 4.9 percent in 1984.[29] During this time, index offense rates (crimes against persons and property) increased, while status offense rates (running away) and drug offenses decreased. Yet these rates may reflect policy changes by local law enforcement agencies rather than actual changes in behavior. It appears that the prevalence of official delinquency has probably not changed very much over the past decade.

## Numbers at Risk

As would be expected from the high prevalence rates, a very large number of young people are at risk of criminal activity. Literally millions of youngsters commit minor offenses all the time (vandalism, truancy, disorderly conduct, curfew violations) and a sizable number get arrested. It was reported that more than 1.7 million arrests occurred among 10- to 17-year-olds in 1986 (Table 3.6). More than half a million of those arrested were age 14 or under (46,000 were under age 10). Of these arrests (charges), 1.3 million ended up as actual cases in the juvenile justice system. More than half a million of the cases were for serious crimes (index offenses).

The number of index offenses committed may be 10 times larger than the number of cases that are discovered and end up in juvenile court. It is estimated that approximately 6 million 10- to 17-year-olds reported that, within a one-year period, they had participated in an act that was against the law; of these, 3.3

TABLE 3.6. Numbers at Risk of Delinquent Behavior by Age in 1986 (in thousands)

|  | Totals Age 10–17 | Age 10–14 | Age 15–17 |
|---|---|---|---|
| *Arrests* | 1,747 | 536 | 1,211 |
| Index crimes | 641 | 238 | 403 |
| Nonserious crimes | 1,106 | 298 | 808 |
| *Disposed cases* | 1,304 | — | — |
| Delinquency | 1,034 | — | — |
|   Index crimes | 504 | — | — |
|   Nonindex | 530 | — | — |
| Status offenses | 270 | — | — |
|   Truancy | 47 | — | — |
| *Self-reported delinquency* |  |  |  |
| Index offenses | 5,800 | 3,300 | 2,500 |
| Truancy | 8,900 | 3,000 | 5,900 |

*Sources:* For arrests: *Uniform Crime Reports, 1986;* for disposed cases: *Juvenile Court Statistics, 1984;* for self-reported delinquency: extrapolated data from D. Elliott et al., 1983; see Table 3.3 using 1976 prevalence applied to 1986 population data.

million were 14 or under. The number of young people reporting truancy numbered almost 9 million, and of these, 3 million were age 14 or under.

Another "number" that should be mentioned here is the annual count of juvenile runaways, estimated at 1 million to 1.7 million children under the age of 17 during 1983.[30] (The NYS showed that 5.9 percent of 11- to 17-year-olds reported ever running away; applied to the youth population, that prevalence rate results in an estimate of 1.6 million young runaways). Less than 100,000 of these youngsters ended up in Juvenile Court.

## Antecedents of Delinquent Behavior

The list of predictors of delinquency is long (Table 3.7).[31] It should be kept in mind that these variables are not necessarily proven to be causes of delinquency, but they are highly associated in repeated studies. The direction and the timing are not always clear—for example, which occurs first, school failure or "acting out"? The variables probably work in both directions: doing poorly in school predicts socially unacceptable behavior, and socially unacceptable behavior predicts doing poorly in school.

In any case, consensus among researchers about the antecedents of delinquent behavior is substantial. The earlier antisocial behavior starts, and the more frequent the occurrences, the more likely that serious offenses will take place during adolescence. Children who act out as early as kindergarten, or are overly anxious, hyperactive, or aggressive, are at high risk of developing antisocial behaviors as they go through life. However, each child who acts out does not become a juvenile delinquent. There are many other factors that predict high risk.

Boys are much more likely to get into trouble than girls. The reasons are complex. Researchers are less likely than in the past to explain the differences as genetic (e.g., chromosome differences) and now look more toward differences in personality and socialization. While boys participate in violent behavior and aggression, girls are more likely to be involved in status offenses such as running away. Family factors such as authoritarian discipline are more likely to be antecedents of delinquent behavior among males, while severe emotional problems and depression are frequent predictors among females. Several psychological factors are known to precede the conduct disorders that can lead to delinquency, particularly hyperactivity and frequent aggression.

Doing poorly in school is highly related to delinquent conduct. Young people who have been adjudicated as delinquents have severe educational handicaps; years behind their modal grades in school, many have dropped out of school, with low basic academic skills and, in particular, poor verbal abilities. They have difficulty communicating their ideas. Young people who have low expectations about school are more likely to show deviant behavior. Moreover, those who engage in substance use at early ages as well as precocious sexual activity are more prone to delinquent acts.

Children who demonstrate antisocial behavior come from very nonsupportive families at two extremes: either the family is repressive and abusive, or it seri-

TABLE 3.7. Antecedents of Delinquency

| Antecedent | Association with Delinquency |
| --- | --- |
| *Demographic* | |
| Age | **Early initiation |
| Sex | **Males |
| Race/ethnicity | Conflicting and incomplete data |
| *Personal* | |
| Expectations for education | **Low expectations, little commitment |
| | *Low participation in school activities |
| School grades | **Low achievement in early grades, poor verbal ability |
| Conduct, general behavior, misconduct | **Truancy, "acting out," early stealing, lying |
| Religiosity | **Low attendance at church |
| Peer influence | **Heavy influence, low resistance |
| Conformity-rebelliousness | **Nonconformity, independence |
| Involvement in other high-risk behaviors | **Early, heavy substance use |
| | **Precocious sex |
| Psychological factors | **Hyperactivity, anxiety, aggressive behavior |
| Congenital defects | *Handicapping conditions |
| *Family* | |
| Household composition | *Inconsistent data |
| Income, poverty status | **Low socioeconomic status |
| Parent role | **Lack of bonding, repressive, abusive, low communication |
| Parental practice of high-risk behavior | *Family history of criminality, violence, mental illness, alcoholism |
| *Community* | |
| Neighborhood quality | *Urban, high crime, high mobility |
| School quality | *Repressive environment |
| | *Tracking ability |
| | *Ineffective school management |

* = Several sources agree that factor is a major predictor.

** = Most sources agree that factor is a major predictor.

*Sources:* S. Henggeler, *Delinquency in Adolescence* (Newbury Park, Calif.: Sage, 1989), pp. 23–62; J. Hawkins and D. Lishner, "Schooling and Delinquency," in E. Johnson, ed., *Handbook of Crime and Delinquency Prevention* (Westport, Conn.: Greenwood Press, 1987), pp. 180–90; R. Loeber and M. Stouthamer-Loeber, "Family Factors as Correlates and Predictors of Juvenile Conduct Problems and Delinquency," in M. Tonry and N. Morris, eds., *Crime and Justice: An Annual Review of Research,* vol. 7 (Chicago: University of Chicago Press, 1986), pp. 29–150; P. Greenwood and F. Zimring, *One More Chance* (Santa Monica, Calif.: Rand Corporation, 1985), pp. 9–13; B. Sommer, "Truancy in Early Adolescents," *Journal of Early Adolescence* 5(1985): 145–60; D. Kandel, O. Simcha-Fagan, and M. Davies, "Risk Factors for Delinquency and Illicit Drug Use from Adolescence to Young Adulthood," *Journal of Drug Issues* 16(1986): 67–90.

ously neglects the child from the early years on. Incarcerated delinquents report excessively high rates of physical abuse, abandonment, severe parental punishment, and neglect. Girls who become delinquent frequently come from stressful home environments where sexual abuse is rampant. Parents and siblings of children who become delinquents are often involved in criminal activities themselves. Family structure (whether two-parent or single-headed household) is not as significant in predicting social deviance as the quality of the parenting relationship.

Communities appear to breed crime. Living in a high-crime area, which also suffers from poverty and dense living conditions, increases the chances that a child will get involved in criminal acts. These communities often have grossly inadequate schools. Children who attend schools that are repressive, arrange them in classes by ability, and are poorly managed are more likely to become delinquents. Peer influence here is strong, and delinquent gangs emerge from such deprived social environments.

Just as the number of different behaviors cumulate to create high risk of negative consequences, so do the antecedents cumulate to create high risk of becoming a delinquent. One of the factors may make little difference, but for a child who lives in a crime-ridden community, surrounded by delinquent peers, who also has low academic basic skills and attends an inadequate school . . . the chances are high that delinquent behavior will follow.

Elliott et al. have demonstrated that peers display a very powerful influence over the behavior of teenagers.[32] In their analysis, having delinquent peers and early delinquent behavior are the most direct antecedents of serious delinquent behavior. The chances of becoming delinquent are greatly increased when one lives in a nonsupportive environment. In a different analysis, of social class differences in regard to delinquent behavior, Elliott and Huizinga show significantly higher incidence rates for serious offenses among lower-class males.[33] While middle-class respondents had higher prevalence rates for nonserious offenses, their frequency of delinquent acts was considerably lower than lower-class youth for every category.

A unique longitudinal study of high-risk children was conducted on the island of Kauai. Although the findings may not be generalizable, they have contributed to our understanding of the predictors of delinquency among low-income families.[34] Werner and colleagues tracked the development of a group of children from birth (in 1955) to age 18 and came to the following conclusions about who was most likely to become a delinquent in adolescence: they came from homes that lacked social and emotional supports and their lives were burdened with stressful events. In addition, high-risk adolescents had many more problems as babies, with perinatal stress and congenital defects or early handicaps. Given a range of social, behavioral, and medical variables, risk of delinquency was defined by having four or more negative predictors. Children from equally economically deprived homes who did *not* become delinquents were characterized by the researchers as full of "hopefulness" rather than "learned helplessness." They were more often first-born children, in smaller, better spaced families, who had access to either their mothers or alternate caretakers in the household who were supportive. These "resilient" children did much better in school and had superior verbal and social skills.

## Summary

Most children at one time or another "act out," doing things that are destructive or troublesome for themselves or other people. If these behaviors occur frequently and at early ages, psychiatrists would diagnose them as *conduct disorders*. If these behaviors result in illegal acts by juveniles, society would label them as *delinquency*. Based on self-reported patterns of behavior, a large number of young people—as many as one in five—are at risk of committing offenses that could result in arrests. Only a fraction of those at risk actually become court cases each year.

High risk of later delinquency is identifiable at early ages. Children who are aggressive and wild in early grades have a high probability of later delinquent behavior. Early delinquent behavior can lead to criminal careers and prison, but a small number of young people are ultimately responsible for a large number of the serious offenses committed and adjudicated.

There is considerable agreement about the antecedents of delinquency. Children who come from families that lack the necessary social and emotional supports to help them resist negative peer influences are extremely vulnerable. Families with a history of criminality, mental illness, or alcoholism produce children at high risk of delinquency. Peer influence is a dominant theme, often resulting in gang behavior. Delinquency follows school failure and is highly related to poor academic skills and the absence of social skills.

Although it is not possible to count how many "juvenile delinquents" there are in the United States, we can see a significant decrease in numbers of juveniles from those who report any kind of delinquent behavior, to arrests, to cases, and, finally, to those who are actually incarcerated. The numbers drop rapidly, from the millions who report minor and major offenses, to the 1.7 million arrests and the 1.3 million cases. According to the Juvenile Court Statistics, about 100,000 of the cases in 1984 were placed in secure detention of some sort. This jibes with the Statistical Abstract, which shows a total of 83,000 juveniles held in custody in public and private juvenile residences and facilities. According to the Bureau of Justice statistics, about 25,000 juveniles are currently confined in long-term, state-operated juvenile institutions.[35] The survey of juveniles held in custody provides a summary of the characteristics of the highest risk youth: 93 percent were males, 40 percent black, and 12 percent Hispanic. This group reported very low educational levels; only one in four grew up with both parents; more than half had a family member who had been incarcerated; 42 percent had been arrested 6 or more times previously; and 60 percent had already been in jail. The mean age at first arrest was 12.8 years. These young prisoners were already heavy drinkers; almost a third were under the influence of alcohol at the time of their current offense. Some 60 percent used drugs regularly, and 39 percent of these were under the influence at the time of arrest. One in four used cocaine regularly.

In Chapter 9, we will review interventions that focus on preventing juvenile delinquency. As we can see from this review of the prevalence of delinquency, the range of behaviors to be prevented is broad. We would expect that programs to prevent conduct disorders would occur early and that family, school, and community factors would receive considerable attention. The necessity for addressing the underlying predictors and antecedents of high-risk behavior has been further documented in this review.

## Notes

1. T. Flanagan and K. Jamieson, eds., *Sourcebook of Criminal Justice Statistics—1987* (Washington, D.C.: U.S. Government Printing Office, U.S. Department of Justice, Bureau of Justice Statistics, 1988).

2. Criteria are set by the American Psychological Association, *Diagnostic and Statistical Manual of Mental Disorders* (Washington, D.C.: American Psychological Association, 1985). See A. Kazdin, *Conduct Disorders in Childhood and Adolescence* (Newbury Park, Calif.: Sage, 1986).

3. L. Robins, "The Consequences of Conduct Disorder in Girls," in D. Olweus, J. Block, and M. Radke-Yarrow, eds., *Development of Antisocial and Prosocial Behavior: Research, Theories and Issues* (New York: Academic Press, 1986), pp. 385–414.

4. Kazdin, *Conduct Disorders*, p. 11.

5. Federal Bureau of Investigation (FBI), *Crime in the United States: Uniform Crime Reports* (annual) (Washington, D.C.: U.S. Department of Justice); also reported in U.S. Bureau of the Census, *Statistical Abstract of the United States* (annual) (Washington, D.C.: U.S. Government Printing Office).

6. H. Snyder, T. Finnegan, E. Nimick, M. Sickmund, D. Sullivan, and N. Tierney, *Juvenile Court Statistics, 1984* (Pittsburgh: National Center for Juvenile Justice, 1987).

7. U.S. Department of Justice, *Children in Custody: Public Juvenile Facilities, 1985* (Washington, D.C.: Bureau of Justice Statistics, 1986).

8. D. Elliott, S. Ageton, D. Huizinga, B. Knowles, and R. Canter, *The Prevalence and Incidence of Delinquent Behavior: 1976–1980* (Boulder, Colo.: Behavioral Research Institute, 1983).

9. J. Donovan, R. Jessor, and F. Costa, "Syndrome of Problem Behavior in Adolescence," *Journal of Consulting and Clinical Psychology* 56 (1988): 762–65.

10. D. Kandel, O. Simcha-Fagan, and M. Davies, "Risk Factors for Delinquency and Illicit Drug Use from Adolescence to Young Adulthood," *The Journal of Drug Issues* 16 (1986): 67–90.

11. D. Farrington and D. West, *The Cambridge Study of Delinquency Development* (Cambridge, Eng.: Institute of Criminology, June 1983); M. Wolfgang, M. Figlio, and T. Sellin, *Delinquency in a Birth Cohort* (Chicago: University of Chicago Press, 1972); M. Rutter, B. Maughan, P. Mortimore, J. Ouston, and A. Smith, *Fifteen Thousand Hours: Secondary Schools and Their Effects on Children* (Cambridge: Harvard University Press, 1979).

12. See Robins, "Consequences of Conduct Disorder," pp. 18–22; Kazdin, *Conduct Disorders*, p. 17.

13. L. Robins and K. Ratcliff, "The Long-Term Outcome of Truancy," in L. Hersov and I. Berg, eds., *Out of School* (New York: Wiley, 1980), pp. 65–82.

14. Kazdin, *Conduct Disorders*, p. 17.

15. S. Menard, Personal communication, July 1989.

16. Kazdin, *Conduct Disorders*, p. 16.

17. Based on a survey of high school students in Chicago, carried out in 1983, 36 percent of the males and 27 percent of the females were characterized as delinquent. See D. Offer, E. Ostrov, and K. Howard, "Self-Image, Delinquency and Help-Seeking Behavior among Normal Adolescents," *Adolescent Psychiatry, Developmental and Clinical Studies* 13 (1986): 121–38.

18. See Elliott et al., *Prevalence of Delinquent Behavior*, pp. 53–509, for detailed cross-tabulations on more than 40 delinquent and status offenses.

19. Cited in J. Rabkin, "Epidemiology of Adolescent Violence: Risk Factors, Career Pat-

terns and Intervention Programs'' (Paper presented at Conference on Adolescent Violence, Columbia University, New York State Psychiatric Institute, February 1987).

20. D. Farrington and D. West, "The Cambridge Study in Delinquency Development, 1980," in F. Dutile, C. Foust, and D. Webster, eds., *Early Childhood Intervention and Juvenile Delinquency* (Lexington, Mass.: D.C. Heath, 1982), pp. 11–21.

21. The number of arrests used to create prevalence rates for Table 3.4 were presented in Flanagan and Jamieson, *Sourcebook of Criminal Justice Statistics—1987,* Table 4.5, p. 372.

22. Flanagan and Jamieson, p. 372.

23. Cited in Rabkin, "Epidemiology of Adolescent Violence," p. 4.

24. Snyder et al., *Juvenile Court Statistics, 1984,* p. 37.

25. A "case" is when a court handles a juvenile charged with a law violation. Many juvenile courts are also responsible for child support, adoption, abuse, and other kinds of cases, but they are not counted here.

26. R. Loeber and M. Stouthamer-Loeber, "Family Factors as Correlates and Predictors of Juvenile Conduct Problems and Delinquency," in M. Tonry and N. Morris, eds., *Crime and Justice: An Annual Review of Research,* vol. 7 (Chicago: University of Chicago Press, 1986), pp. 29–150.

27. D. Elliott, D. Huizinga, and F. Dunford, "Understanding Delinquency and Crime" (Proposal prepared for the Justice Program Study Group of the John D. and Catherine MacArthur Foundation, Behavioral Research Institute, Boulder, Colo., 1983).

28. U.S. Bureau of the Census, *Statistical Abstract of the United States, 1989* (Washington D.C.: U.S. Government Printing Office, 1989), p. 173.

29. Snyder et al., *Juvenile Court Statistics, 1984,* p. 7. Youth-at-risk is defined as the number of children age 10 through the upper age of the juvenile court jurisdiction as defined by legislation in each state.

30. J. Powers, J. Eckenrode, and B. Jaklitsch, "Running Away from Home: A Response to Adolescent Maltreatment" (Paper presented at the meeting of the Society for Research on Adolescents, Alexandria, Va., March 1988).

31. S. Henggeler, *Delinquency in Adolescence* (Newbury Park, Calif.: Sage, 1989); J. Hawkins and D. Lishner, "Schooling and Delinquency," in E. Johnson, ed., *Handbook of Crime and Delinquency Prevention* (Westport, Conn.: Greenwood Press, 1987), pp. 180–90; Loeber and Stouthamer-Loeber, "Family Factors as Correlates and Predictors," pp. 29–150; P. Greenwood and F. Zimring, *One More Chance* (Santa Monica, Calif.: Rand, 1985); B. Sommer, "Truancy in Early Adolescence," *Journal of Early Adolescence* 5 (1985): 145–60; Kandel et al. "Risk Factors for Delinquency," 82–86.

32. D. Elliott and D. Huizinga, *The Relationship between Delinquent Behaviors and ADM Problems* (Report of Research Conference on Juvenile Offenders with Serious Drug, Alcohol and Mental Health Problems, Behavioral Research Institute, Boulder, Colo., April 1984).

33. D. Elliott and D. Huizinga, "Social Class and Delinquent Behavior in a National Youth Panel," *Criminology* 21 (1983): 149–77.

34. E. Werner, "Vulnerability and Resiliency in Children at Risk for Delinquency: A Longitudinal Study from Birth to Young Adulthood," in J. Burchard and S. Burchard, eds., *Prevention of Delinquent Behavior* (Newbury Park, Calif.: Sage, 1986), pp. 16–43.

35. U.S. Department of Justice, *Survey of Youth in Custody, 1987* (Washington, D.C.: U.S. Government Printing Office, Bureau of Justice Statistics, September 1988).

# 4

# Prevalence of Substance Abuse

Quantifying the number of young people who are high risk because of substance abuse is complicated by the ambiguity of existing definitions and the absence of ideal data. Among other definitional problems, the term *substance abuse* covers a multitude of "sins"—smoking, drinking, use of marijuana, and use of a whole range of drugs from over-the-counter diet pills to illicit heroin and cocaine. In recent years, chewing smokeless tobacco and wine coolers have been added to the menu. To add to the confusion, the substance abuse field has not produced an adequate response to the question: Who is at risk of long-term consequences? In the teen pregnancy field, the problem is generally defined using the outcome to be prevented, early childbearing (see Chapter 5). Teen fertility is quantifiable, measured from official statistics (Vital Statistics), and the characteristics of those at risk can be determined by studying the outcome date. In the delinquency field, there are official arrest figures. In the education field, school records and self-reports can be used to define low achievers and dropouts. In the substance abuse field, research suggests that there are important differences between occasional users and those who ever tried these substances (but are not abstainers), and the subset who become heavy users. It is the subset of heavy users who should be the prime targets of interventions, and yet it appears that most prevention is aimed at the larger group.

The task of defining risk groups for substance-abuse prevention programs would be facilitated if one could turn to a data set that had all the requisite parts: a large random sample of 10- to 17-year-olds, followed longitudinally, and rich in detail about precursors and the social environment. From such a resource, we could better understand the antecedents of drug and alcohol use, current use patterns by different subgroups of the population, and the consequences that followed from that use. A number of researchers have produced important work on what they describe as the etiology or the causes of substance abuse,[1] others have focused on the consequences,[2] and many surveys have been conducted to track prevalence patterns.

Much of what is known about the antecedents and consequences derives from the pioneering work of Lee Robins, Ann Brunswick, Denise Kandel, and Richard Jessor. They collected data from variously designed samples of youth during the 1960s and 1970s and followed up subsets of sample populations to track long-term effects. Their studies are important for laying out the theoretical base for understanding adolescent drug use in the context of other behavioral and social phenomena. Robins documented the potent impact of starting substance use at early ages (before age 15) and the persistent effects of frequent early childhood misbehaviors on later adult experience.[3] Brunswick demonstrated the pyramidal nature of substance-use involvement, whereby a small number of young people use a large amount of drugs.[4] Kandel has documented the progression in the uses of substances and anchored the discussion of substance abuse within the framework of adolescent development.[5] Jessor's work centers around the concept of a problem behavior syndrome of which drug abuse is only one factor in a cluster of behaviors; he has sought to define those individual personality variables that make one child more *prone* or *vulnerable* than another.[6] From these works and others, we can start with a few basic assumptions: that there are differential pathways that adolescents follow in their substance-using behavior; that high-risk behaviors are interrelated; and that experimentation with substances must be viewed as one of the developmental tasks of early adolescents.[7]

## Sources of Data

The major current sources for data on substance use by adolescents are shown in Table 4.1. The National Survey of High School Seniors (NSHSS) has been conducted by researchers at the University of Michigan every year since 1975. This annual survey has provided a unique picture of substance-use trends showing important differences by type of substance and by age of initiation. Because of the large random sample survey administered in 130 public and private schools around the country, a number of cross-tabulations have been produced for various social characteristics.[8] Smaller samples have been followed up through young adulthood to track changes in substance use. One limitation of the NSHSS study is that chronic absentees and high school dropouts are not included, only currently enrolled seniors. Furthermore, black students, particularly males, are underrepresented.

The National Survey of Drug Abuse (NSDA) has been conducted periodically since 1971. The household sample includes persons 12 or older living in a household and does not include transient or homeless youth or runaways. This survey is conducted by a personal interview in the home with various members of the family. This High School Survey and the Household Survey are the primary sources used by program planners and analysts to track the prevalence and trends in the field of substance abuse.

Another source of data, the PRIDE National Data Archives, compiles state

TABLE 4.1. Sources of Data on the Prevalence of Substance Abuse

| Source and Subject | Year | Sample Size | Citation |
|---|---|---|---|
| *National* | | | |
| National Survey of High School Seniors: grade 12 | 1975– 1987 | 18,000 | Johnston et al. 1986 |
| National Survey of Drug Abuse: ages 12–17 | 1972– 1985 | 8,038 | NIDA 1988 |
| PRIDE National Data Archives: grades 6–12 (selected states) | 1982– 1988 | 39,417 | Adams 1988 |
| *State* | | | |
| Arizona: grades 7–12 | 1987 | 29,239 | Arizona State School Survey 1987 |
| New York: grades 7–12 | 1983 | 27,335 | Barnes and Welte 1986 |
| Colorado: grades 8 and 12 | 1983 | 3,413 | Search Institute 1985 |
| Oregon: grades 8 and 11 | 1988 | 4,000 | Halprin, Inc. 1988 |
| *Local* | | | |
| Ventura County, Calif.: grades 7, 9, 11 | 1985 | 2,926 | Newcomb et al. 1987 |
| Northern Calif.: grade 10 | 1985 | 1,447 | Robinson et al. 1987 |
| Michigan: grades 5 and 6 | 1985 | 5,680 | Dielman et al. 1987 |

and local surveys that use uniform instruments in schools in the southeastern and southwestern parts of the country.[9] The aggregate is not a national sample but can produce useful cross-tabulations on specific subjects that appear to be consistent with data from national samples.

Four state surveys of substance use are cited in Table 4.1 along with a compilation of data from other states known to have conducted similar efforts. Of the many small-area or small-sample surveys that have been conducted, those listed have been utilized by researchers for their analyses of prevalence, consequences, or antecedents.[10]

## Defining High-Risk Behavior with Substance Use

Most adults and the majority of adolescents in the United States have used alcohol and have tried smoking cigarettes at one time or another. In recent years, with increasing social pressure, smoking has become less acceptable. Nevertheless, drinking "in moderation" is still considered normative behavior in most social circles. For many people, neither of these behaviors have lasting consequences; an occasional cocktail or glass of wine or beer and one or two cigarettes from time to time probably do not produce life-threatening problems.

Excessive drinking and heavy smoking, however, lead to many societal problems. It is estimated there are at least 18 million heavy drinkers aged 18 and over in this country, whose lives are limited by their drinking problems as are the lives of their families.[11] Drunk driving is a major hazard; over 60 percent of all auto fatalities are alcohol related.[12] Smoking is a leading cause of morbidity and mortality; cigarette smokers have a 70 percent higher overall death rate than nonsmokers, and tobacco has been associated with more than 300,000 premature deaths per year.[13]

There is a continuum from not drinking and smoking to doing either or both excessively, and it is somewhere on that continuum that high-risk behavior begins. Some highly placed officials in the alcoholism field maintain the position that only abstinence is safe. "This term 'responsible use' of alcohol should be purged from the lexicon of the field. Use of alcohol by underage youth as a voluntary, recreational activity is never appropriate."[14] A resolution was passed at the White House Conference for a Drug Free America, which called for "no use of any illegal drug and no illegal use of any legal drug."[15] In these strategies, the goal of prevention is never to initiate the behavior. Much of the "saying no" ideology stems from the belief that children can be taught never to drink or smoke. (The results of "saying no" programs are discussed in Chapter 9.)

One argument used to prevent cigarette smoking is that, while light smoking may not be harmful, it can lead to the use of other drugs, particularly marijuana. And the use of marijuana is associated with the use of hard drugs. The progression suggested in the work of Kandel is beer or wine, cigarettes and/or hard liquor, marijuana, and then other illicit drugs.[16] The heavier the use of a seemingly harmless substance in the early years, the more likely that multiple substance use will occur later. Both alcohol and smoking have been characterized as "gateway" drugs by various sources, since they can lead to more serious substance abuse.

In developing estimates of the number of young people who are at risk of substance abuse, we could start with the assumption that all young people are at risk, at least of substance use, if not abuse. But for our purposes, we are interested in high-risk behavior, behavior that will have damaging consequences over time, prevent normal growth and development, and limit an individual's potential for achieving responsible adulthood.

Table 4.2 summarizes the literature on the immediate and long-term consequences of using various substances. Many of the findings cited are based on small samples of drug-addicted individuals during their adult years. The data are inconclusive in regard to the amount of substance use that triggers actual problems. Individual reactions to drugs vary widely; some have sensitivities and allergies that produce serious reactions to small amounts of substances, while others can tolerate heavy use with little damage. Sorting out cause from effect, consequences from antecedents, is also difficult. Do substance abusers fail in school or do young people who fail in school take up drugs? Despite these questions, it is

TABLE 4.2. Consequences of Substance Use During Adolescence

| | Consequences | |
| --- | --- | --- |
| Substance | Short Term | Long Term |
| *Cigarettes*[a] | | |
| Occasional use | Vulnerability to other drugs | Unknown |
| Frequent use | Bad breath | Excess morbidity, mortality |
| | Respiratory problems | |
| *Alcohol* | | |
| Occasional use | None | None |
| Frequent use | Drunk driving, leading to accidents, arrests, mortality | Alcoholism |
| | | Cirrhosis of liver |
| | | Stomach cancer |
| | Impaired functioning in school | |
| | Family problems | |
| | Depression | |
| | Accidental death (e.g., by drowning) | |
| *Marijuana*[b] | | |
| Occasional use | Vulnerability to other drugs | Inconclusive |
| Frequent, high | Impaired psychological functioning | Respiratory problems |
| | Impaired driving ability | Possible adverse reproductive effects |
| | Loss of short-term memory | Decrease in motivation |
| *Illicit drug use* | | |
| Cocaine[a,c] | Physical symptoms, such as dry mouth, sweats, headache, nose bleeds and nasal passage irritation | Drug dependence |
| | | Rhinitis, ulcerated nasal septum |
| | | Hepatitis |
| | Loss of sleep | Psychological effects: depression, anxiety |
| | Chronic fatigue | Convulsions |
| | Feelings of depression | Social and financial problems |
| | Suicidal ideation | |
| *Multiple substance use*[a] | Dysfunction | Drug dependence |
| | Drop out of school | Chronic depression, fatigue |
| | Suspension from school | Truncated education |
| | Motor vehicle accidents | Reduced job stability |
| | Illegal activities | Marital instability |
| | | Crime |

[a]M. Newcomb and P. Bentler, *Consequences of Adolescent Drug Use: Impact on the Lives of Young Adults* (Newbury Park, Calif.: Sage, 1988), pp. 219–22.

[b]R. Peterson, "Marijuana Overview," in *Correlates and Consequences of Marijuana Use* (National Institute on Drug Abuse, *Research Issues* 34, 1984), pp. 1–19.

[c]Based on findings from a study reported by D. Chitwood, "Patterns and Consequences of Cocaine Use," in N. Koxel and E. Adams, eds., *Cocaine Use in America: Epidemiologic and Clinical Perspectives* (National Institute on Drug Abuse, USDHHS, NIDA Research Monograph, 61, 1985), pp. 111–29.

obvious that the more substances that are used and the greater the frequency of use, the larger the damage. Thus, young people who occasionally smoke a cigarette or a "joint" (marijuana), or drink a beer or a glass of wine, will suffer no consequences. However, for young people who get heavily involved in drugs (either dependence on one drug or on several different kinds), the consequences can be devastating, physically and psychologically, and severely limit educational, career, and marital success.

Based on this understanding of the differential consequences of substance use, the target population for preventive interventions would be those young people for whom there is *a high probability of frequent and heavy use.* Thus, we would not be interested in accounting for "ever users" of cigarettes, alcohol, or even marijuana, since almost all young people fit into that category. However, the data on progression from smoking and drinking to hard drugs suggest that frequent users of legal substances may fall into a high-risk category. It is well documented that few young people start their substance "careers" with cocaine or heroin or other stimulants. As we will see when we look at current drug and alcohol prevention programs, almost all of them are aimed at the total population (usually a class or a school), and few concentrate their resources on high-risk children.

For the purposes of estimating target populations for interventions that focus on high-risk behavior, two measures are of interest: *current use*, defined by 30-day prevalence rates (e.g., self-reported use of a substance within the past month), and *heavy use*, defined for each substance:

Cigarettes: daily use
Alcohol: daily use or frequent heavy use
Marijuana: daily use
Cocaine and other hard drugs: any use within past month

The National Survey of High School Seniors is an excellent source of data for examining the amount and use of various substances. Table 4.3 presents the proportions of seniors who reported that they used cigarettes, alcohol, marijuana, and hard drugs (cocaine and amphetamines are included in the table). Table 4.3 compiles the percent who ever used a substance, current use defined as use in the past thirty days, and a measure of regular or heavy use. These data illuminate clearly the differences in prevalence of experimentation and what could be defined as abuse. For example, more than two-thirds of seniors have tried cigarettes, less than one-third smoked in the month prior to the survey, and 12 percent smoked more than half a pack of cigarettes a day. For alcohol, almost all students had tried a drink by the time they reached their senior year, two-thirds had a drink within the past month, and 15 percent reported heavy drinking (five or more drinks in a row three or more times during the past two weeks). The use of marijuana closely mirrored the use of cigarettes, with slightly lower levels; more than half had ever used marijuana, one-fourth had used it within the month, and 5 percent acknowledged regular use (20 times or more in the past 30 days). Some 17 percent of high school seniors had ever used cocaine, 7 percent within the past 30 days, and 3 percent three or more times during the past month. About 26 percent had ever used amphetamines, 7 percent within the past 30 days, and 3 percent three

TABLE 4.3. Prevalence of Substance Use among High School Seniors by Sex and Race, 1985

| Substance Used | Total | Male | Female | White | Black |
|---|---|---|---|---|---|
| *Cigarettes* | | | | | |
| Ever | 69% | 67% | 70% | 70% | 61% |
| Past 30 days | 30 | 28 | 31 | 32 | 19 |
| Daily, ½ pack | | | | | |
| or more | 12 | 12 | 12 | 14 | 4 |
| *Alcohol* | | | | | |
| Ever | 92 | 93 | 92 | 94 | 84 |
| Past 30 days | 66 | 70 | 62 | 70 | 44 |
| Heavy[a] | 15 | 21 | 9 | 17 | 7 |
| *Marijuana* | | | | | |
| Ever | 54 | 57 | 51 | 55 | 49 |
| Past 30 days | 26 | 29 | 22 | 24 | 22 |
| Often[a] | 5 | 7 | 3 | 5 | 4 |
| *Hard drugs* | | | | | |
| Cocaine | | | | | |
| Ever | 17 | 20 | 15 | 18 | 10 |
| Past 30 days | 7 | 8 | 6 | 7 | 3 |
| Often[b] | 3 | | | | |
| Amphetamines | | | | | |
| Ever | 26 | 25 | 28 | 29 | 9 |
| Past 30 days | 7 | 6 | 7 | 8 | 2 |
| Often[b] | 3 | | | | |

[a]Heavy use of alcohol = 5 or more drinks in a row, three or more times in the past two weeks. Heavy use of marijuana = 20 times or more in the last 30 days.

[b]Heavy use of cocaine and amphetamines = three or more times in the past month.

*Source:* L. Johnston, J. Bachman, and P. O'Malley, *Monitoring the Future, 1985* (Ann Arbor, Mich.: Institute for Social Research, University of Michigan, 1986). Extracted from descriptive results.

or more times during the past month. About 1 percent of the sample reported ever using heroin (not shown in the table), and a tiny fraction reported current use. Other drugs currently used by small percentages of seniors included inhalants, hallucinogens (LSD, PCP), sedatives (barbiturates, methaqualone), and tranquilizers. In 1986, 13 percent of seniors had used an illicit drug (other than marijuana) within the past month.

Thus, about two-thirds of high school seniors appear to drink currently and one-fourth currently use cigarettes and marijuana. At least 15 percent of all seniors practice very high-risk behavior, either smoking cigarettes or marijuana daily, drinking heavily, or using hard drugs. Cigarette smokers are more likely to be regular users (40% of current users smoke at least half a pack a day), and about one in four current drinkers drink heavily, while one in five current marijuana smokers do it almost every day.

Although the prevalence of using smokeless tobacco is not included in the senior survey, use is believed to be rising among males. A sample survey in the Midwest found that 9 percent of seventh-grade males were users, as were 22 percent of twelfth graders.[17] Daily use of smokeless tobacco was reported by 3 percent of seventh-grade males and 15 percent of twelfth graders. The average age of first chewing tobacco was 10 or 11, and this practice was associated with the use of other substances as well.

According to the survey of high school seniors, regular smokers and heavy drinkers are much more likely to use hard drugs than occasional smokers or non-smokers or occasional or nondrinkers. One example of the association between these substance-abuse behaviors is that only 3 percent of those who never used any illicit drugs smoked cigarettes regularly, compared with 14 percent of mari-juana users and 36 percent of heavy drug users.[18] As Table 4.3 shows, 15 percent of seniors were heavy drinkers; this measure applied to only 4 percent of those who used no drugs, 15 percent of marijuana users, 33 percent of heavy drug users, and 52 percent of heroin users.

Experimentation with substances starts at very early ages. A recent survey from the *Weekly Reader* found that 26 percent of fourth graders and 42 percent of sixth graders had already tried wine coolers.[19] According to the retrospective re-ports of the high school seniors (class of 1986), one in ten had a drink (more than a sip) by sixth grade, and by eighth grade, one-third had used alcohol. Some 14 percent of the seniors reported daily smoking by eighth grade, and 15 percent had already tried marijuana. Hard drugs were first used in the later grades, usually in the early high school years. These patterns give evidence of the importance of placing interventions in junior and middle schools, before regular use is estab-lished.

## Prevalence Rates and Numbers

To estimate the number of youth aged 10 to 17 at risk of consequences from substance abuse, it was necessary to locate prevalence rates for younger age groups for each of the four substances of interest. Because no one source was identified that could meet these requirements, a "simulated" estimate was derived from a number of sources that had conducted surveys asking about current and heavy use. A range of estimates has been produced, assuming that heavy users are al-ready at high risk of consequences (and in fact would be in the target population for treatment programs), while current users are potentially at risk of conse-quences if they increase their frequency of use or move to harder substances.

For current use, a number of data sources were identified including four recent state surveys, a composite of state and local surveys conducted in the early 1980s, and the Household Interview Survey.[20] While the state surveys report monthly prevalence rates that are relatively consistent (Table 4.4), the results of the House-hold Survey produce lower estimates (Table 4.5). Measures of heavy or daily use are less frequently collected in the state surveys. The estimates shown in Table 4.4 for heavy use were extrapolated from the experience of the high school se-niors, using the ratios of current use to heavy use as a rough guide (Table 4.3).

Based on the findings from this collection of surveys on substance use, esti-mates were made of current and heavy use by age group for each substance.

TABLE 4.4. Estimated Percentages of 10- to 17-Year-Olds Using Substances Currently and Frequently, around 1986–87

| Substance | Current Users by Age | | | Heavy Users by Age | | |
|---|---|---|---|---|---|---|
| | 10–11 | 12–14 | 15–17 | 10–11 | 12–14 | 15–17 |
| Cigarettes | 7% | 15% | 25% | — | 5% | 4% |
| Alcohol | 6 | 25 | 55 | 1 | 6 | 12 |
| Marijuana | 1 | 7 | 20 | — | 1 | 4 |
| Cocaine | — | 2 | 6 | — | 1 | 3 |

*Source:* Extrapolated from selected state and local surveys.

These prevalence rates from Tables 4.4 and 4.5 have been applied to the current population estimates (Table 2.1) to obtain rough estimates of the number of youth between 10 and 17 at risk of the consequences of substance abuse. Estimates for 12- to 17-year-olds based on the 1985 Household Survey findings are also shown. The numbers are high (Table 4.6). Roughly 4.8 million of the nation's 28 million 10- to 17-year-olds have smoked within the past month, 9 million have been drinking, 3 million have used marijuana, and about 800,000 have used cocaine. (The NIDA Household Survey figures are somewhat lower since they do not include the youngest age group and the prevalence rates were generally lower than the composite of the other survey data.) Estimates for the use of other hard drugs might expand these numbers even further, but in all likelihood, they are already covered in one of the categories presented. It is well documented that most of the hard drug users are duplicated in these counts. Cocaine users are most likely to also use marijuana and smoke cigarettes; marijuana users almost always smoke cigarettes; and so on.

The heavy users are at particularly high risk of negative consequences (Table 4.6). This highest risk group includes almost a million regular cigarette smokers, more than two million heavy drinkers, half a million regular marijuana users, and about half a million young people who are using hard drugs including cocaine. In sum, about 1 in 15 of the nation's young people drinks heavily (daily or in frequent binges), and almost 2 percent are confirmed users of illicit hard drugs.

TABLE 4.5. Percentage of 12- to 17-Year-Olds Reporting Use of Selected Drugs during Past Month, 1985

| Substance | Users by Age | | | |
|---|---|---|---|---|
| | 12–13 | 14–15 | 16–17 | 12–17 |
| Cigarettes | 6% | 14% | 25% | 15% |
| Alcohol | 11 | 35 | 46 | 31 |
| Marijuana | 4 | 11 | 21 | 12 |
| Cocaine | — | 1 | 3 | 2 |

*Source:* NIDA Household Interview Survey.

TABLE 4.6. Estimates of the Number of Young People at Risk of Consequences of Substance Abuse by Age, 1987 (in millions)

| Substance | Number Who Are Current Users by Age | | | | |
|---|---|---|---|---|---|
| | 10–11 | 12–14 | 15–17 | 10–17 | NIDA Estimate 12–17 |
| Total population | 6.5 | 10.2 | 11.1 | 27.8 | 21.3 |
| Cigarettes | 0.5 | 1.5 | 2.8 | 4.8 | 3.3 |
| Alcohol | 0.4 | 2.5 | 6.1 | 9.0 | 6.6 |
| Marijuana | 0.1 | 0.7 | 2.2 | 3.0 | 2.5 |
| Cocaine | — | 0.2 | 0.6 | 0.8 | 0.3 |

| Substance | Number Who Are Heavy Users by Age | | | |
|---|---|---|---|---|
| | 10–11 | 12–14 | 15–17 | 10–17 |
| Cigarettes | — | 0.5 | 0.4 | 0.9 |
| Alcohol | 0.1 | 0.6 | 1.3 | 2.0 |
| Marijuana | — | 0.1 | 0.4 | 0.5 |
| Cocaine | — | 0.1 | 0.3 | 0.4 |

*Source:* Prevalence rates from Tables 4.4 and 4.5 applied to population estimates from Table 2.1.

## Trends in Prevalence

Is this situation getting worse or better? Both the Household Survey of 12- to 17-year-olds and the survey of seniors show decreases in lifetime prevalence rates (ever used) between 1979 and 1985 for most substances. However, the Household Survey shows a slight upturn between 1982 and 1985 in current use for all substances, while the seniors showed no change or continuing decreases—with the exception of cocaine use, which went up. Only the senior data are available for the period between 1985 and 1988,[21] which indicate that all drug use decreased including cocaine. The data also suggest that fewer teens are experimenting with substances, but that those who use them, do so more frequently. (For example, there has been a slight upturn in heavy drinking.)

The recent decline in cocaine use among seniors was attributed to changing perceptions among seniors about the risks of using cocaine.[22] For the first time, information was collected on the use of "crack," and the researchers hypothesized that "crack" use was not declining as much as other forms of cocaine. They reported that, in 1987, crack was being used in 75 percent of the high schools in their sample, up from 50 percent in 1986. The data suggests, however, that only a very small number in each school could have been users. About one in three cocaine users reported use in the form of crack.

Inhalants are the only substance shown consistently in both data sets to be on the rise, including substances that are sniffed or inhaled for "kicks" or to "get high" (glue, gasoline, amyl nitrates, and nitrous oxides). The pronounced fadism in drugs reflects peer pressure to follow adolescent crazes, the impact of media, and changes in supply of various drugs. Inhalants are very easy to obtain and cheap.

Throughout the 1970s, there were striking increases in the use of all substances in the lower grades.[23] Age of first use appeared to be getting lower and lower. These data were influential in persuading the American public to get involved in stopping the "drug epidemic." For example, in 1971, about 6 percent of seniors reported that they had used marijuana by eighth grade; in 1978, 20 percent had used it by eighth grade; and in 1987, 14 percent had used it by eighth grade. With the exception of cocaine, teen prevalence rates for drugs such as marijuana peaked in 1978; early smoking peaked in 1976. The timing of first use of alcohol has changed very little since the first data became available in 1972. Each year's report shows that by eighth grade some 30 percent have already used alcohol. First use of cocaine is somewhat later, and there has been little change over the decade in age at first use.

## Antecedents of Substance Use

Based on the National Survey of High School Seniors, substance abuse "problems," defined by heavy use, are experienced more by males, whites, and youth without college plans; and these problems are more common on the East and West Coasts for illicit drug use and less common in the South for all substance abuse.[24] Seniors with low academic averages are more likely to smoke regularly than high achievers: 2 percent of A students were regular smokers compared with 23 percent of D students.[25] Although every study uses a different methodology, there is a large body of knowledge and considerable agreement about the antecedents of substance abuse, which are summarized in Table 4.7.[26] The list of factors that are "risk markers" for later substance abuse on which there appears to be almost complete agreement include:

*Early initiation*: use of any substances at an early age (10 to 12).
*School problems*: lack of expectation that school will be a successful experience, low grades (particularly in the beginning of junior high school), acting out in school, or truancy.
*Family problems*: lack of parental support and guidance.
*Peer influences*: consorting with peers who use substances and lacking resistance to their influences, favoring peers' opinions over parents' and other adults.
*Personality*: being a nonconformist, rebellious, or having a strong sense of independence.[27]

Additional antecedents are important to consider, but the evidence is either incomplete or inconsistent. While earlier studies of substance abuse pointed toward greater usage among young males, more recent studies show a decrease in sex differences. Female high school seniors are more likely than males to smoke and use some illicit drugs, such as amphetamines, and they use alcohol and marijuana at almost the same rates as male seniors (Table 4.3). There is evidence, however, that males are much more involved in heavy drinking and drunk driving than females.

TABLE 4.7. Antecedents of Substance Abuse

| Antecedent | Association with Substance Abuse |
|---|---|
| *Demographic* | |
| Age | **Early initiation |
| Sex | *Males = heavy drinking |
| Race and ethnicity | Conflicting or incomplete data |
| *Personal* | |
| Expectations for education | **Low expectations |
| School grades | **Low achievement in junior high |
| Conduct, general behavior | **Truancy, "acting out," misconduct |
| Religiosity | **Low attendance at church |
| Peer influence | **Heavy influence, low resistance to influences |
| Peer use | **Highly related |
| Conformity–rebelliousness | **Nonconformity, independence |
| Beliefs about risk | **Lack of belief that use will harm |
| Involvement in other high-risk behaviors | *Early delinquency |
| Psychological factors | *Stress, depression |
| Self-esteem | Inconsistent data |
| *Family* | |
| Household composition | Inconsistent data |
| Income, poverty status | Inconsistent data |
| Parental role, bonding, guidance | **Lack of parental support |
| Parental practice of high-risk behaviors | *Parents use substances |
| Culture in home | *Lack of resources in home |
| *Community* | |
| Neighborhood quality | *Urban, high-density area |
| School quality | *Alternative/vocational school |

 * = Several sources agree that factor is a major predictor.

** = Most sources agree that factor is a major predictor.

*Sources:* K. Gersick, K. Grady, E. Sexton, and M. Lyons, "Personality and Sociodemographic Factors in Adolescent Drug Use," in *Drug Use and the American Adolescent* (National Institute on Drug Abuse, USDHHS, NIDA Research Monograph, 38, 1985), pp. 39–45; J. Polich, M. Ellickson, P. Reuter, and J. Kahan, *Strategies for Controlling Adolescent Drug Use* (Santa Monica, Calif.: Rand Corporation, 1984), p. 131; M. Newcomb, E. Maddahian, E. Skager, and P. Bentler, "Substance Abuse and Psychosocial Risk Factors among Teenagers: Associations with Sex, Age, Ethnicity, and Type of School," *American Journal of Drug and Alcohol Abuse* 13(1987): 413–33; R. Hawkins, D. Lishner, R. Catalano, and M. Howard, "Childhood Predictors of Adolescent Substance Abuse: Toward an Empirically Grounded Theory," *Journal of Children in Contemporary Society* 8(1986): 11–47; G. Barnes and J. Welte, "Patterns and Predictors of Alcohol Use among 7–12th Grade Students in New York State," *Journal of Studies in Alcohol* 47(1986): 53–61; D. Murray and C. Perry, "The Prevention of Adolescent Drug Abuse: Implications of Etiological, Developmental, Behavioral and Environmental Models," *Etiology of Drug Use* (National Institute on Drug Abuse, USDHHS, NIDA Research Monograph, 56, 1986), pp. 237–39.

The race issue is complicated by the underrepresentation of black inner-city youth in the two national surveys. Moreover, aggregate black rates are weighted by rural southern blacks, who are much less likely than other black youth to experiment with drugs.[28] In almost every study where race differences are presented, black children present lower rates of substance abuse than white children. The senior survey shows significant differences (Table 4.3). The detailed results of the 1985 Household Survey show that white males and females have the highest current prevalence rates for all substances except cocaine; that black females consistently report the lowest rates; and Hispanic females have rates almost as low as black females. For cocaine, the reported rates are low for all groups: Hispanic males and females report the highest rates (2–3%), while black males and females report the lowest rates (around 1%).[29] One school survey in California reported prevalences of substance use for various ethnic groups: highest use was among Native American and white youth and lowest use was among Asians, Hispanics, and blacks.[30] However, for hard drug use, there were no significant differences. The Arizona state survey showed a similar pattern, with significantly higher rates among Native American youth for all substances except cocaine (where there were no marked ethnic differences).[31] Black youth in Arizona consistently reported the lowest rates on every substance, lower than the group classified as "Oriental."

What we learn from the surveys contradicts the impression we cull from media stories about "crack" houses and drug raids. Much of the illegal activity surrounding crack seems centered in deteriorated urban slums. AIDS statistics support this conclusion, pointing toward inner-city minority youth as the highest risk group for using intravenous drugs. In 1986, one-third of the admissions to emergency rooms for drug episodes were black, as were one-fourth of the individuals who died from drug-related causes.[32] Of those who were admitted to emergency rooms for cocaine use, 50 percent were black.

Untangling the cause-effect relationships in predicting behavior is in itself a high-risk activity. The data on family structure are quite thin. It appears that household composition (e.g., two-parent family versus single-headed family) is not as important as the quality of the relationship between the parent(s) and the child. While it is relatively simple to gather data about family composition, it is difficult to measure the level of attachment among family members. At least one set of researchers believes that family interactions and childrearing practices are the most important predictors of later problems with substances.[33] There is general agreement that lack of loving care and absence of communication between parent and child shape the adolescent's perceptions that drug use may be a rewarding experience. However, no evidence has been found that child abuse leads to substance abuse, although it may well be a factor.

Parental substance use is another hazy area. A great deal of attention has been paid to the genetic factor in alcohol abuse, with the assumption that addiction to alcohol may be inherited. Studies have shown that sons of alcoholics are four times more likely to become alcoholics, but no such evidence has been found for daughters of alcoholics.[34] Studies based on samples of adoptees, twins, and animals have documented a genetic predisposition to alcoholism that is difficult to separate from environmental factors. It appears that only a minor amount of the variation in alcohol use among teenagers can be attributed to genetic factors.[35]

Many people believe that children get involved with substance abuse because they have low self-esteem. The research is inconsistent. There is little agreement about the relationship between the use of substances and either low self-esteem or lack of what has been called "locus of control" (being outer-directed rather than inner-directed). It may be that these concepts are too "soft" to be measured through the crude instruments used in most substance abuse surveys. The association between being in a depressive state and using drugs, however, has been documented in a few studies. Young people in stressful situations are more likely to abuse substances. Although heavy substance abusers may develop serious psychiatric problems (see Table 4.2), it is not clear whether they start out with a predilection toward psychopathology, or whether the use of substances has physiological effects that produce the pathology.

## Summary

Research findings on the etiology of substance abuse among adolescents are rich in some areas. From the large amount of psychological research being conducted, we can now point to the antecedents and consequences of substance use. Yet it is still difficult to find an adequate definition of high-risk behavior that takes into account a certain amount of "non-risk" experimentation. This definition is important for conceptualizing prevention efforts. Official government positions and statements from politicians and program advocates seem to place all young people at risk and call for programs of abstention. Counts of "ever users" are promulgated as public relations symbols for the media and legislators. But, from this review, it appears that only certain subsets of those who are currently using these substances will ever get into any trouble as a result of their experimentation.

We have opted for two measures of current (30-day) and heavy use to produce the range of estimates of the numbers of youth at risk of negative consequences from substance abuse. We do not believe that every young person needs to be in the target population for intensive prevention efforts. However, the subsets are sizable: almost 5 million (17%) of the nation's 28 million 10- to 17-year-olds smoke, 9 million (32%) drink fairly often, about 3 million (11%) use marijuana, and more than 800,000 (3%) have already tried cocaine. Of these youth-at-risk, many are already established smokers and heavy drinkers: almost a million smoke regularly and 2 million drink frequently and in large amounts. These estimates are not additive, since much of substance use involves multiple substances. (In Chapter 7, the question of overlap in problem behavior will be addressed.)

There is a growing consensus among researchers about the antecedents of substance-abusing behavior: early initiation and susceptibility to peer influence are significant markers. Family influences are also important: lack of parental support, involvement, and caring and parental approval of drug and alcohol use are strong markers of risk. Certain personality patterns are significant: nonconformity, rebelliousness, and independence. School problems emerge early, including misconduct, truancy, and low achievement, which gets translated in later years into being "turned off" by school and having low aspirations for further education.

This knowledge base has been used extensively for designing interventions. We will see in Chapter 9 which prevention programs have been successful at preventing behaviors that lead to negative consequences.

## Notes

1. See, for example, National Institute on Drug Abuse, *Etiology of Drug Abuse: Implications for Prevention* (Washington, D.C.: U.S. Government Printing Office, DHHS Pub. No. (ADM) 86–1335, 1986). Sources used for summarizing antecedents include K. Gersick, K. Grady, E. Sexton, and M. Lyons, "Personality and Sociodemographic Factors in Adolescent Drug Use," in *Drug Use and the American Adolescent* (National Institute on Drug Abuse, USDHHS, NIDA Research Monograph, 38, 1985); J. Polich, M. Ellickson, P. Reuter, and J. Kahan, *Strategies for Controlling Adolescent Drug Use* (Santa Monica, Calif.: Rand Corporation, 1984); M. Newcomb, E. Maddahian, E. Skager, and P. Bentler, "Substance Abuse and Psychosocial Risk Factors among Teenagers: Associations with Sex, Age, Ethnicity, and Type of School," *American Journal of Drug and Alcohol Abuse* 13(1987): 413–33; R. Hawkins, D. Lishner, R. Catalano, and M. Howard, "Childhood Predictors of Adolescent Substance Abuse: Toward an Empirically Grounded Theory," *Journal of Children in Contemporary Society* 8(1986): 11–47; G. Barnes and J. Welte, "Patterns and Predictors of Alcohol Use among 7–12th Grade Students in New York State," *Journal of Studies in Alcohol* 47(1986): 53–61; D. Murray and C. Perry, "The Prevention of Adolescent Drug Abuse: Implications of Etiological, Developmental, Behavioral, and Environmental Models," *Etiology of Drug Use* (National Institute on Drug Abuse, USDHHS, NIDA Research Monograph, 56, 1986), pp. 236–56.
2. See M. Newcomb and P. Bentler, *Consequences of Adolescent Drug Use: Impact on the Lives of Young Adults* (Newbury Park, Calif.: Sage, 1988), for a recent review of theoretical constructs as well as research findings, summarized here in Table 4.2.
3. L. Robins, "Sturdy Childhood Predictors of Adult Antisocial Behavior: Replications from Longitudinal Studies," *Psychological Medicine* 8(1978): 611–22.
4. A. Brunswick, "Young Black Males and Substance Abuse," in J. Gibbs, ed., *Young, Black, and Male in America: An Endangered Species* (Dover, Mass.: Auburn, 1988), pp. 166–87.
5. D. Kandel and J. Logan, "Patterns of Drug Use from Adolescence to Young Adulthood: I. Periods of Risk for Initiation, Continued Use, and Discontinuation," *American Journal of Public Health* 74(1984): 660–67; K. Yamaguchi and D. Kandel, "Patterns of Drug Use from Adolescence to Young Adulthood: II. Sequences of Progression," *American Journal of Public Health* 74(1984): 668–72; K. Yamaguchi and D. Kandel, "Patterns of Drug Use from Adolescence to Young Adulthood: III. Predictors of Progression," *American Journal of Public Health* 74(1984): 673–81.
6. R. Jessor and S. Jessor, *Problem Behavior and Psychosocial Development—A Longitudinal Study of Youth* (New York: Academic Press, 1977).
7. It should be noted that most of the studies were conducted more than a decade ago, and were based on selected population samples, either middle-class white suburban students or black urban youth.
8. See L. Johnston, J. Bachman, and P. O'Malley, *Monitoring the Future* (Ann Arbor, Mich.: Institute for Social Research, University of Michigan, annual volumes, 1980 to present).
9. See brochure from PRIDE, National Parents' Resource Institute for Drug Education, Inc., describing questionnaires for grades 4 to 6 and 6 to 12 and services that may be purchased from PRIDE for data compilation and reports (undated). Also, R. Adams, "From the Computer," *Pride Quarterly* (Winter 1988), 4.
10. Citations for Table 4.1 are included in notes 1, 8, 9, 18, and 20, except for T. Robinson, J. Killen, B. Taylor, M. Tekh, S. Bryson, K. Saylor, D. Marton, N. Maccoby,

and J. Forquar, "Perspectives on Adolescent Substance Use: A Defined Population Study," *Journal of the American Medical Association* 258(1987): 2072–75; T. Dielman, J. Shope, P. Campanelli, and A. Butchart, "Elementary School-Based Prevention of Adolescent Alcohol Misuse," *Pediatrician* 14(1987): 70–76.

11. U.S. Department of Health and Human Services, *Alcohol and Health* (Sixth Special Report to the U.S. Congress from the Secretary of Health and Human Services, DHHS Pub. No. (ADM) 87–1519, 1987).

12. E. Ginzberg, H. Berliner, and M. Ostow, *Young People at Risk: Is Prevention Possible?* (Boulder, Colo.: Westview Press, 1988), p. 41.

13. U.S. Department of Health and Human Services, *Health, United States and Prevention Profile, 1983* (Washington, D.C.: U.S. Government Printing Office, DHHS Pub. No. (PHS) 84–1232, 1983), p. 380.

14. Speech by Loran Archer, Acting Director, National Institute on Alcohol Abuse and Alcoholism, published in *Sharing Knowledge for Action* (Proceedings of the 1st National Conference on Alcohol and Drug Abuse Prevention, August 3–6, 1986), pp. 120–28.

15. *PRIDE Quarterly* 9(1988): 9. This is a publication of a voluntary parents' organization (see note 9). This resolution apparently did not address the issue of smoking since there are no laws governing the advertising or sales of cigarettes.

16. D. Kandel, "Epidemiological and Psychosocial Perspectives on Adolescent Drug Use," *Journal of American Academy of Child Psychiatry* 21(1982): 328–47.

17. R. Jones and P. Moberg, "Correlates of Smokeless Tobacco in a Male Adolescent Population," *American Journal of Public Health* 78(1988): 61–63.

18. See Johnston, Bachman, and O'Malley, *Monitoring the Future, 1985* (1986), and prior and more recent publications (1987, 1988) for detailed results of the annual surveys of high school seniors.

19. Reported in *Youth Policy* 9(1987): 58.

20. Arizona State School Survey (unpublished data supplied by R. Jones, The Smith Project for Substance Abuse Education, University of Arizona, 1987); NIDA, *National Institute on Drug Abuse National Household Survey on Drug Abuse: Main Findings 1985* (DHHS Pub. No. (ADM) 88–1586, 1988); Halprin, Inc., *Drug Used by Oregon Public School Students* (Preliminary Report, 1988); average from 12 surveys conducted between 1982 and 1984 summarized in *School Surveys of Substance Abuse* (Internal memo from National Institute on Drug Abuse, Alcohol, Drug Abuse and Mental Health Administration, August 30, 1985); Search Institute, *Colorado Survey on Drug Use and Drug-Related Attitudes* (Minneapolis: Search Institute, 1985); Barnes and Welte, "Patterns and Predictors of Alcohol Use," 53–61.

21. "Seniors Reported Drug Use Lowest in Years," *Education Week,* March 8, 1989.

22. "Sharp Drop Seen in Student Cocaine Abuse," *Education Week,* December 13, 1987.

23. L. Johnston, P. O'Malley, and J. Bachman, *National Trends in Drug Use and Related Factors among American High School Students and Young Adults, 1975–1986* (Washington, D.C.: U.S. Government Printing Office, DHHS Pub. No. (ADM) 87–1535, 1987).

24. Johnston et al., *Monitoring the Future, 1985*, pp. 16–32.

25. Ibid.

26. See sources in Table 4.7.

27. Independence from parental authority but not necessarily from peer influences.

28. See Brunswick, "Young Black Males and Substance Abuse," for a useful discussion of substance abuse among black youth.

29. NIDA, *National Household Survey on Drug Abuse* (1988), p. 49.

30. Newcomb et al., "Substance Abuse," 430.
31. Arizona State School Survey (1987).
32. National Institute on Drug Abuse, *Data from the Drug Abuse Warning Network (DAWN)* (Series 1, No. 6, Annual Data, 1986, DHHS Pub. No. (ADM) 87–1530, 1987).
33. Hawkins et al., "Childhood Predictors," 44.
34. D. Goodwin, F. Schlusinger, J. Knop, S. Mednick, and S. Guzo, "Alcohol and Depression in Adopted-Out Daughters of Alcoholics," *Archives of General Psychiatry* 34(1977): 751–55.
35. Girls Clubs of America, Inc., *Facts and Reflections on Girls and Substance Abuse* (1988).

# 5

# Prevalence of Adolescent Pregnancy

Once a young person experiences coitus, she or he acquires "risk status." Unquestionably, young people who are not sexually active are not at risk of pregnancy, unless they are forced to have sex (which is not a rare event). However, once the decision is made to initiate sexual activity, risk of pregnancy is high for those who do not use contraception consistently. And since no contraception is 100 percent effective, an unplanned pregnancy may occur. Once pregnant, a young woman must decide whether to carry the pregnancy to term. She may decide to have an abortion, if that option is available to her. If a child is born, the mother may decide to give the child up for adoption.

While this series of decisions seems relatively straightforward, there is little consensus in our society about how to intervene at any point along the way and prevent the negative consequences. Differing perceptions of the problem shape the range of solutions. One set of conflicts centers on the morality of premarital sex. Some people believe that the only response to the issue of adolescent pregnancy is to promote abstention. Others believe that premarital sexual activity has become a normative behavior and, therefore, interventions should focus on teaching responsible sexual behavior and providing access to contraception. A second set of conflicts is focused on the abortion issue. Once pregnant, should a girl be required to maintain the pregnancy and encouraged to put the baby up for adoption if she cannot care for it, or should she be assisted to obtain an abortion if that is what she wants?

We can turn to many sources of data to gain insights into these questions. The problem of adolescent pregnancy has received a great deal of attention over the past decade and numerous studies have been produced from which we can learn about the antecedents, prevalence, and consequences of early sexual activity, contraceptive use, and pregnancy among teenagers. In 1987, the National Academy of Sciences (NAS) published a two-volume tome, summarizing research findings gathered over a two-year period for the deliberations of a Panel on Adolescent

Pregnancy and Childbearing.[1] Many of the findings cited in this chapter derive from that work.

## Sources of Data

Table 5.1 summarizes the major sources of data that are used in the adolescent pregnancy field, many of which were tapped for the NAS report. The first epidemiological study of adolescent sexual behavior was conducted by researchers from Johns Hopkins University (John Kantner and Melvin Zelnik) in 1971, and followed by surveys in 1976 and 1979.[2] The two earlier surveys included a national sample of young women, 15 to 19, and the third survey added a sample of males between 17 and 21 and was limited only to metropolitan areas. In 1982, the National Survey of Family Growth (NSFG) of the National Center for Health Statistics included unmarried adolescents for the first time.[3] The NSFG has been tracking the fertility patterns and contraceptive use of American women ages 18 to 44 for many years. The most recent data about teenage sexuality and pregnancy behavior come from the 1983 National Longitudinal Survey of Youth (NLSY).[4] The High School and Beyond Survey (HS&B) has also been used to study the determinants of early childbearing.[5]

Responses to survey questions about sexual activity are not always reliable. Researchers believe that girls may understate their sexual activity while boys overstate. Abortions are significantly underreported. The most reliable survey data are for births, probably because of the actuality of the condition. The results of most recent surveys are consistent with official statistics about births.

TABLE 5.1. Sources of Data on Adolescent Pregnancy

| Source and Subject | Year | Sample Size | Citation |
|---|---|---|---|
| National Survey of Family Growth: females 15–19 | 1982 | 1,900 | Pratt et al. 1984 |
| National Longitudinal Survey of Youth: males and females 14–21 in 1979 | 1979–1986 | 12,686 | Mott 1983 Hayes 1987 Hofferth and Hayes 1987 |
| Survey of Young Women and Men, Johns Hopkins: females 15–19, males 17–21 | 1979 | 2,634 | Zelnik and Kantner 1980 |
| Vital Statistics: births to females <20 | Annual | Count | Ventura et al. 1988 |
| The Alan Guttmacher Institute: abortions to females <20 (age distribution from Centers for Disease Control) | Annual | Count | Henshaw 1987 |
| High School and Beyond: sophomores in 1980 | 1980–1984 | 13,601 | Abrahamse et al. 1986 |

Annual vital statistics are gathered by the National Center for Health Statistics, and their reports produce numbers and rates of births by age and race.[6] Studies based on surveys of providers and state data-collection agencies conducted by the Alan Guttmacher Institute produce aggregate numbers and rates of abortion.[7] The Centers for Disease Control (CDC) analyzes state survey data to produce age/race distributions.[8]

Our knowledge of the role of young males in sexuality and pregnancy behaviors is incomplete.[9] Much of the talk about adolescent pregnancy ignores males, except for the acknowledgment that they are "perpetrators" of the outcomes. Information about almost 40 percent of the fathers of babies born to teenage mothers is missing from vital statistics.[10] Close to 70 percent of the identified fathers in 1986 were over the age of 19 (not surprising since two-thirds of the teen mothers were between 18 and 19). No data are available about the age of the male partners in teen pregnancies that terminate in abortions, but it is probable that those males are younger than the fathers of live births. In any case, males must be included in target populations for pregnancy prevention programs.

## Consequences of Early Pregnancy and Childbearing

Research about the consequences of adolescent sexual activity and pregnancy has been furthered by the work of the National Institute for Child Health and Human Development.[11] Scores of researchers have received grants to produce analyses of census data and other surveys, documenting the consequences of childbearing on adolescents compared with childbearing among older women. One problem that has confronted researchers is the determination of the effects of low socioeconomic status (SES) and race apart from the effects of age. Many of the problems encountered by teen mothers are not unlike those encountered by older mothers who live in similarly deprived economic circumstances. Recent studies suggest that low-income women lack access to quality prenatal care, and that when such care is provided, the negative effects of childbearing are diminished.[12] Another problem is that teenagers enter into pregnancy with many preexisting conditions that may produce negative outcomes, such as drinking, smoking, drug abuse, poor nutrition, sexually transmitted diseases (STDs), and anemia. Thus, the consequences stem from the problem behavior or illness, not from the mere fact of age at conception.

Despite these shortcomings, researchers have been able to "control" their data and to isolate the short- and long-term consequences documented as having a negative effect on teenagers (Table 5.2).[13] Early sexual intercourse places young women at very high risk of health consequences. The younger the age at which a girl first enters into sexual relationships, the more likely that negative consequences will follow. Early sexual initiates have more frequent acts of coitus and multiple partners, and are less likely to use effective methods of contraception. The most deleterious consequences other than pregnancy are sexually transmitted diseases and their related side effects (infertility, cervical cancer, ectopic pregnancies, and infections passed on to newborns). As we have seen in Chapter 2, STD

TABLE 5.2. Consequences of Early Sexual Intercourse and Early Pregnancy

| Behavior | Consequences | |
| --- | --- | --- |
| | Short Term | Long Term |
| *Early Sexual Intercourse* | | |
| Frequent sex with multiple partners | Sexually transmitted diseases (STDs)<br>Pelvic inflammatory disease (PID) | Infertility<br>Ectopic pregnancies<br>Cervical cancer<br>Infections in newborn |
| With use of intravenous drugs, or partner using drugs, or bisexual | HIV positive | AIDS<br>Mortality |
| Contraceptive problems | | |
| Failure of method | Unintended pregnancy | |
| IUD side effects | PID | |
| Pill side effects | Inconsequential, if under medical supervision | Possible long-term health effects (conflicting evidence) |
| Unprotected intercourse | Pregnancy: usually unintended | (see Early Pregnancy) |
| *Early Pregnancy* | Early childbearing<br>*Mother:* complications, toxemia, anemia, prolonged labor<br>If <15, higher risk of mortality | *Mother:* Reduced educational attainment, more subsequent births closer together and unintended, marital instability, lower status jobs, poverty, welfare |
| | *Baby:* prematurity, low birthweight | *Child:* lower achievement, more emotional problems, high risk of becoming a teen parent, life in poverty |
| | Abortion | Possible future spontaneous abortions |
| | Adoption | Effects unknown |

*Sources:* D. Strobino, "The Health and Medical Consequences of Adolescent Sexuality and Pregnancy: A Review of the Literature," in S. Hofferth and C. Hayes, eds., *Risking the Future: Adolescent Sexuality, Pregnancy, and Childbearing, Vol. II* (Washington, D.C.: National Academy Press, 1987), pp. 93–122; C. Brindis and R. Jeremy, *Adolescent Pregnancy and Parenting in California* (San Francisco: Center for Population and Reproductive Health Policy, University of California, 1988), pp. 53–76.

rates are high in certain risk groups. With cases of chlamydia and herpes on the rise, diseases that can affect future fertility and newborns, the results of frequent unprotected intercourse take on serious consequences. AIDS is the most life-threatening consequence; young people who are involved in an array of high-risk behaviors, such as drug use, prostitution, and frequent sex with multiple partners, are extremely vulnerable.

The most direct consequences of early pregnancy are related to childbearing. The birth of a child impacts on both the mother and the baby—and ultimately the father, family, and community—with immediate short-term, long-term, often life-time, consequences. Very young mothers under the age of 15 suffer the worst physical effects, with heightened risks of complications and mortality. Moreover, teen mothers under the age of 18 are more likely to have toxemia, anemia, and prolonged labor. Their babies are at higher risk of prematurity and low birth-weight.

In the years following early childbearing, teen mothers suffer several disadvantages: reduced educational achievement, unstable marriages and high divorce rates, or no marriage, more subsequent births closer together and unintended, lower status jobs, lower incomes and, in some cases, long-term welfare dependency (although as time goes on, welfare dependency decreases). Adverse effects on children of teenage parents include lower achievement, many more behavioral and emotional problems, high risk of becoming teenage parents themselves, and a lifetime in poverty.

Not all teen mothers experience negative consequences as they become mature women. A unique follow-up study of urban black teen mothers by Furstenberg and colleagues found that many of these women had completed high school, found employment, and were not dependent on public assistance.[14] Success was associated with coming from a more economically secure and better-educated family and doing well in school. However, compared with their peers who had delayed childbearing until after their teen years, they were not so successful.

Teenagers experience very few documentable, negative consequences from abortion. There is some evidence of an increased risk of spontaneous abortions in pregnancies that follow abortions, but the risk is no greater (and may be less) for teens than for older women. This applies to other sequillae as well, such as complications and hemorrhaging. In general, the earlier in the pregnancy the abortion procedure, the lower the risk of complications. Teens who suffer negative consequences generally do so because they are more likely to have later abortions (after eight weeks) than older women. There is no evidence in the psychological literature that abortion produces depression or guilt. Most anecdotal reports refer to feelings of relief.

Adoption is a decision that teenagers rarely make following unplanned pregnancies (official adoption rates are currently very low). No studies have been identified that document the psychological consequences of adoption on the teenage mother, such as depression or regret.

From our discussion, we can conclude that young women who delay the initiation of sexual intercourse until they can effectively use contraception to prevent pregnancy are at lower risk of negative consequences. High-risk behavior centers on three critical factors: early intercourse, unprotected intercourse, and early unintended childbearing. Young people who are at risk of practicing these behaviors would make up the target population for interventions.

## Prevalence of Early Unprotected Intercourse

The family planning field has made extensive use of risk estimates as the denominator to be used for program planning. Estimates of the number of women ''at risk of unintended pregnancy and in need of family planning" were introduced in the mid-1960s as evidence of the need for public support of birth control clinics. The legislation that supports family planning, The Family Planning and Population Act of 1970 (Title X of the Public Health Service Law), required from its inception that programs that receive public funds focus on low-income women "in need of subsidized services." Adolescents were specifically included in this regulation after 1978.

A woman in "need" of *organized* family planning services (medical contraception delivered by a clinic or a private physician) has been defined as sexually active, fertile (or fecund, depending on whether one is a demographer or a biologist), and not intentionally pregnant or trying to become pregnant.[15] To establish need for *subsidized* family planning services (free or sliding scale), various measures of poverty have been defined. In the mid-1970s, as attention began to shift from low-income women to adolescents in general, estimates of the number of "teenagers-at-risk" were produced, largely based on the sexual activity factor. It was assumed that all adolescents were medically indigent and needed access to free family planning services.

Few adolescents are known to be functionally or surgically sterile. However, increasing numbers of young girls are probably having coitus prior to their first menstrual periods (menarche). There has been a downward trend in the age of menarche of about four months per decade since 1850.[16] The average age of first menstruation is currently about 12½ years, although peak fertility is somewhat later.[17] Thus, while the age of menarche has dropped significantly over the past century, the rate of early initiation into sexual activity has increased. Some young girls who are sexually active may not be at risk of pregnancy (fecund) at their current ages; however, they will be at risk in the near future.

The prevalence of reported teen sexual activity (coitus) is much higher now than it was two decades ago.[18] In the first study in 1971, about 30 percent of all young women aged 15 to 19 reported that they had experienced sexual intercourse, and this proportion increased dramatically, up to almost half in the 1979 survey. In 1982, the rate appeared to decrease slightly to 47 percent, suggesting a plateauing effect. The 1983 data are based on the different NLSY survey methodology, and although the rate of 56 percent is a little higher, it does not indicate a significant change.

Males were included in the 1979 Johns Hopkins Survey for the first time (but not in the 1982 NSFG). Of all respondents aged 17–21, 70 percent reported that they had premarital intercourse.[19] The 1983 NLSY estimates are also higher for males; more than 70 percent of a younger age group (15- to 19-year-olds) reported sexual activity. Survey data consistently show earlier initiation of sexual intercourse among males than females.[20]

Table 5.3 shows the prevalence of sexual activity by age, sex, and race and ethnicity as of 1983. Almost 1 in 5 boys and 1 in 20 girls reported having had sexual intercourse before the age of 15. Sexual intercourse at early ages is highly prevalent among black males; more than 4 out of 10 said they had sex before they reached their fifteenth birthdays (compared with 1 out of 10 young black females). By age 17, most black males and two-thirds of white and Hispanic males report

TABLE 5.3. Percentage of Teenagers Who Have Had
Sexual Intercourse by Age, Sex, and Race/Ethnicity,
1983

| Sex and Race/ethnicity | Percentage Who Were Sexually Active by Age | | |
|---|---|---|---|
| | 15 | 17 | 19 |
| *Females* | | | |
| Total | 5 | 44 | 74 |
| White | 5 | 42 | 72 |
| Black | 10 | 59 | 85. |
| Hispanic | 4 | 40 | 70 |
| *Males* | | | |
| Total | 17 | 64 | 83 |
| White | 12 | 60 | 81 |
| Black | 42 | 86 | 94 |
| Hispanic | 19 | 67 | 84 |

*Source:* Cumulative sexual activity rates from National Longitudinal
Survey of Youth, reported in S. Hofferth and C. Hayes, eds., *Risking
the Future: Adolescent Sexuality, Pregnancy, and Childbearing, Vol.
II* (Washington, D.C.: National Academy Press, 1987), Appendix A,
Table 16, p. 368.

sexual activity, and by age 19, sexual relationships are clearly normative behavior
for all male groups. Among females, by age 17, 3 out of 5 blacks and 2 out of 5
whites and Hispanics have had sex. By age 19, the vast majority report sexual
relations, including 85 percent of black females and over 70 percent of all others.

It should be kept in mind that having intercourse *once* does not necessarily
place an individual at risk. About 18 percent of "sexually active" 15- to 17-year-
old girls reported no intercourse in the past 3 months, and 21 percent had a frequency of once a month.[21] An unknown proportion of girls' first sexual encounters
result from rape and incest. In a small sample survey, it was reported that almost
one-third of sexually active respondents had unwanted sexual experiences at some
time.[22] More than a third of those who had unwanted sex (about 1 in 10 of those
who were sexually active) had been forced to have sex. The others engaged in
intercourse only to please partners or because of peer pressure.

The earlier a young woman engages in sexual intercourse, the higher the risk
of unintended pregnancy, primarily because these sexually active women are not
using contraception. The 1979 Johns Hopkins Survey found that, among girls who
had sex before they were 15, only 31 percent used any form of contraception the
first time; for those who had first sex between 15 and 17, 52 percent used contraception.[23] Table 5.4 shows the percent distribution of sexually active teenagers
according to the methods they used the first time they had sex, and the methods
they reported using in the most recent survey (the 1982 NSFG).[24] These data show
significant race/ethnic differences in usage at first intercourse. More than three-
quarters of Hispanic and two-thirds of black young women, compared with 45
percent of white young women, did not use any protection the first time they had

TABLE 5.4. Contraceptive Use among Sexually Active 15- to 19-year-old Females: First Intercourse and Current Practice, 1982

| Race and Ethnicity | Percentage of Sexually Active Teens by Method Used at First Intercourse | | | | |
|---|---|---|---|---|---|
| | None | Pill or Diaphragm | Condom | Withdrawal | Other |
| TOTAL | 52 | 8 | 23 | 13 | 4 |
| White | 45 | 9 | 25 | 17 | 5 |
| Black | 64 | 11 | 19 | 5 | 2 |
| Hispanic | 77 | 2 | 13 | 4 | 4 |
| | Percentage of Sexually Active Teens by Method Used Most Recently | | | | |
| | None | Pill or Diaphragm | Condom | Withdrawal | Other |
| TOTAL | 29 | 50 | 15 | — | 5 |
| White | 27 | 51 | 17 | — | 5 |
| Black | 35 | 50 | 9 | — | 7 |
| Hispanic | 32 | 49 | 10 | — | 8 |

*Source:* A. Torres and S. Singh, ''Contraceptive Practice Among Hispanic Adolescents,'' *Family Planning Perspectives* 18(1986): 193–94.

intercourse. White youngsters were much more likely to say that they used condoms or withdrawal at first coitus than other ethnic groups.

The contraceptive practices of teenagers improve significantly over time. Table 5.4 shows the most recent method used by sexually active teenagers who are ''currently exposed to the risk of unintended pregnancy''—that is, they are not pregnant and have had intercourse in the past three months. They report primarily medical methods: pills (45 percent), with a small number reporting diaphragms (4 percent) and IUDs (1 percent). Condom use is less typical after the first sexual encounter, and withdrawal is no longer reported as a method. Nonuse of contraception is greatly reduced and differences between ethnic groups no longer are significant. Still, close to one-third of all sexually active teenage girls continue to have sexual relations without use of birth control, placing them at very high risk of unintended pregnancy.

The earlier the age of first intercourse, the longer the delay in going to a clinic to obtain contraception. In one study of clinic patients, for the youngest girls (below 13), the time elapsed before seeking a contraceptive method was an average of 40 months, compared with 18- to 19-year-olds who only delayed 6 months.[25] If a girl continues to have intercourse without contraception, she is quite likely to become pregnant. Within 6 months of first intercourse, 25 percent of 15- to 19-year-olds conceived if they had never used a contraceptive method, compared with 5 percent who always used a method.[26] At the end of two years, at least half had conceived. Thus, the chain of evidence links together in an obvious pattern: early intercourse, nonuse of protection at first intercourse, long delay prior to obtaining medical methods, early pregnancy.

## Prevalence of Early Childbearing

The most obvious consequence of early sexual intercourse is early unwanted childbearing. Recent research has shown that 82 percent of conceptions that occurred to teenagers in the mid-1980s were unintended, and the younger the girl, the more likely the pregnancy was unplanned.[27] Yet, among those who reported that they did not want to become pregnant at the time, only 31 percent were using contraception. While a few young girls may still consciously become pregnant to ''have someone to love'' or unconsciously become pregnant ''to punish their parents,'' very few conceptions result from planned parenthood among teenagers.

There have been more than 1 million teen pregnancies[28] in the United States annually since 1973, and for the past decade, about one in nine adolescent females has conceived each year.[29] The peak year was 1980, with close to 1.2 million teen pregnancies. During the early 1970s, the teen birth rate declined (from 68 to 56 per 1000), but since 1976 when it reached 53 per 1000, there has been almost no change.[30] The teen abortion rate rose steadily until 1980, but has been about 43 per 1000 ever since. Thus, the teen pregnancy rate has changed very little during this decade, although the proportion of pregnancies that result in live births has decreased each year—from about ⁀⁔ percent in 1973 to 48 percent currently. However, the increase in the number of young women at risk has been even greater than the increase in pregnancies over this same period and, therefore, the rate of pregnancies per sexually active teenager has decreased (from about 270 per 1000 to 230 per 1000). Currently, close to one in four (23%) of sexually active teens experience a pregnancy during the year.

Table 5.5 shows the 1985 birth, abortion, and pregnancy rates per 1000 teens by age and race (and in the discussion, the rates will be converted to percentages,

TABLE 5.5. Birth, Abortion, and Pregnancy Rates per 1,000 Population by Age and Race, 1985

| Age and Race | Birth | Abortion | Pregnancy[a] |
|---|---|---|---|
| *Total* | | | |
| 15–17 | 31 | 31 | 71 |
| 18–19 | 81 | 63 | 166 |
| *White* | | | |
| 15–17 | 24 | 26 | 57 |
| 18–19 | 70 | 55 | 145 |
| *Black* | | | |
| 15–17 | 63 | 53 | 134 |
| 18–19 | 129 | 97 | 261 |

[a]Pregnancy rates include estimated miscarriages as well as births and abortions.

*Source:* S. Henshaw and J. Van Vort, ''Teenage Abortion, Birth and Pregnancy Statistics: An Update,'' *Family Planning Perspectives* 21(1989):85–88.

as described in note 30).[31] Among 15- to 17-year-olds, about 6 percent of white girls and 13 percent of black girls became pregnant in that year; of these, 2 percent of whites and 6 percent of blacks became mothers. Among 18- to 19-year-olds, the rates were much higher, as would be expected: 15 percent of whites and 26 percent of blacks became pregnant and 7 percent of whites and 13 percent of blacks became mothers.

Much attention has been given to the issue of pregnancies among very young women under the age of 15 because the medical consequences can be so much more severe. Practitioners never forget the experience of delivering a baby to an 11- or 12-year-old child. This is, however, a very rare event. About 10,000 girls under the age of 15 delivered babies in 1985 (the same number each year in the past decade). This number represents just 2 percent of all 472,000 births to women aged 15 to 19 in 1985. Girls under the age of 15 who become pregnant are much more likely to obtain abortions than older women.

Data on total pregnancies among Hispanic young women are not available. No estimates are available for abortions among Hispanics, nor are the population data available for denominators. In 1985, according to vital statistics reports, 13 percent of all teen births were to Hispanics (who were white or black), while the census showed that about 9 percent of the teen population was Hispanic. The prevalence rates among Hispanics probably lie somewhere between those of whites and blacks, but there are significant differences among this group depending on point of origin—for example, Cubans have very low teen birth rates, while Puerto Ricans have the highest rates.

The most dominant theme in the discussion of adolescent pregnancy is the striking increase in out-of-wedlock births. While fertility rates in general were on the decline, birth rates for unmarried teen women have been increasing, particularly among young white women. Teenagers no longer marry, not even to legalize a birth prior to delivery. In 1986, fully 3 out of 5 births to women under the age of 20 were out of wedlock. Almost all of the youngest mothers under 15 were unmarried; the percent decreases linearly from 86 percent of 15-year-old mothers to 49 percent of 19-year-olds.

## Number of Teens at Risk of Adolescent Pregnancy

The first estimate of adolescents at risk of pregnancy appeared in a 1976 publication of the Alan Guttmacher Institute, *Eleven Million Teenagers: What Can Be Done About the Epidemic of Adolescent Pregnancies in the United States.*[32] The number included 4 million girls and 7 million boys aged 15 to 19 who were estimated as having already experienced sexual intercourse, based on the 1971 survey data applied to the current population for females, and very rough "guesstimates" for males.

The 1983 National Longitudinal Survey of Youth data on sexual activity has been applied to 1986 population estimates (Table 2.1) to roughly estimate the number of sexually active teenage females and males in 1986. Although the rates may be slightly overestimated, the data base includes males and provides infor-

TABLE 5.6. Estimated Number of Young People at Risk of
Consequences of Early Sexual Activity, 1986 (numbers in 000s)

| Behavior | Age 10–14 | Age 15–17 | Totals Age 10–17 |
|---|---|---|---|
| *Sexually active* | | | |
| Males | 1,452 | 3,614 | 5,066 |
| Females | 407 | 2,404 | 2,811 |
| *Do not use contraception*[a] | | | |
| Females | 200 | 800 | 1,000 |
| *Early pregnancy* | | | |
| Females | 30 | 371 | 401 |
| *Early childbearing* | | | |
| Females | 10 | 168 | 178 |

[a]Estimate that one-half of 10- to 14-year-olds and one-third of 15- to 17-year-olds are not currently using contraception.

*Sources:* Estimates on sexual activity from Table 5.3 applied to population estimates from Table 2.1; pregnancy: estimated by author based on data from K. Moore, *Facts at a Glance* (Flint, Mich.: Charles Stewart Mott Foundation, 1989); childbearing: *Monthly Vital Statistics Report* 37 (July 12, 1988).

mation that can be used to construct a simulated estimate of the younger cohorts (10 to 14) as well as separate estimates for 15- to 17-year-olds.

In 1986, approximately 7.9 million young people in the United States age 10 to 17 had already experienced sexual intercourse at least one time, including 2.8 million girls and 5.1 million boys (Table 5.6). For all 10- to 19-year-olds, the total estimate amounts to 13.5 million (not shown). This represents a sizable increase over the past decade, particularly in the number of girls who are sexually active, reflecting the upward trends in the survey data.

Not all sexually active young people are at equal risk of negative outcomes from their behavior. Older teenagers in stable relationships appear to be able to use effective contraception. Our concern is with younger people who are not adequately protected from the consequences. It would simplify matters if we could select an age when intercourse is appropriate and rule out all other behavior. This is not, obviously, enforceable. Therefore, we can assume that all sexually active young people under the age of 18 are at relatively high risk, and that those who are not currently using contraception and those who have already experienced a pregnancy are at very high risk of negative consequences.

In regard to the 5 million young males under the age of 18 who are at risk, we have little information about their contraceptive use, and even less data on pregnancy patterns among young males. We do know that the characteristics of young fathers are similar to those of young mothers (see Table 5.7, which summarizes antecedents of these behaviors).

Among the 2.8 million young females under the age of 18 who are sexually active, it is estimated that about 1 million are not currently using contraception. Some 400,000 experienced a pregnancy in 1986 and 178,000 became mothers. Almost all the births to these women result from unintentional pregnancies.

## Antecedents of High-Risk Behavior
## Related to Adolescent Pregnancy

Many studies have been conducted from which we can learn about the antecedents of early sexual activity, nonuse of contraception, and early childbearing. As summarized in Table 5.7, it is obvious that many of the antecedents are the same for each of the three high-risk behaviors, but they are not identical. Black young people, especially boys, are more likely to have intercourse at very early ages, even when other factors are taken into consideration. Early pubertal development in males has some influence on age of initiation. Some researchers attribute the higher rates of early sexual intercourse among black youngsters to specific cultural patterns and attitudes in different communities. However, when controls are added for socioeconomic status, much, but not all, of the differences in prevalence disappears. Young people from low-income families, with uneducated parents who are not supportive or communicative are much more likely to initiate sex at early ages. Children who are not engaged in school activities, who have low expectations for school achievement, and hang around with and are easily influenced by friends in similar situations are more prone to early sex. This behavior is often preceded by other high-risk behavior, such as early substance use and truancy. Children who perceive that they may have poor prospects for the future and live in communities that are poor, segregated, and lack employment opportunities are more likely to initiate sex at early ages.

TABLE 5.7. Antecedents of Early Sexual Intercourse, Nonuse of Contraception, and Early Childbearing

| Antecedent | Early Sexual Intercourse | Nonuse of Contraception | Early Childbearing |
|---|---|---|---|
| *Demographic* | | | |
| Age | | **Early sex | **Early sex |
| Pubertal development | *Males | | |
| Sex | **Males | | |
| Race/ethnicity | **Blacks | *Hispanics | **Blacks |
| *Personal* | | | |
| Expectations for education | **Low | **Low | **Low |
| Perception of life options | *Poor prospects | *Poor prospects | *Poor prospects |
| School grades | **Low | **Low | **Low |
| Conduct, general behavior | **Truancy | | **Delinquency |
| Religiosity | **Low attendance | | **Low attendance |
| Peer influence | **Heavy influence | | *Peer attitudes |
| Peer use | | *Emulate peers | |
| Conformity–rebelliousness | *Nonconformity | | |
| Beliefs about risk | | *Unconcerned | |
| Involvement in other high-risk behaviors | *Early delinquency *Substance use | | |
| Psychological factors | | *Impulsive | |
| Self-esteem | | *Lack locus of control | |
| Relationship to partner | | **Uncommitted | |

| Antecedent | Early Sexual Intercourse | Nonuse of Contraception | Early Childbearing |
|---|---|---|---|
| *Family* | | | |
| Household composition | *Single headed | | **Single headed |
| Income, poverty status | **Low income | | **Low income |
| Parental education | **Low level | **Low level | **Low level |
| Parental role, bonding | **Lack of support and communication | **No communication | **Lack of support and monitoring |
| Parental practice of high-risk behaviors | *Permissive parents | | **Mother was teen mom |
| Culture in home | | | *Lack resources |
| Siblings | *Large family | | **Unmarried sisters are teen moms |
| | | | |
| *Community* | | | |
| Neighborhood quality | *Poverty area | | **Poverty area |
| Segregation | *Blacks in segregated schools | | **Blacks in segregated schools |
| Employment situation | *High unemployment | | **High unemployment |

\* = Several sources agree that factor is a major predictor.

\*\* = Most sources agree that factor is a major predictor.

*Sources:* S. Hofferth, "Factors Affecting Initiation of Sexual Intercourse," in S. Hofferth and C. Hayes, eds., *Risking the Future: Adolescent Sexuality, Pregnancy, and Childbearing, Vol. II* (Washington, D.C.: National Academy Press, 1987), pp. 7–35; C. Hayes, ed., *Risking the Future, Adolescent Sexuality, Pregnancy, and Childbearing, Vol. I* (Washington, D.C.: National Academy Press, 1987), pp. 95–122; A. Abrahamse, P. Morrison, and L. Waite, "Single Teenage Mothers: Spotting Susceptible Adolescents in Advance" (Unpublished paper, Rand Corporation, Santa Monica, Calif., 1986), 77–80; N. Maxwell and F. Mott, "Trends in the Determinants of Early Childbearing" (Paper presented at the 1987 Annual Meeting of the Population Association of America, Chicago, Illinois), 1–12; J. Dryfoos, "The Determinants of Early Childbearing and Other Risk Behaviors: Framework for a Prevention Strategy," in L. Lipsett and L. Mitnick, eds., *Self-Regulation, Impulsivity, and Risk-Taking Behavior: Causes and Consequences* (Norwood, N.J.: Ablex, 1990); C. Chilman, *Adolescent Sexuality in a Changing Society,* 2nd ed. (New York: Wiley, 1983), pp. 131–43.

An observer of the contemporary urban scene can easily imagine how this early sex takes place. Many children hang around on street corners even during the school day, being drawn into the street life of gangs, drugs, prostitution, and the vast underground economy (sales of stolen goods, drugs, off-the-books businesses and services). In burned out areas, there are many buildings one can enter to engage in these illicit activities. Even in more affluent areas, children can use their own homes for sexual encounters because family members are often not present during the daytime. The Johns Hopkins Survey found that the living room couch has long since displaced the back seat of the car or the beach as the place of intercourse.

Use of contraception follows a pattern that is linked to early initiation of intercourse and other behaviors. Hispanics are less likely to use contraception either initially or subsequently. Young sexually active teens who do not use contraception are more impulsive and lack an internalized locus of control; they are poor planners. They are more likely to have "casual" sex and not be in committed relationships with partners. These high-risk youngsters have low prospects for the future, low expectations, and low grades. Their parents have limited education and are less likely to communicate with them.

Young women who become teen parents are those who enter into sexual relationships at very early ages (more typical of black youngsters) and use no contraception (typical of Hispanics). Again, they fit the pattern—they are low achievers in school, have poor prospects, and low expectations for the future. Girls who become teen mothers often have friends whose attitudes are accepting of early parenthood. Teen mothers come from poor families, frequently single-headed (mother) households, with low educational levels, and often their mothers were teen mothers as well as their older sisters. Girls who become teen mothers do not have parents who support or monitor them (what one researcher called "talking and tracking"). Their homes are located in poverty areas, with segregated schools and high unemployment rates. Homes lack cultural resources such as books and magazines.

Questions have been raised about whether girls who become teen mothers are less cognitively able than their same-age peers. This question can only be answered in terms of "basic skills," and in this area, teen mothers are at a great disadvantage. Those who have the lowest level of basic skills are many times more likely to become mothers inadvertently and at early ages. Some of the teen mothers appear to be submissive and depressed; motherhood is something that just happened to them. The most graphic description of this phenomenon came from a teen mother in Florida: "I was just standing there and he came along and put his thing in me, and a couple of months later they told me I was gonna' have a baby."

## Summary

The risk of negative consequences deriving from adolescent sexual behavior can be defined at three points: the initiation of sexual intercourse, the use of contraception, and the birth following an unintended pregnancy. Premarital sexual intercourse has become increasingly described as normative behavior during the teenage years. (It is not entirely clear whether such behavior wasn't always normative, or whether the survey methodology has just become more reliable.) Recently, the most dramatic documented changes have been in the age of first intercourse. We have estimated that as many as 5 million boys and almost 3 million girls have already had sex prior to their eighteenth birthdays. Not all of these young people have frequent sexual relations. Others lose their virginity as a result of involuntary experiences, from incest, rape, sexual abuse, and other unwanted sexual activities.

Early sexual activity can lead to very negative consequences, particularly early pregnancy, but also high rates of STDs and high risk of AIDS. There is a growing consensus that interventions should address this issue by presenting arguments and skills for delaying the initiation of sexual intercourse until one is ready to assume the responsibilities for the consequences.

One argument for delay is that early initiates rarely use contraception. The path from nonuse of contraception to subsequent negative consequences is well documented. We have shown that close to 800,000 young sexually active girls under the age of 18 are not using any contraception. Their reasons for nonuse range from lack of planning to lack of access to fear of the health consequences from birth control pills. Nonusers of contraception are particularly ignorant about the risks of STDs and early pregnancy. Young boys are even more ignorant about contraception than young girls. Even among teenagers who have used contraception, many use ineffective methods such as withdrawal and douches, and many use effective methods sporadically or incorrectly. Documentation is strong for interventions that ensure that all sexually active teenagers have adequate information about contraception and access to quality birth control services.

The most compelling data about adolescent pregnancy emerge from the research on the antecedents and consequences. Teen mothers have a myriad of short- and long-term problems, as do the babies they bear, the fathers, their families, and, ultimately, their communities. Among girls under the age of 18, 178,000 became mothers in 1987, for the most part, unintentionally (80%) and unmarried (72%). The research documents and observations verify that teen childbearing has become a "job" for low-income underachievers. Unfortunately, it is a job they are ill-equipped to carry out. Achievers (e.g., girls who are doing well in school and expect to go to college), when confronted with this situation, obtain abortions.[33] Only a few put their babies up for adoption.

One of the most significant research findings in recent years has confirmed the interrelationships between basic skills, poverty, and teen childbearing. Based on an analysis of the National Longitudinal Survey of Youth,[34] the data reveal the percent of 16- to 19-year-olds who were already mothers, by race and according to basic skills and poverty levels:

| Basic Skills:<br>Family Income: | Below Average<br>Below Poverty | Average or Better<br>Above Poverty |
|---|---|---|
| White | 21% | 3% |
| Black | 23 | 3 |
| Hispanic | 21 | 5 |

Girls with low basic skills from poverty families were five to seven times more likely to have become mothers during their teen years than girls with average or better basic skills and not from poverty families. Differences among whites, blacks, and Hispanics were insignificant. This analysis provides strong confirmation for the "underclass" theory—that increasing numbers of young people in the United States are falling behind and being cast in roles that will prevent them from ever catching up and "making it." Although race is a factor, poor nonachieving white youngsters have low odds for success as well.

Our analysis suggests that interventions to prevent early childbearing must encompass the problems of low basic skills and the effects of poverty. This greatly expands the scope of the adolescent pregnancy field into an exploration of what has been called "life options." Our review here demonstrates the validity of pregnancy intervention programs that seek to expand the opportunity structure for these disadvantaged youth.


## Notes

1. C. Hayes, ed., *Risking the Future, Adolescent Sexuality, Pregnancy, and Childbearing, Vol. I* (Washington, D.C.: National Academy Press, 1987); S. Hofferth and C. Hayes, eds., *Risking the Future: Adolescent Sexuality, Pregnancy, and Childbearing, Vol. II* (Washington, D.C.: National Academy Press, 1987).
2. Many articles have been written using data from the Johns Hopkins studies. For a summary article of the 1979 survey, see M. Zelnik and J. Kantner, "Sexual Activity, Contraceptive Use and Pregnancy among Metropolitan-Area Teenagers," *Family Planning Perspectives* 12(1980): 230–37.
3. W. Pratt, W. Mosher, C. Bachrach, and M. Horn, "Understanding U.S. Fertility: Findings from the National Survey of Family Growth, Cycle III," *Population Bulletin* 39(1984): 36–38.
4. F. Mott, "Early Fertility Behavior among American Youth: Evidence from the 1982 National Longitudinal Surveys of Labor Force Behavior of Youth" (Paper presented at the 1983 Annual Meeting of the American Public Health Association, Dallas, Texas). See also analyses by A. Sum in K. Pittman, *Preventing Adolescent Pregnancy: What Schools Can Do* (Washington, D.C.: Children's Defense Fund, 1986).
5. A. Abrahamse, P. Morrison, and L. Waite, "Single Teenage Mothers: Spotting Susceptible Adolescents in Advance" (Unpublished paper, Rand Corporation, Santa Monica, Calif., 1986).
6. S. Ventura, S. Taffel, and W. Mosher, "Estimates of Pregnancies and Pregnancy Rates for the U.S., 1976–1985," *American Journal of Public Health* 78(1988): 506–11.
7. S. Henshaw, "Characteristics of U.S. Women Having Abortions, 1982–1983," *Family Planning Perspectives* 19(1987): 5–8.
8. Centers for Disease Control, Annual Abortion Surveillance Reports, in U.S. Bureau of the Census, *Statistical Abstract of the United States* (annual) (Washington, D.C.: U.S. Government Printing Office).
9. See J. Dryfoos, *Putting the Boys in the Picture* (Santa Cruz, Calif.: Network Publications, 1988), for a discussion of the research on teen male sexuality, contraception, and pregnancy.
10. National Center for Health Statistics, "Advance Report of Final Natality Statistics, 1986," *Monthly Vital Statistics Report* 37(July 12, 1988).
11. The National Institute for Child Health and Human Development (NICHHD) is situated in the National Institutes of Health. Its Center for Population Research has targeted adolescent pregnancy as a priority area for grants and contracts since the mid-1970s.
12. Institute of Medicine, *Preventing Low Birthweight* (Washington, D.C.: National Academy Press, 1985).
13. Sources used for Table 5.2 include D. Strobino, "The Health and Medical Consequences of Adolescent Sexuality and Pregnancy: A Review of the Literature," in Hofferth and Hayes, eds., *Risking the Future, Vol. II*, pp. 93–122; and C. Brindis and R. Jeremy, *Adolescent Pregnancy and Parenting in California* (San Francisco: Center for Population and Reproductive Health Policy, University of California, 1988.

14. F. Furstenberg, J. Brooks-Gunn, and S. Morgan, "Adolescent Mothers and Their Children in Later Life," *Family Planning Perspectives* 19(1987): 142–51.

15. J. Dryfoos, "Women Who Need and Receive Family Planning Services: Estimates at Mid-Decade," *Family Planning Perspectives* 7(1975): 172–79; J. Dryfoos, "A Formula for the 1970's: Estimating Need for Subsidized Family Planning Services in the United States," *Family Planning Perspectives* 5(1973): 145–74.

16. J. Tanner, "Physical Growth," in P. Mussen, ed., *Carmichael's Manual of Child Psychology*, vol. 1, 3rd ed. (New York: Wiley, 1970), pp. 77–156.

17. L. Zabin, Marilyn Hirsch, and Janet Hardy, "Ages of Physical Maturation and First Intercourse in Black Teenage Males and Females" (Paper presented at the Annual Meeting of the American Public Health Association, Montreal, 1982).

18. The pioneering Kinsey studies made 40 years ago reported high rates of sexual activity among "lower class" adolescent males.

19. Zelnik and Kantner, "Sexual Activity, Contraceptive Use, and Pregnancy," 230–37.

20. Boys reportedly initiate sex earlier than girls, but girls report that their partners are two years older than they are. The question rises, with whom do the mass of young boys have sex? Some observers think that a very small number of older girls may have sexual relationships with a very large number of younger boys.

21. Hofferth and Hayes, *Risking the Future, Vol. II*, pp. A-22, 374.

22. P. Erickson and D. Moore, "Sexual Activity, Birth Control Use and Attitudes Towards Premarital Pregnancy among High School Students from Three Minority Groups" (Paper presented at the 1986 Annual Meeting of the American Public Health Association, Las Vegas, Nevada), p. 4, Tables 4 and 5.

23. M. Zelnik and F. Shah, "First Intercourse among Young Americans," *Family Planning Perspectives* 15(1983): 64–72.

24. A. Torres and S. Singh, "Contraceptive Practice among Hispanic Adolescents," *Family Planning Perspectives* 18(1986): 193–94.

25. L. Zabin and S. Clark, "Why Teens Delay Getting Birth Control Help," *Family Planning Perspectives* 13(1981): 205–17.

26. M. Koenig and M. Zelnik, "The Risk of Premarital First Pregnancy among Metropolitan-Area Teenagers: 1976 and 1979," *Family Planning Perspectives* 14(1982): 239–48.

27. C. Hayes, *Risking the Future, Vol. I*, p. 52.

28. The "one million teenage pregnancies" was first calculated "on the back of an envelope" in answer to a question asked of me by the late Fred Jaffe, founder of the Alan Guttmacher Institute. We needed such an estimate for a paper we were writing on the need for services for adolescents. I added the number of births to the number of abortions to teenagers (data that became available around 1973) and then, in consultation with colleagues, worked out a procedure for estimating the number of miscarriages.

29. For a detailed summary of reproductive behavior by women aged 15 to 19 from 1970–1984, see Hofferth, *Risking the Future, Vol. II*, Table 3.1, pp. A-63, 414–15.

30. The convention for measuring fertility events is to present rates per 1000 population, making it difficult for the nonbiostatistician to understand. One way to deal with this problem is to convert rates per 1000 into rates per 100, or percentages. Thus, a fertility rate of 53 per 1000 15- to 19-year-olds can be interpreted to mean "about 5 percent of teens were mothers in a year." This does not account for multiple births, a very rare event in any case, but it certainly improves the comprehensibility of the statistic.

31. For an expert analysis of the demography of adolescent fertility, see K. Pittman & G. Adams, *Teenage Pregnancy: An Advocate's Guide to the Numbers* (Washington, D.C.:

Children's Defense Fund, 1988). This publication was used as a primary source for this chapter.

32. The Alan Guttmacher Institute, *Eleven Million Teenagers: What Can Be Done About the Epidemic of Adolescent Pregnancies in the United States* (New York: Alan Guttmacher Institute, 1976).

33. Hayes, *Risking the Future, Vol. I*, p. 116.

34. See Sum analysis of NLSY data in Pittman, *Preventing Adolescent Pregnancy*, p. 6.

# 6

# Prevalence of School Failure
# and Dropping Out

In this chapter, we turn to the risk behavior that appears to underlie many of the problems addressed so far. Low achievement in school has been shown to be an important predictor of substance abuse, delinquency, and early sexual intercourse. And as we will see, not only are many of the antecedents of poor school performance the same as those for other problem behaviors, so are the consequences. Moreover, low academic achievement is both a predictor and a consequence of other kinds of risk behavior, as well as being a problem in itself. Understanding the epidemiology of school failure and dropping out is fundamental to this book's argument: that high-risk behaviors are interrelated and, therefore, interventions must be comprehensive.

School failure is a process rather than a single risk event. A young person initiates hard drug use or has early unprotected sexual intercourse or first commits a delinquent act at a specific time and place. Usually these actions are voluntary and follow a personal decision (although they are heavily influenced by the social environment). Low achievement results from an array of forces, many of which are outside the control of the child. The quality of the school is, of course, a major factor, as are the actual classroom practices and attitudes of the teacher.

Estimates of the risk of other problem behaviors can be projected based on individual characteristics. Children with certain attributes are more likely than others to get involved in certain behaviors. This is not necessarily the case for estimating the risk of school failure since the probabilities are conditioned by both individual characteristics and the quality of the school. Children from disadvantaged households have been shown to succeed in excellent schools, while some schools are so inadequate that success is an exception.

Unlike the other behaviors, risk of educational failure is measured routinely for almost all children at frequent intervals. Report cards inform children about their progress and, in aggregate, these marks produce a grade point average for each student. An even simpler measure of educational progress is based on modal grades by age. Being more than a year overage for a grade is a strong indicator of educational failure. A widely used assortment of achievement tests and assessments produce comparative scores to measure progress at various grade levels. However, leaving school prior to graduation is a different kind of measure, one that is known to the student but not necessarily collected systematically by school systems. No uniform procedures are required of school districts for tracking school attendance. Even Census data may be inaccurate, since parents who are surveyed may be unaware of their children's actual school status.

## Sources of Data

The education field has produced a vast array of literature on educational failure and school dropout rates. Table 6.1 summarizes the sources of data generally utilized for studying educationally disadvantaged youth. One longitudinal study is the major source for information about school achievement and dropping out: the High School and Beyond Survey (HS&B). This large-scale, follow-up survey of high school sophomores was first conducted in 1980 by the National Center for Educational Statistics.[1] The National Longitudinal Surveys of Labor Market Experience from 1979 to the present have also been used to examine basic skill

TABLE 6.1. Sources of Data on School Failure and Dropout

| Source and Subject | Year | Sample Size | Citation |
|---|---|---|---|
| *National surveys* | | | |
| High School and Beyond: sophomores and seniors | 1980 | 58,000 | Barro and Kolstad 1987 |
| in 1980 | 1983 | 12,200 | Peng 1983 |
| National Longitudinal Surveys of Labor Market Experience: males and females 14–21 in 1979 | 1979– 1986 | 12,686 | Berlin and Sum 1988 |
| National Assessment of Educational Progress: test scores | Annual | All students | U.S. Department of Education 1988 |
| Current Population Survey of the Census Bureau: household survey | Annual | 60,000 | U.S. Bureau of the Census 1988 |
| *Local surveys and studies* | | | |
| Edmonds, Washington: ninth graders in 1983 | 1983 1988 | 1,451 | Brown 1988 |
| Chicago: ninth graders in 1980 | 1980 1984 | 39,500 | Designs for Change 1985 |
| Dade County, Florida: eighth graders in 1980 | 1980 1985 | 18,829 | Stephenson 1987 |

levels and consequences over time.[2] The Current Population Survey of the Census Bureau collects detailed data annually about school enrollment through a household survey.[3] Test scores are compiled by the National Assessment of Educational Progress, conducted by the Department of Education.[4] In addition to national surveys, there are literally hundreds of small studies that focus on educational variables; only a few of these are cited in Table 6.1 as examples of the kinds of data available.[5]

## Consequences of School Failure and Dropping Out

Low school achievement, poor grades, or being overage for a grade all lead to dropping out. However, not everyone who has low grades or is overage drops out. But for poorly equipped graduates, low grades and low test scores may stand in the way of admission to college. In some cases, low grades indicate the lack of basic skills, severely limiting job opportunities and adversely affecting many aspects of the quality of life. Thus, many young people who complete high school still face barriers to success, particularly if they are black or Hispanic.

The consequences of dropping out are well documented (see Table 6.2). School dropouts have significantly fewer job prospects. They make lower salaries and are more often unemployed (some permanently). Dropouts are also more likely to be welfare dependent and more frequently experience unstable marriages. Dropouts are much more likely to be involved in problem behaviors of all kinds, including delinquency, substance abuse, and early childbearing. The chances of becoming an adjudicated criminal and serving time in prison are much higher for dropouts than for graduates, and yet there is conflicting evidence on the association between dropping out and criminal behavior.[6] Earlier studies suggested that, for marginal youths, dropping out helped speed up the transition to adult roles (getting a job, forming a family). More recent studies indicate that failure to achieve a high school education predicts subsequent criminal behavior. This difference probably reflects changing labor force requirements; in the past, dropouts could find legitimate employment opportunities in industrial and service jobs. With increasing technical demands, ill-equipped job-seekers more often turn to illegitimate sources of employment, such as drug dealing and fencing "hot merchandise." Finally, society suffers the consequences of dropping out in terms of lost revenue from diminished taxes and increased welfare expenditures. In more graphic terms, it is unhealthy for a community to have a bunch of alienated undereducated unemployed kids hanging out on street corners getting into trouble.

This understanding of the consequences suggests that risk behavior be measured in terms of two dimensions: risk of failing and risk of dropping out. Three kinds of measures will be used here to estimate target populations for interventions:

- The prevalence of being one or two years behind modal grade (older than the average age in that class).
- The prevalence of low test scores.
- The prevalence of dropping out.

TABLE 6.2. Consequences of School Failure and Dropout

| Behavior | Consequences | |
|---|---|---|
| | Short Term | Long Term |
| Low achievement<br>Poor grades | Nonpromotion<br>Difficulty gaining admission to<br>   college<br>Truancy, absenteeism | Dropout<br>Low basic skills<br>Low employability<br>Lack of a college degree |
| Nonpromotion<br>Left back | Low self-esteem<br>Low involvement in school<br>   activities<br>Problem behaviors<br>Alienation | Dropout |
| Dropout | Unemployment | No entry to labor force<br>Welfare dependency<br>Low-level jobs |
| | Low wages | Low lifetime earnings<br>Repeated job changes |
| | Depression<br>Alienation | Later regrets<br>Poor physical health<br>Mental health problems |
| | Low basic skills | Illiteracy |
| | Delinquency | Criminal career, prison |
| | | Marital instability<br>Divorce |
| | Pregnancy<br>Abortion | Early childbearing |
| | | Social costs: lost tax revenue,<br>   welfare expenditures |

*Sources:* D. Kandel, V. Raveis, and P. Kandel, ''Continuity in Discontinuities: Adjustment in Young Adulthood of Former School Absentees,'' *Youth and Society* 15(1984): 325–52; G. Berlin and A. Sum, *Toward a More Perfect Union: Basic Skills, Poor Families, and Our Economic Future* (New York: Ford Foundation, 1988), pp. 24–38; E. Ginzberg, H. Berliner, and M. Ostow, *Young People at Risk: Is Prevention Possible?* (New York: Ford Foundation, 1988), pp. 105–21.

These probabilities will be applied to individuals to be consistent with the previous estimates. However, it should be kept in mind that certain schools and communities are generators of school failure and produce high-risk children. (In Chapter 12, we will describe schools and communities that have been effective at preventing failure and reducing the dropout rate.)

## Prevalence of School Failure and Dropout

### *Behind Modal Grade*

About two-thirds of U.S. students are in their ''modal grade''—the grade considered the appropriate one for their age. However, at least 4 percent are two or more years behind their modal grade (e.g., they are two or more years older than their classmates) and about one in five is one year behind. The higher the grade, the higher the proportion of enrollees who are behind their grade. About 7 percent are one or more years above grade, a proportion that is relatively constant from kindergarten through twelfth grade. Assuming that some of the 7 percent are above grade as a result of being "skipped," the normal age distribution would be about 5 percent below grade, 90 percent modal, and 5 percent above. The fact that 27 percent of 10- to 17-year-olds are below modal grade suggests that this measure can be used as a rough indicator of educational disadvantage. As many as one in five may have "flunked" a grade at some time.

School policies delineating whether or not a student will be kept back in a grade show great variation and generate considerable controversy. Educators seem to disagree on the effects of such policies on student achievement and personal adjustment. Holmes conducted a metaanalysis of 63 studies in which retained students were compared with promoted students in elementary and junior high schools.[7] He found significant negative effects on the students who were held back, with the largest effect on academic achievement, followed by social adjustment and behavior, attendance at school, and attitudes toward school. These effects were maintained even in studies where the samples were controlled by IQ scores and prior achievement. The higher the grades (up to seven), the greater the effects. Holmes also selected nine of the studies that reported positive effects of grade retention (and lowered the total negative effect score for the aggregate), and these studies were all found to be intensive remediation programs with very small classes in middle-class communities. He concluded, "Those who continue to retain pupils at grade level do so despite conclusive evidence that the potential for negative effects consistently outweighs positive effects."

Falling behind one's age peers in school is strongly predictive of dropping out. Large-scale surveys have consistently demonstrated that many more dropouts than graduates have been held back, usually in the early grades. Smith and Shepard point out that "retention increases the probability of eventually dropping out of school by 20 to 30 percent, even with achievement, socioeconomic status and gender controlled."[8] In one large school district (Austin, Texas), almost half of those who were behind grade dropped out of school compared with 18 percent who were at modal grade level and 5 percent of those who were above.[9] In another school district (Dade County, Florida), 55 percent of those who were two or more years behind dropped out as did 40 percent who were one year behind and 21 percent who were at modal grade.[10]

According to Census data for 1986, almost 5 percent of 10- to 17-year-olds are two or more years behind, and close to 22 percent are one year behind. Hence, three out of ten of the youngsters in this population are in this very high-risk category. Table 6.3 presents these two measures by sex, age and grade, race, and Hispanic origin. The modal grade for 10-year-olds is fifth, ranging up to grade twelve for 17-year-olds. Males are much more likely to have been retained in a grade than females. For the younger cohort, ages 10 to 13 (grades 5 to 8), 31 percent of males are below their modal grade compared with 23 percent of females. For 14- to 17-year-olds (grades 9 to 12), the difference is even greater, 31 percent for males compared with 21 percent for females.

TABLE 6.3. Modal Grade of Enrollment of 10- to 17-Year-Olds, by Sex, Age, Race, and Hispanic Origin, 1986

| Age and Grade | Percentage Two or More Years Behind | | | Percentage One Year Behind | | |
|---|---|---|---|---|---|---|
| | White | Black | Hispanic | White | Black | Hispanic |
| *Males* | | | | | | |
| 10    5 | 3 | 7 | 4 | 26 | 34 | 39 |
| 11    6 | 3 | 6 | 6 | 27 | 30 | 22 |
| 12    7 | 5 | 14 | 10 | 26 | 32 | 40 |
| 13    8 | 4 | 8 | 12 | 26 | 36 | 35 |
| 14    9 | 7 | 11 | 18 | 24 | 38 | 37 |
| 15   10 | 6 | 11 | 13 | 22 | 33 | 18 |
| 16   11 | 6 | 20 | 16 | 26 | 28 | 37 |
| 17   12 | 7 | 16 | 15 | 22 | 30 | 29 |
| *Females* | | | | | | |
| 10    5 | 3 | 4 | 6 | 20 | 25 | 30 |
| 11    6 | 2 | 6 | 4 | 20 | 30 | 22 |
| 12    7 | 3 | 6 | 8 | 16 | 28 | 20 |
| 13    8 | 3 | 6 | 11 | 19 | 28 | 30 |
| 14    9 | 3 | 7 | 9 | 17 | 22 | 28 |
| 15   10 | 3 | 6 | 9 | 19 | 24 | 24 |
| 16   11 | 4 | 9 | 17 | 16 | 22 | 25 |
| 17   12 | 5 | 8 | 17 | 14 | 22 | 24 |

*Source:* U.S. Bureau of the Census, "School Enrollment—Social and Economic Characteristics of Students: October 1986," *Current Population Reports,* Series P-20, No. 429, 1988, pp. 60–62.

Black and Hispanic students have a greater probability of being left back than white students. For most age and sex groups, the probability of being two or more grades behind is at least twice as high among minority children as among white children.[11] The differences between blacks and Hispanics by age and sex groups are not entirely consistent, but the patterns are clear. Among minority males, more than one in ten are two years or more behind grade, and the higher the grade, the greater the evidence of having been left back.

A recent report from the New York City school system showed that 40 percent of ninth and tenth graders were a year or more older than average at the time that they were entering into high school from junior or intermediate school.[12] There were significant differences in the age of entrants according to the type of high school: 61 percent of those entering a general inner-city school were already behind grade compared with 28 percent entering a specialized school for the health professions. School officials claimed that "the age of the student in a particular grade (is) the best indicator of whether the student will drop out."

### Test Scores

Not only are many children being held back in grades, they are also unable to perform on achievement tests up to acceptable norms (which may be one reason they are being left back). The whole subject of achievement tests is, of course, a

TABLE 6.4. Prevalence of Low School Achievement (Reading and Math) by Age, Race, and Hispanic Origin

| Race and Ethnicity | Reading: Percentage Below Intermediate Level Ages | | | Math: Average Percentage of Scores Incorrect Ages | | |
|---|---|---|---|---|---|---|
| | 9 | 13 | 17 | 9 | 13 | 17 |
| TOTAL | 82 | 40 | 16 | 44 | 39 | 40 |
| White | 78 | 33 | 11 | 41 | 37 | 37 |
| Black | 95 | 65 | 34 | 55 | 52 | 55 |
| Hispanic | 95 | 61 | 31 | 52 | 48 | 51 |

*Source:* U.S. Department of Education, *Youth Indicators 1988* (Washington, D.C.: Office of Educational Research and Improvement, 1988). For reading: p. 85, cited to U.S. Department of Education, National Institute of Education, National Assessment of Educational Progress, *The Reading Report Card* (n.d.), for 1983–84 scores; for math: p. 62, cited to Education Commission of the States, *The Third National Assessment: Results, Trends, and Issues* (1983), for 1981–82 scores.

"can of worms." Achievement measurement instruments have been the subject of extended controversy, with claims that they are culturally biased and measure the teacher's abilities more than the students. For the purposes of this discussion, we will review some of the findings put forward by the educational establishment with the caveat that there are many questions about the reliability of these measures.

Table 6.4 shows the percent of students reading below the intermediate level at ages 9, 13, and 17 by race and Hispanic origin according to the National Assessment of Educational Progress (NAEP). Reading ability improves with age, so that by age 17, the majority of young people are relatively literate. In 1984, about 16 percent of 17-year-olds were unable to read at what the NAEP considers a functional level. However, group differences are significant—more than a third of black and 31 percent of Hispanic youth are unable to read even at the intermediate level. Math achievement (also shown on Table 6.4) follows similar patterns, although age differences are not marked. On average, 17-year-olds could answer only 60 percent of the math questions correctly, with an average incorrect score of 40 percent.

A detailed study of the Chicago school system revealed the extent of low test scores and their relationship to type of schools.[13] This study compared Chicago students with the national average for reading below the Minimum Competency Level (MCL: more than 4 years below the national average for reading achievement in the fall of their senior year). In the nation, 18 percent of seniors rank below the MCL. In Chicago, as a whole, 29 percent of seniors fell below that level. Yet there were vast differences according to type of school. In Chicago, a segregated school is defined as one with more than 70 percent minority enrollment. About two-thirds of all Chicago students in public schools are in segregated schools. Only 6 percent attend specialized academic high schools, and the rest attend either integrated, nonselective high schools or vocational schools. In selective academic high schools, only 2 percent of seniors were reading below the

MCL as were 20 percent of the seniors in integrated, nonselective high schools and 16 percent in selective vocational high schools. However, for those seniors who were attending segregated, nonselective high schools, 41 percent were reading below the MCL, at or below the eighth grade level.

### Dropping Out

Although everyone talks about the "dropout rate," there is no common definition. The Bureau of the Census uses one approach and the U.S. Department of Education another. The figure most often stated is that about 1 in 4 of U.S. students do not finish high school. The Current Population Survey (CPS) of the Bureau of the Census produces annual estimates of the proportion of various age groups that are neither enrolled in school nor have graduated from high school by a certain age (Table 6.5). In 1986, 6 percent of 16- to 17-year-olds and 12 percent of 18- to 19-year-olds had dropped out without completing high school.[14] The Center for Educational Statistics (CES) of the Department of Education tracks the number of yearly high school graduates and the number of freshman students enrolled four years earlier in each state. The difference between the two CES figures is assumed to be the number of dropouts. CES estimated "graduation rates" for the nation's public school students in 1985 based on the aggregate for each state adjusted for migration and unclassified students.[15] This produced a graduation rate of 71 percent, and a dropout rate of 29 percent. Areas with low graduation rates (under 65 percent) included all of the South, the District of Columbia, Nevada, New York, Tennessee, and Texas.

Data from the High School and Beyond Survey show that 14 percent of those who were sophomores in 1980 had dropped out prior to graduation in 1982. However, a follow-up survey in 1984 found that 38 percent of those who had dropped out had completed school requirements either by returning to high school or getting a general equivalency diploma (GED).[16] Another 13 percent had returned to

TABLE 6.5. Prevalence of Dropping Out According to U.S. Census by Age, Race, and Hispanic Origin, 1986

| Race and Ethnicity | Percentage Not Enrolled and Not Graduated by Age | | | |
|---|---|---|---|---|
|  | 14–15 | 16–17 | 18–19 | 20–21 |
| TOTAL | 2 | 6 | 12 | 15 |
| White | 2 | 7 | 12 | 14 |
| Black | 3 | 5 | 15 | 18 |
| Hispanic | 4 | 15 | 27 | 35 |
| Inside central city | 3 | 7 | 14 | 18 |
| Suburb | 2 | 5 | 10 | 12 |
| Nonmetro | 2 | 7 | 14 | 16 |

*Note:* For 10- to 13-year-olds, 1 percent are not enrolled in every category.
*Source:* U.S. Bureau of the Census, "School Enrollment—Social and Economic Characteristics of Students: October 1986," *Current Population Reports*, Series P-20, No. 429, 1988, pp. 5–7, 9.

high school, but either failed to graduate or were still there. A study by the General Accounting Office (GAO) arrived at 13 to 14 percent as the estimate of dropouts among youth aged 16 to 24 (derived from both the Census and the HS&B), a "reasonable indicator" of the problem.[17]

Given the fact that high school completion rates have steadily increased over time, one might ask why there is so much concern about the dropout issue. As with all social data, the aggregates hide the problem. In the United States today, there are many school districts where fewer than half of the students complete high school. The special studies tell the story. The Chicago study previously referred to found that there were enormous differences in high school completion rates according to type of school. For the city as a whole the completion rate was 45 percent (compared with 92% in suburban Cook County). The graduation rate was 73 percent for students who attended academic high schools, 65 percent for nonselective, integrated schools, 52 percent for vocational schools, and 38 percent for nonselective, segregated schools. No differences in dropout rates were found between segregated schools that were primarily used by black students (27 schools) and Hispanic students (4 schools). In New York City, 3 out of 4 black students and 4 out of 5 Hispanic students do not complete high school within the traditional four-year period.[18]

High dropout rates are endemic in inner city and segregated schools all around the country.

## Numbers at Risk

The Census figures have been used to produce current estimates of the numbers of young people at risk of failure and dropout. Among the nation's 28 million 10- to 17-year-olds, more than one out of four—7.4 million—are behind their modal grades (see Table 6.6). Of these, one in four—1.4 million—are two or more years behind. This second group is at very high risk of eventually dropping out. According to the Census figures, about 700,000 young people under the age of 18 are already out of school and have not graduated. Some will obtain a general

TABLE 6.6. Numbers at Risk of School Failure and Dropping Out in 1986 (in millions)

|  | Age 10–14 | Age 15–17 | Age 10–17 |
|---|---|---|---|
| Behind modal grade | | | |
| by one year | 3.8 | 2.2 | 6.0 |
| by two or more years | 0.7 | 0.7 | 1.4 |
| Total behind | 4.5 | 2.9 | 7.4 |
| Already dropped out[a] | 0.2 | 0.5 | 0.7 |

[a]Not enrolled or graduated from high school.

*Source:* Prevalence rates from Tables 6.3 and 6.5 applied to population estimates from Table 2.1.

equivalency diploma (GED), but the majority will encounter long-term employment problems in the absence of basic skills.

In the younger cohort, likely to be in middle or junior high school grades, 4.5 million 10- to 14-year-olds are behind grade. Only a small number have already dropped out. As would be expected, the number of dropouts is much higher among older students. At least half a million 15- to 17-year-olds are already out of school.

## Antecedents of School Failure and Dropout

In this discussion of the antecedents of school failure and dropping out, we return once again to the "chicken and the egg" quandary. Which variables precede failure and dropout, and which ones are the results of alienation from school? Comparing the antecedents (Table 6.7) with the consequences (Table 6.2), it is obvious that many variables appear on both lists. For example, delinquent behavior is both a predictor of dropping out and a consequence; acting out in class, truancy, and minor offenses during the early years happen prior to school failure and, once out of school, dropouts are more likely to commit serious offenses than those who stay in school.

The antecedents of school failure and dropping out are similar; it has been well documented that poor grades and being left back often lead to dropping out with a kind of inevitable progression. The literature on the antecedents of dropping out is very rich,[19] but less is known about those who fall behind their modal grades. One multivariate analysis of 1977 Census data showed that the antecedents of being below modal grade were how much income the child's family had and the educational level within the household.[20] As with many more recent studies, other characteristics, such as living with one or two parents, or race, were not significant when socioeconomic status was accounted for. Parental support is a key factor in school performance; several studies document the finding that strong parental guidance is as important as coming from a two-parent family. Milne et al. conducted analyses of two major national data sets that included variables about educational achievement (math and reading scores) as well as parental status. They concluded that the negative effects on achievement of living in a one-parent family were "entirely mediated" by other variables, specifically family income.[21]

Researchers have been interested in delineating among family types in regard to "parenting styles" and looking at differential effects. Baumrind and Black have specified three parenting styles: authoritarian (high in demands, low in responsiveness), permissive, and authoritative (high expectations, firm enforcement of standards, and open communication).[22] Dornbusch and colleagues have related parenting styles to school performance and found that children whose parents have authoritative styles have significantly higher school grades than children in other types of families (with the exception of Asian children).[23] Having cultural resources in the home, such as dictionaries and reference books, makes a difference in school achievement levels as well.

Not everyone who is behind grade will drop out. In any population, a certain

TABLE 6.7. Antecedents of School Dropout

| Antecedent | Association with Dropping Out |
|---|---|
| *Demographic* | |
| Age | **Old for grade |
| Sex | *Males |
| Race and ethnicity | **Native American, Hispanic, Black |
| *Personal* | |
| Expectations for education | **Low expectations, no plans for college |
| School grades | **Low grades |
| Basic skills | **Low test scores |
| School promotion | **Left back in early grades |
| Attitude toward school | **Strong dislike, bored |
| Conduct, general behavior | **Truancy, "acting out," suspension, expulsion |
| Peer influence | *Friends have low expectations for school |
| | **Friends drop out |
| School involvement | **Low interest, low participation |
| Involvement in other high-risk behaviors | *Early delinquency, substance use, early sexual intercourse |
| Social life | *Frequent dating, riding around |
| Conformity–rebelliousness | *Nonconformity, alienation |
| Psychological factors | *Stress, depression |
| Pregnancy | **High rates for childbearers |
| *Family* | |
| Household composition | *Inconsistent data |
| Income, poverty status | **Family in poverty |
| Parental education | **Low levels of education |
| Welfare | *Family on welfare |
| Mobility | *Family moves frequently |
| Parental role, bonding, guidance | **Lack of parental support, authoritarian, permissive |
| Culture in home | *Lack of resources in home |
| Primary language | *Other than English |
| *Community* | |
| Neighborhood quality | *Urban, high-density area, poverty area, also rural |
| School quality | **Alternative or vocational school |
| | **Segregated school |
| | *Large schools, large classes |
| | *Tracking, emphasis on testing |
| | *Public (vs. parochial) |
| Employment | *Higher rates of employment |

* = Cited in selected sources
** = Major predictor

*Sources:* R. Rumberger, "Dropping Out of High School: The Influence of Race, Sex and Family Background," *American Educational Research Journal* 20(1983):199–220; S. Barro and A. Kolstad, *Who Drops Out of High School? Findings from High School and Beyond* (Washington, D.C.: U.S. Department of Education, Center for Education Statistics, May 1987), pp. 25–60; A. Hahn, J. Danzberger, and B. Lefkowitz, *Dropouts in America: Enough is Known for Action* (Washington, D.C.: Institute for Educational Leadership, March 1987), pp. 11–25; R. Rumberger, R. Ghatak, G. Paulos, P. Ritter, and S. Dornbusch, "Family Influences on Dropout Behavior: An Exploratory Study of a Single High School" (Unpublished paper, University of California, Santa Barbara, 1988), 26–27; R. Eckstrom, M. Goertz, J. Pollack, and K. Rock, "Who Drops Out of High School and Why? Findings from a National Study," *Teachers College Record* 87(1986): 356–73.

number of children have congenital physical and psychological handicaps that prevent them from moving through the grades as rapidly as their peers.[24] With special education classes now mandated, many children progress through the system at their own speed, but are not necessarily at high risk for negative consequences.

Nevertheless, being behind modal grade and having low grades are the two strongest predictors of dropping out. As we have seen, males are at higher risk of dropping out than females, and black, Hispanic, and Native American children have higher rates than others. Dropout rates are much higher for children whose primary language is not English, particularly for Hispanics. The higher frequency for minority children is linked to the socioeconomic status (SES) of their families.[25] Children whose families live in poverty or on welfare have significantly higher dropout rates. When controls are added for SES, racial differences in school dropout rates are greatly diminished (but do not disappear entirely). Among SES measures, parental education is the strongest determinant; the more advanced a parent's education, the less likely the child will drop out.

Children who are truant, act out in school, have ever been suspended or expelled, and are involved in other kinds of problem behaviors are much more likely to drop out of school than others. Potential dropouts have low expectations for future schooling, are not involved in school activities, and have friends with similar patterns of behavior. Potential dropouts spend more time dating and, in the suburbs, riding around in cars. Early childbearing or marriage is a significant antecedent of dropping out (but dropping out is also an antecedent of early childbearing). Young people who do not finish high school may also have higher rates of depression.

School quality is an important factor affecting whether or not a child will stay in school. Students have higher dropout rates in segregated schools, public vocational schools, schools with low teacher-pupil ratios, large schools with large classes, and schools with emphasis on tracking and testing. Students who feel shut out of school activities, powerless in adversarial teacher–student relationships, and bored and uninvolved often leave. One survey of dropouts found that 70 percent of leavers might have stayed "if teachers paid more attention to students" and "if we were not treated as inmates."[26] These kinds of schools are most likely to be located either in high-density urban poverty areas or low-density rural areas (not in suburban areas). Urban communities with high employment rates may have higher dropout rates because of the pull of jobs. In light of the miserable conditions in the schools, some young people who drop out have much higher academic potential than those who stay in, but they are unwilling to continue to expose themselves to the daily "hassles," humiliations, and dangers they would have to endure by continuing in school.

## Summary

Millions of young people in the United States are having problems in school. Ample data exist to document that at least 7 million young people are behind grade in school and about 14 percent of every class does not graduate from high school. As a result, the pool of dropouts continues to grow. At the same time, employment opportunities are more limited than ever before for nongraduates. And even among graduates, many have such low basic skills that their employment prospects are also limited.

The facts about school dropout rates are well known, but the measurement of actual rates at the local level is very inconsistent. It is becoming increasingly evident that certain schools in inner cities (and possibly in remote rural areas) have dropout rates that are extremely high—as high as 80 percent. Almost no one graduates.

Children who have a high probability of falling behind in school, receiving low grades, and eventually dropping out are most often from disadvantaged families living in poverty communities. Some of their families can offer them little in the way of support or enrichment. Their parents are too intimidated by the school bureaucracy to interfere. Thus, the children are dependent on the quality of the schools, the same schools that may place their students in jeopardy of failure. Some young people, often those with the most potential, leave these schools because they are too dangerous and alien.

This negative picture of youth at high risk of school failure should not be construed as a picture of all schools in inner cities or disadvantaged rural communities. As we will see in Chapter 12, there are excellent schools and educational programs in all parts of the country that work well to promote achievement among high-risk children. Children who have previously failed in school, or who have low test scores or poor grades, can be kept in school and assisted to graduate. Alpert and Dunham have produced a unique comparison of "marginal" students who stayed in school and dropouts from the same schools.[27] They identified five independent variables that explained the differences: the "stayers" had avoided misbehavior in school, believed that their school experience had relevance to their future jobs, had experienced success in school, had parents who monitored their school performance, and were insulated from peers who had dropped out. We will see how these same variables are addressed in prevention interventions.

## Notes

1. S. Peng, "High School Dropouts: Descriptive Information from High School and Beyond," *Bulletin, National Center for Education Statistics,* U.S. Department of Education (November 1983).

2. G. Berlin and A. Sum, *Toward a More Perfect Union: Basic Skills, Poor Families, and Our Economic Future* (New York: Ford Foundation, 1988).

3. U.S. Bureau of the Census, "School Enrollment—Social and Economic Characteristics of Students: October 1986," *Current Population Reports,* Series P-20, No. 429, 1988.

4. U.S. Department of Education, *Youth Indicators 1988* (Washington, D.C.: Office of Educational Research and Improvement, 1988).

5. L. Brown, "Dropping Out: From Prediction to Prevention" (Paper presented at the Annual Meeting of the American Educational Research Association, New Orleans, April 1988); Austin (Texas) Independent School District, "Mother Got Tired of Taking

Care of My Baby: A Study of Dropouts,'' listed in U.S. Department of Education, Education Resource Information Center (ERIC) # E-D 233102, Pub. No. 82.44, 1982; R. Stephenson, "A Study of the Longitudinal Dropout Rate: 1980 Eighth Grade Cohort Followed from June, 1980 through February, 1985" (Dade County Public Schools, Florida), in Phi Delta Kappa, *Dropouts, Pushouts, and Other Casualties* (Bloomington, Ind.: Phi Delta Kappa, 1987), pp. 41–54; Designs for Change, *The Bottom Line: Chicago's Failing Schools and How to Save Them* (Chicago, Ill.: Designs for Change, Research Report No. 1, 1985).

6. G. Alpert and R. Dunham, "Keeping Academically Marginal Youths in School: A Prediction Model," *Youth and Society* 17(1986): 346–61.

7. C. Holmes, "Grade Level Retention Effects: A Meta-Analysis of Research Studies," in L. Shepard and M. Smith, eds., *Flunking Grades: Research and Policies on Retention* (Philadelphia: The Falmer Press, 1989), pp. 16–33.

8. M. Smith and L. Shepard, "Flunking Grades: A Recapitulation," in L. Shepard and M. Smith, eds., *Flunking Grades: Research and Policies on Retention* (Philadelphia: Falmer Press, 1988), pp. 214–35.

9. Austin (Texas) Independent School District, "Mother Got Tired of Taking Care of My Baby," p. 5.

10. Stephenson, "A Study of the Longitudinal Dropout Rate," p. 48.

11. A study of nonpromotion rates in the Boston schools revealed higher rates for black and Hispanic students than white and Asians. The peak rates were in grades one, six, and nine, reflecting important transition points. The nonpromotion rate from eighth to ninth grade was 25 percent. See Massachusetts Advocacy Center, "Status Report, The Way Out: Patterns of Non-Promotion in Boston Public Schools (1985–87)" (January 1988).

12. "New York's Dropouts-to-Be: A Grim Class Portrait," *New York Times,* April 11, 1989, B1.

13. Designs for Change, *The Bottom Line*, pp. 56–57.

14. U.S. Bureau of the Census, "School Enrollment: October 1986," p. 9.

15. "Databank: State Education Statistics: Student Performance, Resource Inputs, Reforms, and Population Characteristics, 1982 and 1986," *Education Week,* February 18, 1987. Produced by the Office of Education as a "wall-chart" for measuring progress.

16. A. Kolstad and J. Owings, "High School Dropouts Who Change Their Minds About School" (Unpublished paper from U.S. Department of Education, Center for Statistics, April 16, 1986).

17. U.S. General Accounting Office, *School Dropouts: The Extent and Nature of the Problem* (Briefing Report to Congressional Requestors, June 1986).

18. New York State Department of Education, *The Time for Assertive Action* (Albany, N.Y.: Report of the Commissioner's Task Force on the Education of Children and Youth-At-Risk, 1988).

19. Among the many important analyses that have been produced on the determinants of school dropout are R. Rumberger, "Dropping Out of High School: The Influence of Race, Sex and Family Background," *American Educational Research Journal* 20(1983): 199–220; S. Barro and A. Kolstad, *Who Drops Out of High School? Findings from High School and Beyond* (Washington, D.C.: U.S. Department of Education, Center for Education Statistics, May 1987); A. Hahn, J. Danzberger, B. Lefkowitz, *Dropouts in America: Enough is Known for Action* (Washington, D.C.: Institute for Educational Leadership, March 1987); R. Rumberger, R. Ghatak, G. Paulos, P. Ritter, and S. Dornbusch, "Family Influences on Dropout Behavior: An Exploratory Study of a Sin-

gle High School'' (Unpublished paper, University of California, Santa Barbara, 1988).
20. S. Bianchi, ''Children's School Progression: An Investigation of Family Type, Socio-economic and Ethnic Subgroup Differences'' (Paper presented at the Population Association of America in San Diego, California, April 1982).
21. A. Milne, D. Myers, A. Rosenthal, and A. Ginsburg, ''Single Parents, Working Mothers, and the Educational Achievement of School Children,'' *Sociology of Education* 59(1986): 125–39. The data sets were High School and Beyond using the 1980 interviews with 2,720 parents and The Sustained Effects of Title I, carried out in 1977 using interviews with 12,429 families.
22. D. Baumrind and A. Black, ''Socialization Practices Associated with Dimensions of Competence in Preschool Boys and Girls,'' *Child Development* 38(1967): 291–327.
23. S. Dornbusch, P. Ritter, P. Leiderman, D. Roberts, and M. Fraleigh, ''The Relation of Parenting Style to Adolescent School Performance,'' *Child Development* 58 (1987): 1244–57.
24. Approximately 4.4 million handicapped students aged 3 to 21 are enrolled in public schools. Forty-four percent are learning disabled, 26 percent speech impaired, 15 percent mentally retarded, 9 percent emotionally disturbed, and 6 percent other. U.S. Bureau of the Census, *Statistical Abstract of the United States, 1989* (Washington, D.C., 1989), 142.
25. According to Barro and Kolstad, *Who Drops Out of High School,* p. 26, the High School and Beyond Survey produces dropout rates that are significantly related to socioeconomic status (SES). Using a composite SES indicator, the rates by quartile were:

| | |
|---|---|
| First (lowest) | 22.3% |
| Second | 13.2 |
| Third | 10.7 |
| Fourth (highest) | 7.0 |

26. B. Wells, ''Commentary,'' *Education Week,* April 6, 1983.
27. Alpert and Dunham, ''Keeping Academically Marginal Youths in School,'' 346–61.

# 7

# The Overlap in High-Risk Behaviors

The previous four chapters have reviewed the consequences, antecedents, and numbers of adolescents at risk of behaviors in four distinct fields of study: delinquency, substance use, teenage pregnancy, and school failure. It should be apparent that these fields are interrelated since the same variables have emerged time and time again as consequences or antecedents of the diverse behaviors. In this chapter, the commonalities among these fields are analyzed and synthesized. First, we address the question of common antecedents or predictors of behavior. Then, we focus on the overlap in high-risk behavior. How many young people "do it all," and how many don't do any of it? From the wealth of data presented in the preceding chapters and from studies that look at the co-occurrence of these behaviors, a "synthetic estimate" is created that quantifies target groups for comprehensive interventions.

## The Common Characteristics of High-Risk Youth

Chapters 3 to 6 presented summaries of the antecedents of the separate problem behaviors (see Tables 3.7, 4.7, 5.7, and 6.7). A large number of variables were identified in each category. However, some of the antecedents or predictors applied only to one or two of the behaviors. A summary of the four diverse fields of study yields six common characteristics that predict each of the problem behaviors:

1. *Age:* Early initiation or occurrence of any behavior predicts heavy involvement in the behavior and more negative consequences.
2. *Expectations for education and school grades:* Doing poorly in school and expecting to do poorly in school are associated with all of the problem behaviors.

3. *General behavior:*   Acting out, truancy, antisocial behavior, and other conduct disorders are related to each of the problem behaviors.
4. *Peer influence:*   Having low resistance to peer influences and having friends who participate in the same behaviors are common to all of the behaviors.
5. *Parental role:*   Having insufficient bonding to parents, having parents who do not monitor, supervise, offer guidance, or communicate with their children, and having parents who are either too authoritarian or too permissive are all strongly associated with the behaviors.
6. *Neighborhood quality:*   Living in a poverty area, or an urban, high-density community is predictive of these problems.

The research is somewhat ambiguous on several of the variables. Males appear to act out more than females and get into more trouble in school and out, but females have higher rates of smoking and, obviously, pregnancy has more negative consequences for females. In regard to race, the data on early initiation of sexual intercourse, early childbearing, school failure and dropping out are clear: minority youth have much higher rates than white youth. This seems to be the case for arrest rates in the delinquency field, but not for self-reported delinquent behaviors. Substance abuse rates are higher for whites, but this may reflect an inadequate data base rather than actual behavior.

Household status is typically measured by whether or not the youngster is being brought up in a household with both parents, one parent, or some other arrangement. Much attention has been given to single-headed female households. The relationship between this variable and delinquency, substance abuse, and dropping out is not clear: the research suggests that it is more the quality of the parenting than the composition of the family. Thus, one nurturing parent or caretaker can be a more significant influence and guard against high-risk behavior than two nonnurturing parents. The family bonding variable is very strong in all the research. Parental practice of high-risk behaviors is a frequent antecedent of problem behavior in children and suggests the importance of parents as role models. Low "religiosity" (infrequent church attendance) is related to unstable family patterns, and predictive of most, but not all, of the problem behaviors.

Some of the ambiguity in the substance abuse literature about social class variables may reflect greater interest on the part of the researchers in psychological than in social variables. Poverty status and low parental education—two important components of measuring SES—are specific predictors of delinquency, teen childbearing, and school failure. The confusion about the effects of being in a single-parent family stem from the fact that mother-only households are much more likely to be poor. Thus, when controls are added for SES, other variables, such as household composition, have little or no effect. Studies that included indicators of the availability of cultural enrichment in the home (e.g., encyclopedias, magazines, classical music, home computers) suggest an additional aspect of social class influence (and affluence). The more "culture," the less problem behavior.

School quality appears to be another important variable for the categories of delinquency, substance abuse, and dropping out. No studies could be identified that related the quality of the school to teen pregnancy rates, although evidence is strong that the lack of basic skills is a significant predictor of adolescent child-bearing. Studies did, however, link segregated school systems with high pregnancy rates as well as high dropout rates.

It is difficult to summarize the findings on psychological variables in relationship to problem behaviors because of the wide range of variables (and testing instruments) used. Depression is one primary diagnosis about which there is agreement: depression and related stress are documented antecedents of school dropout rates and substance abuse. Hyperactivity, aggressiveness, and other forms of antisocial behavior at early ages often lead to delinquency. Alienation is related to delinquency and dropping out. Lack of conformity and rebelliousness are associated with problem behaviors (except early childbearing). The evidence on genetic predictors and congenital psychopathology suggests some association with substance abuse and delinquent behavior. Boys with alcoholic fathers appear to have a markedly higher prevalence of alcohol abuse. However, there is an ongoing debate about the relative influence of biological versus social environmental factors.

Low self-esteem is believed by many to be an important predictor of problem behavior. The literature, however, does not support that hypothesis. Measures of self-esteem and locus of control rarely reach significance levels in multiple variable analyses. Low self-esteem has been related to substance abuse but found not to relate to dropout rates. Externalized locus of control has been associated with dropping out, but the findings on substance abuse are contradictory.

Each behavioral field employs specific variables that may not be included in more general studies. Delinquency has been related to early conduct disorder and handicapping conditions. Substance abuse is not only related to peer influences, it is also affected by peer use. In this field, young people who do not believe in the consequences of their actions are more likely to be heavy users. In the pregnancy field, it is hypothesized that a low perception of life options is associated with high rates of early childbearing. Girls who do not use contraception are more likely to be in uncommitted relationships with partners (casual relationships rather than going steady). Dropping out of school is specifically related to disliking school, having a primary language other than English, being in a welfare family, moving frequently, and living in communities with high rates of youth employment (exercising a pull away from school).

Many more common antecedents have been identified than uncommon ones. School experience, family support, peer influence, general conduct, and neighborhood quality appear to have a strong impact on the probability that a young person will engage in any of the behaviors at early ages and experience negative consequences.

## Evidence of Overlap from Multivariable Surveys

To sort out the overlap in the behaviors of interest here, we return once again to the major surveys that have been conducted which include at least two of the behaviors. We want to know, in a given population, how often do behaviors co-

occur. Ideally, one survey would tell it all: (1) the proportion who are simultaneously having trouble in school, delinquent, sexually active, and abusing drugs
and (2) the proportion who do some of these things occasionally. No recent survey
meets all of the requirements for this exercise. Therefore, it is necessary to extract
as much as possible from available data sources and then make some assumptions
about the target populations.

The Jessor conceptualization of the problem behavior syndrome dates back to
research on drinking behavior in a tri-ethnic community in the mid-1960s, followed by the seminal longitudinal study begun in 1969 based on a sample of white
suburban junior high school students. In the sample of tenth to twelfth graders
(1972), Jessor found that 28 percent of the males and 16 percent of the females
were problem drinkers,[1] and that there were significant relationships between problem
drinking, marijuana use, nonvirginity, deviance (engaging in socially disapproved
behaviors like shoplifting or truancy), and low church attendance. For example,
virtually none of the alcohol abstainers were marijuana users compared with 80
percent of the problem drinkers. Among males, 5 percent of abstainers were sexually active compared with 52 percent of the problem drinkers, and for females,
the comparable measures were 4 percent and 73 percent. Among abstainers, 64
percent of males and 52 percent of females were high in church attendance compared with 27 percent and 18 percent of the problem drinkers.

These interrelationships between high-risk behaviors have been corroborated
by Donovan and Jessor in analyses of more recent data based on more representative and larger samples. They conclude that there is a common factor underlying
all of these behaviors, and that is unconventionality (as measured by lower religiosity, tolerance of deviance, more liberal views, peer approval of deviant behavior, poor school performance, and so on).[2] Donovan and Jessor's latest work
is based on the Adolescent Health Behavior Study, conducted in the seventh to
twelfth grades of one school district in Colorado with a sample of predominately
white, middle-class youth. They created a Problem Behavior Index (PBI) by sum-
ming up involvement with marijuana and cigarettes, heavy drinking, delinquency,
church attendance, and school behavior and demonstrated the correlation between
the PBI and health behaviors, health attitudes, and unconventionality. Using unpublished data from their survey, we can observe the distribution of problem behaviors and relate the numbers of problems to school performance (Table 7.1).
More than half of the students reported no problem behavior, about one-fourth
reported one such behavior, 18 percent reported two or three, and only 8 percent
reported four or five. The distribution of problem behaviors was strikingly different according to school grades. Fully 27 percent of low achievers (with typical
marks of D or lower) reported four or five problem behaviors compared with only
4 percent of high achievers (with marks in the range of A and B). Only 19 percent
of low achievers reported no problem behavior compared with 61 percent of high
achievers.

Erickson and her colleagues have analyzed data from a sample of middle and
high school students in Los Angeles to show the distribution of multiple-risk behaviors (sex, drugs, and alcohol).[3] In this group, 30 percent were neither sexually
active nor used substances frequently, 17 percent were at low risk, 31 percent

TABLE 7.1. Distribution of Seventh to Twelfth Graders by Number of
Problem Behaviors and School Grades

| Number of Problem Behaviors | | Percentage Distribution | | |
|---|---|---|---|---|
| | Total | As and Bs | Cs | Ds and Lower |
| 0 | 51 | 61 | 40 | 19 |
| 1 | 23 | 23 | 23 | 23 |
| 2–3 | 18 | 12 | 25 | 31 |
| 4–5 | 8 | 4 | 12 | 27 |

*Source:* Unpublished cross-tabulations from the Adolescent Health Survey, the Adolescent Health Behavior Study, 1985. Made available by J. Donovan, Institute of Behavioral Science, Boulder, Colorado.

moderate risk, and 22 percent at high risk because they were both sexually active and used substances frequently. In this sample, 19 percent have never had sex or used any substances. Peterson's study of youngsters in suburban Pennsylvania found that "more than half seemed to be almost trouble-free, and approximately 30 percent had only intermittent problems. Fifteen percent, however, did appear to be caught in a downward spiral of trouble and turmoil."[4]

More typically, in youth studies, one field is the center of research and other behaviors are related to it. The review that follows tracks behaviors in that framework.

### Delinquency and Other Behaviors

Elliott has analyzed the National Youth Survey (NYS) to examine the relationship between delinquency, drug use, sexual activity, and the timing of pregnancy.[5] The relationship between delinquency and drug use is very strong: among 15- to 21-year-olds in 1980, 5 percent were characterized as serious delinquents. This small group accounted for 80 percent of all serious offenses, 94 percent used alcohol, 85 percent used marijuana, and 55 percent used other illicit drugs. Among the multiple illicit drug users (13% of the respondents), about one-fourth had been involved in felonies and more than half in minor offenses. Adding sexual activity as a variable shows the association between the three behaviors (Table 7.2). Among those 11- to 17-year-olds classified as serious delinquents, 46 percent of males and 36 percent of females were sexually active compared with less than 7 and 4 percent of nonoffenders. Young people who used multiple drugs had very high rates of sexual activity, 67 to 71 percent if they were also delinquents and 50 to 43 percent if they were not.

Elliott used the NYS data to show the probabilities of pregnancy within a year of initiation of sexual intercourse according to drug use and delinquency status at the time of onset. For those using multiple and illicit drugs or who were serious delinquents at the time of sexual initiation, the risk of pregnancy was substantially greater at ages 12 to 15.[6] Among those who had first intercourse at age 14, 27 percent became pregnant within a year. For heavy drug users, however, the rate

TABLE 7.2. Prevalence Rates of Sexual Intercourse among 11- to 17-Year-Olds According to Delinquency and Drug Use, 1976

|  | Percentage Sexually Active | |
|---|---|---|
|  | Males | Females |
| *Serious delinquents* | 46 | 36 |
| Multiple illicit drugs | 67 | 71 |
| Alcohol and marijuana | 65 | 33 |
| Alcohol only | 35 | 33 |
| No drugs | 34 | 20 |
| *Nonoffenders* | 7 | 4 |
| Multiple illicit drugs | 50 | 43 |
| Alcohol and marijuana | 21 | 24 |
| Alcohol only | 10 | 9 |
| No drugs | 6 | 2 |

*Source:* D. Elliott and B. J. Morse, "Drug Use, Delinquency and Sexual Activity" (Unpublished paper, Behavioral Research Institute, Boulder, Colorado, undated), Table 2.

was 56 percent, and for offenders 40 percent. Serious delinquency and multiple-drug use are not only related to high risk of pregnancy, they are also associated with self-reported mental health problems. Among 11- to 17-year-olds in 1976, 28 percent of serious delinquents reported mental health problems compared with 9 percent of nonoffenders; 26 percent of heavy drug users compared with 2 percent of nonusers reported mental health problems.[7]

Using data from the NYS, it is possible to distribute the youth population according to several risk groups.[8] Among 11- to 17-year-olds, about 11 percent were at very high risk—either of serious delinquency or heavy drug use; about 40 percent were at moderate risk because they used marijuana or alcohol, had committed a number of minor offenses, or were sexually active. The remaining half were at virtually no risk: they did not report committing serious crimes or engaging in frequent delinquent behavior, they rarely used any substances, and they were not yet sexually active. Among the older cohort, ages 15 to 21, 15 percent were at very high risk, 62 percent were at moderate risk, and less than a fourth were not at risk. The differences in the two distributions reflect a combination of aging and social trends between 1976 and 1980: more substance use of all kinds, increased sexual activity, less serious delinquency, and fewer minor offenses.

From juvenile court records, one can get an idea of the relationship between delinquency and school failure: it is estimated that 85 percent of juveniles who appear in court are illiterate.[9] This extremely high rate may also reflect the differential between those who commit delinquent acts and those who are actually apprehended.

## Substance Abuse and Other Behaviors

Barnes and Welte's study of New York State students found that school misconduct (cutting class, being sent to the principal, etc.) and low school grades were the most important predictors of alcohol consumption; of those students who had 10 or more misconduct events, 93 percent were drinkers compared with 54 percent of students who had no reported misconduct.[10] Among students with failing grades, 82 percent were drinkers compared with 59 percent of A students. As in many studies, the correlations between alcohol use, alcohol-related problems, and drug use were very strong. The Michigan survey of high school seniors provides a wealth of information about the attributes of drug users, showing the high incidence of nonconforming behavior, delinquency, and school problems among users (see Table 7.3). Clearly heroin users are deviant in almost every respect (based on a small sample exclusive of dropouts who were not included in the survey).

The seniors who abstained from drugs, however, did not all lead exemplary lives. One in five self-reported a minor theft, a driving ticket, cutting classes, and heavy drinking. Marijuana users and those who only used other illicit drugs on three or less occasions appeared to report similar patterns of behavior, with almost one-third reporting school and minor delinquency problems. Almost one-half of those students who used illicit drugs but not heroin were cutting school and delinquent, as were up to two-thirds of the heroin users.

TABLE 7.3. Drug Use and Other Behaviors Among High School Seniors, 1985

| | Percentage Reporting Behavior | | | | |
|---|---|---|---|---|---|
| Item | No Use | Marijuana Only | Few Pills | Heavy Pills | Ever Used Heroin |
| *School* | | | | | |
| Average grade C or less | 10 | 15 | 15 | 20 | 25 |
| Cut school in last four weeks | 16 | 31 | 33 | 45 | 58 |
| Cut a class | 21 | 37 | 38 | 47 | 66 |
| *Delinquency* | | | | | |
| *(during past 12 mos.)* | | | | | |
| Trouble with police | 11 | 23 | 23 | 38 | 54 |
| Serious fighting | 10 | 16 | 22 | 28 | 44 |
| Theft <$50 | 19 | 31 | 30 | 46 | 57 |
| Theft >$50 | 3 | 7 | 6 | 14 | 27 |
| Reckless driving, ticket | 20 | 29 | 28 | 39 | 51 |
| *Social life* | | | | | |
| Heavy drinker | 19 | 37 | 40 | 49 | 71 |
| Out more than four times per week | 14 | 22 | 34 | 49 | 61 |
| Date more than four times per week | 7 | 11 | 13 | 19 | 21 |
| *Personal* | | | | | |
| Get a kick out of doing things that are a little dangerous | 22 | 33 | 34 | 49 | 61 |

*Source:* L. Johnston, J. Bachman, and P. O'Malley, *Monitoring the Future, 1985* (Ann Arbor, Mich.: Institute for Social Research, University of Michigan, 1986), pp. 20, 22, 44, 100, 101, 108.

Several researchers have taken a "risk-factor" approach to analyzing drug use data, similar to Donovan and Jessor's Problem Behavior Index. Newcomb and his colleagues have shown that the *number* of different risk factors (what we have called antecedents) is a more important predictor of substance abuse than any single risk factor. In his sample, 17 percent of the high school students abused at least one substance; those with few risk factors were rarely involved in drug use; however, 71 percent of those with seven or more risk factors abused at least one substance.[11] Based on this study, 40 percent of the students had zero or one risk factor, 30 percent had two or three, 19 percent had four or five, and 11 percent had six or more.

Weber and his colleagues produced an analysis from a sample of seventh and eighth graders that clearly differentiated "types": Type I youngsters were "normally socialized" in their patterns of alcohol use and Type II youngsters were "problem prone."[12] The latter group, who made up 20 percent of the respondents, had early onset of alcohol use and frequent drunkenness. These youth were characterized as having poor relationships with parents, school conduct problems, and a psychological profile suggestive of "troublesome psychological functioning."

### Sexual Activity, Pregnancy, and Other Behaviors

The strong positive association between substance use of any kind and early sexual activity has been well documented in the work of Elliott, Kandel, Jessor, and others. Data from the 1981 National Survey of Children (age 15 and 16) shows very strong associations between being sexually active and smoking, using alcohol, using marijuana, having shoplifted, and having run away.[13] For example, among white females, 2 percent who had never smoked and 1 percent who had never used alcohol were sexually active compared with 39 percent who smoked frequently and 27 percent who used alcohol. Marijuana users were nine times more likely to be sexually active than nonusers. Only a small number of the respondents reported ever shoplifting, but among those who did, they were three times as likely to have been sexually active. Only 12 percent of those who had never run away were sexually active compared with 51 percent who had.

Based on a study of Baltimore junior and senior high school students, Zabin created an index of substance abuse and found that it related significantly to sexual activity and being behind grade in school.[14] Chewning showed that among eleventh graders, for the 47 percent of females who had sex, 45 percent smoked daily, while for the 53 percent who had not had sex, 13 percent smoked daily. The same patterns prevailed for males, and for the use of alcohol and drugs.[15]

Using data from Mott and Haurin's analysis of the National Longitutinal Survey of Youth (NLSY), another set of risk groups can be described (as above) based on sexual activity and substance use.[16] Among this sample of 13- to 17-year-olds, about half were not at risk at all, even by the time they were age 17. The proportion involved in the highest risk behaviors (7 percent) was small, while about 40 percent were involved in at least one of the behaviors. The Mott data suggested that if only one behavior was entered into, it was likely to be either sex or marijuana, and the most prevalent combination was sex, alcohol, and marijuana.

The "conventional wisdom" has been that girls drop out of school *because* of pregnancy; this has been described as the most deleterious consequence of early childbearing. Recent analyses suggest that many girls who become mothers drop out *prior* to the pregnancy. A seminar on this subject produced findings from several national surveys: data from the High School and Beyond Survey (HS&B) showed that of all those girls who both dropped out and had a birth, 28 percent had dropped out prior to the conception; a survey of 20- to 29-year-old never married women showed that among those who became both pregnant and dropouts, 61 percent of the pregnancies occurred after the dropout; a survey of very young welfare mothers showed that 20 percent were already out of school before the conception.[17] These and other data led the author to produce a "ball park" estimate that about one-fourth of the dropout–childbearing syndrome occurs prior to conception.

The reasons that dropouts give for leaving school provide insights into these behavioral interrelationships. Based on HS&B data, among girls, 62 percent gave a family-related reason (31% marriage, 23% pregnancy, and 8% to support a family). *But,* 82 percent cited a school-related reason, such as poor grades or dislike of school (more than one reason could be reported). For boys, virtually all cited school-related reasons and an additional 27 percent mentioned work.[18] However, significant differences by race are apparent from the NLSY; when female dropouts were asked the *primary* reason for dropping out, 41 percent of blacks, 15 percent of Hispanics, and 14 percent of whites said pregnancy. However, 4 percent of blacks, 15 percent of Hispanics, and 15 percent of whites said marriage. School-related reasons were primary for 36 percent of white females, 29 percent of blacks, and 21 percent of Hispanics.[19]

Two recent analyses of the national surveys produced substantial new evidence about the association between school achievement and pregnancy. From the HS&B, it was shown that sophomores in each of the three race/ethnic groups with low academic ability (lowest third) were twice as likely to become unwed parents by their senior year as those with high academic ability (highest third).[20] The NLSY data yielded more dramatic differences: females in the bottom quintile of a measure of basic reading and math skills were five times more likely (29%) to become mothers over a two-year period than those in the top quintile (6%).[21] (See also the data at the end of Chapter 5.) In these analyses, racial differences are greatly diminished when socioeconomic status (SES) measures are added to the measures of basic skills.

An earlier analysis of substance use as a predictor of premarital pregnancy found that current and former users of illicit drugs were twice as likely to become premaritally pregnant; having dropped out of school and having poor grades had equal effects.[22] When the premarital pregnancy events were separately analyzed by outcome, the probability of abortion was highly related to illicit drug use and full-time, post-high-school attendance; the probability of having a premarital birth was related to having dropped out of school; and the probability of having a postmarital birth was related to not using illicit drugs.

A unique data analysis of the NLSY investigated the interrelationship between teen fatherhood and problem behaviors. Regardless of race and family income, the study demonstrated that the fathers were much more likely than nonfathers to have been expelled or suspended from school, to have smoked marijuana, to have been involved with the police within the past year, and to have been involved in other forms of delinquency.[23] Elster and his colleagues concluded that adolescent fatherhood may represent a consequence of living in a "high-risk" social environment rather than being independently determined.

### School Failure, Dropping Out, and Other Behaviors

Repeated studies have validated the fact that dropouts were not doing well in school prior to the act of dropping out. Peng's analysis of the HS&B variables shows very large differences: 43 percent of sophomores with mostly Ds dropped out compared with 3 percent with mostly As, and 15 percent of vocational school attendees left compared with 4 percent of academic program attendees.[24] Dropping out typically follows all kinds of trouble in school: cutting classes, truancy, misbehavior, suspension, and expulsion.

Friedman found that illicit drug use was an important determinant of dropping out among a sample of ninth to eleventh graders.[25] More than half of the heavy drug users dropped out compared with one-fourth of those who used no drugs. The heavy drug users (who were more likely to be males) were very dissatisfied with, and doing very poorly in, school and came from disadvantaged families (low maternal education, parents separated, large family size). The authors suggest that drug use should not be considered the cause of dropping out, but rather a "concomitant effect of the more basic state of dissatisfaction."

Johnston et al. attempted to estimate the prevalence of drug use among dropouts (who were excluded from the University of Michigan Survey of high school seniors), but concluded along with a National Institute on Drug Abuse (NIDA) review committee that the estimates of drug use were not substantially affected by the exclusion. Thus, dropouts were not assumed to have significantly higher drug prevalence rates than enrolled students, with the possible exception of heroin use, which Johnston suspects may be higher among dropouts.[26]

Mensch and Kandel analyzed data from the 1984 National Longitudinal Survey of Young Adults at ages 19 to 27 to explore the relationship between dropping out of high school, drug involvement, and other problem behaviors.[27] They found significantly higher rates of substance use among dropouts and took issue with the Michigan survey findings because dropouts and absentees were not included. Their analysis includes tabulations for dropouts who eventually obtained graduate equivalency diplomas (GEDs); these respondents, about 27 percent of all dropouts, were even more likely to have used drugs than either dropouts or graduates. The earlier the involvement in drug use, particularly illicit drugs, and sexual activities, the more likely that dropping out occurred. Some 60 percent of males who used illicit drugs at age 12 or less dropped out compared with 29 percent of those who had never used drugs. For females, 69 percent of those who had experienced intercourse at age 12 or younger dropped out compared with 6 percent who had never had intercourse (by age 19). The impact of alcohol use was not as marked as drug use, although the early initiation of drinking was a predictor. In the words of Mensch and Kandel,

> [The] participation in a variety of activities in adolescence that are deviant because they contravene general societal norms, such as delinquency or the use of marijuana and other illicit drugs, or because they contravene age-related norms, such as sexual intercourse, pregnancy or cigarette smoking, greatly increase the risk of dropping out of school. . . . [E]ach behavior creates unique risks of its own. The role of drug involvement in early school leaving illustrates that participation in one class of deviant activities by itself . . . [significantly] increases the risk of participation in other deviant behaviors and reduces the commitment to conventional institutions, one of which is the school.[28]

They conclude that prevention of drug use might increase the probability of high school graduation.

Few surveys report on the behavior of rural adolescents. One unique study looked at rural, white, low-income eighth- to tenth-grade girls and found that those with high grades and heavy academic involvement were much less likely to be sexually active than those with poor academic performance and low expectations for the future.[29]

### Special Problems and Their Relationship To Other Behaviors

Several special problems of today's adolescents were mentioned in Chapter 2 that also relate to the major topics treated here. Of particular importance are physical and sexual abuse, homelessness, and suicide. About 13 percent of one high school population reported that they had been maltreated (ever abused). Among those who had been abused, their rates of sexual activity, pregnancy, and drug use were significantly higher. Some 45 percent of those who had been maltreated had made prior suicide attempts compared with 9 percent of those who had never been maltreated.[30] Those who had made suicide attempts reported strikingly higher rates of physical and sexual abuse, early pregnancy experiences, and substance abuse.

Homeless youth are typically depressed and under great stress. One study found that almost one-half of homeless youth had ever tried to commit suicide, 29 percent within the previous year.[31] About one-fourth had run away from home because of parental alcohol abuse, and 13 percent had been sexually assaulted within a year.

### Summary of Interrelationships Between Problems

A large number of reports have been reviewed that document the strong interrelationships between the variables of interest. As one researcher attested, "It may not come as a surprise to anyone to hear that a significant amount of drug use by adolescents interferes with academic and career progress. Common sense would suggest this. Nevertheless, it is useful to document carefully, by hard research findings, that this is in fact true.'' [32] The weight of the evidence is substantial; a large number of important studies document the relationships between the factors. [33] Unfortunately, no one study has analyzed how the various separate behaviors overlap, to give us the whole story. In aggregate, these studies confirm the hypothesis that problem behaviors are indeed interrelated:

1. Delinquency is associated with early sexual activity, early pregnancy, substance abuse, low grades, and dropping out.
2. Early initiation of smoking and alcohol leads to heavier use of cigarettes and alcohol, and also leads to the use of marijuana and other illicit drugs.
3. Heavy substance abuse is associated with early sexual activity, lower grades, dropping out, and delinquency.
4. Early initiation of sexual activity is related to the use of cigarettes and alcohol, use of marijuana and other illicit drugs, lower grades, dropping out, and delinquency.
5. Early childbearing is related to early sexual activity, heavy drug use, low academic achievement, dropping out, and delinquency.
6. School failure leads to dropping out. Lower grades are associated with substance use and early childbearing. Truancy and school misbehavior are related to substance abuse, dropping out, and delinquency.
7. The number of risky behaviors that are engaged in is strongly related to the seriousness of the problems that result from the behaviors.

These behaviors are interrelated in complex ways. Which of these behaviors, if any, is the precipitating event? What is the sequencing? From this preliminary review of the literature and from many observations and discussions, it appears that school failure begins to occur at very early ages, and that once failure occurs, other events begin to take place. Doing poorly in school and minor delinquent offenses seem to fit together, and as these high-risk children grow older, substance abuse and sexual activity enter the picture, and the major negative consequences— early childbearing, heavy substance abuse, serious delinquency, and dropping out ensue. Obviously, patterns differ dramatically. However, these data appear to substantiate the hypothesis that a definable group of young people are at risk of the full range of behaviors with the most negative consequences.

## Numbers at Risk of Multiple-Problem Behaviors

### *Summary of Categorical Risk Estimates*

Table 7.4 presents a summary of the numbers and percents of 10- to 17-year-olds at risk of the various categories of behaviors. The top part of the table shows the behaviors which evidence very negative short- and long-term consequences: frequent substance abuse, any hard drug use, unprotected sexual intercourse, pregnancy, being two or more years behind in school, or having already dropped out, and being arrested while a juvenile. From 2 to 9 percent of the youth population

TABLE 7.4. Summary of Numbers and Percentages of 10- to 17-Year-Olds in High-Risk Categories (numbers in thousands)

| Behavior | Number Aged 10 to 17 | Percent of Total |
|---|---|---|
| *Number and Percentage at High Risk of Behaviors with Negative Consequences* | | |
| Arrested | 1,700 | 6 |
| *Heavy substance abuse* | | |
| Cigarettes | 900 | 3 |
| Alcohol | 2,000 | 7 |
| Marijuana | 500 | 2 |
| Cocaine, hard drugs | 800 | 3 |
| *Unprotected sexual intercourse* | | |
| Females | 1,400 | 5 |
| (including pregnancies) | | |
| Males | 2,500 | 9 |
| Two years behind modal grade | 1,400 | 5 |
| Dropouts | 700 | 3 |
| *Number and Percentage at High Risk of Behaviors with Moderate Consequences that Can Lead to Higher Risk* | | |
| *Self-reported delinquency* | | |
| Index offenses | 4,200 | 15 |
| Truancy | 7,200 | 26 |
| *Use substances occasionally* | | |
| Cigarettes | 3,900 | 14 |
| Alcohol | 7,000 | 25 |
| Marijuana | 2,500 | 9 |
| *Sexually active, with contraception* | | |
| Males | 2,500 | 9 |
| Females | 1,400 | 5 |
| One year behind modal grade | 6,000 | 22 |

*Source:* Adapted from Tables 3.6, 4.6, 5.6, and 6.6. Figures have been adjusted to eliminate double counts.

has experienced one of these high-risk behaviors. However, the percentages are not cumulative because some youngsters are counted in several categories.

The bottom half of Table 7.4 summarizes the numbers and percents of young people who are involved in behaviors that could eventually lead to higher risk, but they probably are not currently in danger of negative consequences. These behaviors include occasional substance use, sexual activity (intercourse) among males and females who make use of contraception, being behind modal grade by one year, and self-reported delinquency that is not serious or not yet apprehended. The numbers are much larger in this grouping, ranging from 5 to 26 percent of the population.

## Quantification of Overlap in Problem Behaviors

To produce an approximation of the number of youth with multiple-problem behaviors, we move into the area of simulated estimation. No actual data exist to
precisely quantify risk groups and target populations. Therefore, it is necessary to
extrapolate from what is known to estimate the unknown. This is a process in
which numbers are ''forced'' into a cell based on knowledge of interrelationships,
assumptions, and intuition. A matrix has been created in which the categorical
risk estimates are fitted into four risk groups according to the distributions suggested by the data presented in the literature thus far reviewed. The research produced remarkably consistent groupings of populations.

The risk groups are labeled very high, high, moderate, and low risk. *Very
high-risk youth,* those with multiple-problem behaviors, make up about 10 percent
of the youth population. This group includes: those who have been arrested or
have committed serious offenses, have dropped out of school or are behind their
modal grades, are users of heavy drugs, drink heavily, regularly use cigarettes and
marijuana, are sexually active but do not use contraception. Some but not all teen
parents fit into this category. Most but not all of the highest risk youths ''do it
all.''

*High-risk youth* include another 15 percent of the youth population who participate in many of these same behaviors but with slightly lower frequency and
less deleterious consequences. They commit less serious delinquent offenses, but
are also heavy users of alcohol, cigarettes, and marijuana, mostly engage in unprotected sexual intercourse, and are behind in school. This group of high-risk
youth may be engaged in two or three problem behaviors.

*Moderate-risk youth* make up about one-fourth of the 10- to 17-year-olds.
They are the experimenters: they commit minor delinquent offenses, use substances occasionally but not hard drugs, have sexual intercourse and use contraception, and may be one year behind in school. Most of these moderate-risk youth
are only involved in one of these risk behaviors.

About half of all young people are in the *low-risk* category. They do not
commit any serious delinquent acts, do not abuse substances at all, and are not
yet sexually active. A small proportion drink occasionally and a few are one year
behind their modal grade in school because of their birth dates or for developmental reasons, but their risk of any negative consequences is minimal.

Tables 7.5 and 7.6 show the distribution of the 28 million 10- to 17-year-olds
according to the simulated estimate of risk groups. Almost 3 million young people
are in jeopardy of major negative consequences from their behavior, and another
4 million are at high risk. About 7 million young people are at moderate risk of
consequences; they probably will not be in trouble unless their current behavior
leads to more dangerous behaviors. Some 14 million 10- to 17-year-olds are probably not currently at risk of negative consequences. They appear to be conducting
themselves in patterns that will lead to high school conclusion with relatively high
levels of achievement and relatively low levels of risk from problem behaviors.

We return to the statistics to get a better fix on who and where the 7 million

TABLE 7.5. Distribution of Youth Population
According to Risk Status (numbers in millions)

| Status | Total Number | Percentage |
|---|---|---|
| Very high | 2.8 | 10 |
| High | 4.2 | 15 |
| Moderate | 7.0 | 25 |
| Low risk | 14.0 | 50 |
| TOTAL | 28.0 | 100 |

highest risk children are. While we do not know the exact demographic make-up of the highest risk youth, available data about each of the separate behaviors suggest that more are males than females. They are more likely to live in cities than in suburban or rural areas. Their families are more likely to be poor and have low educational levels.

The percent behind modal grade in school is a powerful measure of risk status for all the problem behaviors. Extrapolated from the distribution of 10- to 17-year-olds who are two or more years behind in school (Table 6.3), it is estimated that among high-risk youth, 44 percent are white males, 25 percent white females, 20 percent black males, and 11 percent black females.[34] Some 13 percent are

TABLE 7.6. Distribution of Categorical Problem Behaviors According to Risk Groups (numbers in millions)

| Behavior | Total | Very High | High | Moderate | Low Risk |
|---|---|---|---|---|---|
| *Delinquency* | | | | | |
| Arrests | 1.7 | 1.7 | | | |
| Other delinquency[a] | 7.2 | 1.1 | 4.2 | 1.9 | |
| *Substance abuse* | | | | | |
| Smoking | 4.8 | 1.5 | 1.5 | 1.8 | |
| Drinking | 9.0 | 2.0 | 2.5 | 2.5 | 2.0 |
| Marijuana | 3.0 | 1.6 | 1.4 | | |
| Hard drugs | 0.8 | 0.8 | | | |
| *Early sexual intercourse* | | | | | |
| Unprotected | | | | | |
| (no contraception) | 3.9 | 2.0 | 1.9 | | |
| Protected | 3.9 | | 0.5 | 3.4 | |
| *School failure and dropout* | | | | | |
| Dropped out | 0.7 | 0.7 | | | |
| Behind | | | | | |
| 2 years | 1.4 | 1.4 | | | |
| 1 year | 6.0 | 0.7 | 3.0 | 1.6 | 0.7 |
| TOTAL | 28.0 | 2.8 | 4.2 | 7.0 | 14.0 |

[a] Assumes overlap between index offenses and truancy.

*Source:* Numbers from Table 7.4.

Hispanic males and 10 percent Hispanic females (most of whom are counted as white). Among all 10- to 17-year-olds, 81 percent are white, 15 percent are black, 4 percent are "other"; 10 percent are of Spanish origin (white or black). Thus minority children are overrepresented in this high-risk group: 31 percent of those who are two or more years behind in school are black compared with 15 percent in the population, and 23 percent are Hispanic although they make up 10 percent of the population. Black and Hispanic youth have higher rates of school failure, early unprotected intercourse and early childbearing, and certain categories of delinquency. However, the numbers of white children aged 10 to 17 who are high risk far exceed the numbers of black and Hispanic children. In round numbers, of the 7 million high-risk youth, we could expect that about 4.8 million are white and about 2.2 million are black. Roughly 1.6 million of the total would be of Hispanic origin. In terms of rates, 21 percent of white 10- to 17-year-olds fall into the group as do 52 percent of black and 59 percent of Hispanic youth. These estimates help clarify the fact that problem behavior is not at all an exclusive attribute of minority children. Given the proven links between poverty and school failure, poverty and early childbearing, poverty and serious delinquency, it is clear that most of these children live in severely disadvantaged households and neighborhoods and, in fact, roughly 10 percent are homeless or living on the streets because their homes are not viable.

## Conclusions from Part I

In many diverse ways, delinquency, early initiation of smoking and alcohol use, heavy drug use, unprotected sexual intercourse, early childbearing, school failure, and dropping out are interrelated. Every young person who has sex at 12 does not become a drug addict or a felon, but most drug addicts experienced early sexual encounters and some form of delinquent behavior. As already stated in the introduction, the goal of interventions is to assist children to pursue a life path that leads to responsible adulthood.

We can visualize the life histories of the various risk groups in this way. A train is leaving a station. Some children are born on the train and stay on until they grow up. They have supportive parents and live in a healthy community with a good school. Some children who are born on the train fall off of it because their families fall apart, or the school fails, or other stressful events occur. Some children are not born on the train and never get on it. They lack parental support, live in a poor social environment, drop out of terrible schools, and are surrounded by hopelessness. Some children are not born on the train but they manage to climb on it. These are the children that Rutter and others call "invulnerable" and "resilient."[35] Almost always these children have had access to a caring individual who assisted them (not necessarily a parent). One prominent black male described how this process worked in his family, "My mother told me when I was very little that I would have to work twice as hard as white kids in order to make it, and she was always right there by my side helping me to do that."

Many of the researchers mentioned here have produced models and path analyses that show the differential effects of family, peers, environment, school, and other factors on these outcomes. Six variables emerge as characteristics of those young people who exhibit all of the four behaviors we examined: starting any of the behaviors early, doing poorly in school, acting out, going around with friends who act out in the same ways, having inattentive parents, and living in a disadvantaged neighborhood. Minority status and low SES appear to compound these behaviors in some, but not all, cases.

The objective of this work is to move away from the traditional categorical approaches to intervention and begin to design a more comprehensive approach. The emergence of common predictors of multiple-problem behaviors lends force to the argument that interventions should focus more on the *predictors* of the behavior than on the behavior itself. Another criterion to consider in prevention programs is the extent to which predictors are *amenable to intervention.* And if there is a developmental progression, it is also necessary to identify *signal* events, for early intervention. These requirements lead to the conclusion that enhancement of early schooling and prevention of school failure should receive high priority not only from those interested in lowering the dropout rate but also from those interested in preventing substance abuse, pregnancy, and delinquency. William Pink posits that

> early in a student's school career, decisions are made about ability and educability that mesh commonplace organizational practices of schools, that is, ability grouping, tracking, and special education, that in turn serve, over time, to solidify both in-school and out-of-school identities for students that finally govern options in both career and life choices.[36]

The director of one of the most "high-powered" substance abuse programs, located in one of the highest SES counties in the country, stated that, of all the students who became substance abusers in his large school system, at least three-fourths could be identified as high risk in the second grade because they were already having school-related problems. He went on to say that by the time they turned to drugs and alcohol in the middle-school years, it was very difficult to help them. The remaining fourth of the abusers were achievers, with problems arising in high school, but much more amenable to counseling, peer pressure, and treatment.

Early identification is not without hazards. We do not want to stigmatize children who are doing poorly by labeling them as "high risk." However, children who are already a year or two behind their peers perceive that something is wrong. What has been clarified here is the high probability that school failure will signal other problem behaviors. Clearly, school behavior derives from a set of circumstances, either personal or within the family or within the school system. "Acting out" in school often is a precursor to school failure and other problems. But not all nonconformity is destructive. It should not be our intention to change all nonconformists into conformists at early ages, but rather to make sure that institutions can facilitate growth that produces acceptable nonconformity, such as creativity and leadership, rather than nonacceptable nonconformity that leads to delinquency.

In Part I of this book, we have reviewed many statistics and research findings about the behavior of young people. In Part II, we take a look at the programs that have been organized to deal with these problems. We will examine interventions to see if they work to prevent the problem behaviors and, particularly, whether they reduce the negative consequences.

## Notes

1. R. Jessor, "Adolescent Problem Drinking: Psychosocial Aspects and Developmental Outcomes" (Presented at the Carnegie Conference on Unhealthful Risk-Taking Behavior among Adolescents, Stanford, California, November 11–13, 1984, and printed in R. Sibereisen, K. Eyferth, and G. Rudinger, eds., *Development as Action in Context* [Berlin: Springer-Verlag, 1986]), pp. 241–64.
2. J. E. Donovan and R. Jessor, "Structure of Problem Behavior in Adolescence and Young Adulthood," *Journal of Consulting and Clinical Psychology* 53(1985): 890–904.
3. P. Erickson, A. Rapkin, S. Scrimshaw, T. Long, S. Pappas, and A. Davis, "Multiple Risk-Taking Behavior in Middle and High School Students in Los Angeles Metropolitan Area" (Unpublished paper, August 5, 1987).
4. A. Peterson, "Those Gangly Years," *Psychology Today,* September 1987, p. 33.
5. D. Elliot and B. J. Morse, "Drug Use, Delinquency and Sexual Activity" (Unpublished paper, Boulder, Colo.: Behavioral Research Institute, undated).
6. Ibid. (See Table 7.2.)
7. D. Elliott, D. Huizinga, and S. Menard, *Multiple Problem Youth: Delinquency, Substance Abuse and Mental Health Problems* (New York: Springer-Verlag, 1988). This volume contains detailed tabulations for each of these variables and shows the interrelationships between them.
8. For details on this process, see J. Dryfoos, "Youth at Risk: One in Four in Jeopardy" (Report to the Carnegie Corporation, June 1987).
9. J. Davidson, "Reducing Adolescent Illiteracy," *TEC Networks* 18(July 1988): 4–5.
10. G. Barnes and J. W. Welte, "Patterns and Predictors of Alcohol Use among 7–12th Grade Students in New York State," *Journal of Studies on Alcohol* 47(1986): 53–62.
11. M. Newcomb, E. Maddahian, R. Skager, and P. Bentler, "Substance Abuse and Psychosocial Risk Factors among Teenagers," *American Journal of Drug and Alcohol Abuse* 13(1987): 413–33.
12. R. Weber, J. Graham, W. Hansen, B. Flay, and C. Johnson, "Rethinking Adolescent Drug Abuse Prevention Strategies: A Tailored Intervention Approach" (Paper presented at the 116th Annual Meeting of the American Public Health Association, Boston, November 1988).
13. K. A. Moore, "Adolescent Drug Abuse and Fertility: Existing Survey Data" (Unpublished paper, Child Trends, Inc., Washington, D.C., undated).
14. L. S. Zabin, J. B. Hardy, E. A. Smith, and M. B. Hirsch, "Substance Use and Its Relation to Sexual Activity among Inner-City Adolescents," *Journal of Adolescent Health Care* 7(1986): 320–31.
15. B. Chewning (Unpublished data from Survey of Minnesota Teenagers, 1986).
16. F. Mott and J. Haurin, "The Inter-relatedness of Age at First Intercourse, Early Pregnancy, Alcohol and Drug Use among American Adolescents," *Family Planning Perspectives* 20(1988): 128–36.

17. J. Dryfoos, "Prevention Strategies: A Progress Report," submitted to the Rockefeller Foundation, May 1985.
18. S. Peng, "High School Dropouts: Descriptive Information from High School and Beyond," *Bulletin, National Center for Education Statistics* (U.S. Department of Education, November 1983), pp. 4–6.
19. R. Rumsberger, "Dropping out of High School: The Influence of Race, Sex and Family Background," *American Educational Research Journal* 20(Summer 1983): 199–220.
20. A. Abrahamse, P. Morrison, and L. Waite, "Single Teenage Mothers: Spotting Susceptible Adolescents in Advance" (Unpublished paper, Rand Corporation, Santa Monica, Calif., 1986).
21. K. Pittman, *Preventing Adolescent Pregnancy: What Schools Can Do* (Washington, D.C.: Children's Defense Fund, 1986).
22. K. Yamaguchi and D. Kandel, "Determinants of Premarital Pregnancy and Its Outcome: A Dynamic Analysis of Competing Life Events" (Unpublished paper, December 1985).
23. A. Elster, M. Lamb, and J. Tavare, "Association between Behavioral and School Problems and Fatherhood in a National Sample of Adolescent Youth," *Journal of Pediatrics* 111(part 1)(1987): 932–36.
24. Peng, "High School Dropouts," p. 3.
25. A. Friedman, "Does Drug and Alcohol Use Lead to Failure to Graduate from High School?" *Journal of Drug Education* 15(1985): 353–64.
26. L. Johnston, J. Bachman, and P. O'Malley, *Monitoring the Future, 1985* (Ann Arbor, Mich.: Institute for Social Research, University of Michigan, 1986).
27. B. Mensch and D. Kandel, "Dropping Out of High School and Drug Involvement," *Sociology of Education* 61(1988): 95–113.
28. Ibid., 112.
29. L. Crockett, "Educational Plans, Current Behaviors, and Future Expectations among Rural Adolescent Girls" (Unpublished paper, 1987).
30. S. Riggs and A. Alario, "Health Related Risk Taking Behaviors and Attempted Suicide in Adolescents Who Report Prior Maltreatment" (Paper presented at the Annual Meeting of the Ambulatory Pediatric Association, Anaheim, California, May 1987).
31. M. Robertson, "Mental Health Status of Homeless Adolescents in Hollywood" (Paper presented at the 116th Annual Meeting of the American Public Health Association, Boston, November 1988).
32. Friedman, "Does Drug and Alcohol Use Lead to Failure," 363.
33. The major studies have been listed in Tables 3.1, 4.1, 5.1, and 6.1, in Chapters 3 to 6, describing the year, sample size, and source.
34. U.S. Bureau of the Census, "School Enrollment—Social and Economic Characteristics of Students: October 1986," *Current Population Reports,* Series P-20, No. 429, 1988.
35. M. Rutter, C. Izard, and P. Read, *Depression in Young People: Developmental and Clinical Perspectives* (New York: Guildford Press, 1985).
36. W. Pink, "Schools, Youth, and Justice," *Crime and Delinquency* 30(1984): 439–61.

# PART II

# THE PREVENTION RECORD: WHAT WORKS AND WHAT DOESN'T

# 8

# Classification and Organization of Programs

Simulated risk estimates (Tables 7.5 and 7.6) provide a quantitative framework for addressing the need of a significant number of children in the United States who are in dire straits: failing in school, delinquent, taking drugs, and having unprotected intercourse. Of the 28 million girls and boys aged 10 to 17, it is estimated that 1 in 10 (almost 3 million) are in critical situations. Another group of 4 million (15%) have excessively high prevalence rates for some but not all of the high-risk behaviors. Thus the future of 7 million youth—one in four in this country—is in jeopardy unless major and immediate changes are made in their school experiences, in their access to opportunities for healthy adolescent development, and in the quality of life in their communities. The children and their families require intensive support services to ameliorate their problems. The school systems must undergo rapid reorganization to respond to the needs of the families in these communities.

Another 25 percent of youth (7 million) are at moderate risk, because of school problems, minor delinquencies, light substance use, and early, but protected, intercourse. These young people would make up the target population for concentrated prevention approaches including school remediation, counseling, and comprehensive services. About half of the nation's youth (14 million) experience few problems and are probably at low risk of negative consequences from their behavior, but they too require general preventive services and health promotion programs. And, of course, effective schools are a social necessity for everyone.

From these rough estimates, it may be possible to conceptualize a more logical, less fragmented strategy for implementing programs aimed at reducing problem behaviors. It is apparent that some children need a great deal of help, others a little, and some not any. Interventions aimed at the common predictors or antecedents of behaviors may have a better chance of success than those that are focused on only one behavior, such as drugs or sex. It seems reasonable to conclude that fewer children would be failing to achieve if the separate categorical interventions of the past had been more successful.


## Classification of Interventions

The next question to be addressed is: What can we learn from these separate categories of interventions that would be useful in buil..ing a more integrated system of youth services? We start by examining the "what works" literature in each of four program areas: prevention of juvenile delinquency; prevention of substance abuse; prevention of pregnancy (early childbearing); and prevention of school failure and dropping out. Each chapter (9 through 12) includes a brief overview of the "state-of-the-art" of program development in the particular field; examples of successful models of prevention; discussion of approaches that have not proven successful at changing behavior; and a summary of concepts that emerge from the overview. The exemplary programs are classified (loosely) into three categories of interventions: early childhood and family (parents), school-based, and communitywide/multicomponent. Table 8.1 outlines the classification scheme in more detail. Each program element is not represented in each field, but there is considerable conformity to the outline, demonstrating the range of programs of all kinds. Part III presents a synthesis of the common themes that arise from the diverse prevention fields and discusses the implications for designing more effective programs.

If rigid scientific criteria had been applied for inclusion of program models, Part II would be very short indeed. As will become apparent, a recurring theme

TABLE 8.1. Classification Framework for Reviewing Exemplary Prevention Programs in Fields of Delinquency, Substance Abuse, Teen Pregnancy, and School Failure/Dropping Out

*Early childhood and family interventions*
Preschool/Head Start
Parent training/support

*School-based interventions*
Curricula
Organization of school
    Teacher training
    School team
    Alternative school
Special services
    Counseling and mentoring
    Health services
    Volunteer work

*Community-based and/or multicomponent*
School–community collaborations
Community education
Multicomponent comprehensive programs

from the various literatures is the absence of proof that programs are effective.[1] Many evaluations show changes in knowledge or attitudes, but these are not sufficiently predictive of behavioral change to accept as evidence that a program "works." Nevertheless, more than 100 programs were identified with proven results, and many more could have been included. The programs described in Chapters 9 to 12 were selected as examples of successful programs currently operating in the various fields of prevention. All of the programs considered here are directed at some form of behavioral change. As the result of an intervention, the client/student/participant is supposed to stop some negative behavior (smoking, having unprotected intercourse, "acting out") and adopt some positive behavior (doing homework, getting higher grades, using contraception).

The evaluation of the program should demonstrate that, in aggregate, more of the participants changed to the desired behavior than matched controls who were not recipients of the intervention. Random assignment to experimental and control groups is an important component of evaluation methodology but often difficult to implement in social programs. Program operators are resistant to the idea of withholding services from someone because it might interfere with the research design. As Menard has pointed out, evaluation research is expensive and time-consuming, and we cannot always wait for results before implementing programs.[2] The usual research approach relies on pre- and post-tests that measure self-reported behavior (substance use, use of contraception). However, school programs can also rely on grades and teachers' reports. It should be acknowledged at the outset that few programs meet all of the criteria set by evaluation methodology.

This book presents a first "cut" in a giant on-going task, which requires sorting through countless references and weighing evidence from personal testimony and observations to accumulate meaningful and powerful perceptions about the "state-of-the-art" of prevention programs. New books, articles in journals and the popular press, organization reports, and presentations at various annual meetings are issued at an increasingly rapid pace, making it difficult to keep abreast of an ever-changing scene. An attempt was made to focus on programs that were no more than a decade old, because life situations for young people have changed so dramatically during the past decade. Since it takes at least five years for program evaluation to enter the literature and some of the most important experiments are longitudinal (15 to 20 years of tracking), this criterion could not always be met in selecting successful program models. Certain important program models may have been missed, but enough material is available to gain an understanding of the current stages of program development in the United States. The primary goal here is to create a framework for devising a *workable and effective* strategy for assisting high-risk youth between the ages of 10 and 17 to gain equal access to responsible adulthood.

## Organization and Funding of Categorical Programs

The landscape covered here is vast. Literally thousands of diverse programs are directed at youth in the community setting. Efforts in four different fields (delinquency, substance abuse, teen pregnancy, and school failure) are summarized in the chapters that follow. Before we turn to the actual program models, however, it may be useful to review briefly the organization of each of the fields by looking at the legislative underpinnings. Each of these areas is in essence a "categorical" program, an initiative, or a group of initiatives, designed at the federal level to respond to a specific social need. It helps to understand the complexity of the local program delivery systems (or nonsystems) if one has a knowledge of the sources of financial support and how that money is transmitted to communities from Washington or the state capitols.[3] With high-quality programming for young people, money isn't everything. But it is an essential component. As a result, organized advocacy for appropriations and policies plays an important part in the youth services scene.

For those unfamiliar with the bureaucratic jungle, a few concepts need to be explained. Federal funds may be forwarded to state and local programs through several channels. *Formula* grants are awarded to states solely on the basis of population characteristics, such as population size or numbers of children or numbers of low-income families. *Block* granting is a mechanism that has been used to consolidate categorical funds (e.g., mental health with drugs and alcohol) and allow states more leeway to decide how to use the funds without federal direction. *Project* grants (discretionary funds) are awarded directly to local programs on the basis of their proposals to meet certain requirements, such as serving runaways or treating drug abusers. In some cases, entire states are treated as projects and receive project grants, and they may in turn award the money to local agencies as *delegates. Contract* funds are awarded by federal agencies to universities, nonprofit research "think tanks," and other organizations for research, technical assistance, and other services. *Reimbursement* payments are used by Medicaid whereby a service provider establishes the eligibility of a client and then bills the state for services rendered. States then collect Medicaid from the federal program on the basis of arrangements for *matching* funds—the amount of money put up by a state or a local agency in order to qualify for federal reimbursement. For example, the federal share for family planning services is 90 percent.

Federal expenditures in 1988 surpassed the 1 trillion dollar mark, and the combined expenditures of state and local governments was around $700 billion. Programs that impact directly on youth receive only a small portion of that huge sum. It is impossible to comb through the federal budget and extract items that apply only to high-risk youth aged 10 to 17. Dollar figures are reported here, but that is just for the purposes of rough comparison. Unless otherwise indicated, the expenditures are for 1988.[4]

### *Delinquency Prevention Programs*

At the national level, the responsibility for delinquency prevention programs rests with the Department of Justice.[5,6] In 1974, as part of a massive reform of the juvenile justice field, the Juvenile Justice and Delinquency Prevention Act was passed. The theory was that delinquency would be diminished by removing juveniles from the jurisdiction of adult courts. The purposes of the federal program were to divert youth from the adult court process, to deinstitutionalize juvenile offenders, and to develop model prevention programs. In 1980, an Office of Juvenile Justice and Delinquency Prevention (OJJDP) was created to carry out the mandates of the legislation.

The major provisions of the act call for formula grants to states (based on the size of the population under 18) for planning and operating prevention, deinstitutionalization, and diversion projects. Some states have created very successful community-based interventions that resulted in reducing juvenile incarceration in adult jails and in discontinuing the detention of status offenders (youth arrested for crimes related to their age, such as running away). Admissions to some state training schools have decreased. But in other states, there is growing evidence of "cracking down on crime," with an increased reliance on correctional institutions resulting in severe overcrowding and reports of mistreatment.

OJJDP also provides grants and contracts to public and private agencies for creating demonstration program models including funds for program evaluation. The first grants went to school-based programs that hoped to provide "alternatives" to crime. OJJDP made funds available to the Alcohol and Drug Abuse Education Program then in the Office of Education to develop a program for the reduction of school crime. The School Team Approach (described in Chapter 9 as a program model) was seen as a promising method of dealing with broader school crime problems. Increasingly, the grants are being directed toward more comprehensive programs emphasizing prevention of substance abuse and enhancing employment opportunities among youth at high risk for delinquent acts. In 1988, 21 new demonstration grants were made, many with a focus on developing community strategies for reducing gang behavior and violence.

Another part of this program gives support to the Runaway and Homeless Youth effort, although the grants are actually administered by the Office of Human Development Services of the Department of Health and Human Services (DHHS). Funds for the runaway program are allocated by state according to the size of their population under age 18. There are more than 300 centers around the country that shelter 85,000 youth and provide services to a total of 300,000 annually. These shelters are reported to be seriously overcrowded.

Although the juvenile justice reform legislation was authorized at $200 million annually, the funding appropriation has never reached that level. In fact, it has been decreased each year since 1980. The Reagan administration tried each year to omit the juvenile justice program from the budget, claiming in recent years that it had achieved the goals of deinstitutionalization and diversion from crime. The expenditure level in 1988 for juvenile justice was $68 million, most of which was passed on to states through a block grant. Another $26 million was earmarked for the Runaway program.

Advocates in the voluntary sector have been successful in keeping the funding in the budget through intense direct lobbying efforts. The National Council on Crime and Delinquency (founded in 1907) has 11,000 members. It provides technical assistance to state governments and promotes community-based programs. An Ad Hoc Coalition for Juvenile Justice and Delinquency Prevention and the National Crime Prevention Council bring together the combined forces of major organizations with an interest in youth, welfare, education, and juvenile justice.

Juvenile justice at the state level is generally the responsibility of a Department of Youth Services. Most of the activities are centered on corrections systems and other control issues rather than prevention.

### Substance Use Prevention Programs

Since the mid-1970s, substance use prevention programs have been the responsibility of the Alcohol, Drug Abuse and Mental Health Administration (ADMHA) in the Public Health Service of the Department of Health and Human Services (DHHS), operating with two separate strands: the National Institute on Drug Abuse (NIDA) and the National Institute of Alcohol Abuse and Alcoholism (NIAAA).[7] States received block grants and were required to spend a small percentage on prevention services (20%), but the bulk of the funding went for treatment and law enforcement. State prevention coordinators were appointed to oversee the grants. It was estimated in 1985 that about $43 million of the ADMHA block grant was expended in states for prevention as well as $114 million in state-generated prevention funds.

In 1986, the passage of the Anti-Drug Abuse Act brought about significant changes in organization and funding. An Office of Substance Abuse Prevention (OSAP) was created to absorb and integrate the prevention responsibilities from NIDA and NIAAA leaving these agencies to concentrate on treatment and research. OSAP was established with the "understanding that prevention can only be as effective as the efforts undertaken at the state and community levels."[8] Its functions include policy review, grants management, workshops, coordination of research in the Public Health Service, training, development of literature, and working with the Centers for Disease Control to reduce the risk of AIDS in intravenous drug users. In its first year, OSAP made 132 project grants, distributing $24 million for model programs to serve high-risk youth. Another $20 million was awarded to contractors for a National Clearing House, Parent Youth Community Programs, Model Community-Based Prevention Programs, and Ethnic–Minority Programs. Technical assistance and evaluation contracts were also given out. At the same time (1986), the bulk of new prevention funds ($200 million) authorized under the Anti-Drug Abuse Act went to the Department of Education for grants to states and local schools for drug abuse prevention programs. OSAP is supposed to coordinate with the Department of Education in training and evaluation of programs funded under the Drug-Free Schools and Community Act of 1986.

A new Anti-Drug Abuse Act of 1988 expanded the scope of OSAP with a proposed budget increase to $79 million for 1989. In addition to continuing grants for high-risk communities, program evaluation, and a Clearinghouse, OSAP initiated new demonstration grants for preventing abuse among women of childbearing age, mobilizing community youth activity programs, and setting up a national prevention training system. The Department of Education was authorized to receive $250 million to continue its work with state agencies, governors, and local districts. However, not all that money is being spent, since many states have failed to use the previous grants for substance abuse prevention in schools.

Advocacy groups play a major role in the substance use prevention field. The National Federation of Parents for Drug Free Youth is credited with raising consciousness throughout the country about the importance of parental involvement in community programs. Other national advocacy groups include Parents' Resource Institute for Drug Education, Inc. (PRIDE), Mothers Against Drunk Driving (MADD), and Students Against Drunk Driving (SADD). The National Council on Alcoholism is one of the professional organizations in the substance abuse field concerned with policy, treatment, and medical issues.

A number of programs at the state level involve both public and private sectors. In Massachusetts, the Alliance for Drugs includes representatives from the departments of health, education, public safety, media, business, sports organizations, and community representatives. In Missouri, the Division of Alcohol and Drug Abuse has set up regional offices that conduct institutes, training, and provide technical assistance around the state. States are required to have a lead agency on substance abuse to receive block grants from ADMHA largely for treatment. Either a separate Office or Division of Substance Abuse has been organized or the responsibility has been assigned to the State Departments of Health, Mental Health, or Human Services. The grants are awarded by the states to designated regional coordinating agencies (e.g., a mental health agency) in county regions that fund local delegate agencies to provide treatment services.

## Pregnancy Prevention Programs

The Adolescent Health Services and Pregnancy Prevention and Care Act of 1978 was the first federal legislation to focus solely on the issue of teen pregnancy.[9] It created an Office of Adolescent Pregnancy Prevention Programs (OAPP) in the Office of Population Affairs (OPA) in the Public Health Service (DHHS). The goal of primary prevention was rapidly restricted by the bureaucracy and, for a short period, the limited funds were granted to local "teen moms" programs to improve the outcomes of teen parenting. By 1981, the appropriation was folded into the Maternal and Child Health Block Grant (MCH). Next came the Adolescent Family Life Act (Title XX), the Reagan response to the problem of teen pregnancy. A limited amount of grant funds ($10 million) were awarded to OAPP demonstration projects for promoting abstention among nonsexually active teens, fostering family-child communication, and promoting adoption among pregnant teens. No provisions were included for contraceptive services for those who were sexually active but not yet pregnant. New legislation is currently being introduced to replace the Adolescent Family Life Act.

The main public funding for pregnancy prevention derives from the Family Planning Services and Population Research Act (Title X) of 1970 which helps support some 4,000 family planning clinics around the country. Since 1978, grant recipients have been required to serve teenagers. Early in the Reagan administration the Title X program was moved out of the Public Health Service along with OAPP and put directly under the Office of Population Affairs. About $138 million was appropriated by Congress in 1988 for Title X and distributed around the country to county health departments, Planned Parenthood Affiliates, community health centers, hospital outpatient departments, and a few community-based youth centers. Local agencies generally receive their project grants through the auspices of State Health Departments. A few states also have put line items in health budgets for family planning services and community education. About 1.5 million teens (a third of the caseload) use family planning clinics every year. An unknown amount of Medicaid and Social Services Block grant funds are collected by local family planning clinics and private physicians to subsidize the care of teenagers. The use of Medicaid by teenagers requires the establishment of eligibility through the family's income status and requires special arrangements to ensure confidentiality.

A number of states have initiated task forces or coordinated teen pregnancy prevention initiatives.[10] In a few, special funds have been committed to this purpose, but most of the interest has been in programs for teen mothers and their babies. Illinois's Parents Too Soon program represents a unique model, combining public and private resources to implement a statewide multiagency program (see Chapter 14).

With the exception of "saying no" programs funded by the OAPP, there are no categorical federal funds earmarked for sex or family life education. States have mandated sex education to be part of the curriculum in 17 states and the District of Columbia, but in no states, except for New York, are special funds available for the implementation of the curriculum at the local level. A few state offices of family planning do fund curriculum development and teacher training in family life education and may offer technical assistance to local districts for implementation. Local school districts are expected to use their general funds (which they may get from the state) to purchase curricula and pay for teacher training.

A recent survey documented that states were much more likely to be involved in AIDS education than sex education.[11] More than 30 states and the District of Columbia mandate that school districts provide their students with information about AIDS. Federal funds are available for this purpose through grants to states from a newly created Division of Adolescent and School Health (DASH) in the Centers for Disease Control (CDC).

The family planning field has a long tradition of advocacy. The provision of federally subsidized contraception to low-income women resulted from an extended battle over 50 years. The Planned Parenthood Federation of America maintains a Washington office to coordinate congressional monitoring, and The Alan Guttmacher Institute provides continuing research on issues related to reproduction among adolescents. The Center for Population Options is focused solely on teenagers and operates a Support Center for School-Based Clinics. The National Organization on Adolescent Pregnancy and Parenting coordinates state groups concerned with programs for teen parents and babies as well as pregnancy prevention.

### School Remediation and Dropout Prevention Programs

Education in the United States is a vast enterprise, with a total annual expenditure at the federal, state, and local levels of about $260 billion (including higher education).[12] At the federal level, the Department of Education (DOE) line-item budget is relatively small, $17.8 billion, and only $7.4 billion of that is for elementary, secondary, and vocational education. Other government departments fund programs in the schools such as school lunches and nutrition (Agriculture), Head Start (Health and Human Services), and job preparation (Labor). In 1986, a total of $146 billion was spent in the United States on public elementary and secondary schools. (Private elementary and secondary schools spent about $13 billion.) Of the public funds for elementary and secondary schools, *only $10 billion came from federal sources* (including funds from agencies other than the DOE)—$71 billion from states and $65 billion from local sources, largely through property taxes. In the United States as a whole, the annual expenditure per child in school was $3,677, but there are significant differences in state levels ranging from $5,616 in New York to $2,305 in Mississippi.[13] New York relies heavily on local property taxes for support, while Mississippi receives a higher proportion of its funds from the federal and state governments.

The relative contribution of federal, state, and local sources to education indicates where the decision-making authority lies. School budgets and teachers' salaries (the largest item in budgets) are tightly controlled at the local level by school boards, and curriculum, licensing, and graduation requirements are closely regulated at the state level by regents or education commissioners. In recent years, states have assumed an increasing proportion of the education bill and have asserted more control over quality issues.

Federal funds are targeted dollars for special interventions, such as teacher training, remediation for disadvantaged students, and services for handicapped children. Emerging differences in educational achievement among children from rich and poor communities led in 1965 to the passage of the Elementary and Secondary Education Act ("Toward Full Educational Opportunity") known as Title 1.[14] It provided federal funds to local school districts for new approaches to meeting the special needs of educationally deprived children. In 1981, early in the Reagan administration, the program's name changed (now called Chapter 1) and local districts were given more autonomy (for example, parent involvement was no longer mandatory). In 1988, about $4.3 billion was expended on Chapter 1 in almost every school district in the country, and almost 5 million school-aged children were served. Chapter 1 is the largest government program that seeks to reduce the inequities between advantaged and disadvantaged children. To be eligible for Chapter 1 services, a student must live in the attendance area of an eligible school, usually an area with a higher proportion of poor students than the district average. If the school qualifies, the student is selected only for certain grades and only if he or she is a low performer. The funds are used primarily for basic instructional services in reading and math, provided by specially trained teachers (see Chapter 12). In addition, in 1988, states received block grants (Chapter 2 grants) of $478 million for school improvement programs, $71 million for magnet schools and $24 million for dropout prevention.

Beginning in 1975, after the passage of the Education for All Handicapped Children Act (Public Law 94–142), schools were required to ensure that every handicapped child between 3 and 21 had the right to a free and appropriate education in the least restrictive environment. In 1988, grants equaling about $1.9

billion were given to states for Special Education, to serve the needs of handicapped children. The Bilingual Education Act provided $192 million for a wide variety of programs. The education budget also included $888 million for vocational education, $86 million for migrant education, and $66 million for Native American education. After the passage of the Drug Free Schools and Communities Act of 1986, funds have been made available through the Department of Education to provide state and local grants for substance abuse prevention programs. An additional $200 million was made available for this purpose in 1988.

It falls to the state departments of education to administer the many different granting mechanisms from which funds must be passed on to localities. A recent account from the New York State Department of Education documented 11 federal and 41 state categorical programs directed toward at-risk children and youth that could be utilized in local initiatives.[15] The largest amounts of state funds were available for compensatory educational services for pupils with low basic skills, special services in the five biggest city school systems, pre-K social and educational programs, bilingual education, school breakfast and lunch programs, dropout prevention, magnet and demonstration schools. Federal funds that were being administered by the Department of Education included Chapters 1 and 2, other bilingual programs, services for migrants and refugees, vocational education, job training, and drug abuse and alcohol prevention education.

The history of organized advocacy for public education mirrors the history of the United States. The never-ending battles around the role of the schoolhouse in the quality of life have involved generations of advocates. Currently, educational advocacy is also a vast enterprise. The National Education Association, founded in 1857, is a powerful group in Washington representing 1.6 million members (mostly teachers) who belong to 10,000 local chapters around the country. The American Federation of Teachers represents more than half a million members. Almost every community has a Parent Teachers Association; there are 26,000 local affiliates with more than 6 million members.

### Youth Employment Programs

Prevention of unemployment has not been treated as a specific categorical issue in this book because the focus is primarily on the prevention of high-risk behaviors among younger adolescents (aged 10 to 17).[16] Few of the target population identified are in the labor force or even trying to enter it. The areas covered in this volume are, however, highly relevant to improved occupational opportunity; almost all youth employment initiatives start with school remediation. Several models that are included in Chapters 9 to 12 rely on funds from youth employment programs.

The Employment and Training Administration of the Department of Labor administers youth services funds through the Job Training and Partnership Act (JTPA) of 1982. A total expenditure of $4.7 billion was reported in 1988, but only a small portion of that involved services for teenagers. Funds reach communities through block grants to states that get passed on to 630 local Service Delivery Areas that are governed by Private Industry Councils (PICs), with heavy representation from local businesses. The services may include classroom training in basic education, on-the-job training, job search skills, and subsidized work experience. The JTPA has been criticized for "creaming," allowing substantial sums of money to be used for the "easy-to-reach." The Department of Labor has been encouraged to promote more outreach in high-risk communities. A separate program provides funds to communities for the Summer Youth Program and another entity administers the Job Corps Centers. The Job Corps recruits 16- to 21-year-olds, most of whom reside at the 107 centers around the country.

The Department of Labor is involved in a number of collaborative projects. It works with the Department of Education on literacy and the Office of Human Development Services on coordinated projects to serve teen parents and provides demonstration funds to projects such as the Summer Training and Education Program (STEP; see Chapter 11) and Job Start.

### Cross-Cutting Programs

Early childhood education and parent training probably fit best under the category of preventing failure and dropout; however, as we will find, these kinds of programs could logically be placed in every category. The primary program—Project Head Start—is administered by the Administration for Children, Youth and Families (ACYF) in the DHHS. Initiated in 1965, Head Start has had its ups and downs. Currently, the program receives about $1.2 billion annually. Some 1300 grantees operate Head Start programs in 2000 communities across the country serving about a half million children. The programs provide a mix of education, health services, parent involvement, and social services.

The Office of Human Development Services (DHHS) administers the Runaway and Homeless Youth grants (mentioned under juvenile delinquency), a number of other child welfare services including Foster Care, Adoption Assistance, Child Abuse and Neglect, and a special grant program for Native Americans (not the same as the Indian Health Service).

It would be so much easier to understand the multilayered bureaucracies if everything fit into neat little boxes, but in the course of responding to various crises, funding initiatives get put into agency budgets for idiosyncratic reasons. AIDS prevention is an important case in point. Funds have been made available through one agency for AIDS education in the schools and through another for coordination. Treatment of intravenous drug users (a major component of AIDS prevention) is apparently being covered by a third agency. The education and information component is under the direction of the Division of Adolescent and School Health (DASH) of the Centers for Disease Control (CDC). DASH has been authorized to distribute project grants of more than $30 million to State Departments of Education and to city school systems that qualify for funds. The coordination item is small ($1.6 million) and is the responsibility of the Public Health Service. DASH has also undertaken the administration of annual surveys of adolescent health with particular emphasis on knowledge and behaviors that relate to AIDS.

In late 1988, Congress approved a new Omnibus Anti-Drug Abuse Act which created an enlarged Alcohol, Drug Abuse and Mental Health (ADMHA) block grant, incorporating the Emergency Drug Treatment Block Grant and a new block grant to reduce the transmission of AIDS by users of illegal intravenous drugs. About $805 million has been appropriated for these purposes, of which $240 million is designated for mental health services allotted to the states by a formula based on state population and per capita income. The AIDS efforts appear to be entirely separate from either substance abuse prevention or teen pregnancy prevention. This is also true of other sexually transmitted diseases. CDC has responsibility for operating the Sexually Transmitted Diseases (STD) program in the Public Health Service; they give $65 million in block grants to states, which is used primarily for surveillance and tracking cases.

Much of the new morbidity in adolescense is related to increasing rates of depression and stress. Thus mental health services are an important adjunct of a comprehensive prevention strategy, but they do not fall into any of the four categories of prevention programs described in this book. Mental health services in the United States at the federal level, as we have seen, have been lumped in with the drug and alcohol services. Beginning in 1984, the National Institute for Mental Health (ADMHA) initiated a grants program, Child and Adolescent Service System Program (CASSP), specifically to address service delivery for emotionally disturbed children and adolescents.[17] Eligibility includes all children up to age 18 who are not functioning, require multiagency services, and have been diagnosed with a psychological problem. States have been encouraged to strengthen their focus on this target population by developing cross-agency (mental health, juvenile justice, child welfare, education, and primary health care) systems of services and stimulating demonstration programs in selected communities, with a particular emphasis on parent involvement. Currently 42 states have grants totaling $7.4 million dollars.

School-based clinics (SBCs) have received a great deal of media attention because some of them include family planning. However, they are primarily comprehensive services and work at preventing all of the problem behaviors categorized here. Several attempts have been made to introduce legislation that would provide funds for SBCs, but none of the bills has been voted out of committee. Currently, SBCs and other community-based youth service agencies are supported by a mix of federal and private funds. The main sources of public funds are state Maternal and Child Health block grants and Medicaid; foundations (e.g., Robert Wood Johnson) have been instrumental in providing start-up funds in high-risk communities. The Early and Periodic Screening, Diagnosis and Treatment Program (EPSDT) of Medicaid is theoretically available for providing medical services to any poor child up to the age of 21.

In addition to food distribution programs, the Department of Agriculture supports the Cooperative Extension Service 4-H program. The Extension service, tied into state land-grant universities, has local offices in most counties. The 4-H youth development program is reported to reach 4.8 million youth, mostly in rural areas. A major national 4-H Youth At Risk initiative was launched in 1988 to focus more on troubled urban communities.[18]

Most comprehensive community-based programs do not fit into just one category of prevention. There are thousands of youth-serving organizations, such as Girls Clubs, Boys Clubs, Y's, and 4-H, that look for support for their wide array of programs in all of these fields. The Children's Defense Fund, the National Collaboration of Youth, and the National Governors Association are examples of national organizations that advocate for a broad array of youth issues.

## Implications for Prevention Fields

Each field has a major federal legislative base with money and regulations flowing down to communities, generally through state agencies according to various regulations. However, there are also grant and demonstration projects that go directly to communities. The complexity of the federal bureaucracy is reproduced in 50 different state governments. Each state has its own idiosyncratic structure with its own set of agencies that are not necessarily coordinated or organized to function efficiently in the best interests of high-risk youth. For each public effort, significant private voluntary efforts are at work, keeping legislatures informed about their issues and monitoring administrative performance to ensure that the appropriated funds are spent according to law. Advocacy groups are often positioned in competition with each other to get the attention and support of the legislators.

In addition to the government agencies, nonprofit service agencies, and advocacy groups, other important institutions shape the way services are organized and delivered. Foundations (e.g., Carnegie, Ford, MacArthur, Grant) play a major role in creating model programs in all areas. They have been willing to initiate large-scale, multisite interventions and support the longitudinal research required to measure effects. Much of the thrust for innovation and change has resulted from foundation-created commissions and task forces. The products of university and "think tank" research (with support from both the government and foundations) have been instrumental in guiding the nation about the behavior of youth and the institutions that affect their behavior.

The organization of delinquency, substance abuse, teen pregnancy, educational, and other relevant programs addressed to youth has been reviewed briefly to set the stage for understanding the complicated status of program development in the United States. The programs described in the four chapters that follow reflect the diversity of categorical legislation, funding, policies, and leadership at the local, state, and federal levels. One central question emerges: Are the needs of youth being well served by these arrangements? If not, what should and can be changed to develop a more comprehensive approach to these issues?

## Notes

1. Many program research reviews comment on the paucity of valid evaluation studies. For example, a review of 5,000 reports on Title 1 and other educational programs

found only 28 with valid evaluations that included achievement test results and program costs (*Phi Delta Kappan* 64[1983]: 339–47); a U.S. Government Accounting Office (GAO) review of dropout prevention programs found only 20 rigorous evaluations out of 452 programs surveyed (*School Dropouts: Surveys of Local Programs,* July 1987); 6,000 abstracts on delinquency prevention yielded only 96 with empirical evaluation (*Journal of Research in Crime and Delinquency* 14[1977]: 35–67).

2. S. Menard, personal communication, 1989.

3. A number of sources have been consulted to try to determine the most current status of federal programs that impact on youth aged 10 to 17. It is almost impossible to get an accurate picture of the federal budget situation at any point in time because of definitional problems on target populations, inaccurate reporting, and differences between appropriations and expenditures. See J. R. Reingold and Associates, *Current Federal Policies and Programs for Youth* (New York: William T. Grant Foundation, 1987); Children's Defense Fund, *A Children's Defense Budget, FY 1989* (Washington, D.C.: Children's Defense Fund, 1988); T. Ooms and L. Herendeen, "The Unique Health Needs of Adolescents: Implications for Health Care Insurance and Financing" (Background Briefing Report, Family Impact Seminar, Washington, D.C., 1989). The monthly publication *Youth Policy* provided added insights.

4. *Budget of the United States, 1990* (Washington, D.C.: U.S. Government Printing Office, 1989).

5. I. Schwartz, "Emerging Trends and Promising Strategies in Juvenile Crime Control in the U.S.," *Youth Policy* 10(1988): 3–8.

6. B. Krisberg, *The Juvenile Court: Reclaiming the Vision* (San Francisco: National Council on Crime and Delinquency, 1988).

7. J. Kushner, "Historical Perspective on Alcohol and Drug Abuse Prevention," in *Proceedings of the First National Conference on Alcohol and Drug Abuse Prevention: Sharing Knowledge for Action,* U.S. Department of Health and Human Services, Washington, D.C., August 3–6, 1986.

8. Office of Substance Abuse Prevention, *OSAP,* Alcohol, Drug Abuse and Mental Health Administration, DHHS (Summer 1988).

9. C. Hayes, ed., *Risking the Future: Adolescent Sexuality, Pregnancy, and Childbearing, Vol. I* (Washington, D.C.: National Academy Press, 1987).

10. See a detailed description of the efforts in California in C. Brindis and R. Jeremy, *Adolescent Pregnancy and Parenting in California* (San Francisco: Center for Population and Reproductive Health Policy, University of California, 1988).

11. A. Kenney, S. Guardado, and L. Brown, "Sex Education and AIDS Education in the Schools: What States and Large School Districts are Doing," *Family Planning Perspectives* 21(1989): 56–64.

12. Expenditure figures for education are derived from the Bureau of the Census, *Statistical Abstract of the United States, 1988* (Washington, D.C.: U.S. Government Printing Office, 1988), tables 186, 215.

13. In the village in Westchester County, New York, where the author resides, the current annual public school expenditure per child is approaching $13,000.

14. Office of Educational Research and Improvement, *The Current Operation of the Chapter 1 Program* (Washington, D.C.: U.S. Department of Education, 1987).

15. The State Education Department, *Current Education Department Programs Serving At-Risk Children and Youth* (Albany: The University of the State of New York, May 2, 1988).

16. For recent information on employment opportunities for youth, see William T. Grant Foundation, *The Forgotten Half: Pathways to Success for America's Youth and Young*

*Families* (Final Report of the Commission on Work, Family, and Citizenship, November 1988).

17. Family Impact Seminar, "Integrated Approaches to Youths' Health Problems: Federal, State and Community Roles" (Background Briefing Report, Washington, D.C., July 7, 1989).

18. J. Irby, "Dealing with Youth At Risk: 4-H Outlines New Initiative," *Corrections Today* (August 1989): 86–91.

# 9

# Prevention of Delinquency

As we have seen in Chapter 3 (Prevalence of Delinquency), the phrase "juvenile delinquency" may refer to the "continuum of behavior that transgresses social norms," ranging from socially unacceptable behavior (acting out in school) to status offenses (running away) to criminal acts (burglary).[1] This broad definition sets wide boundaries on a discussion of prevention. Preventing disruptive behavior in the early elementary grades is quite a different task from preventing major criminal acts among high-school-age gangs. The former focuses more on altering individual and family functioning, while the latter involves alterations in the peer culture, the school experience, and the broader social environment. In any case, a review of the literature on prevention of delinquency produces few programs that can be cited as models of primary prevention at early or late stages. A very small number of programs could generate evidence that they stopped the onset of delinquent behavior. Interventions were cited, however, that have an indirect effect on later delinquency by modifying "acting out" and conduct disorders at very early ages. Many of the programs discussed in the literature focus on secondary prevention, working with adjudicated juvenile delinquents to lower the rates of recidivism (repeat offenses), and almost none of those appear to meet with great success.

The dearth of successful prevention programs in the area of delinquency is not surprising in light of the complexity of the problem and its deep-seated causes. The usual difficulties with evaluation design are compounded in this field by murky definitions. Repeated reviews of literally thousands of studies have produced almost none with adequate evaluations.[2]

Leitenberg's commentary on the "state-of-the-art" is not very encouraging:

> My thoughts about primary prevention programs in delinquency tend to be pessimistic. Unless the larger political, organizational, economic and social issues are addressed . . . we will make small headway. . . . I think the most productive area is not within

the realm of psychology, sociology, psychiatry, social work, or criminology—it is within the area of politics.[3]

And Lundman agrees:

> It is recommended that traditional delinquency prevention efforts be abandoned. Prevention projects don't work, and they waste money, violate the rights of juveniles and their families, inspire bizarre suggestions and programs, and fail to affect the known correlates of urban delinquency (poverty, lack of services and jobs, poor education). Based on the best available evidence, it is time to get out of the business of attempting to prevent delinquency.[4]

Rabkin is only slightly more optimistic in her review of interventions to prevent delinquency, suggesting that individuals within various treatment groups may have made gains that were lost in the aggregate.[5] Greenwood and Ziming cite four programs categories outside of the formal juvenile justice system that appear to be helpful in curbing delinquent or antisocial behavior: preschool interventions, parent-training programs, educational enrichment, and voluntary youth service programs.[6] However, they acknowledge that there is little evidence to support the adoption of these programs specifically as delinquency prevention models. O'Donnell and his colleagues believe that many programs failed in the past because they were targeted exclusively on delinquents whose negative behavior was further enforced by continuing exposure to delinquent peers.[7] For younger high-risk teens, they support the development of programs that reduce peer contact and emphasize individual rather than group approaches. For older youth, they recommend employment programs such as job skills and work study.

Table 9.1 outlines evaluation criteria used in the delinquency field according to the behaviors to which interventions are directed, the indicators that would be used to measure changes in the behaviors, and the sources of data from which the

TABLE 9.1. Measures of Success Used in Evaluation of Delinquency Prevention Programs

| Behavior to Prevent | Measure of Success | Source of Data |
| --- | --- | --- |
| *Conduct disorders* | | |
| Truancy | Better school attendance<br>Fewer suspensions | School records |
| Misbehavior | Improved behavior | Self-report surveys<br>Parent reports<br>Teacher reports |
| *Minor offenses* | | |
| Vandalism | Less destructive behavior | Self-report surveys |
| *Status offenses* | | |
| Running away | Lower arrest rates | Official police statistics |
| Alcohol and drug use | Less abuse | Self-report surveys |
| *Index offenses* | | |
| Homicide, rape, robbery,<br>  burglary, larceny, car<br>  theft | Lower arrest rates<br>Fewer offenses | Official police statistics<br>Self-report surveys |

information would be derived. Most programs identified in the search for success-ful models focus on conduct disorders and minor offenses, behaviors measured primarily from self-reports and reports from schools and parents (rather than offi-cial police records). This fits with the fundamental concept of prevention, getting to the causes of the behavior before it starts, or catching the problem in its earliest stages before it grows into a larger irremediable situation.

One important distinction must be made prior to our review of examples—that is, the difference between *prevention* and *treatment*. Our interest here is in the former. However, because the definition of delinquency is so broad, some pro-grams are simultaneously treatments for existing maladjustment problems and, if successful, preventive of further antisocial behavior.

## Successful Models

### *Early Childhood Interventions*

The link between early childhood experiences and later social behavior has been well established. As we have observed, the earlier the onset of any kind of prob-lem behavior, the greater the consequences as the child ages. We have also shown that early school failure is a critical predictor of conduct disorders, substance abuse, and precocious unprotected sexuality. Increasing attention is being paid to the importance of early childhood (preschool) education so that by the time chil-dren enter elementary school they are adequately strengthened to succeed.

No preschool or Head Start program has been identified that was organized specifically to prevent later delinquency. Instead, the goal has been to enhance cognitive development to improve educational achievement and, through that means, to affect other outcomes. The quality of the research on the effects of preschool on later achievement is much better than in most other kinds of programs, and among the several important evaluations that have been conducted of long-term impacts, one program stands out (and we will return to it in each section). It is the only preschool intervention that tracked experimental and control students over time and measured changes in delinquency variables.

PERRY PRESCHOOL

An early childhood demonstration program operated by the High Scope Founda-tion in Ypsilanti, Michigan, Perry Preschool has received national recognition for its long-term impact on delinquency, education, and pregnancy.[8] This enrichment program, directed by David Weikart, documented that a small random sample of disadvantaged black children who attended a high-quality, two-year preschool pro-gram and received weekly home visits from program personnel had more success-ful outcomes than the controls. Based on official police records, by age 19 the experimental group was less likely to have been arrested than the control group (22 percent versus 38 percent) and reported fewer total offenses as adults. There were significantly fewer chronic offenders in the preschool group; however, no significant differences were observed in the number of convictions that grew out of the arrests. Self-reported behavior at age 19 confirmed the patterns produced by arrest and court records; preschool attendees reported less fighting and less involvement with police than nonattendees.

Analysis of the High Scope data shows that the arrest rates were directly influenced by two variables: educational attainment and teacher rating of social behavior in elementary grades. This suggests that the preschool intervention improved later classroom behavior and intellectual performance and, ultimately, had an effect on the amount of schooling completed; this, in turn, (indirectly) reduced delinquency rates.[9] Leitenberg commented on these findings: "Any positive results in controlled evaluations of delinquency prevention studies are hard to come by and should be savored."[10]

SYRACUSE FAMILY DEVELOPMENT PROGRAM

Day care and family services were provided to low-income families over the first five years of children's lives in the Syracuse Family Development Program.[11] According to a follow-up study conducted 10 years after the intervention, children who participated had a 6 percent rate of juvenile delinquency compared with a 22 percent rate in the control group. Offenses were also less severe in the experimental group, and effects on academic achievement were significant among the girls. Program children were much more likely to expect education to be a part of their lives: 53 percent of them compared with only 28 percent of control children expected to be in school during the next five years (e.g., through high school).

## Family Interventions

A major determinant of conduct disorders and delinquency is the lack of parental support and guidance. One theory is that children act out because their parents do not know how to control them. Preschool interventions typically include a parent education component. Several parent management training programs have been designed for elementary school children, specifically to teach mothers and fathers how to deal consistently with their children, change negative interaction patterns, and administer rewards and punishments.

PARENT TRAINING

The Oregon Social Learning Center (OSLC) trains parents in techniques devised by George Patterson which are meant to monitor and change their children's behavior.[12] Parents start by reading a programmed text, *Living with Children,* and then select a specific behavior to work on with trained therapists. The process teaches parents to record their child's behavior and to administer punishment and rewards consistently and appropriately. Staff have frequent contacts with the families through telephone calls and home visits, and parents are encouraged to take part in structured parent-training groups.

Based on his experience, Patterson has hypothesized that one-third of the families who use the center just need the specific behavior modification skills, another third need to be taught negotiation skills to resolve conflicts, and one-third will fail no matter what is done.[13] Although most reviews mention this program, the critiques raise many questions about its applicability to high-risk populations. Patterson's research is limited to families with young children from Eugene, Oregon, not typical of urban high-crime areas. Highly skilled therapists are relatively easy to recruit and train in a university community. The model has not proven effective with dysfunctional families or families with teenage children, nor can it be used with disinterested or apathetic parents or those who cannot master the educational materials. As Rabkin points out, even Patterson has reservations about costs, durability of effect, and the preferability of working with much younger children. However, Michelson mentions other studies that showed gains from parent management programs in adaptive child behavior, with decreases in aggressive and antisocial behavior.[14]

Hawkins and his colleagues have developed a parent-training program as part of a broader social development approach to preventing delinquent behavior (see the section on Classroom Management which follows).[15] This program, currently operating in Seattle elementary schools, provides seven sessions for parents of first and second graders. Entitled "Catch 'Em Being Good," this program teaches parents what to expect from their children and then how to establish a system of rewards and punishment. This is followed up in later grades with four sessions on "How to Help Your Child Succeed in School," which focuses on parent-child communication skills and homework help. All parents are invited to participate, with special outreach efforts and incentives directed toward parents of high-risk children. Hawkins reported that parents of 43 percent of the children in the experimental schools attended at least one session, with very high retention rates. However, parents of the high-risk black children did not enroll. Preliminary evaluation results show that parents who participated reported better parenting skills, and their children had lower rates of aggressiveness.

## School-Based Interventions

### CURRICULA

Several different kinds of delinquency prevention interventions are provided in schools that fall roughly into the category of curricula. One set of curricula grew out of contemporary psychological theory about preventing antisocial behavior by teaching cognitive problem-solving skills. Increasingly, psychologists are treating child and adolescent antisocial behavior with behavioral modification approaches. The theory is that children who act out lack the cognitive skills required to behave appropriately in given situations. Several new approaches are being used. Using a more didactic approach, teaching adolescents about the legal system is based on the theory that knowing more about consequences of delinquent acts may change behavior.

*Problem-Solving Skills.*    One group of behavioral modification programs focuses on enhancing problem-solving skills by teaching means-ends and causal thinking;

these programs also try to increase sensitivity to and empathy with other people's problems and feelings.[16] Programs such as "Think Aloud," an 8-week program for very young children, and "Project AWARE," a 72-lesson, 6-month program for fourth- and fifth-graders aim at enhancing social competency through small group discussions. Early reports appear favorable and seem to confirm that this training in problem-solving skills improves classroom performance and behavior as well as peer relations. Another program for fourth- and fifth-graders, which included 55 lessons delivered three to four times per week, resulted in reduced antisocial behavior and improved academic achievement.[17] Michelson asserts that, although treatment studies have produced inconsistent results, significant improvements have been shown for maladjusted, antisocial children, and behavioral problems are less likely to emerge among adjusted children. However, only short-term effectiveness has been studied to date. The durability and generalizability of the behavioral improvements are unknown.

*Social Skills Training.* Michelson and colleagues have developed another strategy, *Behavioral Social Skills Training (BSST)*, that teaches behavioral "repertoires" to enhance personal competency—for example, learning to give and receive compliments, acquiring conversational skills, learning to say no, dealing with anger and stress, and so on. Sixty sequential training modules have been produced to reduce aggressive, acting-out, and antisocial behavior through formalizing successful inter- and intrapersonal repertoires. The concepts of instructions, coaching, modeling, rehearsal and practice, feedback and social reinforcement are utilized. The authors report encouraging short-term success with highly disturbed children, but raised questions about generalizability.

Given the potential of both the cognitive (thinking about decisions) and the behavioral (skills for implementing them) approaches, along with the limitations of each, Michelson proposes combined cognitive-behavioral strategies, putting together verbal mediation skills with specific ways of responding to interpersonal situations. A number of small studies support this hypothesis. One larger study of high-risk fourth- and fifth-graders randomly assigned children to four groups: behavioral, cognitive, combined, and control. All treatment groups produced significant improvements in outcome measures. A long-term assessment (six months) concluded that the combined behavioral and cognitive treatment group showed the greatest improvement across a wider dimension of functioning.

Not all experts share Michelson's enthusiasm for social skills training. Rabkin expresses skepticism about such behavioral models, citing the limited effects produced in British studies of incarcerated delinquents. (The British subjects, however, are very different from the subjects in Michelson's studies.) As with many of the interventions discussed in the delinquency literature, there is no strong evidence that social skills training could actually prevent delinquency, but there is evidence that children with minor conduct disorders could be helped to improve their behavior and their social relationships (and even their school performance).

Henggeler's review of the impact of social skills training on delinquent behavior cautions that the development and use of learned cognitive and social skills in laboratory role-play settings may be different for high-risk children in real-life situations in which they interact with members of a dysfunctional family or antisocial peers at school.[18] He suggests that when cognitive and behavioral interventions, such as those outlined here, are integrated into a well-organized intervention program the results are more promising. Henggeler supports the concept of *multisystemic therapy,* an approach to delinquency that recognizes the determinants of the problem as well as the differences between the individuals who act out. This system relies on a highly trained therapist who "packages" the appropriate interventions for each case, intervening directly with the adolescent, family, peers, and school as needed. Approaches may include cognitive and behavioral components, peer group programs, and school interventions. The evaluations of three multisystem programs showed decreased conduct problems among juvenile offenders and lower long-term rates (self-reported) of delinquent behavior and arrests.[19]

*Moral Reasoning Training.*    Group discussions of moral dilemmas have been developed as an approach to helping high-risk adolescents raise their level of thinking and acting about moral issues. Arbuthnot and Gordon evaluated a program for "behaviorally disordered" students that included discussion groups, communication skills, and problem solving on issues such as life extension, property rights, and civil rights. Participants were shown to have made great gains in moral reasoning, to be less tardy at school, to achieve higher grades, and to display fewer behavioral problems.[20]

*Law-Related Education (LRE).*    This type of intervention, organized by the National Institute for Citizen Education in the Law, includes an array of efforts designed to build students' conceptual and practical understanding of the law and legal processes.[21] LRE has been supported by the Office of Juvenile Justice and Delinquency Prevention since 1978. Some aspects of the program have been reported in 40 states. LRE encompasses courses from elementary through high school, mock trials, visits to courtrooms, rides along with police, and work in the community with lawyers, judges, and the police. Law firms are linked with high schools and are involved in mentoring. Community projects have included teaching young children about safety, developing media campaigns, conducting anticrime surveys, and working on victim assistance projects. Special curricula have been built around textbooks, such as *Teens, Crime, and the Community* and *Street Law.*

Evaluations have been conducted on LRE school programs, most recently in Colorado.[22] The LRE course was taught to ninth-graders in two schools for a full class period every day for a semester, replacing the traditional civics course. A police officer joined the teacher as an instructor twice a week. In one school, cooperative team learning was employed as a teaching strategy. Significant differences were found between participants and controls in both schools in regard to self-reported delinquent behavior (reduced school rule infractions, stealing, vandalism, and marijuana use). Success of the LRE program was attributed to the nonthreatening interaction between the students and the police officers and the attention paid to staff training prior to implementation. Other kinds of school-based delinquency prevention programs initiated during the same period were believed to be less successful because they were less direct in addressing normative or moral content.

ORGANIZATION OF SCHOOL

It follows logically that, if preschool interventions can increase cognitive abilities and ultimately influence delinquency rates, then in-school interventions should have the capacity to produce similar effects. However, since patterns of misbehavior are established at such early ages, one could assume that the later the intervention the more powerful it would have to be. While a number of individual and family attributes have been linked to delinquent behavior, another set of attributes relates to the quality of the schools. Certain characteristics of schools are associated with high delinquency rates; these include large school size, absence of individual attention, ability grouping and negative labeling, low teacher expectations, lack of structure, and inconsistent treatment by teachers and administrators. Hawkins and Lishner have documented the strong effects of school environments on the probability of misbehavior and concluded that interventions to prevent delinquency should encompass improvements in academic achievement accompanied by positive peer influence strategies.[23]

There are few evaluations of school-based interventions specifically designed to influence social behavior and delinquency. The examples cited here fall into five categories: classroom management (teacher training), cooperative (student-staff) learning arrangements, school team approach, alternative schools, and special services and counseling.

*Classroom Management.* Instructional strategies that try to promote greater bonding of the student to the school, increase achievement, and lessen antisocial behavior have been tested by Hawkins and Lam as another component of the social development approach to delinquency prevention.[24] Strategies include:

1. Proactive classroom management: Teachers learn how to create and reinforce a positive environment for learning and establish techniques for dealing with incidents of disruption.
2. Interactive teaching: Grades are determined by individual mastery of standards rather than by comparison with other students.
3. Cooperative learning: Students work in heterogeneous teams and receive recognition for group performance.

A study of this intervention was conducted under experimental conditions in a large number of seventh-grade classrooms in Seattle. An analysis at the end of the first year of teacher training and classroom implementation showed very few positive results. While the experimental teachers changed their practices according to plan, students showed little change in bonding (they didn't like school any better). There was, however, some evidence that students were more likely to engage in learning activities, did more homework, did better in math classes, and upgraded their educational expectations. Students whose teachers were trained were less likely to be suspended or expelled from school, but there was no difference in self-reported truancy, theft, or the frequency of getting in trouble at school for drugs or alcohol. The authors hope for more positive outcomes in regard to anti-social behavior as the project continues.

*Cooperative Learning Arrangements.*    The Positive Action through Holistic Education (PATHE) program in South Carolina instituted organizational changes in four middle and three high schools to assist targeted students to improve their behavior and their achievement.[25] The primary interventions were:

1. Participatory decision making in which staff, parents, and student groups were involved in decision making concerning management issues, which included discipline policies.
2. Student team teaching in which heterogeneous students were put together to work on academic tasks in a cooperative climate.

When comparing experimental with control students, the effects were much greater in the middle schools than in high schools. Participants scored higher on achievement tests and received higher grades. Target students in the middle schools reported significantly less delinquent behavior, and the three high schools experienced reductions in self-reported delinquency and in suspensions.

*School Team Approach.*    The concept of joint problem solving has been widely used in the substance abuse prevention field (see Chapter 10). Based on that experience, the school team model was implemented as an approach to delinquency prevention in some 200 schools over a two-year period.[26] These teams consisted of six to eight people including parents, students, school staff, and community residents. The teams were trained in a two-week session to deal with problem behaviors in the school by acting as a group and developing a plan of action. Intervention plans included setting up a time-out room for disruptive students in lieu of suspension, making home visits to problem students, using students as monitors and advisors, and other "commonsense" approaches.

Evaluation results showed that school crime and disruptive behavior were reduced in middle schools, attributed by the evaluators to improved parent–teacher relations and successful handling of discipline and security problems within the schools. Although the results were not as good in high schools, the most effective school teams appeared to improve communication between students and teachers through joint student–teacher problem-solving groups. The largest decreases in school crime were early in the program, described by the evaluators as a "honeymoon effect." The principal was described as a key figure on the team, and the difficulty of maintaining continuity and support were observed to be the biggest problems.

Kimbrough's impression of these school-based interventions is that cooperative team learning impacts on achievement while joint problem-solving groups have an impact on disruptive behavior.

*Alternative Schools.*    One of the most ambitious projects to be discussed in the literature was the School Action Effectiveness Study. Some 17 alternative educational projects in high-crime areas involved reorganization of schools to promote learning, bonding, and prosocial behaviors.[27] Interventions included peer counseling, leadership training, parent involvement, skills lab classes, token economies, vocational education, and school climate improvement. After one year, researchers found that project schools had greater safety, less teacher victimization, and less delinquency. The most successful programs had some of the following components: individual attention, peer counseling, cooperative arrangements between administrators and teachers, and intensity.

Gold and Mann observed the experiences of high-risk tenth-grade students in four alternative schools and compared their subsequent delinquent behavior with that of control students in regular schools.[28] The schools were selected because they served disruptive and delinquent youth, fostered close teacher-student relationships, provided individualized attention, were oversubscribed (popular), and stable (had been in existence for more than four years). These schools tried to change both how the curriculum was taught and the setting in which it was taught. The experimental group fell distinctly into two categories the researchers called "buoyant" and "beset"; the second group was found to be anxious and depressed. The intervention resulted in marked declines in disruptive behavior and delinquency in school but not in the community. Alternative school students after a year changed their attitudes toward school, had higher expectations for future schooling, and greater commitment to school. They described their schools as more flexible and their teachers as more responsive than the control students. The less troubled, buoyant students showed much more significant gain than the depressed, beset students, many of whom showed declines in indicators such as commitment to school. School alone was apparently not a strong enough intervention or, possibly, it came too late in their development.

One strategy for working with misbehaving students is to separate them from other children and place them in separate classes or schools. Laurence et al. describe a year-round day school for truants and delinquents.[29] This program offered self-paced individual instruction, intensive counseling, paid employment, an open "rec room," and "contingency contracting" for behavioral modification. This contracting consisted of a token economy in which good behavior (attendance at school, compliance with rules) was rewarded with points that accumulated to allow various privileges at school and at home. The authors report improvements in attendance and academic performance. Half the participants returned to school or obtained jobs. However, effects on delinquent behavior were described as "inconclusive." They attributed their "success" to the location of the program away from the regular schools, the token economy, and the interactions that took place between the counselors and students.

What the school-based research suggests, and what many observers believe, is that the primary intervention to reduce delinquency must be the upgrading of the quality of education, particularly for disadvantaged children. Based on the growing evidence of the relationship between classroom setting, the school program, and children's behavior, Greenwood calls for establishing school environments in which negative behavior is naturally discouraged and the child's interests are engaged. He cites the literature on effective schools for examples of settings in which poor children have made great gains, despite personal and family characteristics that might stand in their way.

Rabkin warns us that, although delinquents tend to do badly in school and have poor employment records, delinquency may reflect another antecedent variable that increases the probability of all three deviant behaviors (such as lack of parental support). She acknowledges, however, that a number of studies have shown that "good" schools produce fewer delinquents, but that this is not sufficient proof that the schooling is the determining intervention. The appropriate perspective might be that children at high risk of delinquent behavior must be offered quality education, beginning at very early ages, for reasons that transcend delinquency prevention.

*Special Services and Counseling.*   The *Primary Mental Health Project* (*PMHP*) has been functioning for over three decades, first in Rochester, and over the years in hundreds of schools throughout the United States.[30] In this approach, children at high risk of school maladjustment are identified by their teachers in the early grades (Kindergarten to third grade). These children meet with "trainers" either individually or in small groups for an average of 25 sessions. The trainers are paraprofessionals who receive extensive instruction from program administrators. Children are taught to recognize feelings and set limits on their own behavior. Repeated evaluations have demonstrated that this training has resulted in decreased antisocial behavior among those who are shy and withdrawn, but with less success among very aggressive children (see Chapter 12).

### Community-Based Multicomponent Interventions

Many of the young people at high risk of misbehavior and delinquency are so alienated from school that interventions, if they are to be successful, need to be placed in community or neighborhood institutions. One strategy places programs in high-delinquency areas, offering activities that are considered alternatives to delinquent behavior, such as recreation, culture, and academic enrichment. Another strategy targets high-risk youth, referred by juvenile justice authorities, schools, and parents, and makes an array of services available. A number of past efforts to connect juvenile gangs and high-risk youth with social workers who organized meetings, dances, and sports events and referred youths for counseling or treatment were not successful in reducing delinquent behavior.[31] However, more recent programs that offered primarily employment-related activities to older youth have demonstrated some success. O'Donnell et al. believe that employment efforts are successful because they break up gangs by reducing cohesiveness and contacts among delinquent peers.

#### TARGETED OUTREACH

Building on years of experience with delinquency prevention programs, the Boys Clubs of America have created a model effort in their Targeting Programs for

Delinquency Intervention which is called Targeted Outreach and is currently being implemented in 212 local clubs that recruit and "mainstream" high-risk children aged 12 to 18.[32] This model incorporates a case management approach and formal linkages with an array of community agencies. Club staff are trained to recruit high-risk children who have been referred by community agencies and schedule them into club activities. The progress of each participant is carefully tracked. Clubs are encouraged to develop their own service structure, using their own facilities for various group activities, and to work closely with juvenile justice and school systems. In some programs, high priority is given to individual counseling and behavioral contracting; participants are actively involved in planning club programs. With support from the Office of Juvenile Justice and Delinquency Prevention, many of the clubs are expanding Targeted Outreach to include the Boys Clubs prevention curriculum called "Smart Moves" (involving group counseling sessions on decision-making about drugs and sex). As a result of developing a very refined data system, outcomes have been carefully monitored: 39 percent of participants demonstrated a positive change in academic performance and 93 percent who have completed the Targeted Outreach program have not had reinvolvement with the juvenile justice system. This is an interesting example of the interplay between a national organization and local community organizations. Stimulus to initiate the program came from the national level; local clubs added many creative approaches and used the intervention to upgrade their service systems in the community.

JUVENILE COURT VOLUNTEERS

This program works with youth aged 10 to 17 in Houston who have already had contact with the juvenile justice system or have been identified as high risk.[33] Trained volunteers are paired with referred youth and seek to find individualized solutions to the youth's problems. Tutoring, youth advocacy, crisis intervention, and various group recreational activities are offered through collaborative efforts of the county juvenile justice system and local school districts. An evaluation revealed that 44 percent of the youth in the program had no additional referrals to the juvenile justice system and, among the remainder, their offense rate was cut in half. Success is attributed to the introduction of a caring, stable adult (one who is racially matched) into the lives of very disadvantaged youth, who acts as a role model and advocate.

A similar program, *Denver Partners,* also reported positive results.[34] Collaborating agencies included social service agencies, the juvenile courts, police, residential child-care facilities, the district attorney's office, schools, therapists, and mental health workers. The matched pairs—high-risk children and adult volunteers—receive support from program staff through counseling, guidance, life skills training, recreational and social activities, and networking with community resources. A "Health Corp" consisting of dentists, pediatricians, and general practitioners is available for backup support.

CHILD AND FAMILY SERVICE AGENCIES

There are thousands of mental health clinics and family service agencies that work with troubled families and their children. As a result of many of these transactions, positive changes take place in high-risk youth and diminish their risks of negative consequences. While these agencies probably fall under the category of treatment, they may also have an important role in prevention, and yet few of these kinds of interventions appear to enter into the purview of experts on delinquency. The *Pendleton Child Service Center* in Virginia Beach is an example. Youth aged 5 to 12 experiencing behavior problems and their families are served by a multispecialty team including psychologists, social workers, nurses, and teachers.[35] Educational approaches are used to improve parenting skills and children's social functioning. Services include outreach, day treatment, parent counseling, family therapy, behavior management training, services in schools, group counseling, and other treatment modalities. The center has collaborative arrangements with many other community agencies, particularly the schools. Based on staff assessments, 70 to 75 percent of the high-risk participants had no court involvement four to six years after treatment.

RUNAWAY AND HOMELESS YOUTH SHELTERS

About 325 centers receive support to provide crisis intervention, individual counseling, drug and alcohol counseling, long-term foster care, transportation, recreation, and work readiness training to more than 1 million high-risk youth annually. Many of their clients are status offenders because they have run away from home. A study of the network of programs in 1984 found that 57 percent of the youth were reunited with their families, placed in foster care or a group home, helped to attain an independent living arrangement, or placed in some nonsecure detention program.[36] The centers' success in stabilizing the lives of these high-risk children is attributed to the comprehensive mix of services they are able to provide either directly on site or through referral (on the average, 13 different types of services). One such agency, the Travelers and Immigrants Aid of Chicago, operates the *Neon Street Clinic,* a comprehensive service program for homeless and runaway youth under age 21.[37] In addition to the general services, Neon Street serves as a drop-in center for homeless youth, where they are allowed to "hangout" for 15 visits before they subscribe to a "service plan." This clinic allows for contact between social workers and street youth for assistance with social, educational, and vocational problems, AIDS education, and other issues. The program reports that 78 percent of their clients have returned to school, found employment, or are enrolled in prevocational training. Only 7 percent were still living on the streets.

YOUTH SERVICE CORPS

An example of a large-scale employment program that has demonstrated a modest impact on youth behavior is the Conservation Corps. These programs provide work experience, educational remediation, and the opportunity to live away from home with other young adults in a structured environment. Wolf's analysis of the California Conservation Corps' (CCC) impact on short-term measures showed that corps members improved their physical aspects of self-concept, their attitudes toward women in nontraditional jobs, and support of antilittering and recycling efforts, blood donation, and community involvement.[38] No net effects were found in alcohol avoidance, nor in tolerant and altruistic attitudes. The most important benefit of the CCC appeared to be the accomplishment of public works by the participants rather than the upgrading of employment skills.

NEIGHBORHOOD-BASED ORGANIZATIONS

Between 1981 and 1986, a large-scale intervention in six communities with excessively high delinquency rates was sponsored by the Violent Juvenile Offender Research and Development Program.[39] The theory to be tested was that juvenile delinquency resulted from the weakening of social controls and that rates could be lowered by strengthening the bonding between family, school, peers, and the community. Each of the participating areas had to identify a neighborhood organization to act as coordinator, mobilize residents to increase supervision of youth and to liaison with community institutions, and develop specific projects for families and youth. The neighborhood organization was operated by staff and volunteers; it was responsible for developing neighborhood councils and conducting the assessment of needs and action plans. Projects included mediation with schools and law enforcement agencies to change policies, youth activities such as jobs, youth councils, and community service opportunities. Interventions with gangs were a major focus.

This program was carefully evaluated and, according to Fagan, showed positive outcomes in three of the six communities. In San Diego, gang violence was reduced during a targeted summer activities program but, after the intervention stopped, the rates increased again. In the Bronx, intensive neighborhood drug surveillance led to lower arrest rates for juveniles. In Los Angeles, where the focus was on revising the school disciplinary code and conducting community education, violence and vandalism decreased, but suspensions and expulsions increased as a result of enforcement of tougher standards. Many obstacles to success were identified through the community process: it was very difficult to implement family support programs (such as self-help and parenting education) because families were too troubled to spare the time for community activities. Community leadership existed, but demands on the participants' time were excessive and they were not willing to get involved in another project. Those volunteers who were recruited were new to community activity and it was difficult to sustain their participation. School officials were unresponsive to community demands and denied neighborhood groups access to the schools. Police were more willing to cooperate but they did not change policies. On the whole, programs that emphasized advocacy and institutional mediation appeared to be more effective than traditional social services in mobilizing residents to prevent juvenile crime and violence. Project staff concluded that neighborhood organization projects need more persistent efforts and long-range funding to produce greater changes than resulted from these programs.

ADOLESCENT DIVERSION PROJECT (ADP)

A carefully researched intervention, developed by William Davidson and colleagues at Michigan State University, focuses on youth who have already committed delinquent acts but have not yet been formerly adjudicated (entered into the juvenile justice system).[40] The rationale for this program is that early intervention is not adequately selective of high-risk youth. The ADP model is designed to provide empowerment skills to high-risk youth and their families so that they can change the behaviors that are creating problems for them. The approach builds on their strengths rather than their shortcomings. The instrument for change is a "family worker" extensively trained by the project to implement the ADP model, including assessment of desired behavioral change and needed community resources, techniques for behavioral contracting and advocacy in schools and other institutions, and preparation for terminating the service. The worker spends three hours per week with the assigned youth for 16 to 18 weeks. Evaluation results are very positive, showing statistically significant differences between program participants and other delinquent youth in recidivism rates (repeat delinquent acts). In the earlier phases of model development, university psychology students were used as workers. However, recent research shows that community volunteers are as effective as students in working with the youth (although they are more difficult to recruit).

Davidson attributes the success of the program to extensive involvement with the juvenile justice system, including police stations and courts, long-term commitment rather than a short demonstration project, placement of the intervention in the youth's natural environment (home, streets, or school) rather than in an office or a center, close adherence by the staff to a defined and carefully researched model, and availability of close supervision for the staff.

NEIGHBORHOOD WATCH

Programs have been organized in more than 3,000 communities to reduce opportunities for crime and build neighborhood and community cohesion.[41] Stimulated by the National Crime Prevention Council and the Department of Justice, many communities with the help of local police departments have initiated programs either directly or indirectly involved with prevention of delinquency. These programs include block watches, home security inspections, and community improvement efforts. In one community, Neighborhood Watches helped residents after a hurricane; in another, observations led to the confiscation of huge stashes of drugs. Surveys by evaluators have shown that Neighborhood Watch is an effective strategy for involving citizens and building partnerships. There are many available reports on reduced rates of burglaries, vandalism, and other crimes typically committed by juveniles.[42] A Youth Crime Watch Program in Dade County, Florida, instituted a crime reporting system and anticrime rallies and worked with students to instill pride in school and community. School crimes reduced dramatically, including assaults on staff, robberies, sexual offenses, and incidents involving drugs.[43]

### *Programs with Potential but No Research*

"Take a Bite Out of Crime" is a major initiative launched by the National Crime Prevention Council as part of a National Citizens' Crime Prevention Campaign.[44] Funded by the Department of Justice and designed by the Advertising Council, this public relations and media campaign features McGruff, a "trench coated spokesdog." The Council claims that one-half of teens who have viewed the ads on TV have taken crime prevention action and actually changed their own behaviors. However, since no further details on this preliminary evaluation are available, it is hard to tell whether these youth simply stay behind locked doors and not go out on the streets or whether they have changed from delinquent to nondelinquent activities. The initiative has involved millions of citizens in community events, such as crime prevention fairs and forums, speak outs, newsletters, poster and essay contests, cleaning up neighborhoods, mural-painting projects, and community surveys. A number of projects have involved children and teens in planning safe Halloween night celebrations, distributing crime prevention information, promoting local pride, and producing TV shows. A review of materials from this campaign suggests the large demand for crime prevention activities at the local level and the willingness of young people to get involved in creative responses to local problems.

## What Doesn't Work

The literature on delinquency prevention contains considerable documentation of programs that apparently do *not* prevent delinquency.[45] Among those mentioned are preventive casework, group counseling, pharmacological interventions (except for violent behavior), work experience, vocational education, probation officers, use of traditional street corner workers (whether trained or indigenous), social area or neighborhood projects, and "scaring straight" efforts. Earlier delinquency prevention efforts expected that individual psychotherapy would "cure" delinquents of criminal tendencies. This did not prove to be the case. Current use of therapy is much more related to family functioning and individual empowerment, and shows some evidence of success.

One experimental approach to delinquency prevention, Guided Group Interaction, relied heavily on the concepts of peer group counseling. Daily group discussions, facilitated by a trained adult, were built around confronting and censuring negative behavior and supporting and reinforcing positive behavior. Evaluations showed that this program had an adverse effect: the high-risk peers reinforced their negative behaviors.[46]

Current school practices found not to be effective in changing school misbehavior include suspension, detention, expulsion, security guards, and corporal punishment. Interventions of any kind that were exclusively concentrated on de-linquents increased contact between like peers and increased delinquency. The more contact with the criminal justice system, such as probation officers, the higher the probability of serious offenses and eventual incarceration.


## General Concepts of Delinquency Prevention

The programs described in this chapter constitute a cross-section of the *practice* of delinquency prevention. The literature on interventions to prevent delinquency was created by theoreticians as well as practitioners. From the literature, one can extract more general concepts that researchers believe are important in prevention theory. This review yielded eight points on which there appears to be reasonable consensus:

1. Programs should have broader goals than delinquency prevention per se. It is not possible to address delinquency prevention without consideration of the quality of education available to high-risk youth.
2. Programs should have multiple components since no one component has been demonstrated to be the "magic bullet."
3. Interventions should be offered early in the child's development to prevent learning and conduct problems.
4. Schools should play an integral role. The organizational characteristics of safe and orderly schools are well defined and documented: strong governance, fair discipline policies, student participation in decision making, and high investment in school outcomes by both student and staff.
5. Efforts should be directed toward institutional rather than individual change, particularly to upgrading the quality of education for disadvantaged children.
6. While point 5 is true, researchers have established that individual intensive attention and personalized planning are important factors in successfully working with high-risk children.
7. "Treatment integrity," the concept that an intervention should be carried out as designed, should be carefully applied.
8. Program benefits often "wash out" after the intervention stops. Continuity of effort is very important.

This review of the literature on delinquency prevention and the summary of programs that appear to work lead one to agree with the experts: we have not identified many successful models. This review also suggests that there may be many programs out there—for example, mental health clinics and runaway centers—that are having an impact on delinquent youth and have not yet been documented. In any case, the work to date contributes to our aggregate knowledge of youth at risk of delinquent behavior, suggesting that early intervention, intensive individualized attention, and a focus on school arrangements that foster learning are important program concepts. Successful delinquency prevention programs often utilize specially trained personnel, from community workers to behavioral therapists, rather than school counselors or community-agency program staff. Staff training and program development are typically conducted by specialized agencies, such as university research units.

Programs that incorporate more than one approach appear to have a better chance of success (the effects may be additive), but research rarely reveals which of the components are significant. A number of demonstration projects show that communities and neighborhoods can be involved in innovative delinquency prevention efforts, but that most projects lack long-term support and commitment from decision-makers. It is not clear from the research review whether intervention programs should be offered to all children within a disadvantaged or high-crime community or only to specific high-risk children who may have the characteristics of potential chronic offenders.

## Notes

1. H. Quay, ed., *Handbook of Juvenile Delinquency* (New York: Wiley, 1987).
2. P. Van Voorhis, "Delinquency Prevention: Toward Comprehensive Models and A Conceptual Map," *Criminal Justice Review* 11(1986): 15–24.
3. H. Leitenberg, "Primary Prevention in Delinquency," in J. Burchard and S. Burchard, eds., *Prevention of Delinquent Behavior* (Newbury Park, Calif.: Sage, 1986), p. 329.
4. R. Lundman, *Prevention and Control of Juvenile Delinquency* (New York: Oxford University Press, 1984).
5. J. Rabkin, "Epidemiology of Adolescent Violence: Risk Factors, Career Patterns and Interventions Programs" (Paper delivered at the Conference on Adolescent Violence, Stanford University, California, 1987).
6. P. Greenwood and F. Ziming, *One More Chance: The Pursuit of Promising Intervention Strategies for Chronic Juvenile Offenders* (Santa Monica, Calif.: Rand Corporation, 1983).
7. C. O'Donnell, M. Manos, and M. Chesney-Lind, "Diversion and Neighborhood Delinquency Programs in Open Settings," in E. Morris and C. Braukmann, eds., *Behavioral Approaches to Crime and Delinquency* (New York: Plenum Press, 1987), pp. 251–69.
8. J. Berrueta-Clement, L. Schweinhart, W. Barnett, and D. Weikart, "The Effects of Early Educational Intervention on Crime and Delinquency in Adolescence and Early Adulthood," in J. Burchard and S. Burchard, eds., *Prevention of Delinquent Behavior* (Newbury Park, Calif.: Sage, 1986), pp. 220–40. Also, J. Berrueta-Clement, L. Schweinhart, W. Barnett, D. Weikart, and A. Epstein, *Changed Lives: The Effects of the Perry Preschool Program on Youths through Age 19* (Ypsilanti, Mich.: High Scope Educational Research Foundation, #8, 1984).
9. Berrueta-Clement et al., "Effects of Early Educational Intervention," p. 220.
10. Leitenberg, "Primary Prevention in Delinquency," p. 326.
11. U.S. Congress, House Select Committee on Children, Youth and Families, *Opportunities for Success: Cost-Effective Programs for Children: Update 1988* (Washington, D.C.: U.S. Government Printing Office, 1988).
12. Greenwood and Ziming, *One More Chance*, p. 58.
13. Ibid., p. 59.
14. L. Michelson, "Cognitive-Behavioral Strategies in the Prevention and Treatment of

Antisocial Disorders in Children and Adolescents," in J. Burchard and S. Burchard, eds., *Prevention of Delinquent Behavior* (Newbury Park, Calif.: Sage, 1986), pp. 275–310.

15. D. Hawkins, R. Catalano, G. Jones, and D. Fine, "Delinquency Prevention through Parent Training: Results and Issues from Work in Progress," in J. Wilson and G. Loury, eds., *Children to Citizens: Families, Schools, and Delinquency Prevention,* vol. 3 (New York: Springer-Verlag, 1987), pp. 186–204.

16. Michelson, "Cognitive-Behavioral Strategies," pp. 284–305.

17. M. Shure and G. Spivak, "Interpersonal Problem-Solving in Young Children: A Cognitive Approach to Prevention," *American Journal of Community Psychology* 10(1982): 341–56.

18. S. Henggeler, *Delinquency in Adolescence* (Newbury Park, Calif.: Sage, 1989).

19. Ibid., p. 106.

20. J. Arbuthnot and D. Gordon, "Behavioral and Cognitive Effects of a Moral Reasoning Development Intervention for High-Risk Behavior Disordered Adolescents," *Journal of Consulting and Clinical Psychology* 54(1986): 208–16.

21. National Institute for Citizen Education in the Law, *Annual Report 1987–1988* (Washington, D.C.: National Institute for Citizen Education in the Law, 1989).

22. The Colorado Juvenile Justice and Delinquency Prevention Council, *Using School-Based Programs to Improve Students' Citizenship in Colorado* (Denver, Colo.: The Colorado Juvenile Justice and Delinquency Prevention Program, October 1987).

23. D. Hawkins and D. Lishner, "School and Delinquency," in E. Johnson, ed., *Handbook on Crime and Delinquency Prevention* (Westport, Conn.: Greenwood Press, 1987), pp. 179–220. J. Kimbrough, "School-Based Strategies for Delinquency Prevention," in P. Greenwood, ed., *The Juvenile Rehabilitation Reader* (Santa Monica, Calif.: Rand Corporation, 1985), pp. IX, 1–22.

24. D. Hawkins and T. Lam, "Teacher Practices, Social Development and Delinquency," in J. Burchard and S. Burchard, eds., *Prevention of Delinquent Behavior* (Newbury Park, Calif.: Sage, 1986), pp. 241–74.

25. This program was evaluated by D. Gottfredson of the Center for the Social Organization of Schools, Johns Hopkins University. The results are summarized in Kimbrough, "School-Based Strategies," pp. IX, 6–7.

26. J. Grant and F. Cappell, *Reducing School Crime: A Report on the School Team Approach* (Washington, D.C.: U.S. Government Printing Office, Office of Juvenile Justice and Delinquency Prevention, U.S. Department of Justice, 1983).

27. G. Gottfredson, D. Gottfredson, and M. Cook, *The School Action Effectiveness Study: Second Interim Report* (Baltimore: Johns Hopkins University, Center for Social Organization of Schools, 1983).

28. M. Gold and D. Mann, *Expelled to a Friendlier Place: A Study of Effective Alternative Schools* (Ann Arbor, Mich.: University of Michigan Press, 1984).

29. L. Laurence, M. Litynsky, and B. D'Lugoff, "A Day School Intervention for Truant and Delinquent Youth," in D. Safer, ed., *School Programs for Disruptive Adolescents* (Baltimore: University Park Press, 1987), p. 282.

30. Cited as a model for prevention of conduct disorders in A. Kazdin, *Conduct Disorders in Childhood and Adolescence* (Newbury Park, Calif.: Sage, 1987). See also Chapter 12.

31. O'Donnell, Manos, and Chesney-Lind, "Diversion and Neighborhood Delinquency Programs," p. 263.

32. Boys Clubs of America (Briefing Paper, undated). Also, Boys Clubs of America, *Targeted Outreach Newsletter,* vols. III-1 (1987) and II-1 (1986).

33. L. Feldman, ed., *Partnerships for Youth 2000: A Program Models Manual* (Tulsa, Okla.: The University of Oklahoma, National Resource Center for Youth Services, 1988).
34. Ibid., p. 42.
35. Ibid., p. 56.
36. National Network of Runaway and Youth Services, Inc., *To Whom Do They Belong?: A Profile of America's Runaway and Homeless Youth and the Programs that Help Them* (Washington, D.C.: National Network of Runaway and Youth Services, Inc., 1985).
37. Feldman, *Partnerships for Youth 2000,* p. 56.
38. W. Wolf, S. Leiderman, and R. Voith, *The California Conservation Corps: An Analysis of Short-Term Impacts on Participants* (Philadelphia, Pa.: Public/Private Ventures, 1987).
39. J. Fagan, "Neighborhood Education, Mobilization and Organization for Juvenile Crime Prevention," *Annals, American Academy of Political and Social Science* 494(1987): 54–70.
40. W. Davidson and R. Redner, "The Prevention of Juvenile Delinquency: Diversion from the Juvenile Justice System," in R. Price, E. Cowen, R. Lorion, and J. Ramos-McKay, eds., *14 Ounces of Prevention* (Washington, D.C.: American Psychological Association, 1988), pp. 123–38.
41. National Crime Prevention Council, "The Success of Community Crime Prevention," in *Topics in Crime Prevention* (Washington, D.C.: National Crime Prevention Council, 1987).
42. J. Roehl and R. Cook, *Evaluation of the Urban Crime Prevention Program: Executive Summary* (Washington, D.C.: U.S. Government Printing Office, U.S. Department of Justice, National Institute of Justice, 1984).
43. National Crime Prevention Council, "Success of Community Crime Prevention," p. 5.
44. National Crime Prevention Council, "Watch Out, Help Out" (campaign brochure, undated).
45. D. Safer, *School Programs for Disruptive Adolescents* (Baltimore: University Park Press, 1982); Greenwood and Ziming, *One More Chance,* pp. 31–34; Rabkin, "Epidemiology of Adolescent Violence," pp. 81–85; Henggeler, *Delinquency in Adolescence,* pp. 93, 113; Kazdin, *Conduct Disorders,* pp. 106–13.
46. Henggeler, *Delinquency in Adolescence,* p. 102.

# 10

# Prevention of Substance Abuse

The literature on prevention of substance abuse is extensive, diverse, uneven, and difficult to summarize. It encompasses intensive reviews of drug education research in general, well-documented experiments with specific school-based interventions, more cursory articles promoting a program but lacking any outcome data, pamphlets advertising curricula, and assorted other materials. This range reflects the fuzziness of the subject of substance abuse prevention and the specialized interests of those who work on it. Some efforts focus only on preventing cigarette smoking, others on alcohol abuse, a few include all substance-related behaviors. In programs directed toward alcohol abuse, there is no agreement on whether the goal should be abstinence or responsible decision making. There is little agreement about whether programs should focus only on substance abuse or deal with more general issues related to the predictors of substance use, such as family bonding and school failure. One school of thought adheres to the position that substance abuse issues should be dealt with in the context of comprehensive health education.

Another approach to the prevention of substance abuse takes us away from school-based programs into the area of public policy. This view suggests that behavioral change will result from enforcing restrictive laws and policies and creating broader media efforts aimed at the whole society rather than youth. Many people attribute the decline in cigarette smoking to drastic shifts in public opinion about its social acceptability and safety following the release of a Surgeon General's report 25 years ago that documented the negative health consequences of smoking. It is true that the changes in behavior even among adolescents took place in the late 1970s, prior to the initiation of most smoking prevention programs in schools in the early 1980s. Teen smoking behavior has changed much less during this decade than the prior one. The Advocacy Institute has proposed a number of priority policy actions to prevent smoking which include creating smoke-free workplaces and public spaces, increasing excise taxes on cigarettes (assuming a

10 percent increase in tax produces a 12 percent reduction in smoking!), compelling cigarette manufacturers to assume liability for smoke-caused deaths and diseases, neutralizing or reducing cigarette advertising and promotion, and restricting sales to minors.[1] Similar proposals have been made in response to the alcohol problem: charge higher excise taxes, enforce laws on sales to minors, enforce drunk driving laws, and reduce advertising.[2] A growing number of people advocate the legalization of drugs, particularly marijuana, as a means of reducing its profitability and therefore its supply.

The public policy argument has a great deal of merit, and we will pay attention to these issues in the discussion of communitywide efforts in this chapter and in overall strategies, which are taken up in Chapter 14. However, our major interest here is to ferret out those local programs that may have some success in preventing substance abuse. This search focused on identifying programs aimed at delaying or preventing the use of cigarettes, alcohol, marijuana, or hard drugs, with acceptable evaluative data to demonstrate change or modification of actual behaviors and practices. Table 10.1 shows the typical measures of success in relationship to the behaviors in question as well as the sources of data from which conclusions are drawn. Most of the outcome measures are based on self-reported survey data. It is possible that the answers are influenced by either not wanting to admit substance abuse or wanting to please the teacher; however, in those studies that verify smoking claims with saliva tests, there is close agreement with self-reports. Much of the evaluation research is short term, measuring changes in behavior six months to a year following the intervention. The few evaluations that track students over longer times have more dramatic results, either showing larger effects or no effects at all. Almost all of the drug prevention research is classroom based, and the outcomes are presented as aggregates (e.g., the percent of seventh-graders who initiated smoking in year two versus year one). Thus, when a 50

TABLE 10.1. Measures of Success in Prevention of Substance Abuse

| Behavior to Prevent | Measures of Success | Source of Data |
|---|---|---|
| Initiation of any substance use | Increase in percentage of group who report that they never used any substance | Self-report surveys |
| Continuation of smoking cigarettes, using chewing tobacco, marijuana | Reduction in number of current users | Self-report surveys Physical tests (saliva) |
| Misuse of alcohol | Reduction in amount and frequency of use | Self-report surveys |
| | Reduction in arrests for violation of alcohol laws | Police records |
| Driving while intoxicated | Reduction in driving while intoxicated | Self-report surveys Police records |
| Any use of hard drugs | Reduction in use Reduction in arrests | Self-report surveys Police records |

percent reduction in smoking is reported by a program, this may mean that the percent ever smoking in junior high dropped from 10 to 5, based on very small numbers.

This kind of research leads to questions about the intensity of the prevention effects of "successful" programs: Do they primarily deter experimental smoking or drinking among those who would eventually stop on their own? How effective are these programs with "high-risk" users? Goodstadt is convinced that one of the weaknesses of drug education programs is their failure to target subgroups and to measure the differential effects.[3]

One of the most disappointing aspects of the substance abuse prevention field is the large number of health education and counseling programs that can demonstrate only that knowledge was enhanced or attitudes changed as the result of the intervention. It is surprising how many researchers do not even include questions about substance *use* in their psychologically oriented survey protocols (yet there are endless questions about self-esteem and locus of control). There is clear evidence that neither knowledge nor attitude change is sufficiently predictive of behavioral change to accept these indexes as surrogate measures of successful prevention.[4]

In recent years, more than 7000 local groups with concerns about teen drug use have been organized around the country, but no evaluation data could be located to measure their effectiveness at changing behavior. SADD (Students Against Drunk Driving) and MADD (Mothers Against Drunk Driving), PRIDE (Parent Resources and Information on Drug Education), NFP (National Federation of Parents for Drug-Free Youth)), and other parent support groups probably involve millions of parents. Falco attributes the rapid proliferation of these kinds of groups to a perceived lack of government leadership. "Many parents have felt helpless to combat the positive images of substance abuse reflected in the media and the culture and have [organized] countermessages and activities for their children."[5] These programs generally comprise suburban middle-class families and may not reach the highest risk adolescents.

The subject of substance abuse has attracted the attention of a number of the nation's leading social psychologists at several university centers—for example, Stanford, Cornell, Columbia, University of Southern California, University of Michigan, and University of Minnesota. They and their students have produced literally thousands of studies, testing various psychological theories of prevention of substance use (primarily cigarettes). Periodically, other researchers have attempted to synthesize the aggregate of findings through a statistical process known as metaanalysis. Using this method, the results of a large number of studies are added together and treated as one giant pool of data.

A unique meta-analysis of data from 143 adolescent drug prevention programs was conducted by Tobler.[6] Unlike previous efforts, approaches other than curriculum-based interventions were included. Almost all of the programs were in schools; three-fourths were at the junior high level and one-fourth at the high school level. This work compiled published and unpublished research reports and doctoral theses, according to the type (modality) of program. Almost all of the ongoing interventions fall into one or more of five categories of prevention strategy:

1. *Knowledge oriented only.* Based on the assumption that "drug education" will change attitudes that will, in turn, decrease use. Strategy makes use of information on long-term effects, which is presented by instructors; limited group participation; and "scare" tactics.

2. *Affective strategies only.* Based on the assumption that psychological factors place certain children at risk of abuse. Strategy is aimed at social growth; self-esteem building; and values clarification. No mention is made of drugs.

3. *Social influence and life skills.* Based on a combination of approaches that assume that peer pressure is the major factor in abuse.

   (a) *Refusal skills.* Based on the assumption that specific behaviors can be taught to deal with social influences. Strategy teaches interpersonal resistance skills; deals with social pressures; utilizes "saying no" training; and employs peer role models.

   (b) *Social and life skills.* Based on the assumption that generic social skills are needed for problem solving and decision making about substance use. Strategy promotes personal sense of competency; teaches communication skills; uses feedback; introduces values clarification; and teaches coping skills.

4. *Knowledge plus affective strategies.* Based on the assumption that both attitudes and values must be changed to change behavior. Strategy provides information and decision-making skills.

5. *Alternative strategies.* Based on the assumption that changes have to be made in correlates (predictors) of drug use, such as school failure and delinquency.

   (a) *Introduce activities.* Replace negative behaviors with positive activities, such as recreation, jobs, volunteerism.

   (b) *Teach competence in high-risk youth.* Make up for individual deficits using basic skills training, programs such as Outward Bound, and individual attention.

Tobler computed standardized scores for the aggregate of the programs using each of the five strategies on five outcomes: knowledge, attitudes, substance use, skills (problem solving, saying no to peer pressure), and other behaviors (arrests, grades, school attendance).[7] The programs in aggregate had the most effect on knowledge, twice that of any variable, implying that programs could most readily demonstrate an increase in the amount of knowledge about drugs. The programs had relatively little effect on changing attitudes, however. The outcome of interest here, of course, is use, since it reflects behavioral change in regard to substances (see Table 10.1). The effect on changes in substance use was only half the size of the effect on knowledge changes. The change in use was much greater for cigarette smoking than other substances (e.g., programs demonstrated a reduction in smoking).

Of the five different models studied, *social influence and life skills* (peer influence programs) were found to have the largest effect on all outcome measures. The score was 1.3 times the mean score for all programs. The *alternative* programs were second most effective, but the mean score was only half that of the social influence programs. The other three modalities had much lower scores, with *knowledge only* programs having only one-tenth of the mean score. In other words, informational programs showed practically no effect.

The differences among programs in their effect on use were striking. Not only were social influence and life skills programs more effective on the composite drug use score, they were equally effective for each of the specific outcomes (use of cigarettes, alcohol, soft and hard drugs). The other kinds of programs (in aggregate) appeared to affect cigarette use only. While the alternative programs had only an average impact on substance use, they showed a high effect on behavioral measures that predict substance use, such as school grades and attendance (which might have been their primary goals).

Tobler concludes from her research that

> two modalities . . . are effective. Peer programs (social/skills) produced the only results which showed change toward the ultimate aim of reducing drug-abusing behaviors. . . . Alternative programs were equally successful for the special population groups (delinquents, abusers) showing superior results in increasing skills and changing behavior in both direct drug use and indirect correlates of drug use.[8]

In a more recent unpublished analysis, Tobler identified two individual programs that seemed to be more successful than all the others: Life Skills Training Program and The Student Assistance Program[9] (see the following section "Successful Models").

Another recent metaanalysis focused specifically on school-based drug education programs.[10] Bangert-Drowns reviewed 350 such programs and found that only 126 had any kind of evaluation data. After eliminating those with serious methodological flaws or incomparable samples, only 33 entries were acceptable. Like Tobler, Bangert-Drowns found that programs were more successful at changing knowledge than drug use (unlike Tobler, his results were more positive on changing attitudes). Only 14 programs even measured behavorial change and, among these, the amount of change in substance use was minimal. Recent efforts showed greater effects than earlier ones, as did those directed at volunteer students rather than mandatory participants. Peer-taught programs appeared to be more successful than adult-taught ones. However, the new wave of social skills programs were not included in this analysis. Bangert-Drowns concluded:

> As it stands, the public record shows that substance abuse education has failed to achieve its primary goal—the prevention of drug and alcohol abuse. . . . It is unlikely that drug education will ever be withdrawn from the schools, even if it is shown to be ineffective [since] . . . it serves functions such as reassurance of parents that the schools are at least trying to control substance abuse among students.[11]

The findings from these two analyses are strongly supported in the literature. Polich et al. conducted a review of drug prevention programs and concluded that the only hopeful evidence was being produced by the new programs based on the social influence model of adolescent behavior.[12] Mueller and Higgins suggest that funders look favorably on PSST (personal and social skills training) programs

because of their demonstrated preventive effects on cigarette smoking.[13] They believe that this model will ultimately prove effective as a deterrent to other problem
behaviors if it is developed as a component of broader communitywide efforts.
Hitchcock and Schelling, in their review of smoking prevention approaches, support the development of the social influence model but warn that the research
findings still have a "provisional character," since we do not understand how the
model really works, nor for *whom*.[14] They imply that the model may be more
useful for younger than older students, and for delaying initiation of smoking
rather than for stopping smoking among children who already are involved in the
behavior. Leukefeld and Moskowitz summed up a conference on prevention strategies with conditional support for programs that provide training in assertiveness
and decision making as well as information about the social influences that promote substance abuse and the probabilities of negative consequences.[15] They also
question the efficacy of the social influence model on minority populations.

Interestingly, much of the program development and research on the social
influences model was supported by the National Institute on Drug Abuse (NIDA).
A series of NIDA-published monographs presents papers by the major theorists
(primarily psychologists) from which one can track the diffusion of prevention
concepts. Another group of programs is supported by the National Institute on
Alcohol Abuse and Alcoholism (NIAAA). These were primarily directed toward
prevention of alcohol abuse and, to a lesser extent, other problem behaviors. In
1983, the NIAAA selected five prevention models as the "state of the art" in the
alcoholism field.[16] According to the text, the criteria for selection was comprehensiveness, inclusion of both prevention and early intervention, and availability of
documentation (curriculum guides, teacher training manuals, etc.). Evaluation and
evidence of success were not criteria.

Out of these various activities emerged the Office of Substance Abuse Prevention (OSAP). Since 1987, this federal agency has been charged with coordinating
activities from the alcohol and drug prevention fields (taking over from NIDA and
NIAAA). In its first two years, OSAP funded 130 high-risk youth demonstration
projects. A new Division of Evaluation and Research Coordination has been set
up to evaluate the grant programs. Many evaluation activities are getting under
way, but no data have yet been released for public consumption.

## Successful Models

The programs described here are a sampling of interventions that appear to have
some potential to prevent substance abuse or decrease the problems associated
with it. This is *not* an inventory of all programs currently in the field that have
prevention goals. There are literally thousands of them. Almost every school district has some form of drug prevention activity, typically a substance abuse curriculum at the high school level. Every state government has at least one substance
abuse office, and some have more (one for alcohol and the other for drugs). Most
youth-serving agencies offer some programs in this area, and many curriculum
manufacturers heavily market prevention materials.

## Early Childhood and Family Interventions

Few early childhood programs were identified that were designed with the intent to prevent later substance abuse. The Perry Preschool Program (described in Chapter 9), although not specifically focused on preventing later substance abuse, compiled data on a wide range of behaviors in adolescence. Although there were significant differences in delinquent behavior and arrests, no significant difference between the two groups in substance use was found. Nonsignificant findings showed lower marijuana use among the experimental group, but this group reported higher hard drug use than the control group.[17]

Family involvement with prevention of substance abuse is considered very important. A number of programs are specifically aimed at children of alcoholics (COAs) and are conducted in conjunction with adult programs such as Alcoholics Anonymous (AA). However, these kinds of efforts fall more into the domain of treatment. While parent involvement in community education and prevention programs is significant, as already pointed out, no specific program evaluation could be identified that showed effects on behavioral changes among the children of participating parents.

## School-Based Interventions

Schools appear to be the primary locus for substance abuse prevention, not only in the area of curricula but also in school-based individual counseling programs through specialized counselors and school-based clinics.

CURRICULA

As has been stated, most of the research on prevention of substance abuse has been conducted on school-based curricula. Botvin's work in this area has received recognition as a model, most recently by its selection as 1 of 14 showcase programs by the American Psychological Association's Task Force on Promotion, Prevention and Intervention Alternatives in Psychology.[18] Botvin's Life Skills Training program was the only drug prevention intervention selected, out of a field of 300 nominees, based on criteria that included substantive evaluation and replication.

*Life Skills Training Program (LST).* This program approaches substance use as socially learned, purposive, and functional behavior. To address the complex social and personal factors that are involved, it is necessary simultaneously to reduce pressure to smoke, develop general personal competence, and learn specific skills for resisting peer pressure. Botvin embraces problem behavior theory and recognizes the necessity for addressing the underlying determinants of substance use in relationship to other forms of "acting out."

The LST curriculum includes five major components:[19]

1. Information on the short- and long-term consequences of substance abuse; biofeedback experience that illustrates the immediate effects of cigarette smoking.

2. Decision-making skills to foster critical thinking; formulation of counter-arguments to advertising appeals.
3. Coping skills for dealing with anxiety.
4. Social skills training for resisting peer pressure; communication skills; dealing with shyness, dating, and other teen situations; assertiveness skills.
5. Self-improvement; developing a positive self-image using learned principles of behavioral change.

The 20-session program was designed primarily for junior high students, to be provided by a classroom teacher using a Teacher's Manual after receiving one day of inservice training. Older peers (in eleventh and twelfth grade) are also used as teachers after extensive training and with on-site monitoring by the LST staff.

A number of evaluations have been conducted by Botvin showing reductions in new cigarette smoking among junior high school students. Studies showed higher rates of success for more intensive programs and those with "booster" sessions. The most recent published data indicate a reduction in alcohol and marijuana use, as well as tobacco use, with the greatest impact in peer-led sessions. Botvin told the Select Committee on Children, Youth and Families that there are "over 20 studies showing 30 to 75 percent reductions in new junior high school cigarette, marijuana and alcohol users (compared to groups that received no treatment) using the new [psychosocial] prevention techniques."[20]

*Interpersonal Skills Training.*  This training program was developed by Schinke and Gilchrist to address the lack of communication skills among high-risk teens with regard to substance use, teen pregnancy, and other aspects of their lives (see Chapter 11). A specific curriculum aimed at cigarette smoking among fifth- and sixth-graders utilized trained graduate students (social workers) to present a 10-hour intervention.[21] One group received the entire package, including information about smoking, problem-solving skills, self-instruction in modeling and practicing refusal skills, interpersonal communication, and media analysis. Refusal skills involved a four-step model: skills to stop, think, decide, and act when tempted or urged to smoke. A comparison group received the same information but no skills training (the time was spent on quizzes, games, and debates). Compared with both the control group and the information group, those who had the skills training showed significant differences in smoking, and the differences increased over a two-year period.

A similar program focused on preventing substance abuse in general among a population of Native American youngsters, incorporating a Native American instructor and bicultural illustrations.[22] Preliminary evaluation results after six months showed significantly lower rates of tobacco, alcohol, and drug use among the experimental group.

*Alcohol Misuse Prevention Study (AMPS).*  This is a unique curriculum that focuses entirely on the misuse of alcohol. Developed by Dielman and associates, the assumption is that a more rational approach to the prevention of consequences is to teach adolescents how to use substances responsibly rather than to stress abstention.[23] The fifth- and sixth-grade level programs incorporate the social skills "inoculation" approach and teach peer resistance and the immediate effects and long-term consequences of alcohol misuse. Evaluation results showed no differences in experimental and control groups for either baseline abstainers or users at the initial follow-up survey. However, when a follow-up was conducted two years after the intervention, significant differences emerged for prior users; the experimental group had lower rates.[24] These findings support the importance of studying subgroups and suggest that interventions have different effects on abstainers than on users.

*Drug Abuse Resistance Education (DARE).*   A joint project of the Los Angeles Police Department and the Los Angeles School District, this collaborative program uses trained instructors (80-hour seminar plus inservice) who are police officers placed on full-time duty to the DARE project. The fifth- and sixth-grade curriculum is adapted from SMART (Self-Management and Resistance Training), with 17 sessions that also include practices for personal safety at home and in the neighborhood.[25] At the completion, students take a stand against drug abuse with personal essays and public pledges. Certificates of participation are awarded in a schoolwide assembly.

Evaluation of a group of students who took DARE in sixth grade compared with nonparticipants one year later showed less total use of substances since sixth grade.[26] However, when type of substances was examined, there were significant differences in use of hard alcohol and cigarettes, but no differences from controls in use of marijuana, hard drugs, beer, or wine. Further analysis showed effects for boys but not for girls. The results provided an interesting example of a program that apparently had some effect on behavior (for males) but no effect on knowledge, attitudes, or self-esteem.[27] This program is being widely replicated throughout the country.

*Growing Healthy.*   A comprehensive health education program for kindergarten through seventh grade, Growing Healthy integrates substance abuse prevention with general health issues and other school curriculum—for example, reading, physical education, arts, and sciences.[28] This program, originally developed by the American Lung Association and promoted by the National Center for Health Education (NCHE), is in wide use around the country. It has a planned sequential curriculum, which includes the study of body systems, safety, nutrition, hygiene, fitness, mental health, and health life-styles. The requisite teaching materials include audiovisuals, models, materials for workshops, and techniques for involving parents. An important goal is to enlist a broad base of school, parent, and community support for healthy living. Implementation by a school requires the availability of a school team (two teachers, the principal, and one other) for extensive training by NCHE staff in each state. Research tracking ninth graders who received all or part of the K–7 curriculum shows reduced alcohol, drug, and cigarette use.

## SUPPORT SERVICES AND COUNSELING

*The Student Assistance Program (SAP).*   Developed and implemented by Ellen Morehouse almost a decade ago, SAP uses full-time professional counselors to provide alcohol and drug abuse intervention and prevention services to junior and senior high school students. This program, one of five selected by NIAAA as models that should be replicated in local communities, has four basic components:[29]

1. Group counseling sessions (8 to 20 sessions) for students with alcoholic parents. These focus on increased self-esteem and improved academic, behavioral, social, and emotional functioning.
2. Individual, family, or group counseling services for students who are using alcohol or drugs dysfunctionally. Referral to community treatment programs, if available.
3. Counseling services for students who exhibit poor school performance (and are therefore at high risk for alcohol abuse).
4. Work with parent and community groups to develop ways of dealing with substance abuse problems.

Although a school-based program, SAP's counselors are all employed, supervised, and trained by an outside corporation, such as a county mental health department, and therefore do not operate under the same constraints as school guidance counselors (e.g., they can maintain confidentiality and have more time for individual students). However, the schools and their principals must be firmly committed to the program and provide space, equipment, open communication with the staff, and other supportive policies.

An important aspect of this program is its training of teachers, parents, and other gatekeepers to be sensitive to student problems and to refer them appropriately to the counselors. Mandatory referral is required if students are found under the influence of alcohol or drugs on school grounds.

The Student Assistance Program was evaluated by an outside consultant in its early years.[30] The unpublished summary report stated that the program was very effective in preventing nonuser students from taking up alcohol and marijuana and in reducing or stopping the prevalence among users. Alcohol users improved their attendance at school, and there was some evidence that the larger the number of individual counseling sessions, the greater the success. No effect was shown for users of hard drugs. This evaluation did not include data from control schools.

A recent pilot evaluation of the Student Assistance Program from one urban school district has produced very encouraging results.[31] However, this model uses school staff, not outside social workers, as counselors. The students who used the program were, prior to the intervention, at very high risk because of heavy substance use (particularly marijuana), poor school performance and attendance, and low self-esteem. More than three-fourths of the SAP students smoked daily compared with less than a fourth of a comparison sample.

A follow-up survey found significant reductions in alcohol and marijuana use, reductions in quantities of alcohol consumed and days "drunk or very high" (reduced from 5.5 to 3.2!), and significant increases in grade point averages (but not attendance). No effect was shown on self-esteem measures. Services received by the participant students included a screening interview (85%), in-school individual counseling or therapy (44%), in-school use/abuse group (36%), other in-school groups (20%), external groups or individual assessment or counseling (16%), outpatient treatment (7%), inpatient treatment (9%), and AA or Alateen (7%). As these figures suggest, SAP combines a preventive counseling approach with treatment for high-risk users.

This program has gained great acceptance across the country; principals are among the greatest supporters. They appreciate their role in selecting the counselors, are happy to gain an additional professional staff member without cost, and perceive that the programs enable them to establish a school climate conducive to combating student substance abuse.[32] An implementation manual assists schools and community agencies to organize this program. Morehouse attributes much of the program's success to the use of trained social workers who are accessible to the students, to the independence of the program from the school, and to the collaborative spirit that has developed between the schools and the program.

SCHOOL-BASED CLINICS

A rapid rise in the initiation of school-based clinics has taken place throughout the country; currently more than 160 junior and senior high schools have them (see Chapter 11). A few of the emerging school-based clinics have substance abuse prevention as a primary goal, but most are more generalized. More than three-fourths of all school-based clinics reported having some form of substance abuse programs, and almost all provide mental health and psychosocial counseling.[33]

*The Adolescent Resources Corporation (ARC).*   Three clinics are operated by ARC in high schools in Kansas City. This program places high priority on teaching healthy life-styles and discarding risk-taking behaviors through group and individual counseling. The schools report a substantial drop in substance use during a two-year period. Never-use of alcohol went from 59 to 64 percent, never-use of marijuana from 69 to 79 percent, and nonsmokers increased from 87 to 95 percent of the clinic clients.[34] These success rates have not been published and should be interpreted as preliminary.

THE SCHOOL TEAM APPROACH

The concept of the school team, successfully used in delinquency prevention, had its roots in the U.S. Department of Education substance abuse prevention efforts. From 1972 to the early 1980s, some 4500 communities organized school teams involving 18,000 personnel which affected more than 1 million youth annually.[35] A team consists of 5 or more members, including parents, school staff, students, and community residents. After the teams were locally selected, they were trained by professionals from one of five regional national training centers and continued to receive technical assistance and support in implementing local programs. Services differed according to when the program was implemented, and the particular needs of the community were taken into consideration. The centralized training aspect of this intervention is considered critical. In the evolution of the model, as urban areas became interested, the program required that four teams or clusters be sent for training and that the school principal be a member of each team. A full-time coordinator was also required (who would relate to the 21 team members).

Several models are described in the source material that include evaluation data. In Lee, Massachusetts, a number of activities were stimulated in the high school by the School Team there. A ninth-grade curriculum emphasized the social and legal ramifications of alcohol use. During Prom Week, all students were exposed to a class on the dangers of drinking and driving, and contracts from SADD were sent home to all parents. Seniors were involved with many activities related to graduation, including pledges, parties, and concerts (alternatives to drinking). Parents were asked to sign a pledge not to serve alcohol to children. Attention was paid to heightening community awareness through media and publications. The results were positive: no alcohol- or drug-related accidents, deaths, or arrests were reported during the "targeted time period." Police reported a "calm" atmosphere in the community, and 50 percent of seniors and 70 percent of other students signed a pledge.

In Solem, North Dakota, a community with many high-risk students, particularly Native Americans, the School Team developed a high school drug education program, alternatives to drug use (such as a Community Fun Night), and training in decision-making skills. It was reported that school attendance increased, and there were substantial decreases in the arrest rate, dropout rate, and in coming to school drunk.

Wichita, Kansas, conducted the most comprehensive evaluation on its School Team model.[36] Over the years, 94 five-member teams have been trained in that community, and almost every high school is covered. Based on administrative and law enforcement data, there have been significant reductions in drug abuse as reported by school nurses, fewer suspensions for abuse, a decrease in juvenile arrests for abuse, and no alcohol- or drug-related fatalities caused by juvenile drivers in over a four-year period. A student survey revealed that schools with high team activity had significantly lower substance abuse rates than schools with low team activity.

### Comprehensive and Communitywide Efforts

THE DOOR

A private, nonprofit, multicomponent youth center located in a large facility in New York City, the Door is designed to address the multiple problems of high-risk youth through a range of services, including alcohol and drug education which is offered in the evenings for all clients.[37] Truancy and academic problems are addressed in a Learning Center; delinquency, family problems, and personal problems are treated through intensive psychological counseling and group counseling. Creative and physical arts (pottery, woodworking, gym, break dancing, music, art, theater, and video workshops), sexual health counseling, physical exams, nutrition counseling, English as a Second Language, social services, and crisis intervention are all available to help at-risk youth find alternatives to self-destructive life-styles involving substance abuse. Free nightly meals are served to participants. Program statistics show that large numbers of youth reduced their drug and alcohol experimentation as a result of these services. However, no control group data are available.

The Door has been used as a model for comprehensive youth services since its inception in 1970. Its design is built around the concept of a "community of concern" furthered by a staff deeply committed to a holistic approach to helping young people. In its earlier years, much of its public funding derived from family planning sources but, in recent years, other sources of funds have been added, most recently for substance abuse prevention and treatment. Because of the array of services it offers, The Door could just as well be cited in any of the other prevention chapters (although little data are available on its effectiveness beyond client statistics). The Bridge Over Troubled Waters in Boston and Aunt Martha's Place in the Chicago area are similar multiservice agencies. The 300 shelters that are part of the Runaway and Homeless Youth Network also offer drug-related prevention and treatment services along with a wide array of crisis intervention, suicide prevention, educational and employment services, family and individual counseling, and referrals for medical and legal assistance.[38]

MIDWESTERN PREVENTION PROJECT (MPP)

A large-scale, comprehensive, community-based intervention developed by Mary Ann Pentz and colleagues at the University of Southern California, this drug abuse prevention and research project involves over 100 middle schools in Kansas City and Indianapolis in a broad program that addresses resistance and competence skills as well as environmental support strategies that involve youth, families, and communities.[39] In Kansas City, the program is called STAR, Students Taught Awareness and Resistance. It has five major elements that are being sequentially introduced:

1. *School-based curricula,* which consist of 10 sessions in sixth or seventh grade that focus on drug resistance skills and require 10 homework sessions involving interviews and role-playing with family and others.
2. *Parent programs,* which involve parent-student-principal groups to promote a drug-free environment in the school.
3. *Community organization,* in which community leaders are trained in drug prevention strategies and encouraged to develop agency task forces, mass media appeals, community events, awards ceremonies, networking, and referrals.
4. *Health policy change,* which works with government officials to promote antismoking policies, enforce drunk driving laws, and create neighborhood watches for drugs.
5. *Mass media* efforts, in which press kits, commercials, news features, and other television programs are utilized to promote drug prevention.

This massive program is supported by private donations and foundation grants as well as government sources and has a complex long-term research design to test single element and cumulative effects. In addition to research, staff members from the University of Southern California provide extensive training for teachers, parent groups, and community leaders and pay particular attention to quality control.

An evaluation in 42 of the Kansas City schools showed that, after 18 months, the prevalence of cigarette, alcohol, and marijuana use was significantly lower than in control schools, and parents reported lower use not only for their children but for themselves.[40] Pentz et al. attribute their success in implementing this program in Kansas City to the endorsement and support of the power elite (the head of a leading foundation chaired the advisory committee and recruited participants); the continual feedback from the project to the community; the community's commitment to participating in research; and a design that enhances cooperation between agencies rather than competition.[41] It also appears that the project is unusually well designed, comprehending much of the knowledge of "what works" (see the section "General Concepts of Prevention of Substance Abuse") and is strengthened by the on-site presence of professional staff for training, technical assistance, and support.

CAMBRIDGE AND SOMERVILLE PROGRAM
FOR ALCOHOL REHABILITATION (CASPAR)

A school and community program operated out of a community alcoholism treatment program since 1974, CASPAR has been widely replicated. It has been cited as a model by NIAAA and the National Diffusion Network of the Department of Education. It has six components:

1. School curriculum for grades K to 12 entitled "Decisions about Drinking" (10 sessions per year). Activities are designed to stimulate youth to explore their own ideas and attitudes about drinking in a nonjudgmental atmosphere. Emphasis is on participatory activities such as debates, role play, puzzles, and so on. Each grade level repeats concepts in progressively greater depth.
2. Alcohol education courses for teachers in grades K to 12, in 24- to 30-hour workshops.
3. School- and community-based alcohol education workshops for youth. Workshops during school hours for grades 2 to 6 are co-led by a trained school staff member and a CASPAR staff member. After school, general workshops for grades 7 to 12 meet at CASPAR's facility for education on alcohol; children from alcoholic families are offered special workshops.
4. Training workshops for peer leaders. Selected students are trained and then paid as staff adjuncts for assisting in surveying, conducting alcohol education classes, and conducting community outreach.
5. Training sessions and consultation for the staffs of local youth-serving agencies.
6. Community education to raise community awareness.

The Decisions about Drinking curriculum has been replicated in at least 3000 school systems around the country. The central CASPAR program has stimulated a number of research efforts, and in its report summarizes all of the efforts "rather than hand picking the success stories."[42] In general, the students in classrooms that implemented the curriculum showed improved attitudes and knowledge changes, and in the one school that measured use, a decrease in alcohol consumption. Involved teachers initiated more referrals to community agencies. The program claims that Decisions about Drinking "is the most thoroughly evaluated, most consistently proven school-based alcohol education program available in this country."

THE CLASS OF 1989 STUDY

Developed by Cheryl Perry and colleagues at the University of Minnesota as part of the Minnesota Heart Health Program, this unique study follows the health behaviors of adolescents in two communities—one with a specially designed health education program in the schools aimed at improving nutrition and physical well-being and reducing smoking and drug abuse.[43] Three programs were devised on the basis of proven prevention theory related to peer group norms, alternative healthy role models, and social skills training. Elected peer leaders were trained as instructors. In grade 7, participants were offered *Keep It Clean,* a six-session course highlighting the immediate negative consequences of smoking. In grade 8, students were involved in *Health Olympics,* a booster approach that included exchanging greeting cards on smoking and health with peers in other countries. The grade 9 curricula, *Shifting Gears,* included six sessions focused on social skills. Students critiqued media messages and created their own videotapes. At the same time as the school intervention took place, a communitywide smoking cessation program and diet and health awareness campaign were initiated. Techniques included mass media campaigns, risk factor screening, and community organization.

An extensive evaluation was conducted after five years, comparing the community with the educational interventions to the reference community. Smoking, marijuana, and alcohol use were substantially lower in the educated community. Perry et al. believe that this intervention demonstrates the viability and the desirability of changing school curricula to complement communitywide prevention efforts. Unfortunately, this research does not tell us whether the communitywide campaign in the absence of the school curricula interventions would have been equally successful in changing behaviors.

## Potentially Successful Models

A number of curricula and other kinds of programs have been identified that make a great deal of sense, but success has not been documented in terms of prevention of substance abuse.

PROJECT ALERT (ADOLESCENT LEARNING EXPERIENCES
IN RESISTANCE TRAINING)

Developed by the Rand Corporation and based on the social influence model, Project ALERT adapts methods proven successful in preventing cigarette use and applies them to other forms of substance abuse.[44] This curriculum for seventh and eighth graders includes 11 classroom sessions, 8 in year one and 3 booster sessions in the following year. It is currently being tested in 30 schools, using health educators in one group and adding teen leaders to another group.

SEATTLE SOCIAL DEVELOPMENT PROJECT

We have referred previously to the Social Development Model of Hawkins and his colleagues which addresses the *risk factors* for drug abuse and delinquency rather than the specific behaviors. It has been shown that antisocial behavior, academic failure, lack of commitment to school and, most important, weak social bonding to families and school place youngsters at high risk for substance abuse.

This experiment directed toward strengthening family bonding and parenting skills addresses key risk factors at developmentally appropriate times and has a longitudinal evaluation design.[45] The intervention starts with parents in grades 1 and 2 and a curriculum called "Catch 'em Being Good," which teaches parents how to recognize and reward positive behavior in their children. In grades 2 and 3, parents learn "How to Help Your Child in School." In grades 5 and 6, the curriculum is called "Preparing for the Drug Free Years" and consists of involving parents in a series of four workshops and in the use of a Family Activity Book containing alcohol and drug education materials. The program teaches specific decision-making and coping skills, assisting parents to communicate with their children. Home videotapes and workbooks for parents who don't want to come to the program are made available. In addition to the parent workshops, teachers are trained in better classroom management to promote positive classroom behavior in students. School liaison workers communicate with teachers, principals, parents, and students and help with family problems by trying to implement a plan for improvement.

Preliminary results of these efforts showed no effects on drug use (or delinquent behavior). However, there were significant effects on the *risk factors* for adolescent drug abuse in the early grades. Second-grade boys were less aggressive and girls were less self-destructive. Participants in grades 1 to 4 had more commitment to school, and by the end of seventh grade, higher achievement scores and higher educational expectations were reported, particularly in children who were initially low achievers. The participants were also less likely to be suspended from school.

SKILLS FOR ADOLESCENCE

An aggressively marketed program developed by Quest National Center (a nonprofit educational organization) for students in grades 6 to 8, this multimodal model has been endorsed by Lions International, the American Association of School Administrators, and the National PTA.[46] It is now being implemented in more than 500 school systems around the country. (A new positive youth development model—called Skills for Growing—for use in grades K to 5 is currently being introduced.) Communities are invited to participate by sending school and community teams made up of four to eight members to a Quest Training Institute, where they learn to implement this program. Local Lions Clubs raise money to subsidize the cost of training and materials. Adopting the curriculum involves an 80-lesson plan (a semester course), a student workbook and original textbook, a notebook for student reflections, and a teacher training manual. The curriculum includes training in decision-making skills, help in resisting peer pressures, work on developing self-confidence, lessons on communicating with parents and peers, instruction on dealing positively with rejection, loneliness, and fear, and methods for setting and achieving goals. Students are expected to perform community services as part of the curriculum. An advertisement describes the program as focusing on the skills to "say no" and providing the motivation to "say no." Parents are invited to four evening sessions at which they receive a book about adolescent development.

A search for published evaluations of Skills for Adolescence met with little success. In an unpublished summary of evaluations conducted to date, almost all of the reported outcomes were attitudinal.[47] One community reported less vandalism and absenteeism and lower suicide rates. Similar research has been conducted on the prior version of this program, Skills for Living, a more holistic approach to decision-making skills and career planning that has been implemented in more than 900 school systems under Quest guidance. One community showed improved school attendance, achievement, and behavior. No data could be located showing that either of the Quest curricula resulted in significantly lower use of substances, but there is evidence that the curricula have an impact on the indirect variables that place children at high risk. In any case, numerous testimonials from responsible officials cite Skills for Adolescence as "the best program of its kind we've seen." In response to the lack of documentation about the effects of Skills for Adolescence, Quest International has launched a major multisite evaluation.[48] Preliminary results suggest an improvement in school attendance by participants, but final results on drug usage are not yet available.

"HERE'S LOOKING AT YOU, TWO" (HLAY)

A K to 12 comprehensive school curriculum and teacher training program, HLAY was developed by health educators in Seattle, Washington, and is considered a model program by the NIAAA because of its breadth, the teacher training component, and "its ability to demonstrate impact through formal program evaluation."[49] The curriculum is self-contained at each grade level and designed to have a cumulative effect. It covers the following four areas:

1. Information: Learning about the physiological, psychological, and social implications of alcohol and drug use.
2. Analysis: Developing skills for identifying problems, understanding the consequences of choices, and acting on the basis of this information.
3. Coping: Developing skills for dealing with stress.
4. Self-Concept: Increasing self-awareness and recognizing feelings.

Teachers must agree to a 30-hour training program (four in-service days), and while the manual offers great flexibility, the program is typically taught in four sessions a year, integrated into health education or other courses.

HLAY in its earlier stages was evaluated in a careful 3-year study.[50] Hopkins et al. concluded that the curriculum did not work. There were a few short-term effects on knowledge and self-concept, but in the follow-up study, there were no effects on substance use and the effects on other variables disappeared. Although some teachers were found not to have fully implemented the curriculum, even in the classrooms where the teachers were committed, the children did no better. Hopkins and colleagues cite another unpublished evaluation of HLAY, Two (an improved version, whose description is given here) which also found no effects from the curriculum.[51] Kim conducted a recent evaluation of the effects of HLAY over time, tracking students from fifth through tenth grade according to whether or not they had received the program.[52] He found in both the short term (posttests) and long term (by tenth grade) that actual drinking patterns were not affected by taking the course, although there were some positive changes in knowledge and attitudes.

An abstract of a recent study conducted by Swisher et al. in Pennsylvania has been circulated by the company that markets the HLAY curriculum. The results from a pilot program in one school show significant reductions in use of substances following the implementation of the curriculum.[53] Follow-up discussions with the program developers revealed that the "model" curriculum had been revised and updated and is now called "Here's Looking at You, 2000."[54] The new approach is based on research on risk factors (Hawkins),[55] and the revised curriculum attempts to influence more generic coping skills and to heighten the degree of bonding between the child and the school.

NATURAL HELPERS PROGRAM

Developed and marketed by the Comprehensive Health Education Foundation, this program builds on an existing network within a school system. High schools select 25 students and 5 staff members to be trained as "skilled listeners" in a school setting, and these participants provide information, referral, or arrange for professional intervention for the rest of the school. Natural helpers receive 30 hours of training, starting with a three-day retreat; a school nurse or counselor acts as program coordinator. No evaluation data were located, but a survey of school personnel suggested that the students who were trained appeared to receive the most benefit from the program.

SCHOOL SPORTS STARS AS PEER LEADERS

In one community, football and basketball players were trained in peer leadership skills at a three-day retreat.[56] Three kinds of contracts were to be promoted in the school: individual social contracts in which students agreed not to use drugs, team contracts in which sports goals were specified, and academic contracts in which achievement goals were spelled out. These trained peer leaders set up programs in the earlier grades, including cross-age tutoring and mentoring. The program organizers reported that reductions in substance abuse and negative school behavior occurred as a result of the program, but no data were presented to support this claim.

THE STARR PROJECT (SUMNER TOBACCO AND ALCOHOL
RISK REDUCTION PROJECT)

A joint project of the county alcohol/drug prevention program and the Sumner, Washington, School District, this program is cited by NIAAA as *the* model for a communitywide intervention. It consists of the basic "Here's Looking at You, Two" curriculum in the schools, a parent education program (Social Development Model) in the community, and a peer support program (Natural Helpers). In addition, six community-based approaches include: (1) working with community agencies to develop substance-free alternative activities for recreation such as a Disco, a videogame center, a "battle of local rock bands"; (2) promoting contact with positive adult role models (called SuperSTARRS); (3) training school and community personnel; (4) training local barkeepers to reduce the availability of alcohol to teens; (5) use of mass media including a Newsletter to promote family health; and (6) working with law enforcement agencies to deal with drunken driving.

According to the program coordinator, no evaluation has been conducted, but the program is considered successful on the basis of "gut reactions to what makes sense."[57] A Fact Sheet does present project successes over four years in terms of program statistics, and the numbers and range of efforts are impressive.

## What Doesn't Work

The history of substance abuse prevention is replete with failed models. Every review starts with an inventory of programs that have not proven successful in lowering usage rates including: information or cognitive approaches alone; attitude change alone; self-esteem enhancement or affective methods; scaring tactics; and "Just Say No" media campaigns.[58] Many reasons for these failures have been documented. Some of the curricula cited in this chapter were offered in situations where the teachers did not have adequate training or the amount of time spent was too brief. The ineffectiveness of affective programs that attempted to raise self-esteem has been attributed to the lack of psychiatric training and requisite therapeutic skills among the teachers and counselors charged with implementation. One study reported that "teenagers are saying no to the just say no advertising campaign against drugs [preferring] commercials that emphasized the effects of drug use on students' family relationships or offered strategies for resisting offers of drugs."[59]

Single modal programs almost never produce positive results and may harm more than they help. An example of this kind of "one-shot" approach is "Save a Sweet Heart." The goal was to get high school students to sign a pledge (on Valentine's Day) that they wouldn't smoke. A peer committee was formed that organized the campaign through media, posters, school announcements, and so on. A three-year follow-up found that the intervention had little effect (more on boys than girls).[60] What is surprising is that, even after negative evaluations are published, the purveyors of the curriculum or the program continue to promote their wares. Often the rationale for not filing the program away under "failed efforts" is that the research was faulty or not long term.

In some instances, the theory and the applications both seem to be right on target, and yet the program has no effect. "Amazing Alternatives" was a well-designed curriculum for seventh-graders based on the best and latest scientific evidence. It addressed itself to the reasons that teens use drugs (e.g., to become more adult, to have fun, to be accepted, to solve personal problems) and combined social skills and alternatives approaches. Nine sessions were implemented by trained teachers and peer leaders. A two-year follow-up revealed no differences between experimental and control groups. Murray theorizes that the program "was simply not effective in altering the normal development of drug use in the adolescent population."[61] It is possible that the program focused too closely on alternatives and too little on skills training and rehearsal time. Nine sessions may have been too few.

According to a recent review, "There is a growing feeling among observers that classroom programs, to be effective, must also involve the family, community, and even society."[62] A panel of students told a recent White House Conference for a Drug Free America that, while "just saying no" might be the ultimate goal, the drug problem in schools and communities is bigger and more pervasive than overcoming peer pressure.[63]

## General Concepts of Prevention of Substance Abuse

The review of the *practice* of substance abuse prevention revealed an interesting cross-section of programs that were successful in slowing down the aggregate rates of initiation into substance use of various groups of children. A review of the literature indicated that the theoreticians (many of whom are also the practitioners) agree on a number of concepts about prevention:

1. The issue of substance abuse has to be approached in a broad social and environmental context. Interventions should be directed at the risk factors for drug abuse, such as lack of family support and poor school achievement, rather than at the specific behaviors.
2. Comprehensive communitywide prevention efforts must be simultaneously directed at all the major social influences and institutions: schools, parents, peers, role models, media, police, courts, businesses, vendors of cigarettes and alcohol, and youth-serving agencies.
3. No one intervention or program has been shown to independently bring down substance abuse rates over a long term.
4. School systems have become the central agency for substance abuse prevention programs. Early intervention is believed to be more effective, before the onset of the behaviors. Middle school grades (5 to 7) are often

mentioned as the time of implementation, prior to the traumatic transition to high school.

5. However, school-based substance abuse prevention requires a K to 12 approach, with age-appropriate components available. Whenever school prevention programs are offered, the students need follow-up and continuous attention. For educational components, this means "booster" programs in future years. For counseling, this means availability throughout the school years.

6. The marketing of substance abuse curricula has become a huge industry. It does not appear that purchasers demand evidence of effectiveness, since the impacts of some of the most utilized curricula are not supported by research.

7. Teacher training is a critical element in school-based programs. The best designed curriculum is ineffective in the hands of an inadequately prepared teacher. School systems must provide time and resources for in-service training and supervision.

8. Most successful programs have a full-time coordinator. Social workers, counselors, and other gatekeepers may require specialized training to work in substance abuse prevention. Health educators appear to be underutilized in the programs reported on.

9. Social skills (coping and resistance) training is the most promising of the new wave of school-based curricula. However, care must be taken not to get carried away with a "bandwagon" effect and ignore other approaches. The "state of the art" is incomplete; we do not know how effective these programs will be in the long term, nor do we know if they will be as effective with high-risk children as with others.

10. Peer-led programs appear to be more successful than teacher- or counselor-led efforts, but the research is far from definitive on this point. The most effective arrangement uses older students (senior high) as teachers and role models for younger students (junior high). It is probable that the peers who are selected and trained for these programs gain many benefits, but their influence on others is not clearly documented.

11. A focus on schools has shaped the configuration of the substance abuse prevention program. If one thinks about the range of prevention interventions that should make up the package at the community level, there seems to be a bifurcation between general school-based programs addressed to a whole class or school and targeted programs in a school or community addressed to high-risk children. Most of the work in this field (and probably most of the funds) appears to be directed toward the former, yet the intensity of the need is among the high-risk population.

12. Experience with preventing substance abuse among high-risk children suggests the need for individual attention and intensive counseling.

13. The model programs are aimed at preventing the use of "old drugs," particularly cigarette smoking; there are no models that specifically address the use of "crack." While AIDS prevention education is mandated in every state, there is no evidence as yet that these new curricula have had any impact on intravenous drug use.

Out of an enormous collection of programs directed toward preventing substance abuse, only a small proportion could be identified that actually demonstrated changes in behavior. Three types of programs emerged as the most successful: school-based social-skills curricula, school-based counseling services, and multicomponent collaborative community programs. The most effective curricula concentrate on teaching social and life skills, are peer taught, use adult role models, and include media analysis. The services focus on individual counseling by social workers, school liaison workers, and "skilled listeners." Often these staff members are brought in by outside agencies, who train and supervise them. School teams are used, often combining the outside staff with school-based psychologists, social workers, guidance counselors, and teachers. Principals are key individuals on the team, in collaborative community efforts, and in programs that attempt to change school climate. Successful models offer a wide range of training and education approaches within schools and in the community. Parental involvement is achieved through advisory committees, school teams, and parent education.

## Notes

1. Advocacy Institute, "Priority Strategies for Smoking Control: Public Policy Awareness Education and Initiation" (Report to the Kaiser Family Foundation, June 5, 1986).
2. E. Johnson, S. Amatetti, J. Funkhouser, and S. Johnson, "Theories and Models Supporting Prevention Approaches to Alcohol Problems Among Youth," *Public Health Reports* 103(1988): 578–85.
3. M. Goodstadt, "School-based Drug Education in North America: What is Wrong? What Can Be Done?" *Journal of School Health* 56(1986): 278–81.
4. J. Polich, P. Ellickson, P. Reuter, and J. Kahan, *Strategies for Controlling Adolescent Drug Use* (Santa Monica, Calif.: Rand Corporation, 1984).
5. M. Falco, "Preventing Abuse of Drugs, Alcohol and Tobacco by Adolescents" (Working Paper, Carnegie Council on Adolescent Development, June 1988).
6. N. Tobler, "Meta-Analysis of 143 Adolescent Drug Prevention Programs: Quantitative Outcome Results of Program Participants Compared To a Control or Comparison Group," *Journal of Drug Issues* 16(1986): 537–67; N. Tobler, "Adolescent Drug Prevention Programs Can Work: Research Findings" (Paper presented at Parsons/Sage Fall Institute, Albany, N.Y., 1987).
7. Tobler, "Meta-Analysis," p. 551. The mean effect size for all the drug prevention programs on all outcome measures is 30.

| Outcome | Effect Size Score |
|---|---|
| Total score | 30 |
| Knowledge | 52 |
| Attitudes | 18 |
| Use | 24 |
|   Cigarettes | 38 |
|   Alcohol | 17 |
|   Marijuana | 14 |
|   Hard drugs | 21 |
| Skills | 26 |
| Behavior (other than use) | 27 |

8. Tobler, "Meta-Analysis," p. 561.
9. Tobler, "Adolescent Drug Prevention Programs Can Work," Table 4.
10. R. Bangert-Drowns, "The Effects of School-Based Substance Abuse Education: A Meta-Analysis," *Journal of Drug Education* 18(1988): 243–64.
11. Ibid., p. 260.
12. Polich et al., *Strategies,* pp. 159–61.
13. D. Mueller and D. Higgins, *Funder's Guide Manual: A Guide to Prevention Programs in Human Services* (Saint Paul, Minn.: Wilder Foundation, 1988).
14. J. Hitchcock and T. Schelling, "Social Norms and Cigarette Smoking among Young People" (Unpublished paper, Institute for Study of Smoking Behavior and Policy, Cambridge, Mass., 1986).
15. C. Leukefeld and J. Moskowitz, "Conclusions and Recommendations," in T. Glynn, C. Leukefeld, and J. Ludford, eds., *Preventing Adolescent Drug Abuse: Intervention Strategies* (National Institute on Drug Abuse, USDHHS, NIDA Research Monograph, 47, 1985), pp. 250–55.
16. National Institute on Alcohol Abuse and Alcoholism (NIAAA), *Prevention Plus: Involving Schools, Parents, and the Community in Alcohol and Drug Education* (Washington, D.C.: Department of Health and Human Services, Public Health Service, 1984).
17. J. Berrueta-Clement, L. Schweinhart, W. Barnett, D. Weikart, and A. Epstein, *Changed Lives: The Effects of the Perry Preschool Program on Youths through Age 19* (Ypsilanti, Mich.: High Scope Educational Research Foundation, #8, 1984).
18. R. Price, E. Cowen, R. Lorion, and J. Ramos-McKay, eds., *14 Ounces of Prevention* (Washington, D.C.: American Psychological Association, 1988).
19. G. Botvin, "Substance Abuse Prevention Efforts: Recent Developments and Future Directions," *Journal of School Health* 56(1986): 369–74.
20. G. Botvin (Cornell University Medical College), "Infancy to Adolescence: Opportunities for Success," Hearing Summary, Select Committee on Children, Youth and Families, April 28, 1987.
21. S. Schinke and L. Gilchrist, "Preventing Substance Abuse with Children and Adolescents," *Journal of Consulting and Clinical Psychology* 53(1985): 596–602.
22. S. Schinke, M. Bebel, M. Orlandi, and G. Botvin, "Prevention Strategies for Vulnerable Pupils," *Urban Education* 22(1988): 510–19.
23. T. Dielman, J. Shope, P. Campanelli, and A. Butchart, "Elementary School-Based Prevention of Adolescent Alcohol Misuse," *Pediatrician* 14(1987): 70–76.
24. T. Dielman, J. Shope, and A. Butchart, "Adolescent Attitudes and Prevention Strategies" (Paper presented at the Annual Meeting of the American Public Health Association, Boston, November 16, 1988).
25. SMART is a social-psychological and behavioral-based experimental approach to drug abuse prevention developed by C. Anderson Johnson and associates at the University of Southern California. Components include: use of peer leaders, emphasis on immediate rather than long-term consequences of behavior, socratic method of instruction, modifying normative beliefs, resistance skills training, rehearsal, and public commitment not to smoke. This curricula is included in several of the interventions described here.
26. W. DeJong, "A Short Term Evaluation of Project DARE: Preliminary Indicators of Effectiveness," *Journal of Drug Education* 17(1987): 279–94.
27. One description of DARE contains the following. " 'This is our self-esteem balloon,' Officer says, smiling, 'When good things happen to us, our self-esteem grows. But when bad things happen, what happens to our self-esteem balloon?' He lets out the air making a loud rasp." W. DeJong, "Project DARE: Teaching Kids to Say "No" to

Drugs and Alcohol," *National Institute of Justice: Research in Action* (reprinted from NIJ Reports/SNI 196, March 1986).

28. National Diffusion Network, *Education Programs that Work,* 12th ed. (Longmont, Colo.: Sophris, 1986).

29. NIAAA, *Prevention Plus,* pp. 188–94.

30. "A Study of Westchester County's Student Assistance Programs Participants' Alcohol and Drug Use Prior to and after Counseling During School Year 1982–83—Summary" (unpublished). Provided by E. Morehouse, Director, SAP.

31. D. Moberg, "Evaluation Results for a Student Assistance Program" (Paper presented at the Annual Meeting of the American Public Health Association, Boston, November 14, 1988).

32. D. Flood and E. Morehouse, "The Principal's Role in Preventing and Reducing Student Substance Abuse," *NASSP Bulletin* (February 1986): 10–15.

33. S. Lovick and R. Stern, *School-Based Clinics: 1988 Update* (Washington, D.C.: Center for Population Options, 1988).

34. G. Kitzi, Presentation at Conference on School-Based Clinics, Denver, 1986.

35. U.S. Department of Education, *The School Team Approach,* Alcohol and Drug Education Program, August 1984.

36. J. Scheurich and G. Davis, "The Wichita, Kansas Public Schools' Comprehensive Substance Abuse Prevention Program," in *Sharing Knowledge for Action: Proceedings of the First National Conference on Alcohol and Drug Abuse Prevention* (Department of Health and Human Services, Public Health Service, 1986): 28–29.

37. "Alcohol and Substance Abuse Prevention and Treatment Programs," The Door, undated report.

38. The National Network of Runaway and Youth Services, Inc., *To Whom Do They Belong?* (Washington, D.C.: The National Network of Runaway and Youth Services, July 1985).

39. M. Pentz, C. Cormack, B. Flay, W. Hansen, and C. Johnson, "Balancing Program and Research Integrity in Community Drug Abuse Prevention: Project STAR Approach," *Journal of School Health* 56(1986): 389–93.

40. M. Pentz, J. Dwyer, D. MacKinnon, B. Flay, W. Hansen, E. Yang, and C. Johnson, "A Multi-Community Trial for Primary Prevention of Adolescent Drug Abuse: Effects on Drug Use Prevalence," *Journal of the American Medical Association* 261(1989): 3259–66.

41. Midwestern Prevention Project, Workshop Handout, undated.

42. "Decisions About Drinking: The CASPAR Alcohol Education Program" (Report resubmitted to The Joint Dissemination Review Panel, February 1987). Made available to author by R. Davis, Director.

43. C. Perry, M. Hearn, D. Murray, and K. Klepp, "The Etiology and Prevention of Adolescent Alcohol and Drug Abuse" (Unpublished paper, University of Minnesota, 1988).

44. P. Ellickson, *Limiting Nonresponse in Longitudinal Research: Three Strategies for School-Based Studies* (Santa Monica, Calif.: Rand Corporation, March 1989).

45. D. Hawkins and R. Catalano, "The Seattle Social Development Project: Progress Report on a Longitudinal Prevention Study" (Paper presented at the National Institute on Drug Abuse, Science Press Seminar, Washington, D.C., March 1987).

46. E. Gerler, "Skills for Adolescents: A New Program for Young Teens," *Phi Delta Kappan* (February 1986): 436–39.

47. Listing of evaluations on Skills for Living and Skills for Adolescence provided by Quest National Center, Columbus, Ohio, 1988.

48. Quest International, "Evaluation Report," December 7, 1988.
49. NIAAA, *Prevention Plus,* pp. 2–15.
50. R. Hopkins, A. Mauss, K. Kearney, and R. Weisheit, "Comprehensive Evaluation of a Model Alcohol Education Curriculum," *Journal of Studies on Alcohol* 49(1988): 38–49.
51. Cited by Hopkins et al. from J. Boyce, "All Things Considered . . . A Summary of the Evaluation of the 'Here's Looking at You, Two' Drug and Alcohol Abuse Prevention Curriculum" (Seattle, Wash.: Educational Service District No. 121, September 1984).
52. S. Kim, "A Short- and Long-Term Evaluation of Here's Looking at You Alcohol Education Program," *Journal of Drug Education* 18(1988): 235–42.
53. J. Swisher, C. Nesselroade, and C. Tatanish, "Here's Looking at You, Two Is Looking Good: An Experimental Analysis" (Unpublished abstract, undated).
54. M. Starkman, Roberts, Fitzmahan and Associates, personal communication, 1987.
55. D. Hawkins and R. Catalano, "Risk-Focused Prevention: From Research to Practical Strategies," *OSAP High Risk Youth Initiative* 2(1989): 2–4.
56. G. Edwards, "NE Regional Training Center," in *Sharing Knowledge for Action,* p. 68.
57. N. Frausto, personal communication, 1987. Also STARR Project Factsheet, undated.
58. See, for example, U.S. Government Accounting Office, *Drug Abuse Prevention: Further Efforts Needed to Identify Programs that Work* (Washington, D.C.: U.S. Government Accounting Office, GAO/HRD 88–26, 1988).
59. Health column, *Education Week,* June 24, 1987, 6.
60. G. Bennett, D. Austin, and R. Janizewski, "Save a Sweet Heart: A Smoking Intervention in Senior High School" (Unpublished paper, American Heart Association, Wisconsin affiliate, undated).
61. D. Murray, "Final Report: Tailoring Drug Abuse Prevention to the School Setting" (Washington, D.C.: National Institute on Drug Abuse, 1987).
62. Art Levine, "Drug Education Gets an F," *U.S. News & World Report,* October 13, 1986, 63.
63. *Leadership News* (American Association of School Administrators) (March 15, 1988), 5.

# 11

## Prevention of Adolescent Pregnancy

The literature on prevention of adolescent pregnancy has a somewhat different tone than the two sets of literature we have just reviewed on delinquency and substance abuse prevention. While those fields were dominated by psychiatric studies (delinquency) and psychologically oriented school-based interventions (substance abuse), the discussion of teen pregnancy tends to focus much more on broader sociological and moral issues. During the past decade, a great deal has been said in the press and on TV specials about preventing teen pregnancy; the subject has been aired at endless conferences and in Congressional Committee hearings.[1] A number of books have been published on the subject, typically collections of previously published articles or chapters provided by authorities.[2] In this literature, certain strategies appear to have been accepted among most of the commentators: that the major focus of prevention should be sex education in the schools and access to contraceptive methods, with little mention of evaluation of these approaches.[3]

It would be a gross overstatement to imply that there is a consensus in the United States about what to do about adolescent pregnancy. As in every other facet of American life, there is a significant difference between "liberals" and "conservatives" about appropriate interventions. The conservatives take the position that only abstention will solve the problem, and it is up to families to produce the moral climate necessary to help their children maintain their virginity until marriage. Mosbacher, in a report for the Family Research Council of America, calls for molding children to "reflect virtue, self-control, and self-sacrifice in services to others."[4]

Clearly, when sex enters the scene, the situation becomes complicated. Scholars may be frightened away. Universities do not have departments and big names associated with the evaluation of pregnancy prevention interventions. There is, however, extensive "population research," focusing on demographic studies of changes in vital rates, with some work on the determinants and consequences of adolescent pregnancy (see Chapter 5). Evaluations of family planning programs are mostly being conducted overseas in developing countries.

This lack of attention to evaluation was highlighted in a recent report (1987) by the National Academy of Sciences. After two years of intensive study, an expert Panel on Adolescent Pregnancy and Childbearing observed a significant gap between what people believed to be solutions to the problems of adolescent pregnancy and the "state-of-the-art" of evaluation of the effectiveness of these interventions.[5] Nevertheless, they concluded that adequate knowledge existed on which to base recommendations. Their report stated "because there is so little evidence of the effectiveness of the other strategies for prevention, the panel believes that the major strategy for reducing early unintended pregnancy must be the encouragement of diligent contraceptive use by all sexually active teenagers."[6] The panel also concluded that, even though substantive proof of "what works" is lacking, two other strategies should be pursued: delaying the initiation of sexual intercourse and enhancing "life options" for teenagers.

The concept of "life options" has been proposed in light of the seeming intractability of teen pregnancy rates, despite prolonged efforts to expand sex education and contraceptive services.[7] The association between social disadvantage and teen parenthood (documented in Chapter 5) gives evidence that changes in the social environment are a necessary precondition to opening the opportunity structure for deprived youngsters and giving them a reason for wanting to prevent early childbearing. To use Schorr's words to describe the impact of this perception of the teen pregnancy problem:

> Across a wide ideological spectrum, there is a new commitment to finding ways to combat early childbearing that go beyond making contraception more available. The rhetoric and action implied by this new commitment . . . have been given new life and new meaning by civil rights activists, child advocates, social reformers, and professionals who work directly with teenagers.[8]

Marion Wright Edelman, president of the Childrens' Defense Fund, has been frequently quoted: "The best contraceptive is a real future."[9]

To produce scientific evidence about the effectiveness of an intervention in the pregnancy prevention field, it is necessary to measure changes in adolescent pregnancy rates and attribute those changes to some program, or even a specific curriculum or type of counseling, offered by a specific agency.[10] While information about births is relatively easy to collect in a given population, abortion rates are elusive because of underreporting. Few of the available studies of programs have included comparable experimental and control groups; in some instances, the results were contaminated because control group members gained access to services during the study period.[11] The complexity of evaluation is even further compounded by the demands of testing the effects of life options interventions. In light of these methodological shortcomings, our understanding of "what works" to prevent pregnancy must be informed by using "surrogate" measures of effectiveness, such as delay in the initiation of sexual activity and the use of contraception at initial intercourse and thereafter. Table 11.1 shows the measures used

TABLE 11.1. Measures of Success in Prevention of Adolescent Pregnancy

| Behavior to Prevent | Measures of Success | Sources of Data |
|---|---|---|
| Early initial intercourse | Percent not sexually active | Self-report survey |
| Unprotected intercourse | Percent using method of contraception | Self-report survey |
| Unintentional pregnancy | Reduction in unintended pregnancy abortion | Self-report survey Vital statistics |
| Early childbearing | Reduction in early births | Self-report survey Vital statistics |

for evaluating pregnancy prevention programs and the sources of data. As in the other fields, much of our knowledge derives from self-reported behavior. Many questions have arisen about the reliability of self-reports on sexual activity. Are the figures for males overestimates and for females underestimates? Most analysts believe that their questionnaires are designed to elicit valid responses.

## Successful Models

### *Early Childhood and Family Interventions*

As we have seen in the previous chapters on prevention programs, research during the past 20 years on the effects of early childhood education has yielded a number of positive outcomes experienced by children who attended Head Start type programs: better grades, less failure, higher probability of completing high school and going on to higher education, reduction in welfare dependence, and improvement in students' self-confidence and self-esteem.[12] It seems like a reasonable assumption that Head Start participation because of its direct effect on school achievement would indirectly lower the probability of teen parenthood for high-risk children. In fact, the Perry Preschool participants had significantly lower pregnancy rates at age 19 (64 per 1000) than the control group (117 per 1000); however, this finding was based on a very small sample of females ($n = 49$).[13] Only one other early childhood education program has reported data on pregnancies. The Early Training Program in Murfreesboro, Tennessee, found no effect on pregnancy rates, but it did find that among those who attended the early training program and became childbearers, 88 percent completed high school compared with only 30 percent who had not attended preschool.[14]

The Office of Adolescent Pregnancy is strongly committed to the theory that improved parent-child communication will help children improve their decision-making skills and delay the initiation of intercourse. A number of family communication programs have been initiated with OAPP grants, but no models have been identified with evaluation data.

*School-Based Interventions*

CURRICULA

It has been well documented that sex education courses improve knowledge, but there is little conclusive proof that behavior is influenced by taking courses. The rate of sexual activity does not appear to change as a result of information, nor does the efficacy of contraceptive use.[15] There is no evidence that pregnancies have been prevented as an outcome of any specific sex education curriculum.[16] Sex educators have responded to these disappointing research results by developing and incorporating new approaches into their courses, such as decision-making skills and life planning.[17]

*Life Skills.*    Schinke and Gilchrist have used their Life Skills Counseling methodology to teach problem solving and assertiveness skills as they are related to sexual behavior.[18] Their "cognitive–behavioral group work" approach involves a four-step process:

1. Access to information on which to base decisions and behavior.
2. Accurate perception, comprehension, and storing of this information, using rehearsal, quizzes, and social reinforcement.
3. Personalizing and using the information in making effective decisions.
4. Behavioral skills, to implement these decisions in social situations, and role playing.

For a very small sample, they were able to show improved knowledge, more positive attitudes toward family planning, and better use of contraception. Compared with a control group, participants had fewer incidences of unprotected intercourse a year later. Schinke et al. provide an important insight into a significant component of successful interventions: "One young man wanted to get hold of reliable birth control. He and his partner settled on condoms and foam and decided he would pick them up within the week. Mission accomplished, he called in a report and brought his purchases to the next group."[19] Cognitive changes were translated into direct action.

*Life Planning.*    This approach combines materials on vocational guidance with exercises designed to lead to less risk-taking behavior and more rational decisions in school, social, and family settings. Extensive worksheets produce personalized planning guides for careers, based on course materials, research, interviews, and individual preferences. Several curricula are available to schools and community groups including Life Planning Education, which was developed by the Center for Population Options in Washington,[20] and Choices, developed by the Girls' Clubs of Santa Barbara, California.[21] A high degree of student and teacher satisfaction has been reported by users of these materials; research on the impact on behavioral outcomes is under way, but not complete.

*Life Skills and Opportunities (LSO).*    A component of a comprehensive school remediation Summer Training and Education Program (STEP), LSO was designed and implemented by Public/Private Ventures (PPV) in five urban communities (and currently is being replicated in many more).[22] PPV is a nonprofit research and program development agency in the area of youth services. Other STEP components include two summers of school remediation and job placement, as well as one winter of school remediation and personal counseling (see Chapter 12). The Life Planning Education curriculum has been revised specifically for a low-income, largely minority population. The focus is on the world of work and issues of sexual and reproductive development, feelings, and behaviors. An informational visit to a clinic is part of the curriculum. Evaluation results from the use of the LSO curriculum show significant gains in knowledge of contraception and sexuality. Participants were more likely to use contraceptives if they were sexually active than youth in the control group, but the differences were not large enough to achieve statistical significance in a follow-up survey. PPV believes that the results of the demonstration project confirm the critical need for increased and intensive interventions such as LSO, aimed at enhancing sexual responsibility among high-risk youth, along with educational enrichment and job training.

*George Mason High School, Falls Church, Virginia.*    The Falls Church school system offers a family life and sex education program to all sixth to ninth and eleventh and twelfth graders.[23] Mary Lee Tatum, a trained sex educator who created much of this course, is employed full time by the school district to teach it. As the nation's most respected "hands-on" sex educator, she also trains teachers in the Virginia school system and in many other parts of the country.

The sixth-grade component, taught by classroom teachers, is included as part of the general Family Life and Health Education course and focuses on puberty and social relations. The core course taught by Tatum is divided up over seventh, eighth, and ninth grades as part of the Life Science curriculum and students receive one credit in general science. It includes communication and problem-solving skills; basic biology and genetics; fetal development, childbirth, and the reproductive system; and psychological development. For the last two years of high school, a quarter-long elective Seminar in Human Sexuality is offered that includes a history of sexual attitudes, the role of the family, more on psychosexual development, decisions about life goals, and cultural and religious views on gender, contraception, and abortion.

These courses have received high ratings from students, their parents, and the school administration. One measure of satisfaction has been that 100 percent of the student body elect to take all of the courses offered. An evaluation of the ninth-grade course indicated significant success in the areas of knowledge, communication, and decision making; the twelfth-grade seminar students were shown to be much better users of contraception.[24] These courses have the strong support of the Family Life and Sex Education Council, appointed by the School Board to review the family life program.

*Saying No Programs.*    The prototypical "Saying No" to sexual intercourse program, developed by Marion Howard at Emory University, was designed to provide eighth-grade youth with information and decision-making skills to help them resist peer pressure. In the ten-session Postponing Sexual Involvement curriculum, human sexuality issues are covered by nurses and counselors while the skill-building component is presented by older teen leaders.[25] Preliminary evaluation found that only 5 percent of low-income eighth-grade girls had initiated sex by the end of the school year compared with 15 percent who did not take the course.[26] No long-term effects have been reported.

SPECIAL SERVICES AND COUNSELING

*Fifth Ward Enrichment Program.* A school-based program focused on teaching sexual responsibility to 11- to 13-year-old-boys has been organized as part of the Urban Affairs Corporation, a school-based clinic program in Houston, Texas. Created and operated by Ernest McMillan, an all-male staff works with high-risk youth using a system of positive reinforcement, intensive counseling, daily tutoring sessions, field trips, life skills workshops, and academic guidance. The program, which includes the full services of the health center, functions in the summer as well as during the school year. Preliminary evaluation suggests that the participants are doing better in school and display a lower incidence of conduct disorder than nonparticipants.[27] Staff report increased recognition among the boys that "they won't have children if they can't support them."

*Teen Outreach Project.* Started by the Junior League of St. Louis, this after-school program is being replicated in 75 schools around the country. The American Association of School Administrators is now a co-sponsor. The model includes group classroom and counseling sessions and weekly volunteer community service assignments. Small group discussions are held using a specially developed curriculum, which emphasizes life planning and goal setting. Most participants are aged 14 to 16 in grades 9 and 10.

According to a three-year evaluation, young people in Teen Outreach had fewer pregnancies, fewer live births, and were less likely to fail, drop out of school, or get suspended than comparison students.[28] (The evaluation is not based on random selection, and the comparison group is largely made up of friends of participants.) An analysis of each year of data substantiates these impacts on students who start out with many markers of high risk (more than half had failed a grade in the previous year). The success of the program is attributed to measurable inputs, such as number of volunteer hours worked and attendance rates, as well as intangibles, such as the growth in self-esteem and self-awareness that the program seeks to develop.

*Teen Choice.* A pregnancy prevention/sex education program operated by Inwood House (a voluntary social service agency) in the New York City public schools uses specially trained professional social workers who staff three components of the program: small groups, individual counseling (and referral), and classroom dialogues.[29] The small groups meet once a week for a semester and cover sexuality issues, birth control, values clarification, peer pressure, among other things. The workers are assigned to a school and are on site 3 to 5 days per week in seven schools. The most common problems that arise in counseling sessions include pregnancy scares (25 percent of cases), birth control, relationship and family issues, and general mental health evaluation.

A recent evaluation showed that Teen Choice students were generally at high risk of pregnancy.[30] In addition to positive changes in knowledge and attitudes, participants were shown to have significantly improved their use of contraception following their group experiences and maintained these practices over time. Strengths of the program cited by the evaluators included that the program was school based and thus convenient, students are respected and although abstention is encouraged, contraceptive use is recommended for those who choose not to abstain.

SCHOOL-BASED CLINICS

The search for more effective interventions to prevent pregnancy has led to the promulgation of comprehensive school-based health clinics. Early reports from a school-based program in St. Paul, Minnesota, first drew attention to the potential of this model for preventing pregnancy.[31] Currently, the St. Paul School Health Program, operated by Healthstart, Inc., provides primary and preventive services during school hours in four public schools; over 70 percent of the student body is enrolled in the clinics.[32] Services include athletic physicals, emergency care, immunizations, mental health, nutrition, and social work counseling as well as family planning. Healthstart reports that birth rates in the schools have dropped from 79 per 1000 in 1972–73 to 35 per 1000 in 1985–86. We do not know how this significant decrease compares with either a control group or the population as a whole in that area, nor do we have any information about abortion rates.

The staff attribute the success of their program to the following factors:

1. Clinics are accessible, available, and confidential.
2. The program is "adolescent-focused"; no problem is too minor to be taken seriously by the staff.
3. A unique combination exists between education in the classroom and clinic services (staff provide sex education in the school).
4. Because the clinic has a primary-care focus, no stigma is attached to preventive reproductive health services.
5. Staff is linked to school and community through school nurses, faculty meetings, and parent advisory meetings.
6. One individual in each clinic is always there, known to students and approachable.

The effect of school-based clinics on the reduction in birth rates has been reported by several other programs, including the West Dallas Youth Clinic and the Muskegon, Michigan, school-based program. Mention of similar findings in Jackson, Mississippi, and rural Colorado and North Carolina have not been supported with documentation.

Numerous studies of the impacts of school-based clinics are now under way, but the results at this stage are preliminary. Controlled studies that encompass changes in pregnancy rates are difficult to conduct in every setting; pregnant girls may drop out of school and be hard to track, or they may stay in school and have abortions that are unknown to the staff. One problem with school-based clinics is the small number of users of the family planning services component (10 to 20 percent), which reduces the effect in aggregate statistics.[33]

Research on the question of the effect of clinics on the incidence of sexual activity among the students has yielded no evidence that the rates increase after the clinic opens. A two-year follow-up survey in Kansas City revealed almost no change in reported sexual behavior.[34] Following the three-year school-clinic demonstration project in Baltimore (see the next section, Self-Center), Zabin et al. found a postponement of first intercourse that averaged seven months among program participants.[35] A survey of students in a school that is part of the Houston school-based clinic program showed that school clinic attendance was an important determinant of the frequency of contraceptive use.[36] Clinic users were more than twice as likely to use contraception every time they had sex as compared with those who had not been to the clinic, and they were less than half as likely never to use contraception.

Among students who were already sexually active, clinic patients in Kansas City showed higher rates of contraceptive use than nonpatients as well as a striking increase in use of condoms among males. In Baltimore, younger female students and males in the experimental schools were much more likely to use birth control than those in the control schools. And in St. Paul, female contraceptive users had an extremely high rate of continuation; 91 percent were still using the method (mostly the pill) after a year, and 78 percent after two years of use.[37] (Free-standing family planning clinics report a 12-month program dropout rate of close to 50 percent.[38])

These preliminary evaluation and monitoring results produce evidence of heavy use of clinics for a wide range of adolescent health needs. There is no evidence that making contraception available through school clinics increases the likelihood of early sexual activity. Among students who are sexually active, those who obtain birth control services appear to improve their use of contraception. The evidence that all of these factors lower pregnancy or birth rates is still inconclusive. Experience to date suggests that evaluation of the impacts of school-based programs on pregnancy rates presents large methodological problems. It is difficult to conduct surveys in schools, random assignment is not possible, students are a highly mobile population, and abortion is underreported.

*Self Center.*   One program that demonstrated reductions in pregnancy combined sex and contraceptive education, as well as individual and group counseling in the schools, along with family planning services in a nearby clinic site.[39] The staff, a social worker and a nurse practitioner, worked in both places. Considerable effort was made to involve parents, but none showed up for informational meetings. Research had a high priority. At the end of the three-year demonstration period, pregnancies among students in the experimental schools decreased 26 percent compared with a substantial increase in the control schools (from 32 to 51 percent). The evaluation also showed a significant postponement of first intercourse and very high utilization of the clinic and of contraceptives, especially among junior high school students. Zabin and her colleagues attribute the success of the program to the amount of attention the students received from the staff and the clinic.

## Community-Based Programs

### FAMILY PLANNING CLINICS

The National Academy of Sciences Panel was persuaded by the survey research base that established the connection between the use of contraception and the nonoccurrence of unintended childbearing to teenage females.[40] Data from the 1979 Johns Hopkins Survey of Young Women showed that only 7 percent of those sexually active teens who always used a medical method had experienced a pre-marital pregnancy compared with 62 percent of those who had never used a method.[41]

Family planning clinics are the primary sites used by 1.5 million teenagers annually to obtain medically prescribed contraception. However, no controlled studies have been conducted that compare matched samples of clinic users with nonusers to demonstrate the efficacy of a specific program model. Repeated studies of family planning services for teenagers have concluded that convenience, confidentiality, and lack of "hassle" are important predictors of utilization, while special teen sessions and "rap groups" are appealing to only very young clients. And yet, in many clinics half of the patients fail to make a return visit. Continuation on a method (typically the pill) is often related to satisfaction with the method.[42]

Nathanson and Becker have shown that in those clinics where teenage patients expect that the nurses will give them "authoritative guidance" about contraceptive methods, and where nurses expect to give that kind of service, contraceptive continuation rates were significantly greater.[43] The authors cite this style of staff-patient interaction as evidence that young women initiating sexual activity may want and need more direct personal guidance about contraception than they currently receive.

### MANTALK

This program for teen males, operated by the County Health Department in Winston-Salem, North Carolina, at two community sites and two alternative schools took as its goals to promote positive life-styles and to encourage responsible sexual decision making.[44] Skills training is offered in career development, parenting, academic goal achievement, self-esteem, and job marketing. Issues such as sexism and racism are addressed, and adult male volunteers are used to facilitate discussions at meetings, share their life experiences with the boys, and arrange cultural and social activities. Community support is provided through the donation of tickets for local events, provision of transportation, arrangement of on site job visits, and the promotion of the program in the local media. Program evaluation based on over 200 males shows an increase in knowledge and awareness, improved contraceptive use, and no known cases of paternity. In the school-based programs, the participants had improved attention and grades. The staff believe that the programs in the alternative schools (one a middle and the other a high school) were more effective because participation was facilitated and outreach and recruitment unnecessary.

MULTICOMPONENT/MULTIAGENCY PROGRAMS

*School/Community Program for Sexual Risk Reduction among Teens, South Carolina.*[45]    This demonstration project in a poor, rural school district involves various segments of the community in a comprehensive adolescent pregnancy prevention program. It is located in a portion of one county with comparison populations in the other half of the county and three similar counties. The program was initiated in 1982 by staff from the School of Public Health of the University of South Carolina. The hypothesis to be tested was whether the high pregnancy rates could be reduced following an intensive saturation of the community with large quantities of pregnancy–prevention messages. Prior to implementing programs, a community/school assessment of needs and resources was undertaken and advisory groups organized.

The project started out with two major objectives: to delay the initiation of sexual intercourse and to promote the use of consistent contraception. It was recognized that such factors as decision-making skills, interpersonal communications, self-esteem, and knowledge of reproduction and contraception had to be incorporated into all approaches. The first step was to educate the adults in the target community. School district teachers were provided with tuition-free graduate level courses related to sex education, and these trained teachers, assisted by project staff, then implemented K through 12 sex education in integrated courses (e.g., units of sex education were added to biology, science, social studies, and other courses). At the same time, clergy, church leaders, and parents were invited to attend minicourses (10 hours) that would help them improve their skills as parents and role models for the youth in the community. Some of the churches initiated appropriate classes and special events.

Program staff utilized local media and a speaker's bureau to promote messages about pregnancy prevention. Community awareness activities focused on National Family Sexuality Education Week. Attention was given to broad-based health issues, beyond those that were sex related, with an emphasis on problem solving, risk taking, and personal responsibility.

After several years, pregnancy rates in the school district appeared to drop significantly, even when compared with neighboring areas. The estimated pregnancy rates for 14- to 17-year-olds in the target area dropped from 61 to 25 per 1000 during the project period (1981–85), while in comparison areas, the rates rose from 35 or higher to around 50 per 1000. The researchers attribute success to the involvement of the community at large, including parents, teachers, and clergy. This model is heavily influenced by the availability of professional staff from a school of public health and funds from outside the community.

*Planned Parenthood of East Central Georgia, Jasper County, South Carolina.*[46] The Planned Parenthood agency received a foundation grant in 1985 to develop a comprehensive pregnancy prevention program in a poor rural county in South Carolina. The intervention began with the development of a K through 12 health education curriculum and an advisory committee of parents, teachers, and local agency representatives. The model implemented focused on life skills, including health, nutrition, substance abuse, and decision making.

During the second phase of the program, teen peer counselors were trained to work in junior and senior high schools. In 1987, the third phase of the program initiated a Family Life Center on the school grounds. Services include health education, referral, treatment, vocational training and job placement, and support group services for troubled teens. The County Departments of Health, Social Services, and Youth Services participate along with a private nonprofit youth-serving agency. Preliminary data suggest that pregnancy rates for 14- to 17-year-olds (both births and abortions) decreased from 54 to 42 per 1000, while in a similar county with no services they increased from 62 to 75 per 1000.

*IMPACT 88: Dallas's Countywide Plan for Reducing Teen Pregnancy.*[47] This broad community intervention grew out of earlier work by the Community Council of Greater Dallas's Coalition on Responsible Parenthood and Adolescent Sexuality (CORPAS). With a strong push from the mayor's wife, a new Task Force on Adolescent Health and School Age Pregnancy brought together in 1984 some 175 representatives from business, government, media, religious organizations, civic groups, health and social services, and the teen population (including different racial, ethnic, and socioeconomic groups). Nine subcommittees were formed to study the problem from various viewpoints:

1. Adolescent and Family Organizations: compiled a list of all services for adolescents and identified gaps and needs.
2. Business: addressed the issue of economic impact of teen parenthood; developed child-care strategy and a plan to meet employment needs.
3. Education: increased awareness regarding needs.
4. Community Service Organizations: surveyed volunteer groups about services and strategy to match agencies with adolescent needs.
5. Media: developed public awareness campaign to inform the community about the problems of teen pregnancy.
6. Medical: compiled a list of health services for adolescents and identified gaps.
7. Religious: focused on ways to reach adolescents and their families through church and to increase spiritual education relative to adolescent sexuality.
8. Political and Legislative: gathered information on current legislation and made plans to increase awareness of legislators on issues.
9. Funding: explored ways to secure funding for implementing the plan.

These committees worked for almost a year and drafted a 40-page comprehensive three-year IMPACT 88 Plan outlining eight areas for concerted attention: recreation, health education and care, housing for teen parents, a countywide community awareness campaign, family and peer support systems, employment opportunities for youth, sex education, and child care for teen parents.[48] A detailed statistical report documenting the problem of adolescent pregnancy in Dallas was simultaneously released by CORPAS. The IMPACT 88 Plan was endorsed by 36 local organizations, and one group (Southwest Osteopathic Physicians) funded the establishment of an IMPACT office at the Community Council.

Many activities have resulted in Dallas stemming from this comprehensive fact-finding and planning process: a large-scale countywide public information and awareness campaign; the establishment of a TEENLINE information and referral system; creation of a more centralized referral and clearinghouse office; development of an interagency case-management system for teen moms; establishment of a voucher program for providing child care; increased programming on sex education in some of the school districts and in the community; United Way funding for pregnancy prevention services; establishment of volunteer mentors and summer youth employment programs for teen parents; among other activities.

Sandoval attributes the success of the project to making enough room in the process for people with different viewpoints and ensuring that varied approaches were taken at the community level to address the overall problem.[49] He also points to the importance of the data base that allowed the community to gain understanding that teen pregnancy was not only a problem among minorities but affected all groups. Another obstacle to overcome was the perception that teen parent programs might make life too easy; videotapes of the plight of these young people were used to document their critical needs.

No formal evaluation has been conducted of the statistical effects of this project. However, teen birth rates in the Dallas area have decreased and the IMPACT project believes that it had some influence here. Given the breadth of the approach, it is hard to imagine that it had no impact. The three-year planning cycle is now completed and the project is no longer funded. However, CORPAS continues to function as previously and the central office will now be moved to a joint project of the YMCA and the YWCA.

An important outgrowth of IMPACT 88 has been the development of a model Youth Impact Center, a neighborhood-based, multiservice program in a high-risk area. The design of the model center builds on the collective knowledge gained from the planning experience of the program. At least 16 public and nonprofit health, social, and youth-serving agencies have signed on to co-locate services at the center where case management, educational, and social services will be offered and referral coordinated. Target youth will be involved in center management as part of the decision-making training.

PROGRAMS WITH MULTIPLE GOALS

Programs that include educational enhancement, job preparation, *and* family planning are being initiated in response to the more general objective of helping high-risk youth. These approaches view early childbearing as only one symptom of disadvantage and assume that more comprehensive treatments are necessary to help children achieve their educational, career, and ultimately, family goals.

*The Children's Aid Society Adolescent Pregnancy Prevention Program.* A program that encompasses a multiple-goal approach has recently been initiated by Michael Carrera in New York City and the Children's Aid Society as the lead agency.[50] There are eight "Primary Prevention Programmatic Dimensions":

1. On site primary health services: Complete physical exams, contraceptive counseling, and prescriptions; weekly follow-up counseling of contraceptive patients.
2. Self-esteem enhancement through the performing arts: Weekly workshops with parents and teens led by professionals from the National Black Theater. Issues include conflict resolution, school experiences, job problems, family roles, gender roles, and racism.
3. Skills training in individual sports: Squash, tennis, golf, and swimming— skills that emphasize self-discipline, self-control, and a precise mastery.
4. Academic assessment and homework help program: Complete educational needs assessment and prescriptions for individual and group tutorials, given by volunteers and educational experts.
5. College admission program: Every teen and parent participant receives a certificate at the beginning of the program guaranteeing a place as a freshman at Hunter College with all costs subsidized, following teen pregnancy prevention program and graduation from high school.
6. Family life and sex education unit: A 15-week program, with separate units for parents and teens, that present a holistic view of sexuality, using readings, films, role playing, and lectures.
7. Job club and career awareness program: Weekly session conducted by employment specialists to explore career possibilities, secure a social security card, complete working papers, and apply for jobs. Each teen secures a paid job or takes part in an Entrepreneurial Apprenticeship Program. Each participant opens a bank account and contributes to it monthly.
8. Individual counseling: The focus is on decision making, family, peer, and school issues. Serious problems are handled by clinical staff or referred to the Children's Aid Society mental health program.

Only descriptive evaluation results are available to date. Since the program began five years ago, of 250 clients, five girls have become pregnant and, according to the staff, one of the boys has fathered a child. Fewer than 10 percent of the participants have dropped out of school, a much lower rate than in the Harlem community where the program is located. A number of graduates are enrolled at Hunter College (8 teens and 7 parents).

*Other Comprehensive Programs.* There are numerous interesting and innovative comprehensive youth-serving programs that include pregnancy prevention among their goals. Multiservice centers such as the Door, the Hub (both in New York City), Aunt Martha's (5 centers and 2 group homes in the Chicago area), and the Bridge (in Boston) provide medical, educational, social, and recreational services. The Summer Training and Educational Program (STEP; see previous discussion) involves low-income underachieving 14- and 15-year-olds in two summers of educational remediation and paid part-time work which includes life-planning workshops.[51] During the intervening school year, mentor-counselors offer guidance and referral.

Recent recognition of the interrelationships between problem behaviors, particularly early unprotected intercourse and school failure, has led many youth organizations to move in new directions. The national Girls' Clubs of America has initiated a research project testing the efficacy of four alternative pregnancy prevention programs to identify models to add to its roster of afterschool activities. The National Urban League has initiated a program through the black fraternity Kappa Alpha Phi, combining school remediation, recreation, community service activities, and counseling on responsible sexual activity.[52]

PROGRAMS TO ASSIST TEEN PARENTS AND THEIR CHILDREN

When people talk about "adolescent pregnancy programs," they often mean programs directed toward ameliorating the consequences of teen parenthood rather than prevention. However, prevention of second pregnancies is often a goal of the program, since the consequences of first births are greatly compounded by subsequent births.[53] Many organizations and agencies focus their attention exclusively on "teen moms." Services may include prenatal and postpartum care, infant care, remedial education, counseling, job preparation and placement, and case management. A number of these comprehensive programs have been evaluated and have shown varying degrees of effectiveness in influencing outcomes, such as repeat pregnancies, retention in school, and employment. This knowledge of "what works" to remediate is relevant to prevention of first pregnancies. The question has been raised whether programs of the same complexity and intensity currently directed toward reduction of subsequent pregnancies might be more cost beneficial if they were focused on preventing first pregnancies. One interesting observation is that the price of entry into these comprehensive health and social service programs is to have a baby. In some of the teen mother programs, the high repeat pregnancy rate is attributed to the fact that the only time disadvantaged girls get any attention or caring is when they first become mothers. And in fact most programs only provide the services during the prenatal period and for one year after the birth of the child.

One of the most thoroughly researched programs was Project Redirection, a multisite comprehensive intervention for mothers under age 18, on or eligible for welfare. The Manpower Demonstration Research Corporation (MDRC) tracked participants over a five-year period and found that they were doing better than a comparable group in employment, in getting off of welfare, and in parenting skills, but they were still very disadvantaged and living in poverty.[54] The researchers concluded that:

1. The comprehensive approach had the most effect on those who were most disadvantaged at the beginning of the program, on those in a long-term welfare situation, and on those who had low basic skills.
2. The program was least successful in education and family planning. The education component was probably inadequate, since it did not offer wide choices or individualized attention. The family-planning message was in competition with the parenting message and was probably weakened by community women who acted as mentors and may not have been strongly committed to pregnancy prevention.
3. Services located in central facilities, particularly parenting and employability skills, were the most successful and the most popular. Thus, they were specifically tailored by the staff to the needs of the clients, while the delivery of the services by outside agencies were not.

The Teen Pregnancy and Parenting Project (TAPP), a comprehensive program with 30 participating agencies in San Francisco, demonstrated successful outcomes in school attendance and prevention of repeat pregnancies.[55] A variety of approaches were used (single site and multiple sites for services) to ensure access to needed services. All clients received case-management services for three years (or until age 19) from Continuous Counselors who acted as the primary contacts between clients and service networks. This model program produced strong evidence of the efficacy of case management in working with high-risk youth.

A summary of teen parent programs found a number of characteristics common to the most effective programs:[56]

1. A full range of comprehensive services under one roof, including education, job preparation, and parenting education.
2. Long-term support.
3. Assertive outreach to encourage participation.
4. Involvement of significant others, such as partners and family.
5. Staff that can offer strong emotional support.
6. Integration of pregnancy prevention into programs.

## Potentially Successful Models

The criteria for selecting the program models for inclusion in this chapter required that they had demonstrated positive outcomes (see Table 11.1). There are many programs offered that have never been substantively evaluated and yet rate very highly in the opinion of experts in the field and surveys which report "satisfied customers." Several sex education programs are frequently cited as outstanding.

POSITIVE IMAGES: A NEW APPROACH
TO CONTRACEPTION EDUCATION

This program is oriented toward reproductive knowledge and contraceptive use unlike most school-based sex education curricula.[57] The teaching manual created by Peggy Brick includes 17 lessons on the history of contraception, development of sexuality, understanding of parental attitudes, training in decision-making involving contraception use, and skills for acquiring birth control. The lessons involve role playing and skills development.

FAMILY LIFE EDUCATION, IRVINGTON BOARD OF EDUCATION,
IRVINGTON, NEW JERSEY

One of the few communities in the United States that offers family life education beginning in the earliest grades and continuing through high school, this program is part of the school system's commitment to sex education. All participating classroom teachers receive in-service training on school time. The curriculum was developed out of a long community process, starting with New Jersey's mandate that sex education be provided, and is being implemented by a full-time Family Life Education Coordinator.

In the early grades, emphasis is put on the family; in grades 4 to 6 content includes decision-making skills, peer relationships, the nature of sexuality, and a unit on child abuse, sexual assault, and incest. Grades 7 to 9 concentrate on a deeper understanding of the same issues, with more emphasis on dating, pregnancy, family planning, abortion, and self-esteem. In the high school curriculum, more consideration is given to relationships, life-planning issues, and parenting. Parents have been included on advisory committees from the outset, and almost all parents have consented for their children's participation. No evaluation data are available.

THREE-FOR-FREE

One of the few large-scale programs that distributes condoms has been initiated by the Maryland State Health Department. In an attempt to decrease the barriers to condom use, free condoms and instructions are made available for anonymous pick-up.[58] In addition to local health department sites, the "Three-for-Free" programs have expanded to drug and alcohol counseling centers, community mental health centers, and other social agencies. Local health departments advertise with flyers and public-service announcements. Many condoms are being distributed under this program, but the possibility of evaluating the impact of a mass-distribution program, beyond numbers, is extremely limited. In recent years, there has been an upsurge of interest in programs for males, but most of the results have been too insignificant to evaluate.[59] Despite innovative outreach efforts, young males are reluctant to use family-planning clinics because they perceive them to be "woman-oriented" programs. One of the programs uses videotapes of neighborhood sports events as a lure to an all-male clinic that employs medical students as mentors. Programs designed to reach young males typically conduct outreach on the "street," utilizing older males as role models or peer outreach workers.

TEEN-LINK

According to Mary Vernon, the director of the program, Teen-Link provides comprehensive preventive and primary health care to disadvantaged 10- to 18-year-olds who live in the community. This four-year demonstration project in the Lincoln Community Health Center in Durham, North Carolina, includes:[60]

1. General health services.
2. Group meetings on nutrition and fitness, family life education (including contraception and STDs), strategies for healthy living, risky business (truancy, drugs, etc.), teen parenting and child care, and parents of teens.
3. Peer health educator program (training and outreach).
4. Community Youth Councils, in participating public housing projects, churches, and schools, who elect representatives to County-Wide Teen-Link Advisory Council.
5. Activity groups which feature karate and cosmetics workshops, cultural and sports activities, and a Black Manhood Wakening Club.
6. School outreach program with on site health promotion and services on school premises provided by Teen-Link staff in four middle schools and two high schools.
7. Community outreach including forums, workshops, work with volunteers, and sponsored Teen's Health Nite Out for recreation.
8. The Church Connection Project involves a training program for church members in adolescent health problems.

Teen-Link expects to produce outcome data on health indicators and to show reductions in pregnancies and STDs. At this stage, service statistics show that the program is being used by the target population. A very high number of gonorrhea cases have been identified as well as abnormal Pap smears. Teen-Link clients who chose contraception are staying with their method of contraception longer on average than those who did not receive counseling. A very high number of pregnancy tests have been completed at the center.

URBAN MIDDLE SCHOOLS ADOLESCENT PREGNANCY
PREVENTION PROJECT (UMSAPP)

Eight large urban school districts were awarded grants in 1986 to develop programs in middle schools in collaboration with one or more community agencies. Planning and technical assistance has been provided by the Academy for Educational Development (AED). Each district produced its own variation of a life options approach to pregnancy prevention. Funds were used for teacher and staff development of a sex education program; establishment of school teams; training of young men in decision-making skills; life-planning education in the middle schools; development of and support for mentoring programs; afterschool activities for high-risk youth in a drop-in center; and linking issues related to adolescent pregnancy with dropout prevention. Most projects included several of these components.

While each project was required to develop a data collection component, it is unlikely that outcome data will be forthcoming. However, AED in its review of the demonstration projects has produced information on "lessons learned"—for example, about dealing with community controversy in regard to sexuality issues; the difficulty of designing meaningful programs that will be utilized by high-risk youth; difficulties in recruiting staff and identifying leaders; and the "over-whelming nature of many problems in big city schools such as lack of supplies, limited security, competition from gangs and other forces pulling on youngsters, and constant staff changes."[61]

Most important, UMSAPP has proven that middle schools are ready to get involved with the issue of pregnancy prevention, and school systems are ready and willing to work with other community agencies to develop collaborative programs. A wide array of agencies have been involved in these projects, including colleges, health departments and centers, Planned Parenthood affiliates, Urban Leagues, the March of Dimes, Y's, and others. Clearly, none of these projects handed out contraceptives in the schools, but they moved school systems much further along toward meeting the needs of middle school children who will require skills to become sexually responsible.

Building on these collaborative models, the American Association of School Administrators is developing a similar multischool Primary Prevention of Adolescent Pregnancy initiative. This project will offer middle school students a number of coordinated activities over the span of the middle school years including summers. Two or three urban school districts will be selected to implement a module of services to be staffed by a full-time coordinator in every participating school.

### Other Promising Programs

Several other comprehensive programs are currently being developed that appear to be based on an accurate understanding of the potentially successful models described here. However, they have not yet produced outcome data to indicate whether or not they will really be able to achieve their goals. One of the most significant undertakings is the New Futures Initiative sponsored by the Annie Casey Foundation. Five cities have been awarded large grants to develop comprehensive programs that will address multiple goals, including prevention of pregnancy, dropping out, and unemployment (see Chapter 12). These collaborative projects will involve an array of community agencies and various approaches to pregnancy prevention.

## What Doesn't Work

The delinquency and substance abuse literatures are full of examples of what doesn't work, but this is not true in the pregnancy prevention field. The sense here is that we don't really know *what* will work. We have already reviewed a number of programs that have given some evidence of success, and others that show great promise. We can only make some assumptions about what doesn't work based on very partial evidence or hearsay.

As mentioned previously, researchers have not found that sex education programs increase contraceptive use or prevent unplanned pregnancy.[62] While it is true that sex education courses per se have never been proven to have had any direct effect on pregnancy rates, it is probable that the knowledge base they provide is an important element in pregnancy prevention. Stout and Rivara conclude from their review that it is unreasonable to expect a classroom course alone to change sexual behavior and compete with the adolescent's sexual world as shaped by the media.[63]

Media campaigns are very popular, but there is no direct evidence linking posters that "Just Say No" to any effect on behaviors. And yet posters and TV and radio ads that include a hotline number or another source of care can dramatically increase requests for contraceptive services.[64]

Peer counseling approaches and teen theater groups are also popular, but there are no recent data to show their impacts. Talbot et al. summarized the experience in over 50 peer programs around the country and found a wide range of functions that teens performed, such as assisting in clinics, counseling peers, and outreach.[65] In general, it appears that those who are trained to become peer counselors benefit most from the experience. There is no evidence that programs that only attempt to raise self-esteem have been successful in this prevention area.

Much attention has been paid to involving families in communication programs and clinic services. There is some evidence that parent-child communication programs helped parents and their children talk about sex, but these programs did not encourage parents to discuss birth control.[66] Moreover, these kinds of programs have not involved high-risk youth. One evaluation found that parents of teenagers visiting family-planning clinics were almost impossible to recruit into a family counseling model.[67] The evaluators were unable to document a link between sex-related communications in the family and more effective contraceptive use among adolescent clients.

Although many practitioners are interested in involving males in family planning, there has been little success in recruiting males as patients of family-planning clinics.[68] A recent intervention at a comprehensive health center with an existing teen male caseload showed little impact on sexual behavior or condom use, although there was a slight improvement in pill use among the partners of the experimental group.[69] Great interest has been expressed in enforcement of child support regulations as a pregnancy prevention intervention; however, no evidence has been forthcoming that it is possible to track down the absent fathers of high-risk teen mothers. Some practitioners feel that it is more important to try to involve the young fathers in parenting than to try to extract payments from a largely unemployed population.

## General Concepts of Teen Pregnancy Prevention

The concepts presented here represent a consensus among those who share the position that the goal of adolescent pregnancy prevention programs should be to promote responsible decision making about the timing of sexual intercourse, the use of effective contraception, and the prevention of negative outcomes, particularly early unintended childbearing. General points of agreement include the following:

1. Early intervention is essential, no later than the middle school years.
2. No one program component will be sufficient. In every community, young people should have access to a package of services that include both capacity-building and life-option components. This can be ensured through communitywide planning that includes provider agencies, schools, decision-makers, media, parents, and youth.
3. There must be a public commitment to pregnancy prevention by local officials and community leaders.
4. Males need to be included in these efforts.
5. Pregnancy prevention cannot be effective without ensuring confidential access to contraception. Programs may need greater intensity and sharper focus on outreach, counseling, and other aspects of birth control services. Many teenagers do not use pills or condoms because of myths and fears. Follow-up of contraceptive users is essential to be sure that they maintain their chosen methods.
6. Access to pregnancy testing, counseling, and abortion services is essential.
7. Parents should be involved if possible, but this is a very difficult task. Where this is an unrealistic goal, some form of nonparental mentoring should be substituted.
8. The role of schools in pregnancy prevention is critical and can include not only sex and family life education, but social skills training, counseling, educational enhancement and, in some communities, act as the locus for clinics.
9. Recently developed sex and family life education curricula that include attention to social skills and life planning should be implemented. To do so requires extensive teacher training in workshops and in-service sessions.
10. Outside organizations should be encouraged to come into schools to offer sex education, general health and mental health services, individual and group counseling, and family planning. Collaborative arrangements can be worked out for space, staffing, funding, and maintenance.
11. Crisis intervention and referral mechanisms must be in place. The system should include a 24-hour hotline and formal arrangements to provide services in referral agencies.
12. Young people at high risk of early childbearing may need an array of comprehensive services, including alternative schools, preparation for employment, job placement, and case management.

A number of programs have been identified as models for pregnancy prevention; however, with rare exceptions, these programs can demonstrate only that use of contraception improved among sexually active youngsters or that the initiation of sexual intercourse was delayed. Very few programs could document reductions in teen birth rates. These outcomes are sufficiently positive to claim some success in this field, but it should be understood that our knowledge is limited about whether they prevent the pregnancies that are terminated by abortions.

The successful models fall primarily into three categories: school curricula, special services in schools, and communitywide multicomponent programs. The model curricula combine an interest in life skills and life planning, with training in social skills and decision making. Some utilize peer instructors. Confidential counseling with individuals is important, as is group counseling and discussion. The multicomponent programs encompass a range of services and approaches. Most actively link school and health services—for example, classroom sex education with contraceptive counseling in school-based or nearby clinic sites. Collaborative arrangements are made to bring staff into schools from outside organizations or to provide training for teachers and youth workers on a variety of issues including sexual development. Parent involvement is sought, in some cases, through home visits, and parents may serve on advisory boards along with youth, school personnel, and community representatives. Volunteer and peer mentoring, as well as tutoring, is often offered, with the linking of dropout prevention and pregnancy prevention.

## Notes

1. Senate Committee on Human Resources, *Adolescent Health Services and Pregnancy Prevention and Care Act of 1987*, 95th Cong., 2d sess., 1978, S. Rept. 2910.
2. C. Chilman, *Adolescent Sexuality in a Changing American Society* (New York: Wiley, 1983); P. Smith and D. Mumford, eds., *Adolescent Reproductive Health Care: Handbook for the Health Professional* (New York: Gardner, 1985); I. Stuart and C. Wells, eds., *Pregnancy in Adolescence: Need, Problems and Management* (New York: Van Nostrand Reinhold, 1982); F. Furstenberg, R. Lincoln, and J. Mencken, eds., *Perspectives on Adolescent Pregnancy* (Philadelphia: University of Pennsylvania Press, 1980).
3. See for example, The Alan Guttmacher Institute, *Teenage Pregnancy: The Problem that Hasn't Gone Away* (New York: Alan Guttmacher Institute, 1981), based on work of R. Lincoln and J. Dryfoos.
4. B. Mosbacher, *Teen Pregnancy and School-Based Health Clinics* (Washington, D.C.: Family Research Council of America, 1986).
5. C. D. Hayes, eds., *Risking the Future: Adolescent Sexuality, Pregnancy, and Childbearing, Vol. I* (Washington, D.C.: National Academy Press, 1987).
6. Ibid., p. 7.
7. J. Dryfoos, "A Time for New Thinking about Adolescent Pregnancy," *American Journal of Public Health* 75(1985): 13–14; M. Edelman, *Adolescent Pregnancy: An Anatomy of a Social Problem in Search of Comprehensive Solutions* (Washington, D.C.: Children's Defense Fund, 1987); Hayes, *Risking the Future*, pp. 266–69.
8. L. Schorr, *Within Our Reach* (New York: Doubleday, 1988), p. 56.
9. Ibid.
10. See L. Zabin and M. Hirsch, *Evaluation of Pregnancy Prevention Programs in the School Context* (Lexington, Mass.: Lexington Books, 1988), for a detailed description of evaluation of a demonstration program.
11. J. C. Quint and J. A. Riccio, *The Challenge of Serving Pregnant and Parenting Teens: Lessons from Project Redirection* (New York: Manpower Demonstration Research Corporation, 1985).

12. House Select Committee on Children, Youth and Families, *Opportunities for Success: Cost Effective Programs for Children, Update 1988* (Washington, D.C.: U.S. Government Printing Office, 1988).
13. J. Berrueta-Clement, L. Schweinhart, W. Barnett, D. Weikart, and A. Epstein, *Changed Lives: The Effects of the Perry Preschool Program on Youths through Age 19* (Ypsilanti, Mich.: High Scope Educational Research Foundation, #8, 1984).
14. Ibid., p. 104.
15. Data from one large scale survey (National Survey of Family Growth) suggests that those teens who had taken a sex education course were more likely to use contraception "the first time" but not consistently. However, these aggregate statistics did not shed any light on the quality of the programs offered. See D. Dawson, "Effects of Sex Education on Adolescent Behavior," *Family Planning Perspectives* 18(1986):162–70.
16. D. Kirby, *Sexuality Education: An Evaluation of Programs and Their Effect* (Santa Cruz, Calif.: Network, 1984).
17. K. Pittman and C. Govan, *Model Programs: Preventing Adolescent Pregnancy and Building Youth Self-Sufficiency* (Washington, D.C.: Children's Defense Fund, 1986).
18. S. Schinke and L. Gilchrist, *Life Skills Counseling with Adolescents* (Baltimore, Md.: University Park Press, 1984).
19. S. Schinke, B. Blythe, L. Gilchrist, and G. Burt, "Primary Prevention of Adolescent Pregnancy," *Social Work with Groups* 4(1981): 121–35.
20. C. Hunter-Geboy, L. Peterson, S. Casey, L. Hardy, and S. Renner, *Life Planning Education: A Youth Development Program* (Washington, D.C.: Center for Population Options, 1985).
21. J. Quinn, "Preventing Adolescent Pregnancy: A Proposed Research and Service Program Developed by Girls' Clubs of America, Inc." (Unpublished paper, Girls' Clubs of America, New York, 1985).
22. C. Sipe, J. Grossman, and J. Milliner, *Summer Training and Education Program (STEP): Report on the 1987 Experience* (Philadelphia: Public/Private Ventures, 1988).
23. M. Tatum, personal communication, 1988.
24. Kirby, *Sexuality Education,* p. 170.
25. Pittman and Govan, *Model Programs,* pp. 12–13.
26. Reported in summary in National Organization on Adolescent Pregnancy and Parenting, Inc., *Network* (Spring 1987): 14. Detailed evaluation data have not been published or made readily available.
27. E. McMillan (Remarks presented at the National Conference on School-Based Clinics, Kansas City, Mo., November 1987).
28. S. Philliber, J. Allen, N. Hoggson, and W. McNeil, "Teen Outreach: A Three-Year Evaluation of a Program to Prevent Teen Pregnancy and School Dropout" (Unpublished report to Association of Junior Leagues, 1988).
29. Inwood House, "Community Outreach Program: Teen Choice. A Model Program Addressing the Problem of Teenage Pregnancy" (Summary Report, 1987).
30. M. Stern, "Evaluation of a School-Based Pregnancy Prevention Program," *TEC Newsletter* 19 (1988): 5–8.
31. L. Edwards, M. Steinman, K. Arnold, and E. Hakanson, "Adolescent Pregnancy Prevention Services in High School Clinics," *Family Planning Perspectives* 12 (1980): 6–14.
32. Healthstart, Inc., "Information About the St. Paul School Health Clinics" (St. Paul, Minn., undated).
33. J. Dryfoos, "School-Based Health Clinics: Three Years of Experience," *Family Planning Perspectives* 20(1988): 193–200.

34. G. Kitzi (Remarks presented at the Third Annual Conference of the Support Center for School-Based Clinics, Denver, 1986).
35. L. Zabin, M. Hirsch, E. Smith, R. Streett, and J. Hardy, "Evaluation of a Pregnancy Prevention Program for Urban Teenagers," *Family Planning Perspectives* 18 (May/June 1986): 123.
36. C. Galavotti and C. Lovick, "The Effect of School-Based Clinic Use on Adolescent Contraceptive Effectiveness" (Paper presented at the National Conference on School-Based Clinics, Kansas City, Mo., November 1987).
37. L. Edwards and K. Arnold-Sheeran (Unpublished data from St. Paul presented at the Annual Meeting of the American Public Health Association, November 1985).
38. J. A. Shea, R. Herceg-Baron, F. Furstenberg, Jr., "Clinic Continuation Rates According to Age, Method of Contraception and Agency" (Paper presented at the Annual Meeting of the National Family Planning and Reproductive Health Association, March 1982).
39. Zabin et al., "Evaluation of a Pregnancy Prevention Program," pp. 119–20.
40. Hayes, *Risking the Future,* p. 49.
41. M. Zelnik and J. Kantner, "Sexual Activity, Contraceptive Use and Pregnancy among Metropolitan-area Teenagers," *Family Planning Perspectives* 12(1980): 230–37.
42. J. Shea, R. Herceg-Baron, and F. Furstenberg, Jr., "Factors Associated with Adolescent Use of Family Planning Clinics," *American Journal of Public Health* 74(1984): 1227–30.
43. C. Nathanson and M. Becker, "Client-Provider Relationships and Teen Contraceptive Use," *American Journal of Public Health* 75(1985): 33–38.
44. M. Jalloh and S. Alston, "Mantalk: A Pregnancy Prevention Program for Teen Males" (Paper presented at the Annual Meeting of the American Public Health Association, Boston, November 1988).
45. M. Vincent, A. Clearie, and M. Schlucheter, "Reducing Adolescent Pregnancy through School and Community-Based Education," *Journal of American Medical Association* 257(1987): 3382–86; M. Vincent, A. Clearie, C. Johnson, and P. Sharpe, *Reducing Unintended Adolescent Pregnancy through School/Community Educational Interventions: A South Carolina Case Study* (Washington, D.C.: Department of Health and Human Services, Centers for Disease Control, 1988).
46. Planned Parenthood of East Central Georgia, "Teen Pregnancy Prevention Program for Rural America—a Study of an Approach that Works" (Unpublished paper, undated).
47. Jesus Sandoval, "Impact '88: Dallas' Countywide Plan for Reducing Teen Pregnancy," *SIECUS Report* 16(1988): 1–5.
48. Community Council of Greater Dallas, *IMPACT '88: A Cumulative Report to the Community* (September 1987).
49. Sandoval, "Impact '88," p. 1.
50. M. Carrera, "Multi-service Family Life and Sex Education Program" (Report from Children's Aid Society, New York, 1987).
51. Sipe et al., *Summer Training and Education Program,* pp. 1–2.
52. Hayes, *Risking the Future,* p. 178.
53. In 1986, almost 11 percent of births to girls under the age of 18 were second or higher order births.
54. D. Polit, J. Quint, and J. Riccio, *The Challenge of Serving Teenage Mothers* (New York: Manpower Demonstration Research Corporation, October 1988).
55. C. Brindis, R. Barth, and A. Loomis, "Continuous Counseling: Case Management with Teenage Parents," *Social Casework* (March 1987): 164–72.

56. P. Nickel and H. Delany, *Working with Teen Parents: A Survey of Promising Approaches* (Chicago: Family Resource Coalition, 1985).
57. P. Brick, *Positive Images: A New Approach to Contraceptive Education* (Hackensack, N.J.: Center for Family Life Education, 1987).
58. State of Maryland, *Promotion of Condom Use in Maryland: Three-for-Free* (Baltimore: Department of Health and Mental Hygiene, 1987).
59. J. Dryfoos, *Putting the Boys in the Picture* (Santa Cruz: Network, 1988).
60. "Teen-Link Health Promotion and Disease Prevention for Youth in Durham Community" (Program description provided by Mary Vernon, director, 1989).
61. Academy for Educational Development, "Urban Middle Schools Adolescent Pregnancy Prevention Program: Briefing Report" (May 1988).
62. Kirby, *Sexuality Education,* pp. 394–95.
63. J. Stout and F. Rivara, "Schools and Sex Education: Does it Work?" *Pediatrics* 83(1989): 375–79.
64. A. Radosh, Office of the Mayor, New York City Adolescent Pregnancy Prevention Program, personal communication, 1987.
65. J. Talbot, L. Rohrbach, C. Coan, and S. Kar, "The Status of Teen Peer Advocate Programs in the U.S." (Unpublished paper, Los Angeles Regional Family Planning Council, 1982).
66. P. Higgins, "Teenage Pregnancy: An Intractable Problem? A Literature Review" (Saint Paul, Minn.: Wilder Foundation, May 1988).
67. R. Herceg-Baron, F. Furstenberg, Jr., J. Shea, and K. Harris, "Supporting Adolescent Use of Contraception: A Comparison of Clinic Services" (Unpublished report, Family Planning Council of Southeastern Pennsylvania, 1984).
68. J. Dryfoos, *Putting the Boys in the Picture,* pp. 56–63.
69. R. Danielson, "Reproductive Health Consultation and Contraceptive Practice of Male Adolescents" (Final Report to the Office of Family Planning, Kaiser Permanente Center for Health Research, September 1988).

# 12

# Prevention of School Failure and Dropping Out

At least three different kinds of interventions are suggested in discussions of schools and high-risk children: preventing school failure, preventing school dropouts, and finding and reinstating students who have already dropped out. The first set is touched on in the effective schools literature, assuming that improving the quality of education will result in higher achievement for all children. Thus, the interventions are primarily aimed at school reform and organization. The second set is described in the dropout prevention literature, with much more attention to individual needs and support services, along with alternative school structures. Because official dropout statistics are generally calculated only for high schools, most of the interventions are directed toward older students, although there is increasing recognition of the need for early intervention. Reinstating students in school is approached largely through employment and "recovery" programs for young people over the age of 18. Because this book is focused on 10- to 17-year-olds, the third set of interventions relating to job placement and programs for older youth will not be included. That subject has been thoroughly addressed by the Grant Foundation Commission on Work, Family, and Citizenship and other sources.[1]

The public has been deluged with studies focusing on the crisis in American education. The rationale for intensified concern is that unless the quality of education is improved we as a nation will not be able to compete with foreign countries (the Japanese educational system is most often cited as a model). One source reported that more than 275 education task forces had been organized in the mid-1980s and "reform literature [has become] a cottage industry among scholars."[2] States enacted more than 700 pieces of legislation between 1983 and 1985, mostly stressing a return to basics.[3] Most recommendations directed toward raising quality call for higher standards for graduation from high school, higher college admission standards, teacher competency tests, and changes in teacher certification requirements. Some experts believe that the educational reform movement "may exacerbate the problem instead of alleviating it . . . and may adversely affect students who already are at risk because they do not meet previous, lower standards.''[4] Reforms in some states may result in fewer rather than more minority teachers. Levin summed up the state of the art in school reform succinctly: "A major shortcoming is that the proposed reforms have relatively little to offer educationally disadvantaged students."[5]

In reaction to the perceived elitism of the reform movement in general, a number of reports have been issued by commissions and task forces specifically concerned about high-risk youth. (As we have seen in Chapter 6, the prevalence of school failure is significantly higher among disadvantaged children living in poverty areas.) One analysis summarizes 15 such reports conducted between 1985 and 1987 by the Council of Chief State School Officers, the National Education Association, National Governors Association, U.S. General Accounting Office, and other organizations.[6] Groups such as the National Coalition of Advocates for Children have for many years been addressing issues related to equity in education and growing gaps between socioeconomic groups.

The outpouring of reports, articles, and books has produced an overwhelming amount of material to sort through in order to identify successful prevention models. An attempt has been made to discriminate between the more general "effective" schools literature and the literature on schools and high-risk youth. The latter has served as the primary source for this chapter.[7]

Although the production of educational research appears to be a major industry in this country, there is the same dearth of long-term evaluation that limits the other prevention fields. Hamilton conducted a review of reports generated through the Educational Resources Information Center (ERIC) and was disappointed to find only a few that offered both program descriptions and data indicating program effectiveness.[8] A planning guide to be used by grantees in a new foundation initiative presented 21 dropout prevention program descriptions, of which only 13 even mentioned evaluation.[9] Lipsitz's important work on successful middle schools for young adolescents does not include any actual data on outcomes.[10] However, there are many examples of school programs cited in journals and manuals that have resulted in better short-term outcomes—for example, higher grades, less truancy, and higher retention.

Table 12.1 shows the measures of success and the sources of data used in the evaluation of programs to prevent failure in school and dropping out. Improved achievement and continued retention can be measured both in youth surveys (such as needs assessments) and from official school records. The overlap in problem behaviors becomes a significant issue when we address the subject of school failure. Certain school-related behaviors are also considered delinquent acts (truancy), while some of the outcomes (higher achievement) may be necessary preconditions to the prevention of other problem behaviors, such as substance abuse and early unprotected intercourse. In a sense, the interventions described here may be the "bottom line" for high-risk children, without which few of the other interventions will be successful.

The scale of the public educational enterprise in the United States is very large: 15,000 school districts with 60,000 elementary schools and 22,000 high schools. A recent government report identified more than 1000 dropout programs

TABLE 12.1. Measures of Success in the Evaluation of Prevention of School
Failure

| Behavior to Prevent | Measures of Success | Source of Data |
| --- | --- | --- |
| Poor grades | Improvement in grades | School records<br>Self-report survey |
| Low achievement | Improvement in test<br>scores | School records |
| Low expectations<br>for achievement | Higher expectations | Self-report survey<br>Teacher report |
| Nonpromotion | Improved grade<br>retention | School records |
| Dropping out | Improved grade<br>retention | Self-report survey |
| | Higher high school<br>graduation rates | School records |
| | Higher General<br>Education Degree<br>(GED) rates | Self-report survey<br>Census |
| Truancy | Improved daily<br>attendance | School records |
| Suspensions and<br>expulsions | Lower rates of<br>suspension | School records |

mostly directed toward the provision of basic education and personal counseling;
about three-quarters included career counseling and efforts to involve parents.[11]
Raywid identified 2500 alternative schools in 1982 and received survey reports on
about half of them.[12] A number of surveys have reported periodically on the implementation of Chapter 1 (formerly Title I of the Elementary and Secondary
Education Act), the federal program that provides local school districts with funds
to offer compensatory educational programs for low-achieving children in poverty
areas (see Chapter 8).[13] About three-fourths of all public elementary schools and
one-third of middle and secondary schools provide Chapter 1 services, mostly as
instruction in reading and math in the earlier grades.

## Successful Models

Clearly, one section cannot do justice to all that is happening in schools and in
communities around the country to enhance the educational outcomes of high-risk
students. There are thousands of programs. Some schools report that they offer as
many as 200 different specialized enrichment programs.[14] The models presented
here have been selected as a cross-section of what appears in the literature. The
programs were chosen within categories based on the completeness of their evaluation data and the frequency they were mentioned as models.

The selection presented here is limited to programs offered in the United States.
Some of the most impressive evidence on work with high-risk youth comes from

other countries. One of the important studies of effective schools was conducted by Michael Rutter and his colleagues who tracked students over five years in London inner-city schools.[15] They found that schools where the students had consistent successful outcomes (behavior, attendance, grades) had marked institutional characteristics: an emphasis on academic work, defined teaching roles, flexibility, systems of incentives and rewards, and arrangements whereby students could take responsibility for their own behavior. Success was not related to the size of the school or the physical characteristics. Most important, the whole ethos of the social institution seemed to be more significant than the sum of its parts, a quality often referred to in the United States as "school climate."

## Early Childhood and Family Interventions

The documented effects of preschool programs on later achievement have been referred to in the reviews of delinquency and pregnancy prevention programs in Chapters 9 and 11. Other models in addition to the Perry Preschool have been evaluated and found to have positive impact on later education.[16] These programs rely heavily on family involvement and teaching parenting skills. A meta-analysis of 11 preschool programs conducted by Lazar and Darlington in 1982 showed that early education significantly reduced placement in special education classes and being left back and improved academic performance in the short term.[17]

### THE CAROLINA ABECEDARIAN PROGRAM

Targeted at newborns in high-risk families, this intervention continues from birth through third grade.[18] Developed by Craig Ramey of the University of North Carolina, an intensive all-day child-care intervention began at 3 months and provided cognitive stimulation and socialization skills until kindergarten entry. Children were placed in small groups of three to seven per teacher. After that, until third grade, families had access to a home-school resource teacher to act as an advocate, help mothers tutor children, and conduct enriching summer activities. Research is available up to second grade (it will continue throughout the school years) and shows that both components had an impact on intellectual performance, achievement, and promotion. The preschool component apparently had a greater effect than the K–3 experience—for example, most of the differences between the experimental and control groups occurred very early on, in the first year. However, these differences were maintained, suggesting the importance of program continuity.

### BROOKLINE EARLY EDUCATION PROJECT (BEEP)

A carefully researched school-based intervention, this program was developed for families with newborns who were interested in preparing their children over a five-year period for school entry.[19] An early education center was organized by the project designed to prevent learning and adjustment problems. Staff were identified as "teachers" who worked with parents in discussions and workshops, made frequent home visits, and arranged for child care for the parents. The center, open to all enrollees from the area, had a lending library of toys, play groups for 2-year-olds, and daily prekindergarten classes for 3- and 4-year-olds. Evaluation results were positive. By second grade, BEEP children did twice as well as comparison children (there was no formal control group) in reading and mastery skills, and their parents were more likely to be involved with the school in regard to the child's progress. The effect was much greater for families with lower educational levels than for those with higher education.

## PARENTS AS TEACHERS

A program developed, evaluated, and disseminated by the Missouri Department of Education,[20] this pilot project was first conducted in 1982 in four local school districts. Based on its success, this program is now available in every school district in Missouri for new parents, until their children reach age 3. Parents receive regular home visits from trained parent educators who teach them to be more knowledgeable about childrearing and child development. Staff are encouraged to intervene with family problems and help to improve high-risk situations. Parents also attend group meetings, and their children receive periodic monitoring and formal screening to detect health problems and other handicapping conditions. A referral network helps parents who need special assistance beyond the scope of the program. Evaluation of the 1982 cohort of program children at age 3 showed that they scored higher on achievement, verbal and language ability, and had greater social competence than a carefully controlled comparison group. The program appeared to change the trajectory for high-risk youth, proving that they could perform well regardless of socioeconomic disadvantages and other measures of high-risk status. Further evaluation is currently in progress.

## School-Based Interventions

### CURRICULA

Most of the interventions for prevention of substance abuse fit into the category of "curricula," as does the entire field of sex education. Yet "curricula" do not appear to get much attention in the literature on academically high-risk students. A recent publication of the Department of Education on "best bets" for dropout prevention details efforts under way in 32 school districts with exemplary programs, but none of the models cited is specifically a change in curriculum.[21] Of course, it is difficult to make a distinction between curriculum and school organization—that is, to make a distinction between *what* is taught and *how* it is taught. The National Diffusion Network, which compiled "proven exemplary educational programs and practices," listed many interesting programs.[22] A number of school systems use "laboratory" teachers who are equipped to conduct diagnostic testing, spend individual time with low-achieving students, and identify challenging instructional materials. Follow-Through programs in a number of communities identify high-risk children, place them in small groups, train teachers in individualized instruction, and use specialized teaching materials and instructional programs. Children are encouraged to work independently and to learn to work with others. Some Follow-Through programs include home visiting by teachers and others use parents as classroom assistants.

Slavin and colleagues have been involved in many aspects of the design and implementation of cooperative learning techniques. Using these methods, two to six students are grouped in a team to help one another learn academic material. A "state-of-the-art" review of 60 well-designed evaluation studies of cooperative learning situations showed that most efforts produced positive effects on achievement.[23] The specific components that produced results included simultaneously setting group goals and arranging for individual accountability.

In 1986, Congress mandated a national assessment of the effectiveness of Chapter 1 programs; the report acknowledges the methodological problems in evaluating what is actually a supplement to the regular school program for selected children and presents the evidence that was compiled despite all of the evaluation difficulties.[24] In general, the most successful efforts to raise the reading and math scores among disadvantaged children occurred in schools where teachers emphasized academic instruction, expected students to master the curriculum, and allocated most of the time available for Chapter 1 remediation to the acquisition of basic academic skills. Research showed that Chapter 1 interventions helped reduce the gap between disadvantaged and advantaged students. However, on the average, the Chapter 1 students were still below the median scores after a year of remediation. Additional years of remediation did not improve the situation. The higher the grades, the larger the gap. Over summers the gap widened, with actual losses in scores among low-income students. Summer programs had little effect because they were not academically rigorous.

*Comprehensive Competencies Program.*    A computer-based individualized instruction approach to teaching basic skills was developed by Robert Taggart based on extensive research with disadvantaged youth.[25] This franchised system includes computerized management and testing techniques and is being used in 250 schools and community-based agencies in combination with other education and job training. The package includes self-paced instructional materials and integrates all modes of teaching, workbooks, and audiovisual materials. Teachers are encouraged to spend as much time as possible with individual students. Multiple evaluation results have shown significant gains in reading and math after 28 hours of instruction time.

*Computer Utilization in Education (CUE).*    A remedial reading and math program for educationally disadvantaged students in grades 3 to 8, this project was developed in the Central Square New York school system.[26] This intervention involves a sequentially organized curriculum of enrichment that is administered in short daily sessions in a laboratory setting. Students showed great gains in reading scores.

SCHOOL ORGANIZATION

*The Comer Process.*   A school-based management approach to making school a more productive environment for poor minority children, this process, developed by James Comer from the Yale University Child Study Center, has been success-fully implemented in several inner-city elementary schools in New Haven and is being replicated widely throughout the country.[27] The program attempts to transfer mental health skills to schools where "change agents" must be created by strengthening and redefining the relationships between principals, teachers, par-ents, and students. Four elements are involved:

1. School Advisory Council: Representative management and governance are the function of this elected council. In addition to the principal, 12 to 14 representatives of teachers, teacher aides, and parent groups serve on this board. A member of the Mental Health Team acts as consultant.
2. Mental Health Team: A school psychologist and other support personnel provide direct services to children and advise school staff and parents. Two examples of their input: setting up a Discovery Room for giving children hands-on experiences, and initiating the idea that teachers stay with classes for two years to promote continuity.
3. Parent Participation Program: A parent is hired at the minimum wage to work in each classroom on a part-time basis. In addition to serving as representatives to the School Advisory Council, parents are encouraged to volunteer as teachers' aides, librarians, newsletter staff, and social activity organizers.
4. Flexible Academic Program: One example of change was the development of a social skills curriculum, integrating the teaching of basic skills with teaching of "mainstream" (middle-class) arts and social skills.

Evaluation results show that children in the project schools went from low achievement levels to grade-level norms and attendance rose dramatically. Com-pared with students in other schools, the demonstration project children scored significantly higher on basic skills tests. According to Comer, "We haven't had a serious behavior problem in the schools we have been involved in in over a de-cade." He has pointed out that the strength of this project is its focus on the entire school rather than on any one particular aspect, and its attention to institutional change rather than individual change. This is one of the few models that has successfully engaged parents in school programs.

*Success for All.*   This demonstration project in a Baltimore City elementary school was initiated by the Center for Research on Elementary and Middle Schools, part of Johns Hopkins University.[28] Based on the best available research, the program restructures the entire school with "one commitment in mind: Do everything nec-essary to insure that all students will be performing at grade level . . . at the end of third grade." Interventions include half-day preschool and full-day kindergar-ten, a Family Support Team, an effective reading program, reading tutors, indi-vidual academic plans based on frequent assessments, a full-time program facilitator and coordinator, training and support for teachers, and a school advisory committee that meets weekly. The reading program regroups all students in grades 1 to 3 for 90-minute daily periods, with no more than 15 students at the same reading level. Children are encouraged to work in pairs to help each other. The tutors, who are certified experienced teachers, work one-on-one with priority given to first graders. The Family Support Team, consisting of two full-time social workers and a parent liaison worker, provides parenting education and support assistance for day-to-day problems, such as nutrition, getting eyeglasses, attendance, and problem behaviors.

Evaluations following the first year of the program matched the Success students with those from a nearby school having similar characteristics. Success for All students outscored control school children on multiple measures of reading readiness and reading comprehension. The effects were the strongest in the third grade. In grades 1 to 3, only one child (of the 300 in the program) was retained in a grade, compared with the previous year's level of 12 percent, and the number of children referred for special education also dropped very significantly. Staff are optimistic about these first results, which demonstrate that it is possible to restructure on urban elementary school so that all children will be on grade level by the end of third grade. Success for All is currently being replicated in seven other Baltimore schools and one in Philadelphia.

*Region 7 Middle School.*    A magnet school in Detroit was designed to give students a great amount of choice and to require an equal amount of self-direction and responsibility.[29] Teachers are organized by teams and students rotate among teams every nine weeks. Time is set aside for independent study; students may select from over 100 courses. Ungraded minicourses in Scrabble, chess, swimming, art, journalism, African folk tales, and other subjects proposed by the students round out the curriculum.

Behavioral standards are clear and strict. Students are involved in school policy decisions, and the principal is highly visible. Parental involvement is sought by teachers, the guidance counselor, and an outreach worker. The students are evaluated based on skill areas and work habits, not by grades.

The school reports that average daily attendance is much higher than in other schools. Students have shown marked improvements in reading scores, but not in math achievement.

*Transition Project.*    This intervention was designed by Robert Felner et al. to reduce the problems (feeling lost in a larger impersonal environment, alienation, fear of change) encountered by disadvantaged youth during the transition from junior to senior high.[30] Project freshmen were assigned to homerooms with selected teachers who provided guidance, individual counseling, and maintained extensive family contacts in addition to teaching classes. Project students took all of their academic courses together to facilitate peer support within the complex environment of a large urban school. At the end of ninth grade, participants had higher grades and fewer absences than control students. During the same period, control students' grade-point averages lowered, demonstrating the impact of the transition experience without the intervention. Felner and colleagues believe that this study demonstrates the feasibility and effectiveness of low-cost changes in the roles of teachers, with only minor shifts in organizational arrangements.

*Effective Middle Schools in New York City.*  Advocates for Children reviewed 180 middle schools and selected 4 exemplary schools on the basis of a number of criteria: serving poor and minority children, consistency of achievement on city-wide math and reading scores, high daily attendance, strong leadership, staff involvement, and positive school climate.[31] *Intermediate School 174* is one example of a strong principal's approach (all four chosen schools appeared to have impressive leaders). Incoming fifth-graders receive particular attention; their classrooms are grouped around the principal's office, so he can provide a nurturing atmosphere as well as monitor academic progress. Teachers develop the curriculum and operate a "buddy" system, pairing more experienced teachers with newer teachers. The decision-making process is described as open, with few formal rules. There is no discernible ability grouping. A study team found a high level of student trust and camaraderie. The principal's stress on academic improvement is credited with raising test scores.

Observers reported a number of practices in the four schools that contributed to effectiveness: commitment to achievement, rewards for academic achievement through honor rolls, rewards for nonacademic achievement through honor assemblies and a "climate of celebration" involving parents and the community, stipends to teachers who develop curricula, a sense of ownership, master teachers assigned only to staff development, community involvement with merchants, and recruitment of senior citizens as tutors. One school divided into four minischools, with a coordinator and family worker assigned to each unit.

SPECIAL SERVICES AND COUNSELING

*Primary Mental Health Project (PMHP).*  A well-established program for early detection and prevention of school adjustment problems was pioneered in 1957 by Emory Cowen and colleagues from the Center for Community Study in Rochester (see also Chapter 9).[32] PMHP identifies primary-grade students with adjustment problems through screening procedures. Trained nonprofessional child-aides provide individualized attention and support to referred children through weekly sessions in a special project playroom located outside of the classroom. Children are also seen in group sessions; for example, one group dealt with parental divorce. The associates are all volunteers, carefully trained and supervised, who learn to become a special friend to troubled children. The program is operated by a core team including a psychologist or social worker responsible for the screening procedures, senior-aides who are experienced and can manage the program, child-aides who work with the children, and a program consultant from the Center.

Many evaluations have been conducted over the years to document the positive effects on school achievement and behavioral adjustment over the long term as well as short term. This program has been widely replicated and is now being offered in 100 districts in New York and 350 around the world. It was selected by the National Mental Health Association as the outstanding prevention program in mental health in 1984.[33]

*Absentee Prevention Program.*    An intervention focused on chronically absent K–4 students, this project was developed by staff at the Community College of Beaver County, Pennsylvania.[34] Chronic absentees are systematically identified, assessed, and treated by a Prevention Specialist (a teacher with special training) who arranges for individual counseling and group experience in decision-making and social skills. For each child, another school staff member acts as an in-school support person. Families are involved through home visits, school conferences, classes, and referrals. School personnel actively support parents by providing transportation to meetings and services (e.g., for drug and alcohol treatment). The Prevention Specialist also arranges for in-service training for other teachers and acts as liaison between home and school. Program evaluation showed significantly improved attendance among identified children.

*"Twelve-together."*    An intervention for ninth-graders in 20 Detroit high schools, this project was organized by the Metropolitan Detroit Youth Foundation for the purposes of peer counseling and support.[35] At each site, 12 students are selected, half at high risk and half not at high risk. They receive orientation at a weekend retreat and then attend 20 to 30 weekly two-hour peer counseling sessions, led by trained adult volunteer advisors. In the counseling sessions, the discussion of any problem concludes with agreement on a plan of action to overcome the problem. These students pledge to study 1½ hours a day. Participants also have access to monthly academic forums, and some receive more intensive tutoring using the Comprehensive Competencies Program (see p. 204). Parents are involved at a family reception, and businesses contribute space and incentives.

Evaluation data reflect the program's success: the promotion rate of Twelve-together students in 1984–85 was significantly higher than the promotion rate of a control group of similar students. Attendance and achievement also showed marked improvements.

*Student Assistance Model (SAM).*    Another version of the Student Assistance Program, described in the substance abuse prevention chapter, this project has been developed under the auspices of the Wheeler Clinic (Plainville, Connecticut) to address more general problems of low achievement and school discipline problems.[36] In this model, counselors (master's level social work or psychology) are either brought into a school system under contract with a community mental health association, or a school staff counselor is trained to be a Student Assistance Counselor. A school team is formed involving the administration, guidance, social services, and nursing; they are trained in referral techniques and meet frequently to share information. Students are referred to the counselors for assessment, individual or group counseling, support groups, or outside treatment. SAM is built around a basic life skills curriculum.

Evaluation, based on a small sample, showed that the more in-school assistance the student received, the greater the improvement in achievement and discipline. Two-thirds of the participants showed an increase in grades, and half improved their attendance records. The staff believes that "a significant adult in a nurturing environment can indeed motivate a student to attend school."[37] Students who were referred initially because they appeared to be depressed or had family problems made the greatest gains. The staff felt that they had the least impact on regular alcohol and drug users because the students and their families denied the problem. The staff also found it hard to assist students from severely dysfunctional families without more resources for counseling and support.

Another version of the Student Assistance Program favored by the Pennsylvania Department of Education emphasizes a system of early identification and referral for treatment of high-risk students.[38] A Student Assistance Case Management group composed of school counselors, administrators, a nurse, and a psychologist meets weekly to assess students' needs. Crisis intervention is supplied by the Student Assistance Core Team. This group includes the district central office administrator, a counselor, a nurse, a Student Assistance Program coordinator, and teacher—all trained in SAP and referral techniques. An essential element is coordination with community social and health agencies. In one year, the program had intervened with 20 percent of the students.

*Remedial Instruction and Counseling.*    Caliste reports on a study of high-risk students in ninth to twelfth grades, randomly assigned to experimental and control groups.[39] Participants met over a 12-week period with tutors and teachers in the language arts or math, who provided remedial instruction. They were also assigned to group counseling conducted by a school counselor. Counseling centered on motivation, academic problems, career goals, and study habits. Based on pre- and posttests, including a six-month follow-up, the experimental group had significantly lower rates of absenteeism or dropping out than the control group. However, no changes were demonstrated in attitude measures, such as self-concept, suggesting to the researchers that "affective variables may be unrelated to the subsequent decision of students to withdraw from school." From this research, it is not possible to determine whether the effect was created by the remedial tutor or the counselor.

*The Valued Youth Partnership.*    This program in San Antonio, Texas, trains high-risk Hispanic students to serve as tutors and peer counselors for younger children.[40] Program components include classes for student tutors (skills for tutoring as well as basic remediation), tutor sessions with students in lower grades, field trips for tutors and tutees, exposure to community-based adult role models, and parental involvement through teacher home visits or parental conferences. The tutors work five to eight hours per week and receive the minimum wage for their labor. Results indicate a significant decline in absenteeism and dropout rates and an improvement in grades.

ALTERNATIVE HIGH SCHOOLS

The label "alternative schools" covers a wide spectrum, from rigid, "reform school" type classrooms for delinquent students to loose, permissive "arty" centers for gifted children. What these schools have in common is that they are set up to provide options within a school system for students who do not fit into the mainstream. Alternative schools are typically small, either separate entities or defined areas or houses within a larger school. Foley's study of eight alternative schools in New York City showed that students were performing better than they had in their previous schools, and the improvements in both attendance and credit accumulation lasted for the four semesters covered by the study.[41] The success of these schools in serving high-risk students "seems to lie in their well-focused academic programs and their capacity to engage students and teachers in a dialogue that reaches beyond the formality of roles and fosters creative human relationships."

*The Peninsula Academies.*   The alternative model of a "school within a school" is located in two sites in Redwood City, California.[42] Directed toward potential dropouts in grades 10 to 12, these academies provide specialized vocational education in electronics and computer technology, along with basic high school courses. Classes are small and tutoring available. Volunteer mentors from local industry are involved. Evaluation results are positive: academy students were more likely to graduate from school and their academic performance was higher than a comparison group.

*Reuther Alternative High School (REAL).*   In Kenosha, Wisconsin, this high school attracts underachievers from two local high schools.[43] About 25 students are selected each year because of high risk for failure and enter the REAL program. Their activities are self-contained, with one full-time counselor and three half-time teachers. The curriculum emphasizes real-world experiences, group process, and group identity. An experiential component requires daily work in day-care centers and nursing homes, backed up with courses in child development and aging, and the keeping of a journal. Other components involve building renovation in conjunction with local industry and small business undertaking based on the Junior Achievement model.

Wehlage describes six alternative programs in Wisconsin, all with intensive group processes, individualized support mechanisms or experiential components. He claims that they are all effective in reducing truancy and increasing the possibility of graduation; however, no actual data are cited. In another paper, Wehlage et al. describe an evaluation of this model at 10 sites using a pre-postsurvey instrument that was limited to attitudinal questions.[44] Three of the sites appeared to have significant positive effects (self-esteem, bonding to school, aspirations, etc.) on their students, while one had negative effects. The other six showed few changes. No data are presented on achievement or retention.

SYSTEMWIDE MULTICOMPONENT PROGRAMS

*Pueblo, Colorado, School District 60 System.*   A major effort is under way to reduce the dropout rates in a working-class community where half the students are Hispanic.[45] Centralized coordination rests with the director of pupil personnel. School-community liaison specialists actively retrieve dropouts. Resource teachers are relieved of classroom duty and spend their time counseling and supporting students and their families as well as school staffs. Early identification and intervention (as early as preschool) is a high priority, facilitated by a computerized tracking system.

One approach used to involve parents is a "Summer Linkage Motivational Workshop" for new ninth-grade students and their parents to meet and interact with adult and peer role models. Mentoring by volunteer adults and peers is stressed throughout the system. Rules on suspension have been changed because of this initiative; students who commit minor disciplinary offenses are no longer suspended, but they are isolated for up to five days and monitored by a paraprofessional supervisor.

As in most systems, dropout prevention programs were already in place but they were having little effect. In Pueblo, two existing vocational training programs were strengthened through the interventions of the resource staff. In one, pupils meet daily with a work study teacher who assists them in developing good work entry skills. Afternoons, the students are employed at a community work training site. In the other program, high-risk ninth- and tenth-graders take core subjects from a teacher who guides and motivates them and helps place them in summer jobs. These is also a teen mother program housed at a continuing education center, along with a program for dropout reentry for all students.

Dropout rates have fallen significantly in the Pueblo school system during the two-year period reported on. The retention rates for Hispanics showed marked improvement, with greater changes than for other students.

## Communitywide Multicomponent Programs

### ADOPT-A-STUDENT

The Atlanta Partnership of Business and Education is an umbrella organization focusing on a number of programs.[46] One that has received much attention is Adopt-a-Student, whereby volunteers from 40 local businesses are paired with low-achieving high school juniors and seniors. These volunteer consultants meet with the students weekly to share an activity, and together attend a monthly job preparation workshop. Consultants are expected to take the students to see their worksites and discuss careers. Participants have high graduation rates compared with controls and an excellent record for job placement.

### SUMMER TRAINING AND EMPLOYMENT PROGRAM (STEP)

A national demonstration project directed at high-risk 14- to 16-year-olds has been implemented in five communities by Public/Private Ventures in collaboration with school systems, the Summer Youth Employment and Training programs, and other community-based agencies.[47] Three components, offered over a 15-month period, included intensive remediation over two summers and during the school year using individually paced instruction in basic reading and math skills; classes in "Life

Skills and Opportunities" stressing responsible social and sexual behavior (see Chapter 11 on pregnancy prevention); and half-time summer job placement.

Carefully documented research at this stage provides encouraging results about successive cohorts of participants compared with randomly selected controls. The most recent STEP group showed significant gains in reading and math after only one summer of the program. The second group, after 15 months of participation, also showed reading and math gains. The third group, who had completed the program and were in eleventh grade at the time of the latest survey, had higher math scores and were more likely to have been promoted. Dropout rates were slightly lower for this group, but no effects were detected in reading, attendance, suspensions, or rates of employment. The strongest impacts on dropout rates were shown by Hispanics and females. In the first year of the program, the results were not so encouraging; most of the participants appeared to experience learning losses over the summer (lower achievement scores). However, the loss was less among the experimental group than among the control group. Improvements in outcomes over time were attributed to changes in the curriculum design.

## "I HAVE A DREAM"

Eugene Lang's promise to a sixth-grade East Harlem class of subsidized college study in the event of high school graduation has "become one of the country's most celebrated private-sector initiatives for disadvantaged youth."[48] In addition to the promise of subsidy and Lang's personal attention, the students receive support from a full-time social worker, services from Harlem's Youth Action Program, and volunteers who act as mentors. Most of the original participants are expected to graduate from high school this year.

Nine new incentive projects have started in New York City and in at least 22 cities around the country. The impact of this kind of program may ultimately be measured by the influence of decision-maker millionaires who get drawn into the educational problems of high-risk youth. Several states have begun similar programs: New York State offers "Liberty Partnerships" that promise high school students subsidies for college tuition on graduation.

## THE BOSTON COMPACT

Virtually every report on new approaches to high-risk youth cites the Boston Compact as a reform that makes a difference.[49] Through a series of arrangements between Boston's public schools and local government, business, labor, higher education, and community groups, collaborative efforts have been undertaken to improve school attendance, academic achievement, and post-high-school opportunities. Activities include school-based planning, preapprenticeship training, a sequence of career development, scholarships, teacher training, and postgraduate follow-up. Employers pledge to give priority to hiring graduates of Boston's schools as well as providing summer jobs and part-time employment during the school year. All of this has resulted in higher rates of employment.

While there has been some improvement in school attendance and achievement, dropout rates continue at an unacceptable level. A new plan is being initiated to put special emphasis on teacher involvement, student support teams, alternative education, and parent outreach. The Boston Compact is widening its scope to bring it into closer touch with middle schools and community organizations.

This model is being replicated throughout the country. In the Los Angeles Genesis program, every inner-city youth with a good high school record will be guaranteed a job or college admission. Similar projects are under way in Albuquerque, Cincinnati, Indianapolis, Louisville, Memphis, San Diego, and Seattle.[50]

## Programs with Potential that Have Not Been Evaluated

As should be clear to the reader by now, there is no shortage of ideas about what to do in schools to enhance the educational outcomes of high-risk children (or in some cases, for all children). A list produced by the Los Angeles school system and circulated by the newly created National Dropout Prevention Center mentioned 60 ideas about how to keep students in school. Some of the most appealing ideas have not been evaluated, or at least the evaluations have not been made available.

### COALITION OF ESSENTIAL SCHOOLS

This is a consortium of schools that have reorganized to incorporate the principles derived from the work of Ted Sizer.[51] Based on his experience studying American high schools, he has concluded that the most important task for schools is to teach students mastery of their schoolwork. Sizer believes that it is more important for children to learn a few important ideas "deeply" than to be exposed to fragmented and ineffectual teaching.

### CENTRAL PARK EAST

This school, located in East Harlem in New York City, exemplifies Ted Sizer's philosophy. Designed and operated by Deborah Meier, this innovative public school will eventually house 500 students in grades 7 to 12 (it currently has students in grades 7 to 10). Students in grades 7 to 10 are exposed to an intense classical curriculum in arts and sciences and in the humanities. The last two years of high school will be offered as an institute, with individual programs for each student which may involve courses in other places, field work, and projects. Electives such as dance, music, art, and languages are offered before 9 A.M. or from 3 to 5 P.M., thus engaging students for a full day. Field trips are encouraged as is exposure to computer-assisted learning.

Teachers work together to create a comprehensive curriculum. They also act as coaches and counselors for the students; each day begins with an advisory group of 15 students where any subject may be brought up and shared with other students. Students are required to perform two hours per week of school or community service, working in the library, tutoring, fixing appliances, or whatever they chose.

T-LC MENTORS PROGRAM

A program in Ann Arbor, Michigan, is considered a model for using elder mentors as tutors and friends of high-risk junior high school students. A center has been set up in a junior high school where community volunteers (who must be 55 or older) work with assigned children at least once a week in a variety of projects including school remediation, arts, and career awareness. Interviews with elder volunteers and youth confirmed the high degree of satisfaction. The young people liked the elders because they were not professionals or police, and the mentors enjoyed the autonomy of the program in which they were allowed to devise creative solutions to the youth's problems (of which they had many) and to work "one-on-one."[52]

YOUTH SERVICE PROGRAMS

There is a high level of interest in the idea that students should perform community service as a requirement for graduation or as part of a volunteer program.[53] The thrust for these programs is being driven by the belief that they will combat the prevailing powerlessness and the "consequent preoccupation with self"[54] and help young people feel more valued by the community. Supporters have organized various advocacy activities, and many different models of youth service programs around the country have been identified: 50 conservation and youth service corps, 400 college campus-based programs, and 3,000 school-based programs.[55] Some 50 of these programs offer full-time community service opportunities, typically to school dropouts. The proponents think that well-structured community service programs are an effective intervention strategy for at-risk students, but no hard data could be located to prove this assumption with regard to school achievement.

CITIES-IN-SCHOOLS (CIS)

This national nonprofit organization is devoted to curb dropout rates through partnerships between schools, local government, and businesses.[56] The documented interrelationships between school dropout rates, high-risk behaviors, and social disadvantage inform the conceptual basis for this intervention. CIS operates in more than 25 communities with 130 sites to facilitate a process of collaboration to bring health as well as social and employment services into schools for high-risk youngsters. National CIS staff work with a local board of directors, presided over by a prominent local businessperson, to assess needs and raise funds to put together a professional team approach to discourage potential dropouts. In most programs, a case manager is assigned to each high-risk child. Communities vary in program design; some operate alternative schools, and some offer special CIS life skills classes and other forms of remediation and tutoring. A wide array of partnerships have been established through CIS programs and have involved Boys Clubs of America, VISTA, the United Way, and the Junior League.

Unfortunately, only limited evaluation data are available from local CIS programs. Several of the CIS programs have achieved national prominence. For example, Rich's Academy in Atlanta (one of six CIS schools in that community) is an alternative school held in conjunction with a department store. New York City CIS operates in three school districts teaming up caseworkers from the Human Resources Administration with recreation workers from the Department of Parks and Recreation. In Miami, the CIS program is operated by the Private Industry Council and offers remediation at 13 local high schools.

## THE EARLY ADOLESCENT HELPER PROGRAM

Developed by Joan Schine, this project is currently operating in 20 middle schools. Students are assigned to work as volunteers in senior citizen centers, nursery schools, or afterschool centers. They attend a weekly seminar in school with a trained school staff member (usually a guidance counselor) who works with them on issues such as child development, social skills, and other questions that come up in the course of the experience. *Magic Me* uses a similar approach: 11- to 14-year-old high-risk students are recruited to spend one hour per week during school time with a senior citizen. A coordinator furnishes transportation and acts as a counselor.

In the Atlanta school system, all students are required to perform 75 hours of community service and write an essay about the experience in order to graduate. At least 200 community agencies are involved in the field placements. In Kansas City, high-risk 14- to 17-year-olds have been involved in intensive full-time summer service projects. Around the country, young people are volunteering their services through organized efforts in hospitals, social agencies, day care centers, playgrounds, as well as in cross-age tutoring. Many of the projects emphasize building youth leadership skills in initiating, organizing, and carrying out service programs.

The importance of a "reflective" component in youth service programs has been highlighted, particularly for middle schoolers.[57] Methods proposed include verbal debriefing by skillful and sensitive staff members, written journals and diaries, videotaping, readings, group discussions, and recognition ceremonies.

## NEW FUTURES

A five-year demonstration project of the Annie E. Casey Foundation, this program has awarded grants to five cities to develop comprehensive programs for the prevention of dropping out, teen pregnancy, and youth unemployment.[58] Each city has organized a different model for coordination, either a new nonprofit umbrella organization, a school district, or an official Youth Commission. The major thrust of the interventions appears to be school based: restructuring middle schools, basing social and health services in community schools, using team approaches to coordinate educational and other services, and setting up case-management systems to track high-risk youth. Extensive monitoring and evaluation are planned over the life of the projects.

NEIGHBORHOOD IMPROVEMENT AND YOUTH EMPLOYMENT PROJECT

A joint undertaking of the Philadelphia School District, the West Philadelphia Partnership (a large consortium of organizations and businesses), and the University of Pennsylvania, this complex program has several components:[59]

1. Involvement of students in an afterschool and summer community improvement program. Students from three local inner-city schools participate in neighborhood and school projects (landscaping, painting, etc.).
2. Development of a teacher-designed curriculum (Constructing Your Neighborhood) that focuses on the community and stresses participatory learning. At the elementary level, the curriculum integrates social studies, math, science, and language arts. In high school, science and math are emphasized. All students engage in career exploration activities.
3. Active participation of teachers at every level. In addition to designing curriculum, teachers work with students on community projects and meet with local residents to discuss needs.
4. Attention to incentives in the form of salaries or stipends and recognition in the community.
5. Access to university interns to work with students and conduct research in the community.

Participants in this project believe that its success can be measured by the wide base of community and institutional support demonstrated in the formation of the West Philadelphia Improvement Corps and an active community council for one school.

## What Doesn't Work

The extensive educational literature has yielded a number of examples of what doesn't work to reduce failure in school or dropout rates. Three major strategies that are consistently portrayed as ineffective are mandated promotion, ability grouping, and one-shot interventions.

STATE-MANDATED PROMOTION POLICIES

This policy calls for strict adherence to the use of testing results for determining promotion. Evidence is accumulating to show that if standards and requirements are raised without support for school improvement, and particularly without personal attention to high-risk students, the effect will push more children out of school than we are currently seeing. Higgins and Mueller summarize the effects of grade retention policies as costly, ineffective in preventing poor achievement, ineffective in preventing dropping out, and discriminatory.[60]

ABILITY GROUPING

Being labeled average or below average has an adverse effect on students' self-concept. The psychological costs of ability grouping for the lowest achieving students do not seem to be justified by the uncertain benefits of the practice.[61] Pink cites numerous studies that document that "students in the low trajectory consistently perform poorly, academically and behaviorally, compared to their high trajectory peers."[62] Placement in low ability groups is associated with low teacher expectations and low amounts of learning.

EARLY INTERVENTIONS WITHOUT FOLLOW-UP

Although Head Start and High Scope programs have been found to have long-term effects, without continuing support and follow-up throughout school years, many students will not succeed. Even with the Perry Preschool/High Scope program, the experimental group reported very high rates of delinquency, dropping out, and pregnancy, lower than the controls but much higher than the rates for all children.

In addition, a number of other practices and policies have been described as detrimental to educational enhancement. These include:

Basic skills teaching by itself; work experience and on-the-job training with no other interventions. Some kind of individual attention or mentoring is required.

Grafting additional staff and programs onto existing structures that don't work, such as extending the school day or adding more courses.

Increasing the number of attendance officers to cut down on truancy.

Finally, a caveat that probably applies to all programs: even excellent programs do not work for everyone. For example, many students drop out of alternative schools. It is hypothesized that the intervention comes too late in the schooling experience to remediate past problems.[63]

## Common Concepts in Prevention of School Failure and Dropping Out

The schools literature is list prone. Most of the studies end with sets of recommendations. In fact, the education field presents its concepts in a much more confident language than the other fields. The experts, and the task forces, and the commissions do not always agree; yet there is an amazingly strong consensus on the points which follow.[64] Nevertheless, we will also touch on some important subjects on which there is not complete agreement.

1. No single approach or component has been demonstrated as most effective. Schools and communities need a variety of strategies with different programs for different needs. The key word is flexibility.
2. Early intervention is of critical importance for the prevention of learning and development problems. Communities must have preschool programs and opportunities for parenting education in child development.

3. Early identification of high-risk students must be expedited and progress monitored through a longitudinal K–12 data system. Particular attention should be paid to transitions to elementary school, to junior high, and to senior high.

4. Small size of school and classes appears to be beneficial to high-risk students. Class size is not as important as how the teaching is organized.

5. Individualized attention and instruction are necessities for children with problems in school. Every student should have an individual instructional plan or contract.

6. Program autonomy is very important. The principal, the key individual in a school organization, should have authority to manage the school. Teachers should be involved in policy and curriculum development and held accountable for progress of students. Instructional practices should be flexible; for example, cooperative learning and team teaching have been shown to be effective.

7. Committed teachers must have high expectations for students and be sensitive to gender, race, and cultural issues. Priority must be given to hiring minority teachers, particularly those who can meet the needs of non-English speaking students. Teachers and other school personnel should be adequately rewarded for their students' progress. Teacher training should be revised to meet the needs of high-risk students.

8. Strong vocational components should make the link between learning and working using experiential education and out-of-class learning, community service projects, and paid work experience. Businesses can be involved in job placement and mentoring.

9. Intensive, sustained counseling is essential for high-risk students who need assistance with personal and family problems and, in many cases, on-site health and social services.

10. Positive school climate should be encouraged through a ''family'' atmosphere and a safe, secure, and nonthreatening environment. Behavioral guidelines and standards should be developed and implemented by students, school personnel, and parents.

11. School–community integration is essential. Collaborative programs for educational, family, social, and health services as well as job placement must be planned and implemented. The community must take responsibility for the complete package of services needed.

Many more items appear in the literature than are included here. Some were emphasized by only one expert—for example, Rutter's finding that students needed opportunities to participate in the running of the school,[65] or Garvin's finding that effective schools had an emphasis on applied and fine arts.[66] Levin has presented a whole list of ideas about augmenting home resources so that the home is used as a learning environment—for example, school systems could provide educational materials for parents to use at home.[67] According to Sizer, specialized counselors are unnecessary in schools; teachers should be the agents of social support.[68]

Some recommendations are unique to certain task force reports. A recent New York State Education Commissioner's Task Force pointed out the impact of racism on creating two different systems of education (effective and ineffective) and recommended that mechanisms be developed to implement supportive policies that further equity in education, to provide adequate resources to disadvantaged communities, and to monitor state and local compliance.[69]

There are several important ideas about which consensus is lacking. Although alternative schools have very strong proponents,[70] some observers feel that separating high-risk youth from students who are having successful experiences in school is both a mistake and a "copout." It may remove the troubled youths from positive peer role models, stigmatize them, and have less long-term effect than individual attention within the regular school. It has also been suggested that systems want to remove disruptive students from the regular school and setting up a separate unit serves that purpose. As we have seen, there are many successful models among alternative schools and thousands of high-risk students prefer to attend these smaller institutions with more caring teachers and individualized attention.

A related unresolved issue emerges from the studies of the effectiveness of Chapter 1 supplemental programs. It has been suggested that the impact might be greater if the funds were targeted on disadvantaged school districts rather than on individual students within schools.[71] In this way, resources could be used to change the entire school climate and culture. The practice of pulling children out of their classes for remediation for no more than a few hours per week would be discouraged. Specialized training for working with disadvantaged children might be made available to all teachers in a school system rather than to only a few, and Chapter 1 funds could be used for needed school reorganization.

Henry Levin and his colleagues at Stanford University have reacted to the continuing failure of the schools to educate high-risk children. "The premises of the remediation approach are demonstrably false," according to Levin, and the consequences are debilitating.[72] They have initiated demonstration projects in elementary schools that are rich in curriculum content relevant to students' lives. The goal is to accelerate learning prior to sixth grade so that disadvantaged students catch up while they still can. Rather than drill lessons, children are exposed to literature, problem solving, and a range of cultural experiences. Techniques such as cooperative learning, peer tutoring, and community outreach are incorporated. Parents, staff, and students enter into contractual relationships defining the obligations of each.

Whether the extension of the school day or the school year would have a positive effect on high-risk students is not known. Some experts are very supportive of the idea, believing that more intense instruction is required even to teach basic skills. Others maintain that students who can hardly get through the current short school day may have even greater difficulty over an extended day. However, programs that offer remediation during the summer have been shown to stem the learning loss experienced by high-risk students during that time. It has also been proposed that an additional school year be added to enable high-risk students to make the transition to college.

The concept of offering financial incentives for school completion is very attractive in some communities. It is not clear whether it is the actual money, or the individual attention, that creates the motivation to finish high school. Critics of the idea question whether it offers a viable long-term solution to ineffective school systems.

Open school choice is another intervention that is achieving heightened attention. In several states, initiatives have been created legislatively that allow students to go to any school they choose, with the state education dollars following them. Concern has been expressed that this shifting of populations from poor inner-city schools to more appealing suburban schools will further decimate the decaying inner-city systems. Instead, the effort might be better served if schools in disadvantaged communities were improved.

We conclude this section by turning to the late Ronald Edmonds, the noted guru of school effectiveness.[73] His oft-quoted short list of the most "tangible and indispensable characteristics of effective schools" includes: strong administrative leadership; a climate of expectation; an orderly environment without being rigid; emphasis on pupil acquisition of basic skills; and frequent monitoring of pupil progress. Edmonds's view in 1979 of the state of the art was that "we already know more than we need . . . to teach all children whose schooling is of interest to us." From even a cursory review of current efforts, this statement appears to have continuing validity.

## Notes

1. The Commission's final report sums up the findings from four information papers and 15 working papers: William T. Grant Commission on Work, Family, and Citizenship, *The Forgotten Half: Pathways to Success for America's Youth and Young Families* (Washington, D.C.: Youth and America's Future, 1988). See also G. Berlin and A. Sum, *Toward a More Perfect Union: Basic Skills, Poor Families and Our Economic Future* (New York: Ford Foundation, Occasional Paper 3, 1988).
2. D. Orlich, "Education Reforms: Mistakes, Misconceptions, Miscues," *Phi Delta Kappan* (March 1989): 512–17.
3. L. Darling-Hammong and B. Berry, *The Evolution of Teacher Policy* (Santa Monica, Calif.: Rand Corporation, 1988).
4. Education Commission of the States, *Communities Respond,* Youth at Risk Program, 1987.
5. H. Levin, "The Educationally Disadvantaged: A National Crisis," Working Paper #6, The State Youth Initiatives Project (Philadelphia, Pa.: Public/Private Ventures, July 1985).
6. "Children at Risk: A Summary Report of Selected Research Documents" (Prepared by the Superintendent's Analysis Team of the Syracuse City School District, January 1988).
7. Several recent publications have been used as primary sources for ideas about program models, including M. Orr, *Keeping Students in Schools* (San Francisco: Jossey Bass, 1987); U.S. Department of Education, *Dealing with Dropouts: The Urban Superintendents' Call to Action* (Washington, D.C.: Office of Educational Research and Improvement, 1987); National Dissemination Study Group, *Educational Programs that Work,* 12th ed. (Longmont, Colo.: Sopris West, 1986).

8. S. Hamilton, "Raising Standards and Reducing Dropout Rates," *Teachers College Record* 87(1986): 410–29.
9. Center for the Study of Social Policy, "The Annie E. Casey Foundation's New Futures Initiative: Strategic Planning Guide" (Unpublished report, 1987).
10. J. Lipsitz, *Successful Schools for Young Adolescents* (New Brunswick, N.J.: Transaction, 1984).
11. W. Gainer (Associate Director, Human Resources Division, U.S. Government Accounting Office), "Education's Chapter 1 and 2 Programs and Local Dropout Prevention and Reentry Programs," Testimony before the Subcommittee on Elementary, Secondary and Vocational Education, Committee on Education and Labor, House of Representatives, March 3, 1987, pp. 1–7.
12. M. Raywid, "The Current Status of Schools of Choice in Public Secondary Education," Hofstra University, Project on Alternatives in Education, 1982.
13. Office of Educational Research and Improvement, *The Current Operation of the Chapter 1 Program* (Washington, D.C.: U.S. Department of Education, 1987).
14. One principal in an inner city school showed me a list of hundreds of programs coming into his school from the outside, including computer use, dance, cooking, self-esteem, etc. But he said he had no idea what they did, who utilized them, and whether any of them were any good.
15. M. Rutter, B. Maughn, P. Mortimore, and J. Ouston, *15,000 Hours* (Cambridge, Mass.: Harvard University Press, 1979).
16. U.S. Congress, House Select Committee on Children, Youth and Families, *Opportunities for Success: Cost Effective Programs for Children, Update 1988* (Washington, D.C.: U.S. Government Printing Office, 1988).
17. I. Lazar, R. Darlington, H. Murray, J. Royce, and A. Snippev, "Lasting Effects of Early Education," *Monographs of the Society for Research in Child Development* 47:No. 1–2(1982).
18. Described in P. Higgins and D. Mueller, "The Prevention of Poor School Performance and School Failure: A Literature Review" (Unpublished report, Amherst H. Wilder Foundation, St. Paul, Minn., May 1988).
19. D. Pierson, "The Brookline Early Education Project," in R. Price, E. Cowen, R. Lorion, and J. Ramos-McKay, eds., *14 Ounces of Prevention* (Washington, D.C.: American Psychological Association, 1988), pp. 24–31.
20. Missouri Department of Elementary and Secondary Education, *New Parents as Teachers Project* (Jefferson City, Mo: Missouri Department of Elementary and Secondary Education, October 1985).
21. U.S. Department of Education, *Dealing with Dropouts,* pp. iv–v.
22. National Dissemination Study Group, *Educational Programs that Work,* Sections D–G.
23. R. Slavin, "Cooperative Learning and Student Achievement," Center for Research on Elementary and Middle Schools, Johns Hopkins University (1988).
24. M. Kennedy, B. Birman, and R. Demaline, *The Effectiveness of Chapter 1 Services* (Second Interim Report, Office of Educational Research and Improvement, U.S. Department of Education, July 1986).
25. R. Taggart, *Solving the Basic Skills Crisis* (Washington, D.C.: Remediation and Training Institute, 1987).
26. National Dissemination Study Group, *Educational Programs that Work,* p. F–6.
27. Dr. James Comer, Hearing before the Select Committee on Children, Youth and Families, "Improving American Education: Roles for Parents," June 7, 1984 (Washington, D.C.: U.S. Government Printing Office), 55–60.
28. Center for Research on Elementary and Middle Schools, "Success for All," *CREMS Report* (Baltimore, Md.: Johns Hopkins University, February 1989).

29. Lipsitz, *Successful Schools,* pp. 59–92; Center for Study of Social Policy, "Annie E. Casey Foundation's New Futures Initiative," Appendix D.
30. R. Felner, M. Ginter, and J. Primavera, "Primary Prevention During School Transitions: Social Support and Environmental Structure," *American Journal of Community Psychology* 10(1982): 277–90.
31. Advocates for Children of New York, *Meeting Adolescents Needs: Four Effective Schools* (New York: Advocates for Children of New York, 1986).
32. E. Cowen and A. Hightower, "The Primary Mental Health Project: Alternatives in School-based Preventive Interventions," in T. Gutkin and C. Reynolds, eds., *Handbook of School Psychology,* 2nd ed. (New York: John Wiley, 1989), pp. 775–95.
33. National Mental Health Association, "A Proud Tradition: The Lela Rowland Award Winners 1980–1988," *NMHA Prevention Advocate* 1(1988): 5–6.
34. Pennsylvania Department of Education, *Achieving Success with More Students: Addressing the Problem of Students at Risk, K–12* (Harrisburg, Pa.: Pennsylvania Department of Education, 1987). This manual, prepared in conjunction with Research for Better Schools, Philadelphia, Pennsylvania, describes theories and practices of effective prevention programs.
35. Orr, *Keeping Students in Schools,* pp. 28–38; Center for Study of Social Policy, "Annie E. Casey Foundation's New Futures Initiative," Appendix A; "Dropout Prevention," in *Network News* (New York: Academy for Educational Development, 1986).
36. Wheeler Clinic, "Student Assistance Model" (Plainville, Conn.: Wheeler Clinic, undated).
37. Ibid., p. 3.
38. Pennsylvania Department of Education, *Achieving Success with More Students,* pp. 111–17.
39. E. Caliste, "The Effect of a Twelve-Week Dropout Intervention Program," *Adolescence* 19(1984): 650–57.
40. Description from *IDRA Newsletter* (San Antonio, Tex.: Intercultural Development Research Association, May 1986). Also cited as a model in Committee for Economic Development, *Children in Need: Investment Strategies for the Educationally Disadvantaged* (New York: CED Research and Policy Committee, 1987). The CED report is one of the most influential of the many on the high-risk youth crisis.
41. E. Foley and P. Crull, *Educating the At-Risk Adolescent* (Report of the Public Education Association, 1984).
42. U.S. General Accounting Office (GAO), *School Dropouts: Survey of Local Programs* (Report to Congressional Requesters, BAO/HRD 87–108, 1987).
43. G. Wehlage, *Effective Programs for the Marginal High School Student* (Bloomington, Ind.: Phi Beta Kappa Educational Foundation, 1983).
44. G. Wehlage, R. Rutter, and A. Turnbaugh, "Evaluation of a Model Program for At-Risk Students" (Reprinted in Phi Delta Kappa, *Dropouts, Pushouts and Other Casualties* [Bloomington, Ind.: Center on Evaluation, Development, and Research, 1987]).
45. E. Vallejo, "How to Curb the Dropout Rate," *School Administrator* (September 1987), 21–23.
46. Committee for Economic Development, *Children in Need,* p. 69.
47. C. Sipe, J. Grossman, and J. Milliner, *Summer Training and Education Program (STEP): Report on the 1987 Experience* (Philadelphia, Pa.: Public/Private Ventures, 1988).
48. M. Freedman, "No Simple Dream," *Public Private Ventures News* (Winter 1987): 2.
49. Designs for Change, *The Bottom Line: Chicago's Failing Schools and How to Save Them* (Chicago School Watch, Report #1, 1985). This is a compelling description of an inner city school system and the relationship between segregation and school out-

comes. The Boston Compact is also described in Orr, *Keeping Students in Schools,* pp. 177–89; Committee for Economic Development, *Children in Need,* p. 72.

50. "Across the Nation," *The School Administrator* (September 1987), 5.

51. T. Sizer, *Horace's Compromise* (Boston: Houghton-Mifflin, 1984).

52. Public/Private Ventures, *Partners in Growth: Elder Mentors and At-Risk Youth* (Philadelphia, Pa.: Public/Private Ventures, Fall 1988).

53. A. Lewis, *Youth Serving the Young* (Washington, D.C.: Youth Service America, 1987).

54. Grant Commission on Work, Family, and Citizenship, *The Forgotten Half,* pp. 79–90.

55. "Profile: Bush's Bully Pulpit," *Streams* (January 1989), 1–2.

56. Cities-in-Schools, "Fact Sheet" and "Questions About Cities in Schools" (Washington, D.C.: Cities-in-Schools, 1988).

57. D. Sawyer, "Think Piece: Reflection, Renewal and Service," *Streams* (September 1989), 4.

58. J. Bacon, "New Futures Project Focuses on Teen Troubles," *USA Today,* March 9, 1988, 8A; news release from Annie E. Casey Foundation, March 9, 1988.

59. Pennsylvania Department of Education, *Achieving Success with More Students,* pp. IV, 26–29.

60. Higgins and Mueller, "The Prevention of Poor School Performance and School Failure," p. xii.

61. Carnegie Council on Adolescent Development, *Turning Points: Preparing American Youth for the 21st Century* (New York: Carnegie Corporation, 1989). This report includes recommendations for the transformation of middle schools.

62. W. Pink, "Schools, Youth and Justice," *Crime and Delinquency* 30(1984): 439–61.

63. National Coalition of Advocates for Students, *Steps* 1(1989): 1–9.

64. There is considerable overlap in the membership of national task forces and commissions which may account for the high level of agreement.

65. Lipsitz, *Successful Schools,* p. 5.

66. J. Garvin, "Common Denominators in Effective Middle Schools," in *Schools in the Middle: A Report on Trends and Practices* (Washington, D.C.: National Association of Secondary School Principals, 1986).

67. L. Olson, "Stanford Professor Aims to 'Speed Up' Learning for the Disadvantaged," *Education Week,* June 10, 1987, 12.

68. Personal communication, Theodore Sizer, October 1987.

69. *The Time for Assertive Action* (Report of the Commissioner's Task Force on the Education of Children and Youth at Risk, New York State Education Department, 1988).

70. Raywid, "Current Status of Schools of Choice," pp. 26–28; Foley and Crull, *Educating the At-Risk Adolescent,* pp. viii–xiii; G. Wehlage, R. Rutter, and A. Turnbaugh, "A Program Model for At-Risk High School Students," *Educational Leadership* 44(1987): 70–73.

71. U.S. Department of Education, *The Current Operation of the Chapter 1 Program* (Final Report from the National Assessment of Chapter 1, Washington, D.C.; Office of Educational Research and Improvement, 1987).

72. R. Colvin, "California Researchers 'Accelerate' Activities to Replace Remediation," *Education Week,* November 30, 1988, 6.

73. R. Edmonds, "Effective Schools for the Urban Poor," *Educational Leadership* 11(1979): 15–23.

# PART III

# SHAPING A STRATEGY FOR PREVENTION OF HIGH-RISK BEHAVIOR

# 13

# Common Concepts of
# Successful Prevention Programs

The review of four major fields—prevention of delinquency, substance abuse, teen pregnancy, and school failure (in Chapters 9 to 12)—yielded about 100 different programs that appear to have potential for changing behavioral outcomes.[1] Most of the selected programs reported evaluation data that showed improvements in social behavior or school achievement or reductions in substance abuse or unprotected sexual intercourse.[2] However, 20 of the programs were included as examples of new interventions based on proven theories of behavioral change but with incomplete evaluations. These programs represent a cross-section of thousands of efforts to change the lives of children and youth in all parts of the country.

In each chapter, the programs were loosely categorized by type. Among all the models discussed, about 10 percent fell into the category of early child or family intervention, 60 percent were school-based interventions, and 30 percent community-based or multiagency programs. Among the school-based programs, one-third involved specialized curricula, one-third provided nonacademic services in schools, and one-third dealt with school organization or were alternative schools.

As we will see, the successful programs share a number of common elements, more than might be expected given the extensive differences in size, complexity, goals, and level of documentation. Among the program models are those directed at very small groups of selected high-risk children and those directed at an entire school or community. Some of the programs had a single purpose (smoking prevention), while others had multiple goals (dropout and pregnancy prevention). Some were offered at one site, while others were multisite. The criterion of primary prevention was loosely applied; some of the most successful models combined identification and counseling or teaching of potential high-risk children with treatment of those who already had the problem.

The evaluation of some of the programs accepted here as models was admittedly less than ideal, demonstrating only short-term effects with imperfect control groups. However, for other models, the evaluation meets scientific standards. More than half of the evaluations were carried out by the "designers" of the programs, typically testing their own curricula in schools. Other evaluations were conducted by outsiders from universities, government agencies, and research organizations. In sum, what we have here is an assortment of diverse programs that appear to work, at least better than other programs.

What are the lessons that can be learned from this exercise? We can examine two sources of information, first the actual successful models and then the concepts of the experts about successful interventions, as outlined at the end of each of the program chapters (Chapters 9 to 12).

## Common Components of Successful Prevention Programs

### *Lessons from the Models*

To analyze the 100 programs of interest, an effort was made to extract from each of the program descriptions the specific items that characterized the intervention. For some programs, information about components was compiled from monographs or site visits and was rich in detail. For other programs, information was compiled from the literature, organization reports, or responses to telephone queries (see references for Chapter 9 to 12). What follows therefore is definitely not an operational evaluation but rather an impressionistic overview of available data. Many diverse program components were identified in the program descriptions that fell into categories such as timing, staffing, participants, program operations, personal support, specific skills, and incentives. Each program was characterized by four to six items. Those components that were most prevalent in each of the four different fields conclusively surfaced to the top and are described in the following discussion as the common components of successful programs. The most significant finding from this exercise was the remarkable co-occurrence of specific components in each of the diverse fields of prevention.

Some 11 common program components emerged from an analysis of the reported practices in successful intervention programs. Of these, the first two appeared to have the widest application: *the importance of providing individual attention to high-risk children and the necessity for developing broad communitywide interventions.* These items represent two points at either end of a wide spectrum that extends from individual one-on-one support to institutional changes in the community. This finding supports the view that the needs of high-risk children must be met at the personal level within the context of broader changes in the social environment.

#### 1. INTENSIVE INDIVIDUALIZED ATTENTION

In successful programs, high-risk children are attached to a responsible adult who pays attention to that child's specific needs. This theme was operationalized in each of the fields in several different kinds of programs. In substance abuse prevention, a student assistance counselor was available full-time for individual counseling and referral for treatment. In delinquency prevention, a family worker from the alternative diversion project gave "intensive care" to a predelinquent and the family to assist them to make the necessary changes in their lives to avoid repeat delinquent acts. In pregnancy prevention, a full-time social worker placed in the school system was available for individual counseling and referral. In school remediation, a prevention specialist worked with very high-risk children and their families to improve school attendance.

Various techniques were used, including individual counseling and small group meetings, individual tutoring and mentoring, and case management. Both professionals (psychologists, social workers, counselors, teachers) and nonprofessionals (community aides, volunteers) were utilized in these efforts. Personal counseling and support were offered in preschool settings, school classrooms, "time-out" rooms, school-based clinics, alternative schools, afterschool programs, community agencies, and through home visits and outreach.

## 2. COMMUNITYWIDE MULTIAGENCY COLLABORATIVE APPROACHES

The operating hypotheses of these communitywide programs is that, to change the behavior of young people, a number of different kinds of programs and services have to be in place. This theme was exemplified in the substance abuse prevention field by a communitywide health promotion campaign that used local media and community education in conjunction with the implementation of substance abuse prevention curricula in the local school. In the delinquency prevention field, the neighborhood development program involved local residents in neighborhood councils, working with the schools, police, courts, gang leaders, and the media. A successful model in pregnancy prevention concentrated on community education through media and a speaker's bureau, training of parents, clergy, and other community leaders, and development and implementation of a comprehensive sex and family life education program in the schools. The problem of dropping out of school was addressed by an all-out community effort involving the schools with local businesses, local government agencies, and universities in planning, teacher training, and student training and job placement.

The multicomponent methodology builds on significant successes among community programs for heart disease prevention.[3] Experience with collaborative programs appears to be growing in all fields of prevention. Partners in the models included schools, community health and social agencies, businesses, media, church groups, universities, police and courts, and youth groups. The composition of the coalition depended on the particular "crisis" to which the community was responding (e.g., drugs, dropout rates, teen pregnancy, crime, suicide, etc.). Typically, multiagency efforts have representative advisory councils and use volunteers from the community for various tasks (e.g., planning, community information, grants), as well as for personal mentoring. Cooperation with local media is generally used for gaining access to channels through which education and consciousness-raising efforts can be brought to the community. Local businesses offer mentors, equipment, and incentives, act as role models for career education, and help with job training and placement.

## 3. EARLY IDENTIFICATION AND INTERVENTION

Reaching children and their families in the early stages of the development of problem behaviors demonstrated both short- and long-term benefits. One well-documented preschool program (Perry Preschool) served as a model for delinquency, pregnancy, and substance abuse prevention, as well as for school achievement. (In this case, careful longitudinal tracking of a very small sample produced significant results.) Other successful programs were directed toward preschoolers living in disadvantaged neighborhoods or elementary school students who were acting out in early grades or falling behind in achievement. Early needs assessments and computerized systems for tracking high-risk students over time are utilized in several programs.

## 4. LOCUS IN SCHOOLS

Many of the successful prevention models are physically located in schools. We would expect that most school remediation and much of the substance abuse prevention would take place on school sites. However, it is of great significance that so many of the delinquency prevention and pregnancy prevention interventions were also located in schools. Of course, the goals of the interventions are interrelated, with the acquisition of basic skills as the bottom line for most high-risk children. The idea that a healthy, safe school climate and effective school organization contribute to prevention of negative behavior extends beyond the education field to the other prevention fields as well. Programs in which the principal is considered one of the key elements of success may be found across the various fields—for example, in school reorganization, on school teams for delinquency and substance abuse prevention, as facilitator for school-based clinics, and as liaison with student assistance counselors. Alternative schools and schools within schools have demonstrated improved behavioral as well as educational outcomes for high-risk youth.

## 5. ADMINISTRATION OF SCHOOL PROGRAMS
## BY AGENCIES OUTSIDE OF SCHOOLS

In each of the fields, agencies or organizations outside of the schools carried the major responsibility for exemplary programs that were implemented within the schools. Four types of arrangements were exemplified among the models: (1) the program was designed by a university-based researcher (e.g., James Comer at Yale or Cheryl Perry at Minnesota) who obtained a grant to implement the program and conducted evaluation research in the school or community agency; (2) the model was designed by a nonprofit youth services and research organization (e.g., Public/Private Ventures or the Academy for Educational Development) and implemented in multiple demonstration projects in schools or communities with support from foundations or government agencies; (3) a model was initiated by a foundation (e.g., Robert Wood Johnson, Annie E. Casey) or a government agency (e.g., Office of Substance Abuse Prevention, New Jersey Department of Human

Services) which issued a Request for Proposals calling for comprehensive collaborative programs in schools; (4) a program was developed by a local health or youth service agency in collaboration with a school (Adolescent Resources Corporation in Kansas City) and obtained funds from a state health agency (Missouri Health Department) and foundations. In these types of interventions, project staff may work for the outside agency or be responsible for training and supervising on-site staff. Curriculum materials are usually created by program developers who also are available to provide technical assistance. In all cases, research is conducted by the outside agency. Schools typically provide space, maintenance, and coordination between outside agency staff and school personnel.

### 6. LOCATION OF PROGRAMS OUTSIDE OF SCHOOLS

Not every successful program is located within a school. The staff of certain program models believe they are more effective because they are community rather than school based. Young people who are "turned off" by the school system were reported to have participated in programs in community and church centers, businesses, and a large array of youth service programs. Community-based youth-serving agencies appear to have greater latitude in offering controversial services, such as family planning, and can facilitate weekend and summer programs. Youth programs located outside of schools were able to offer a very wide range of services; for example, many community centers had extensive arts programs with theater groups and painting classes. Others were geared up to serve the most high-risk populations, such as homeless and runaway youth, often providing overnight shelter.[4]

### 7. ARRANGEMENTS FOR TRAINING

Many of the successful programs employ special kinds of staff, professional or nonprofessional, who require training to implement a program. Often they are called on to use a certain protocol (behavioral therapy) or a new curriculum (Life Skills training). School reorganization entails complex concepts such as school-based management, team teaching, and cooperative learning. These approaches require extensive in-service training and ongoing supervision. A number of the model programs have established school teams, generally made up of the support personnel (social worker, psychologist, counselor), the school principal, in some instances parents, and occasionally students. These teams also require training and orientation to carry out the mandates of the intervention. Several model programs employ full-time staff to coordinate teams, curriculum development, treatment services, and referrals, as well as to expedite research protocols.

### 8. SOCIAL SKILLS TRAINING

A number of variants of personal and social skills training have emerged in this review (and more exist than have been discussed). The approach generally involves teaching youngsters about their own risky behavior, giving them the skills to cope with and, if necessary, resist the influences of their peers in social situations, and helping them to make healthy decisions about their futures. Techniques such as role-playing, rehearsal, peer instruction, and media analysis are typically employed. While much of the impetus for these curricula emerged from successes in smoking prevention, curricula currently in use are designed to prevent a range of behaviors with negative consequences. Examples have been given that resulted in delaying initiation of alcohol and marijuana use, delaying initiation of sexual intercourse, improving use of contraception, and improving behavior in school. Few of the social skills programs have demonstrated positive effects with high-risk children. What the research has documented is significant changes among participants that are maintained over a few years, especially if they are exposed to booster (repeat) sessions in subsequent years of school.

## 9. ENGAGEMENT OF PEERS IN INTERVENTIONS

Program designers in every field are aware of the importance of peer influences on adolescent behavior. Research on the efficacy of using peers in prevention interventions has produced mixed results. However, several successful models emerged from this review. The most successful approaches use older peers to influence or help younger peers, either as classroom instructors (in social skills training) or as tutors and mentors. In some programs the peer tutors are paid. The training and supervision of the students are important aspects of this component. Students selected to act as peer mentors gain the most from the experience, probably because of the intensive individual attention and enrichment they receive.

## 10. INVOLVEMENT OF PARENTS

While programs report less success in involving parents than they would like, a number of models across the various fields have demonstrated that programs directed toward parents can be successful. Two approaches have shown documented results: home visits that provide parent education and support, and employment of parents as classroom aides. Outreach to the homes of high-risk families has proven effective for adolescents as well as for preschool and other age children. Parents have also been recruited as members of school teams and advisory committees. It appears that the more defined the expected role for parents, the more likely that participation will occur. Invitations to attend meetings and workshops have failed to recruit the parents of high-risk children. Parent-training programs have been shown to be effective with selective groups.

## 11. LINK TO THE WORLD OF WORK

Programs in a variety of fields use innovative approaches to introduce career planning, expose youngsters to work experiences, and prepare them to enter the labor force. Successful models offered various components: combining life-planning curricula with school remediation and summer job placement; creating opportunities for volunteer community service; and paying high-risk youth to become tutors for younger children. These components were most often combined with group counseling and seminars to help students interpret and integrate the experience.

## Recommendations from the Experts

A list of concepts at the close of each of the prevention chapters (Chapters 9 to 12) was based on the ideas and recommendations by experts about what to do about the specific problem. In general, the experts' opinions confirm the lessons learned from the models. This is not unexpected when one considers that a number of the experts are responsible for the theoretical constructs that shape the models. There is an overlap between those who conduct the research and create the literature and those who are on the panels of experts that make recommendations to commissions and task forces. What is more important here than chicken-and-egg questions (Does the theory drive the practice or does the practice shape the theory?) is the significant agreement among the four diverse fields about concepts. Again, there is a striking consensus among experts from widely divergent disciplines about what needs to be done to help high-risk children.

## Common Concepts among Experts

Six major points surfaced in each of the problem areas, demonstrating the high level of agreement about solutions among the experts from different fields. These theoretical concepts strongly support the lessons learned from successful programs.

### 1. THERE IS NO ONE SOLUTION TO THIS PROBLEM

There is no single program component (no "magic bullet") that by itself can alter the outcomes for all children at high risk for delinquency, substance abuse, teen pregnancy, and school failure.

### 2. HIGH-RISK BEHAVIORS ARE INTERRELATED

Prevention programs should have broader, more holistic goals. Interventions should be directed at risk factors rather than at categorical problem behaviors.

### 3. A PACKAGE OF SERVICES IS REQUIRED WITHIN EACH COMMUNITY

The package must contain multiple components that respond to the particular needs in that community. Communitywide planning is a requisite for bringing all the institutions together to determine what must be done.

### 4. INTERVENTIONS SHOULD BE AIMED AT CHANGING INSTITUTIONS RATHER THAN AT CHANGING INDIVIDUALS

The main thrust of prevention should be in the schools because low achievement is a major risk factor for each of the problems. The acquisition of basic skills is fundamental. Furthermore, schools should be the locus for nonacademic interventions that deal with health, welfare, and support because that's where the children are located, at least in their earlier years.

5. THE TIMING OF INTERVENTIONS IS CRITICAL

Preschool and middle school periods are significant transition points in a child's life when major setbacks can occur. The middle school years have received the least attention in the past. Most interventions start too late to have any effect.

6. CONTINUITY OF EFFORT MUST BE MAINTAINED

"One shots" do not have any effect. Follow-up services, staff supervision, and booster curricula are necessary to insure that whatever changes take place are maintained.

## Do Components of Successful Models Differ From Experts' Opinions?

The differences between the theory of what works and the practices in exemplary programs are not substantive. The experts' opinions are more general than the specific program components extracted from reviews of model programs. The strongest area of agreement is in the efficacy of collaborative communitywide multicomponent programs using a variety of approaches. Exemplary programs demonstrate that large-scale interventions that combine school and community agencies are feasible.

This review suggests that actual programs adhere to the concept of intensive individualized attention but that this focus has not often been articulated by the experts. Although many reports mention the importance of "caring," few recommend the specific approaches that are being used in some of the most successful programs.

The experts appear to place more emphasis on the concept that prevention programs should focus heavily on high-risk children and deal simultaneously with multiple problems. The program designers tend to start with a specific problem behavior and, in addressing that problem, come to understand the importance of a broader, more holistic approach.

The experts recognize the importance of communitywide interventions and broader youth-at-risk programs, but their recommendations do not encompass operationalizing these practices. Few experts view the solution to "their" categorical problems as a joint responsibility of several agencies from different fields, reflecting the "tunnel vision" syndrome in categorical programs. Experts tend to concentrate narrowly on what their categorical colleagues should do and focus less on broader social issues. For example, conferences on substance abuse prevention rarely include experts on school remediation or poverty. Task forces on school remediation rarely pay attention to pregnancy prevention. Schools of education rarely train administrators or teachers to acquire the necessary skills to understand

and cope with the ''new morbidities.'' Meetings of researchers on adolescent behavior almost never include program practitioners.

The importance of training, highlighted by many of the models, gets short
shrift in experts' recommendations. Although most recommendations call for committed and sensitive teachers, social workers, community aides, and other staff
and volunteers, little attention is paid to giving them the necessary orientation,
skills, and supervision to activate their commitment.

## Unresolved Issues

The area of agreement about what works in the four diverse fields is substantial.
We can gain important insights that will help us design more effective strategies
for the future. But this exercise still leaves a number of issues that are unresolved.

### *"Comprehensiveness" Is Not a Magic Bullet*

Although this review produces strong support for the concept of comprehensive
multicomponent approaches to high-risk children, each field has its own imperatives that must be met. It is important to recognize the limitations of comprehensive thinking, as well as the advantages. Important categorical program components can be eliminated in the quest for more holistic approaches to children. The
most obvious and controversial area is pregnancy prevention.

Experts in the adolescent pregnancy field generally agree and several of the
models demonstrated that access to contraception in school and community clinics
is an essential component. In addition, sexually active teenagers who do become
pregnant need access to confidential pregnancy testing. If they opt to continue the
pregnancy, they need access to prenatal care and other services; and if they make
a decision to terminate the pregnancy, access to safe abortions. Commitment by
public officials and community decision makers to the concept of prevention of
pregnancy and early unintended childbearing is considered a fundamental requirement for successfully launching communitywide efforts. This principle was not
given high priority in the recommendations made by experts in any of the other
fields, though there was acknowledgment that the problems of teen pregnancy,
delinquency, school failure, and substance abuse were interrelated. Concern has
been expressed that folding family-planning programs into broader communitywide efforts will reduce visibility and, possibly, effectiveness.

Recommendations in the education field included many unique elements, ranging from systemwide school reorganization and school-based management to self-
paced instructional materials, cooperative learning, team teaching, and opportunities for personal evaluation based on individual progress rather than standardized
test scores. Many of the interventions in the other fields incorporated educational
enhancement as the major program component. In fact, the prevention of delinquency appears to be embedded in the prevention of school failure. Whether delinquency prevention is actually a field in itself or whether it should be subsumed
under the rubric of educational remediation is an unresolved issue. To a great

degree, this may be true of prevention of substance abuse and teen pregnancy as well. The acquisition of basic skills at appropriate ages appears to be a primary component of all prevention. One might ask, based on this analysis, if school failure were eliminated, and all children were achieving well in school, would the other categorical interventions become obsolete?

## The "War on Drugs" as a Political Football

The whole direction of the substance abuse field appears to be an "unresolved issue." Currently, a "war on drugs" is being launched in the political arena with heightened rhetoric on the scourge of drugs and how this is the "number one" problem in this country. Recent reaction to increasing drug wars and inner-city homicides have led to proposals about harder punishments, including the death penalty. The evidence presented in this book suggests that almost none of the proposed measures will have much effect on the abuse of drugs, particularly crack cocaine, among high-risk adolescents.

The drive toward abstention as a goal has resulted in the massive use of resources on low- and no-risk youth. Perceptions are slowly changing about priorities for program development, but the major activity out in the field is heavily weighted with "saying no" interventions that bypass potentially alienated youth. Unlike the other fields, substance abuse prevention must deal with two sides of a complex equation: supply and demand. Some experts believe that it is a waste of time to foster prevention efforts unless very strong measures are taken to contain the supply. Eliminating subsidies for tobacco growers and placing high taxes on cigarettes and alcohol have been proposed, as well as heightened efforts to stop the flow of hard drugs at our borders. Measures to enforce laws on drinking age and drunk driving have proven effective at lowering rates of motor fatalities among teenagers. At the same time, some experts believe that the only solution to the drug problem is the legalization of drugs.

## Targeting of High-Risk Children

This overview of program models and expert opinion has not resolved the question of targeting high-risk children. The two disparate positions are: (1) changing social institutions, particularly raising the quality of education in the nation, should impact on all children; and (2) resources are so scarce they should be rationed to focus on the needs of high-risk and disadvantaged children. We can gain an overview of current targeting practices from the reviews of successful interventions. Programs to prevent delinquency and school failure were most likely to focus on high-risk children, or at least on schools or neighborhoods with many disadvantaged families. Programs to prevent substance abuse focus largely on all children in certain school grades who are offered 5 to 20 sessions of a prevention curriculum. However, a few exceptional programs concentrated services on identified high-risk youth or known drug neighborhoods. School-based sex and family life education programs to prevent pregnancy were also offered to all children in a grade, clinic programs were available to all potential users of contraception, but more recent comprehensive interventions were aimed at high-risk youth or communities with high pregnancy rates.

Many of these differences spring from interpretations of who is at risk of what. School failure is easily measured and, in fact, every student from kindergarten to twelfth grade carries markers of risk status right on his report card. It is not so easy to identify those who are at high risk of negative consequences of substance abuse, unprotected intercourse, and acting out. However, new techniques for needs assessments make identification feasible in early grades.

In any case, concern is often expressed about the effects of stigmatization resulting from targeting high-risk youth. Classification systems in general, such as ability grouping in classrooms, have produced negative effects on learning as well as lowered self-esteem among all but the highest achievers. Some experts believe that school reorganization that allows *all* children an equal opportunity for cognitive development and mastery of essential skills and areas of knowledge (Sizer model) should be the goal. Others believe that the only solution to the problems of high-risk youth lies in social and economic changes involving state and federal educational, employment, housing, and welfare policies. Although there is no consensus on this matter, the majority of those concerned with high-risk youth seem to take the position that resources should be targeted on high-risk neighborhoods and school districts, but not on specific high-risk children.

### Special Cultural Considerations for Different Ethnic Groups

An issue related to targeting is whether it is necessary to develop special programs (curricula, skills training, and so on) for specific racial or ethnic groups in this heterogeneous society. The key phrase here is "sensitivity to cultural diversity." This perception has led to the development of Black Heritage clubs for young boys, social skills training that is built around Hispanic concepts (e.g., "dignidad" = self-worth), the use of Native American instructors for Native American students, contraceptive education that assumes Hispanic males are "macho," and there are many other examples. The related (but not the same) issue of bilingual education is, of course, exceedingly controversial. There is enormous tension between those who believe in separate language classrooms and those who believe in total immersion in English. In any case, the deleterious effect of the absence of black and Hispanic teachers and administrators in disadvantaged school districts has been well documented.[5]

To assist high-risk youth, some experts believe that the primary issues to be dealt with are social and economic disadvantage. They believe that if school systems, social systems, and the economy dealt with all communities equally, racial and ethnic differences in achievement would be reduced. They maintain that solutions must involve allocations of massive resources for the problems of the disadvantaged, not just the development of special programs for racial groups. This does not mean that they oppose affirmative action, but it does mean that they believe in large inclusive coalitions that will advocate legislatively for broad-scale interventions in education, employment, housing, and welfare.

As for sensitivity, the model programs demonstrate conclusively that this is an essential attribute no matter who the client is. Programs that pay attention to cultural diversity and life-style as well as individual diversity are more likely to succeed.

### Continuation of Programs that Have Proven Not to Work

A brief summary of the kinds of programs that were reported as ineffective for changing behavior was included in each of the prevention chapters. Common themes emerged about what doesn't work as well as what does. The universal experience is that no one intervention appears to have much impact on high-risk behavior unless it is accompanied by other interventions. For example, information alone and media alone have no proven effect on behavior. Thus, posters that "Just Say No" may be a wasted effort. Affective programs that tried to raise self-esteem and make young people "feel better" about themselves were not successful in any of the fields. "Scared Straight" programs produced poor results among delinquents and substance users. Basic skills training or job training without personal attention had little positive effect. Many school practices and policies, such as ability grouping, grade retention, suspensions, and expulsions, were found to have negative effects. Family involvement programs that tried to get high-risk parents to come to meetings or workshops at schools, clinics, or community centers were not successful.

The most discouraging field appeared to be delinquency prevention where some of the programs that were effective with nondelinquents, such as intensive case work, community interventions, and behavioral therapy, did not seem to work. It was hypothesized that most programs aimed at delinquency were initiated much too late in the young person's life to change the trajectory. It was also pointed out that programs that group delinquents together with their peers probably reinforce delinquent behavior. One of the successful models focused on working with individual high-risk youth in their home settings in order to avoid the influence of delinquent peers.

In the substance abuse field, the concept of "treatment integrity" was emphasized. This issue was raised in two ways: concern about replication of prevention programs based on evaluated curricula that were being implemented without adequate teacher preparation and training (which therefore had no effect), and the massive marketing and utilization of unevaluated curricula. While marketing practices are most obvious in the substance abuse field, the same problem applies to sex education curricula, school remediation curricula, computer programs, and many other products that are sold without any testing or certification.

It is important to reiterate that no program, no matter how well designed it is, works equally well for all participants. None of the successes reported on here changed behavior for everyone; they were able at best to show greater positive changes among experimental groups than control groups. Despite Father Flanagan's assertion that "there is no such thing as a bad boy," the experience of even the most skilled practitioners is that a few children (and their families) just seem to be irremediable.

## Cloning Charismatic Leaders

The term "charismatic leader" has not worked its way into any of the prevention literature. Yet most of the successful programs mentioned are associated with an individual. This person is often a researcher who designed a curriculum and then administered its implementation. We cannot discern from the literature how much of the positive effect may have derived from the personality of the individual and how much can be attributed to the actual program. This is, of course, why replication is so important, and why the phrase "treatment integrity" is so often mentioned in regard to curricula.

Several of the most successful educational and cultural programs are directed by truly charismatic individuals. They have great sensitivity to children. Often one observes them "laying on hands," coming into a roomful of youngsters, distributing hugs, and knowing each of them by name. However, these people do more than "loving." They have high expectations for the children and work very hard to impart the skills and the knowledge that the children will need in order to "make it." Many of them also appear to have mastered the art of "grantmanship"; they know how to appeal to funders and are exceptionally articulate about their programs.

Training administrators, teachers, nurse-practitioners, counselors, and others who work with children to develop the qualities of the program innovators is rarely addressed. Yet the need for adequately trained managers and other personnel is substantial. If programs are expected to recruit enough personnel to initiate and maintain the agenda implicit in these findings, problems such as low salaries, "burn out," and lack of prestige must be dealt with.

## Incentives

The idea of offering financial or other rewards as incentives for achievement is certainly not new. The most highly publicized approach involves a wealthy sponsor who offers high-risk children college tuition if they stay in school. Another comprehensive program guarantees college admission and tuition for youth who don't drop out and don't become parents. While the incentive approach seems more relevant to dropout prevention, elements are also found in the substance abuse field. Schools are given recognition for being drug free, and program participants who sign a pledge of abstinence are awarded tee-shirts and banners. Pregnancy prevention programs have offered records and other merchandise in exchange for continued visits. In a current highly publicized effort, young women are being offered one dollar for every day they do not become pregnant, collectible weekly at a family-planning agency. In delinquency prevention, we find the concept of the "token economy," accumulating points for good behavior.

Given the documented successes of some of the incentive programs, why does it appear here as an unresolved issue? The problem is twofold. First, it is difficult to determine whether the intervention is really the material reward or the amount of social support made available along with the incentive. It may be that young people would respond equally well to intense individual attention. The second concern has to do with the incorporation of fiscal incentives in public programs, particularly educational systems. If large amounts of funds are available, it may be more effective to use them to reorganize the system rather than to pay a small number of youngsters to cope with the system.

### Evaluation Problems

A frequently reiterated point bears mentioning here: there is a shortage of acceptable evaluations of interventions in the various fields. Of the thousands of prevention programs, only a few in each field have been rigorously evaluated. Many of the evaluations that meet scientific standards were conducted by university-based researchers who devise theories, design curricula or other interventions, and then submit them to fairly limited testing. The available literature on program effects is weighted by the university system. College professors have to "publish or perish," which accounts for the endless production of articles in learned journals, particularly in regard to substance abuse and educational psychology, documenting changes in attitudes and knowledge, but not in behavior. Much of the university research is supported by government grants from categorical agencies that are looking for specific effects (such as the Office of Adolescent Pregnancy's interest in abstention programs and the earlier National Institute on Drug Abuse's interest in delaying initiation of first substance use). One impression gained from this exercise is that the more involved the researcher is in demonstrating a positive outcome, the more likely a success. Thus, programs that have an on-site researchers who can suggest program improvements over time have shown better results. A small number of the most impressive programs have been designed and operated by nonprofit research and program development companies, generally with support from foundations. Large-scale demonstration projects involving multiple sites, control groups, and longitudinal design are very expensive, but the evidence gathered here suggests that these kinds of experiments are necessary to yield that quality and quantity of data necessary to make judgments about what works.

Many programs with a great deal of potential have not been evaluated because they are operated by administrators whose priorities are elsewhere. Unless their funding requires evaluation, there is no incentive to conduct research, which is often perceived as intrusive and time consuming. Not until program evaluation research receives the requisite attention and support from both the public and private sectors will we have sufficient data to fine tune some of the program components outlined here.

### Media

The impact of media is very difficult to evaluate. The literature suggests that, as a single approach, media has little effect. Yet, in combination with other approaches, it can be effective. For example, posters and TV commercials can encourage certain behaviors, such as using condoms to prevent AIDS. However, if the ad does not contain any information about where to get the services being promoted, it provides little opportunity for the viewer or listener to act to change behavior.

## Summary: What Works

Information on about 100 different successful programs has been compiled from the fields of delinquency, substance abuse, teen pregnancy, and educational remediation. A number of important lessons and concepts have been extracted from the model program descriptions and from the opinions of experts in these fields. The level of consensus between the different disciplines about what works to prevent high-risk behavior is remarkable.

The program experience documents the importance of early and continuous intensive individualized attention. And many models exist that link responsible professional and nonprofessional adults to high-risk children. At the same time, the context of community is strongly reinforced by this review. There is solid agreement that effective communitywide prevention programs must include an array of program components and involve multiple community agencies in collaborative arrangements, with a view toward changing institutional roles. The particular package of services required in any one community can be determined by a process of planning that identifies who needs what services and how resources can be allocated to meet priorities.

School failure is increasingly recognized as the common marker of high-risk status. Schools are viewed as both the primary institution that impacts on the lives of the children and the locus for other supportive services. Many models exist that demonstrate successful academic remediation in disadvantaged communities. The principles underlying effective school organization are well known. Other model programs rely on outside health and social service agencies and local universities to bring nonacademic services, staff, curricula, and technical assistance into schools.

Other components of successful interventions include attention to staff training and development; use of personal social skills training in teaching students coping mechanisms; engagement of high-risk youth in peer interventions; involvement of parents through home visits and in specific defined roles; and linkages to the world of work through curricula, job experience, and volunteer community service. While many of the model programs are school based, significant models are community based, reflecting the importance of addressing the diverse needs of high-risk youth.

It would be nice if the comprehensive framework that emerges from this analysis could incorporate all prevention concepts from the extensive array of efforts and experience and wrap them up in a neat package. However, there are clearly some loose ends. We cannot put all of the categorical efforts out of business, at least not for a long time. Because there are so many special cases, attention has to be focused by program developers and advocates on the specific requirements in these different prevention efforts: sexually active young people need contraception, children of alcoholics need support services, runaways need shelter, and so on.

Although many model programs pay attention to training and supervision, the lack of additional personnel sufficiently trained to implement replications of these models, or create new ones, must be addressed (probably by academic institutions responsible for graduate programs). Additional evaluation research is clearly needed to further define what works. We have mentioned uncertainty about the impact of media and incentives. Many other questions about evaluation have been raised throughout this review and elsewhere. Much of the ongoing research does not address what seem to be compelling issues, such as whether or not an intervention results in behavioral changes. And, as we have seen, even when programs have been shown to be ineffective (e.g., information alone), they continue to be implemented.

It is interesting at this juncture to compare these findings about what works (and what doesn't) with those of others who have attempted comparable analyses across disciplines. Schorr extracted lessons from successful programs that reached and helped disadvantaged children and families (maternal and child health services, child care, family services, and teen pregnancy) and came out with a similar list.[6] Her key words for success were intensive, comprehensive, and flexible (in contrast to ineffective programs that were fragmented, meager, and uncoordinated). As in the model prevention programs described in this book, Schorr found that effective interventions had caring staffs and provided convenient and accessible services. She placed particular emphasis on the importance of flexibility in professional roles, pointing out that there was a "fundamental contradiction between the needs of vulnerable children . . . and the traditional requirements of professionalism and bureaucracy." In the most successful interventions, professionals were willing to step out of their bureaucratic molds and were guided by the needs of their clients (e.g., helping families with household problems, not imposing eligibility criteria for services). None of the programs identified by Schorr was a product of the "normal functioning of a large public or private system"; instead, they operated in unusual constraint-free conditions with unusually gifted leaders (what we have called charismatic leaders).

Another analysis of prevention programs has been conducted by the Task Force on Promotion, Prevention and Intervention Alternatives of the American Psychological Association (APA). In a search for model prevention programs, 300 interventions were reviewed, 52 met the stringent criteria including evaluation, and 14 were selected and described in a casebook for practitioner (psychologists') use.[7] Five of the programs were early childhood interventions, five were directed at youth (social skills, social supports), and the other four were for adults and the elderly. According to Price and colleagues, the model programs shared certain characteristics. All of them were based on strong theoretical frameworks and knowledge of risk behavior. They were targeted toward altering the life trajectory of the participants and expected that the resultant changes would be long term. These models offered new skills for coping more effectively and provided social support in the face of life transitions. These findings overlap with our program review and, in fact, several of the APA models are described in this text.

Another comprehensive view of what works comes from the National League of Cities. In an effort to provide city officials with practical descriptions of effective programs that have potential for replication, a number of experts compiled descriptions of 30 local programs (child care, youth employment, homelessness, and teen pregnancy).[8] In summarizing the experiences of communities in addressing the needs of children and families, Kyle identified critical elements of successful programs: strong leadership, often one person (the charismatic leader again); a strong data base; collaborations between the public and private sectors; coordination between service agencies; involvement of the target community in policymaking and program development; crucial role of schools; and the importance of evaluation. Again, the findings are substantially the same as from our program review.

Finally, we turn to the *Funders' Guide Manual* from the Amherst Wilder foundation, a report on prevention programming in human services directed toward helping other foundations evaluate proposals. With an approach similar to that found in this book, Mueller and Higgins conducted extensive reviews of the literature in four problem areas: child abuse and neglect, poor school performance and school failure, teen pregnancy, and teen substance abuse.[9] They found a number of common factors that influence the effectiveness of prevention programs, including the ability to identify and target high-risk youth; appropriate timing (early) and sufficient intensity; involvement of parents (but they are skeptical about feasibility); availability of well-trained and highly skilled staff; incorporation of experiential learning and personal social skills training; and integration or coordination with other efforts in the community. They recommend broader more generic interventions for younger children but believe that, as specific problems emerge in early adolescence, programs should have a more narrow focus (e.g., explicit education on birth control). The Mueller-Higgins study, covering much of the same territory as this book, confirms many of the concepts and conclusions found here—that the highest priority should be given to developing comprehensive, multifaceted prevention efforts within communities. In these authors' words, "ideally, prevention programs should address risk factors across the multiple environmental levels that surround the at-risk individual—i.e., the personal or psychological level, the family level, the school and community level and the broader social level."[10]

It should be clear by now that, despite shortcomings in program evaluation, enough is known to greatly improve the potential life course for high-risk children in the United States. In Chapter 14, this knowledge of common (and uncommon) concepts is used as a framework to develop strategies for building stronger, more intensive programs that will be effective at making substantive changes in children's lives and in their communities.

## Notes

1. Many more programs were identified than could be included.
2. It should be kept in mind that many of the program descriptions are based on secondary sources and the results could have been overstated. The author did not have access to the actual evaluation data in most cases.
3. For a review of three major comprehensive communitywide prevention programs, see

C. Johnson and J. Solis, "Comprehensive Community Programs for Drug Abuse: Implications of the Community Heart Disease Prevention Programs for Future Research," in T. Glynn, C. Leukefeld, and J. Ludford, eds., *Preventing Adolescent Drug Abuse: Intervention Strategies* (National Institute on Drug Abuse, USDHHS, NIDA Research Monograph, 47, 1985), pp. 76–114.

4. A number of very impressive community programs were not included in the program models because they have never been evaluated or they didn't fit into any specific categorical notch. For example, *El Puente* (a Holistic Center for Growth and Development in Brooklyn, N.Y.) serves large numbers of Hispanic youth and their families with health services, classes in karate and aerobics, a wide range of arts classes, counseling, and legal and social services; *Project Spirit* is a family-oriented church-based program operated by the National Congress of Black Churches in 15 churches in three cities. The project offers after-school tutorials, cultural enrichment, parent education, and a pastoral counseling education component. These programs, and many others, are described in the publications of the Adolescent Pregnancy Prevention Clearinghouse of the Childrens' Defense Fund.

5. R. Reed, "Education and Achievement of Young Black Males," in J. Gibbs, ed., *Young, Black and Male in America* (Dover, Mass.: Auburn, 1989), pp. 37–96.

6. L. Schorr, *Within Our Reach* (New York: Doubleday, 1988), pp. 259–60.

7. R. Price, E. Cowen, R. Lorion, and J. Ramos-McKay, *14 Ounces of Prevention* (Washington, D.C.: American Psychological Association, 1988).

8. J. Kyle, ed., *Children, Families and Cities: Programs that Work at the Local Level* (Washington, D.C.: National League of Cities, 1987).

9. D. Mueller and P. Higgins, *Funders' Guide Manual: A Guide to Prevention Programs in Human Services* (Saint Paul, Minn.: Amherst Wilder Foundation, 1988).

10. Ibid., p. 23.

# 14

## Strategies for Preventing High-Risk Behavior

This book began with the hypothesis that a definable segment of America's youth is so disadvantaged that this group will not be able to grow up into productive adults unless they receive immediate attention. An analysis of successful prevention programs has documented that enough information is now available to launch the necessary interventions to change the prospects for many of these young people. In Chapters 3 to 7, the prevalence and overlap in high-risk behavior were described and quantified; Chapter 8 reviewed the organizational structure that defines categorical programs; and Chapters 9 to 13 compiled extensive information on successful prevention programs. In this final chapter, we build on those findings to outline specific procedures that may lead to the development of more rational and effective strategies for changing the life trajectories for millions of children. These strategies rely heavily on the concept of centralized Youth Development Agencies, at the local, state, and federal levels. Such structures would be empowered to package the various program components so that they would have greater impact and efficiency.

### Who Is At Risk?

It should be well understood by now that approximately one in four children of the 28 million aged 10 to 17 are in dire need of assistance because they are at high risk of engaging in multiple problem behaviors—in other words, of being substance abusers, having early unprotected intercourse, being delinquents, and failing in school. Based on current population estimates, this means that 7 million young people living primarily in disadvantaged neighborhoods are in the target population for intensive care. Minority youth have higher prevalence rates and are more visible in densely populated urban areas; nevertheless, the majority of these multiproblem youth are white (and male). Another 7 million young people—25 percent—practice risky behavior, but to a lesser degree, and are therefore less subject to negative consequences. And, it is estimated that about half of the youth population, 14 million, are not currently involved in high-risk behaviors and appear to be moving through the educational system at expected levels. However, their problem-solving skills need sharpening and they need access to a higher quality of education, as do all children.

## What Are the Underlying Antecedents of High-Risk Behavior?

The evidence that the different problem behaviors have many common antecedents is substantial (see Chapter 7). Six characteristics were shown to be associated with each of the problem areas:

1. Early age of initiation.
2. Poor achievement in school and low expectations for achievement.
3. Acting out, truancy, antisocial behavior, and conduct disorders.
4. Low resistance to peer influences.
5. Lack of parental support.
6. Living in a deprived neighborhood.

Other variables that frequently predict multiple problem behaviors include rebelliousness and nonconformity, low religiosity (infrequent attendance at religious services), low socioeconomic status, parental practice of high-risk behaviors, lack of cultural enrichment in the home, segregation in school and community, and poor performance in school. Clearly, there is some redundancy in this analysis (poor school achievement predicts school failure), but this reflects the time sequence of most studies (early failure predicts later failure). Studies that include psychological variables such as self-esteem and locus of control present inconsistent findings with regard to problem behaviors. However, the few studies that have included depression and stress as variables show a consistent relationship to high-risk behavior.[1]

The antecedents of delinquency and of school failure are the most highly correlated. Factors leading to early childbearing and school failure are also highly correlated. The data on substance abuse yield lower correlations with some of the variables of interest. This may reflect shortcomings in the data sets. The national studies of substance use do not elucidate the characteristics of very high-risk youth (for example, they don't include school dropouts). Yet repeated studies of incarcerated youth show that almost all of them were on hard drugs.[2] However, it is important to understand that, while most delinquent youth may be substance abusers, not all substance abusers are delinquents. All sexually active youth are not failing in school. All those behind their modal grade do not engage in precocious sex. In every statistical analysis, we are looking at probabilities that behaviors will co-occur; this probability is never 100 percent.

## Which of These Factors Can Be Changed,
## and What Works to Change These Behaviors?

In Chapter 1, a framework was presented to convey the concept that interventions should be responsive to the factors that put children at risk rather than to the problem behaviors themselves. Table 14.1 shows the most important antecedents matched to the concepts derived from successful prevention programs (Chapter 13). The match between the risk factors and the intervention concepts is striking. For each of the six common antecedents of problem behaviors, there are types of programs that have been proven to change behavior.

Starting from the top of the list of common antecedents of high-risk behavior, we cannot change the age of an individual, but lowering the age at which identification and intervention occur has a striking effect on life trajectories. A strong case has been made for *preschool education* such as Head Start and *enhanced parenting skills* through home-visiting by trained parent educators. Low school achievement and low expectations for schooling were shown to be highly predictive of heightened risk of all problem behaviors. Many models exist that demonstrate the feasibility of changing the effectiveness of schools—for example, *school reorganization, school-based planning, individual tutoring, team teaching, and cooperative learning. Experiential education,* including community service and part-time job placements, has proven effective at upgrading school performance as well as preventing other high-risk behaviors. *Intensive individual attention and support* has been shown to be a requisite for helping children improve performance and succeed. This component is essential as a basic "right" for high-risk children. The consensus among all the fields of research and practice is far-reaching:

TABLE 14.1. Framework for Developing Strategies for Prevention of High-Risk Behavior

| ANTECEDENTS————→ | SUCCESSFUL INTERVENTIONS FOR PREVENTION OF HIGH-RISK BEHAVIORS |
|---|---|
| *Demographic* | |
| Age | Early interventions |
| *Personal* | |
| Expectations for education | School reorganization |
| | Experiential education |
| School grades | Basic skills remediation |
| Conduct, general behavior | Intensive individual attention |
| Peer influence | Personal social skills training |
| Peer use | Engagement of peers in programs |
| *Family* | |
| Parental role, bonding | Involvement of parents or parent surrogates |
| *Community* | |
| Neighborhood quality | Communitywide planning |
| | Provision of comprehensive health, social, and support services in schools and other community agencies |
| School quality | School reorganization |

*every child needs to be attached to a responsible adult who pays attention to that child's individual needs.*

Children can learn how to resist the negative influences of their peers through *social skills training;* these new curricula have demonstrated improvements in social competency and decision making. High-risk youth can gain strength from programs that *engage peers in defined roles*—for example, as tutors for younger students and as classroom instructors. Parents of high-risk children can become more supportive if they are involved in programs that also give the *parents defined roles;* for instance, involving parents as paid classroom aides or as participants on school teams give them real decision-making responsibilities. School reorganization planning requires the participation of parents as well as teachers and administrators.

Neighborhood quality can be addressed through *multicomponent community-wide planning and programming.* Implicit in this approach is the targeting of disadvantaged neighborhoods rather than disadvantaged children whereby social institutions, particularly schools, become the focus of interventions. Increasingly, communities are developing collaborative approaches to provide the range of health, educational, social, and support services that are needed to improve the quality of life in these neighborhoods. This reflects the growing understanding of the concept that there is *no one solution to any of these problems. A package of services is required.* Each community has its own configuration of needs and existing services that must be considered in developing the package. Collaborative arrangements between schools, social agencies, businesses, media, and community-based organizations can facilitate the process.

While our knowledge base on the prevalence of high-risk behavior is far from complete, our understanding of the characteristics of high-risk children and the components of successful prevention programs is surely adequate to use as a framework to develop strategies. How would one go about applying this knowledge to implement changes at the community, state, and federal level?

## The Focus of Strategy

Past experience suggests that changes in youth policy and practice only come about through a lengthy and complicated political process. As pointed out in Chapter 8, many of the programs in youth services are bureaucratic responses to crises, epidemics, and campaigns. It is not within the scope of this study to resolve the debate about whether interventions have to start from the "bottom up" in the community or from the "top down" in the White House. The descriptive material presented about current systems for addressing youth issues leads to the conclusion that changes must take place at every level. It is also clear that changes do not take place overnight; there are no miracle cures for social ills.

Modern American history gives us several instances in which national problems were effectively addressed by the exercise of strong national leadership. Franklin Roosevelt assumed office in 1933 by galvanizing the nation with his assertion that "one third of this nation is ill fed, ill housed and ill clothed." Thus began the

New Deal, an era of federal action on economic and social policy that used the power of central government to put in place the safety nets under the vast army of the unemployed and the poor. The brief Kennedy years opened with the call to "Ask not what your country can do for you. Ask what you can do for your country." We cannot know the full impact of a Kennedy presidency, but he used his pulpit to inspire Americans, particularly the young, to serve national goals rather than personal and parochial ones.

Lyndon Johnson's assumption of the presidency brought a renewed emphasis on national solutions and called attention to the need to eradicate institutionalized racism. The Great Society and the War on Poverty used some of the same rhetoric of the Roosevelt years. The federal poverty program, labeled as "social engineering" by detractors, worked to empower the disadvantaged at the community level so that they could plan and operate programs that would help them to become more self-sufficient.

Since the 1960s, we have seen a growing disenchantment with massive bureaucracies. Despite the efforts by a few legislators and other national figures, there has been little leadership in Washington that could direct new large-scale interventions that would help deprived communities gain a real share in the American dream. Since voters appear to reject the old rhetoric and are much more influenced by "me first" concerns, aspiring politicians avoid any mention of broad social programming and funding for disadvantaged families. Thus, issues that appeal to the middle classes, such as the "drug war" and child care for working mothers, receive most of the attention. Education demands are now being phrased in the rhetoric of "what's good for business."

As mentioned in Chapter 8 with regard to the organization and funding of youth services, more and more responsibility is being shifted to states, especially for that big-ticket item—education. States are gaining more authority through block grant mechanisms that allow them to decide what to fund and where. This situation is exacerbated by the historical "downstate–upstate" conflicts between urban and suburban–rural interests; often large cities with major problems are short-changed in the process. State governors can and do exert a great deal of influence on behalf of their constituents. As we will see, certain states have moved ahead in their commitment to youth-at-risk issues. Yet there is no uniformity in the effectiveness of state governments. The average annual educational expenditures per child is twice as high in the more advantaged states as in the less advantaged states. The same is true for welfare subsidies and Medicaid payments. Although we do not have a grasp of total expenditures for youth in each state, there is clear evidence that the needs of a disadvantaged child in one state will not be met with equal support in another state.

What happens in communities reflects to a certain degree the level of commitment of state and local governments to youth programs. In fact, the organizing principles for developing youth policies are similar at every level. But as exemplified in several of the model programs, there is an additional human element that must be considered. Individuals in communities can have large impacts by articulating problems and solutions, offering leadership, and bringing people together to deal with their own neighborhoods. Even without outside assistance, some communities are able to pull themselves together to reorganize schools, promote recreational and cultural events, fight drugs and crime with neighborhood watch programs, promote "fair" housing, and beautify their streets. However, community leaders and residents can do even more if they have the necessary resources to rebuild their schools and other social institutions, to pay the people who work in them, to refurbish their housing and subsidize rentals or purchases, to create the job opportunities and make sure they are filled.

## Implications at the Community Level

This is such a vast and heterogeneous country that it is admittedly foolhardy to try to generalize.[3] There are, nevertheless, particular common characteristics of communities that impact on the lives of children. Neighborhoods in cities are similar in many ways to small towns in rural areas and villages in suburbia. Every community has public schools. Just about all have churches, usually more than one. Almost every area is covered by a police department and some form of public health and social services, generally under county jurisdiction. Every citizen, theoretically, gets to vote for a local governing body, a mayor and council, or county commissioners. The array of official youth-serving agencies offering local programs is impressive: Scouts, Girls and Boys Clubs, Y's, 4-H Clubs, Lions Clubs, public recreation and cultural programs, among others. Many communities have their own home-grown variety of community-based organizations that take an interest in their own youth: ethnic pride groups, church social groups, fife and drum corps, sports teams, and so on. Today, children in every community are exposed to national network radio and TV and an array of local networks.

On the other hand, there are significant differences between communities because of social stratification and geography. A common attribute of inner-city neighborhoods and rural communities is the dwindling number of social institutions: no local groceries or candy stores or medical facilities or library branches. The only business that is left is the corner bar. Legitimate jobs for youth are hard to find. The economy has gone "underground," where drug selling is the best job going. Gang warfare and homicide, long a hazard of inner-city life, have been further exacerbated by the crack industry. The absence of adequate housing has reached crisis proportions. Inner cities that began to decay years ago have never been rebuilt, and whatever once flourished, is rapidly disappearing. Social agencies have moved out to the malls because they are safer and busier. Poor rural communities, often slighted in these discussions, have always had fewer resources; their population is moving out, and the people left behind have to travel farther and farther to gain access to needed services. Suburban areas, the enclaves of achievers, have many resources for children. Schools in suburban areas are the most heavily supported and financed; failure and dropout rates are consequently lower. But in the suburbs, high-risk children with nonfunctioning parents are often overlooked. They too lack access to cultural and educational enrichment programs and need attention just as the children in poverty areas.

The picture in high-risk neighborhoods is grim. The social conditions here are not conducive to achievement, and children are growing up with no hope of ever getting out. Whatever resources exist are fragmented and uncoordinated. Programs directed toward youth are invariably categorical, not surprising given the funding arrangements (see Chapter 8). Legislatures seem to respond only to crises; one year it's school reform, the next year drugs, and this year it's AIDS. Social agencies tend to protect their turf and their fiefdoms, an operating principle that is a direct consequence of intense competition for funding. As a result, there is little communication between agencies within the same community. And this lack of communication is intensified in rural areas where distance creates barriers to collaboration.

Despite all these problems, in all parts of the country one will find dedicated and committed people, working under difficult conditions with little emotional or fiscal support, gaining few "points" from society. In the most troubled communities, one will find effective parents who are rearing successful children. The goodwill and readiness for change are there waiting to be tapped and organized into a more effective strategy.

## Comprehensive Communitywide Multicomponent Programs

A very strong case can be made for multicomponent programs that address broad objectives. Categorical programs that focus on only one behavior, such as substance abuse, delinquency, or pregnancy prevention, are important, but unless they are linked together into a more rational approach to reach young people, they will continue to have limited effects. The quality of education emerges from this study as the veritable *bottom line*. Early school failure is the *signal event* that predicts almost insurmountable barriers to life's opportunities. Whatever package is put together, the primary institution has to be the local public schools. At the same time, categorical programs that aim only at improving basic skills will not work unless other components such as individual attention and a structured learning environment are included. The package, in a kind of *parallel thrust,* has to encompass both educational services and services that focus on the critical health, social, familial, and cultural needs of high-risk children in poor neighborhoods. What may emerge are school-centered community interventions that link all the necessary components together so that they are both effective and accessible for disadvantaged children and their families. The outcome of implementing these new program approaches may look like new institutions with broader goals and broader governance.

Based on the knowledge gained from the model programs and the experts' opinions summarized in Chapter 13, as well as past experience with community planning and program development,[4] a number of concepts are outlined here that are known to produce changes at the community level and that should help achieve the goal of assisting every child to grow up into a responsible and productive adult.

1. Formal administrative arrangements are required to assure coordination of youth services.

A comprehensive approach to the prevention of high-risk behavior implies that a whole package of services, such as those displayed in Table 14.1, have to be obtainable, but not necessarily under one roof. This concept requires a central administrative structure that makes sure adequate services are in place. To assemble a comprehensive delivery system, existing services may need upgrading or new services added where they are nonexistent, of low quality, or inaccessible.

Many communities already have committees and task forces that bring together agencies to discuss common problems. However, arrangements between agencies tend to fall apart unless agreements are contractual. For reasons already cited, collaboration is an "unnatural act" in an environment where agency hegemony has to be protected. Until recently, school systems operated in an entirely separate environment from other social agencies. Fragmentation of youth services is such that two separate noncommunicating agencies—one for prevention of drug abuse and the other for prevention of alcoholism—may operate in the same community. Even though family-planning programs may see more high-risk teenage clients than many of the other agencies, they are rarely invited to meetings about coordination. A comprehensive system involves the participation of schools, community centers, social service agencies, health agencies, youth-serving agencies, employment programs, and other relevant institutions.

2. A designated lead agency is required to perform organizational functions.

A system for developing a comprehensive youth program requires that a central administrative structure be located in one agency in a community, in an agency that has the strengths required to coordinate the work of other agencies. This lead agency would have to have a broad view of program goals and not be limited in scope to only one or two of the program areas. For example, youth employment agencies have little interest in family planning; family-planning agencies have little experience with school remediation; public health programs do not deal with social supports; and so forth. School systems, while inextricably involved in all of these efforts, are generally not willing to take on large-scale noneducational projects. The lead agency would have to have the confidence of the target community and represent parents, children, and local community organizations, and be acceptable to them.

Few existing agencies meet the lead agency criteria (comprehensiveness, community-based). For this reason, in some communities a new entity would have to be created to serve as a *Youth Development Agency* (YDA), which would be governed by a representative board. A YDA could be freestanding, nonprofit, and voluntary. It could also be connected to an agency such as a community council, a United Way, the Urban League, or an existing social planning agency. It could also be chartered by the mayor or county executive as a public commission, or it could be a unit of government, created by a mayor's office or city council. In some communities, Youth Bureaus were created to coordinate juvenile justice programs.

The purpose of the YDA approach is to enable the development of a multiservice program targeted to assist youth with educational, social, and health problems. This agency would have the capacity to assess needs, plan the necessary package of services, receive funds, allocate funds, provide technical assistance, and monitor compliance. It would be constituted to serve the youth of the community at large, not to promote the interests of any one particular program, and to set priorities objectively on the basis of needs.

3. The framework for a communitywide prevention program is a plan based on the particular needs of the community and the existing service systems.

The first major function for a YDA or any communitywide prevention program is planning. Communities must gain a better understanding of who is at risk of what. As we have seen, many current interventions have little effect because they are not focused on the problems in high-risk communities where the needs are the greatest. The most flagrant example is in the area of substance abuse prevention where millions of dollars are being poured into curricula for suburban schools, while inner-city children using crack are not reached at all. In pregnancy prevention, scarce resources are being used to promote "saying no" to young people who are already sexually active and at high risk of pregnancy and STDs. Few resources are being used for early mental health interventions, least of all in rural areas where mental health needs among adolescents are significant.

As observed in model programs, the program-planning process starts with needs assessment and quantification, even if it produces very crude estimates. Most communities have access to official records on juvenile arrests, drug-related arrests, emergency room visits, school achievement scores, and births to teens. All schools could compute the number of children who are behind modal grade in each class (an excellent surrogate measure for high-risk status since being older than other students is the strongest predictor of school failure, and school failure is a predictor of other problems). In addition, measures of poverty by neighborhood are available from the U.S. Census. Anecdotal accounts from school counselors, youth workers, police, local reporters, and the children themselves can enrich an overall description of what is going on.

The point here is that *putting together the available facts in any community can produce enough information to begin to assign priorities to interventions.*[5] Additional local surveys of the prevalence of substance abuse, low educational expectations, unprotected intercourse, and other risk behaviors may increase reliability of needs assessments. However, individual patterns of behavior do not differ that markedly from one disadvantaged community to another. Although it is a difficult concept for most Americans to accept, *the prevalence of poverty is the overwhelming statistical fact that differentiates the quality of life in the neighborhood.*

In addition to developing estimates of the numbers of high-risk youth and targeting neighborhoods for attention, the planning process requires some understanding of what programs are currently in place. Annual reports, budgets, and existing studies can be compiled. A careful look at the quality of the schools might entail comparisons with state and national standards. Social, health, and other agency programs could be reviewed in detail to determine what they are doing, whom they serve, how they are financed and governed, and their capacities for expansion. An appraisal of unmet needs and service gaps can then be produced, documenting the approximate numbers of high-risk children who are not getting what they need. The job of the planning body is then to identify existing institutions with the capacity to meet the assessed needs of the community, or to document the necessity for new institutions.

4. The planning process should define the package of services required to meet the needs of high-risk children and their families.

Many community groups go through all of the work of gathering data about the needs of high-risk youth, but after the results are compiled, get bogged down in figuring out what to do next. A planning group would systematically address the questions: What are the actions this community must take in order to assure that all children are allowed to grow up into responsible and productive adults? What actions have the highest priority?

The answers are not a mystery. Many ideas were presented in previous chapters about successful programs and summarized in Chapter 13, and there are many sources for ideas about other approaches.[6] The common components of successful prevention programs that have been identified imply a heavy focus on schools. The package of services required in most disadvantaged communities would probably include some form of school reorganization and institutional change. In addition, schools can be the setting for many of the other important components: Head Start and prekindergarten classes, experiential education, social skills training, peer engagement programs, parent involvement, and training programs. We have seen successful models of school-based health clinics and mental health programs, where services are located in schools but are operated by other community agencies. However, in some communities, services may also be needed in community-based settings or in alternative schools for children and their families who feel alienated from the schools.

Finally, based on the findings from this research, the package must include arrangements for attaching a responsible adult to every high-risk child to ensure adequate individual attention. In some programs, this component is called "case management," but that phrase does not adequately express the quality of caring required. Disadvantaged children should not be stigmatized as "cases" that need "treatment." The role of the adult can be compared with a "Sherpa" who will guide the child over the rough spots and run interference against the barriers to personal success, such as an insensitive school system or overwhelming family problems. Existing models show that this component can be implemented through school systems, starting with personal needs assessments conducted at entry to the earliest grades. Some models use teachers as volunteers to act as mentors for small groups or "families" of students. Or a community-based agency could be responsible for recruiting, training, and supervising adult mentors (community aides, social workers, volunteers) and matching them with children, similar to the Big Brothers-Big Sisters approach.

An important emerging program model is the school–community center that encompasses many of the concepts presented here. We have referred to it as the *parallel thrust:* strengthening the educational system so that disadvantaged children can achieve and, at the same time, addressing the major social environmental barriers that otherwise would prevent the children from benefiting from the system. In this model, a whole range of services are co-located in or next to the school, so that the child and the family do not have to shop around for health programs and services, afterschool recreation, intensive counseling, the welfare office, or whatever else they need. The school building remains open afternoons, weekends, and summers. Children know that there is a safe place to go where someone will look out for their interests.

The package of services that fits with a community's needs is the backbone of a comprehensive plan for a communitywide multicomponent program. The community dialogue should lead to the designation of institutional responsibilities and the setting of priorities. The plan should spell out in detail how agencies will interrelate and the formal arrangements needed to enhance collaboration.

5. The community must make a commitment to obtain funding for implementing its plan.

The lack of funds is universally cited as the barrier to creating a system that addresses the needs of high-risk children. It is true that budgets are very tight in every one of the fields reviewed; the only new money in recent years has been appropriated for substance abuse prevention and AIDS education (see Chapter 8). School systems in many communities have to bear the brunt of tax resistance since their budgets are voted on locally. State budgets for education and health are subject to the vagaries of legislatures.

One of the most important functions for a YDA would be to assist with the development and coordination of funding proposals. A community with a documented comprehensive plan might stand a better chance of securing funds from foundations, local and national, than an individual agency. The YDA could also take the responsibility for seeking categorical grants for communitywide projects and distributing the funds to constituent agencies according to the plan. A major function could be facilitating the use of Medicaid within local agencies to subsidize health and counseling services for eligible children. Common management information and accounting systems would greatly enhance the efficiency of many small agencies. New sources of state and federal funds may begin to materialize as the nation becomes more committed to the idea of comprehensive programs for high-risk youth. Increasingly, local businesses are willing to contribute funds or services to communitywide interventions that show promise of improving the quality of the future labor force.

In addition to serving as a fiscal agency, a YDA could be responsible for monitoring agencies to ensure that services are provided; for offering technical assistance and training to constituent agencies; for developing advocacy for youth in the community; and for bringing program results to state and federal legislators to keep up the demand for support.[7]

### Precedents for the Youth Development Agency Model

In the descriptions of categorical program models, a number of exemplary communitywide multicomponent efforts were cited, including Neighborhood Improvement in Philadelphia (prevention of school failure), Impact '88 in Dallas (prevention of teen pregnancy), and Midwestern Prevention Project in Kansas City (prevention of substance abuse). They all include planning, recruitment of leadership from the important local decision makers, broad community involvement, a package of services, and the ability to document impacts on target populations.

Today an increasing number of interventions are being designed and implemented that are aimed simultaneously at multiple behaviors, typically dropout prevention, teen pregnancy prevention, and enhancement of employment opportunities. The Annie E. Casey Foundation's New Futures program has created large-scale demonstration projects in five middle-size cities to test the validity of comprehensive planning and program development that may lead to institutional change.[8] The five selected programs differ, but they all encompass collaborations between schools, employment programs, health and child welfare providers, and local government. Each community was required to designate a lead agency (for one a school district, for another the city commission, the third chose a public authority, and two new nonprofit agencies were formed by the two other programs) to assume the responsibility for planning and administration as well as organizing case-management systems.

Many of the new wave of comprehensive programs for prevention of high-risk behavior are focused on elementary and middle school populations. The Edna McConnell Clark foundation has launched a Middle Grades Initiative that encourages community involvement in the personal and educational development of disadvantaged students. The Institute for Responsive Education has implemented a "Schools Reaching Out" program in two inner-city elementary schools, to increase community and parental involvement by using laboratory schools to pilot approaches that will build up the roster of community resources available in schools.[9] Staff of the on-site parents' center will coordinate the work of paid parent outreach workers in the community and will enlist social and mental health agencies to bring services into the schools. A recent study by the National Center for Education Statistics gives evidence of the increasing numbers of collaborative arrangements between schools and other institutions. According to their figures, 40 percent of public schools participated in partnership agreements in 1988, compared with only 17 percent five years earlier.[10] The study projected that a total of 140,800 agreements were in effect last year in 30,800 public schools—half with businesses, about one-fourth with civic groups, and under 10 percent with either government agencies or colleges and universities.

One community, Indianapolis, is working toward the creation of a mayorally appointed commission responsible for comprehensive coordination of youth services in the metropolitan area.[11] A task force study of youth services determined that there were over 300 organizations and more than a dozen school systems operating in six very separate and fragmented delivery systems: education, employment, health, mental health/social services, juvenile justice, and recreation. No one agency could be identified that could draw all these forces together to organize youth services in a more rational way. A lengthy and "tortuous" community process organized by the local Community Service Council resulted in a proposal for a new body, the Greater Indianapolis Commission on Youth (GICY), composed of representatives from the six service delivery systems, local government, major funding bodies, local experts on youth services, youth advocacy groups, parents, and youth. GICY's major functions will be to develop plans and establish policies regarding the coordination of services; provide a community forum; facilitate training programs; foster interorganizational relationships; and develop new sources of funding and joint funding approaches. The commission will require a full-time staff, funded jointly by the city, United Way, and local foundations. The preliminary planning body recommended that the mayor's office act as the lead agency for implementation. The local city council appears to be divided over the requested initial funding appropriation ($75,000), and commission staff have not yet been hired.

As we will see, several states have taken the initiative in encouraging communities to develop collaborative programs for serving high-risk youth in low-income communities.

## Implications at the State Level

Much of the fragmentation in youth services derives from the way programs are funded. States rely primarily on federal grants to support human services, and their policies for allocation are often determined by federal regulations about eligibility. In the past, states were rarely held up as models for program innovation. People who worked in state health and education departments in the 1960s and 1970s gave the impression that they didn't want to "make waves." Several major federal funding efforts (Community Action Programs, Neighborhood Health Centers, Family Planning Programs, Runaway Centers) were designed specifically to bypass state governments by using the project grant mechanism to get funds directly to communities. Advocates in and out of Congress did not trust state governments to use categorical funds for the designated purpose and, in fact, were fearful that state funds would not get out to the communities most in need.

The "Reagan Revolution" with its "new federalism" has had a large impact on state governments. As the federal role diminished and funding was withdrawn from human services, states began to become much more responsive to the needs of low-income populations. The quality of state government administrators greatly improved, as young people who were interested in public administration and policy were recruited by state agencies. A number of governors have offered outstanding leadership in their commitment to solving the problems of high-risk youth, mostly in the field of educational reform. (Most states define risk status on the basis of educational achievement.) Nevertheless, bureaucracies are slow to change and, in most states, key agencies still do not communicate with each other.

The focus of this book has been on local programs. To gain an overview of states, we now turn to a number of different studies that document that states differ widely in their responses to the problems of high-risk youth. In a recent study prepared for the Charles Stewart Mott Foundation, a research organization (MDC, Inc.) found that about half of the states have recently issued policy statements calling for attention to the educational problems of at-risk youth; yet no single state had an "overarching" policy.[12] MDC estimated that 30 percent of all students were at risk of not receiving an adequate education; yet only 5 percent of state education funds were being used specifically for services to at-risk children. They found no state where the governor had vested responsibility to a single cabinet-level agency or arm of the state government to implement and coordinate the recommendations that were coming out of the large number of investigative commissions and task forces.

The implications at the state level for developing a large-scale initiative to put together a service system capable of helping high-risk children are that a state counterpart to the local Youth Development Agency is necessary. Appointed by the governor, a statewide *Youth Development Commission (YDC)* would be broadly representative of the public and private sectors. To ensure comprehensiveness, the commission would have to be quasi-independent or placed in one agency that would act as the lead (e.g. one agency with the major responsibility). Its goal would be to foster the development of multicomponent communitywide programs that were responsive to local needs. The commission would foster collaborations between schools and other social and health agencies. Moreover, such a commission would need legislative assurance that its tenure would outlast the current gubernatorial term.

To implement its tasks, the YDC would require the commitment by the governor and the state legislature of funds for the statewide initiative on youth development. Additional funds could be put together from state agency budgets; for example, health, education, mental health, labor, "drug money," and juvenile justice funds could be assembled for collaborative demonstration projects. These funds could be distributed to communities through an RFP (Request for Proposals) process. (This involves the issuance by the state-funding agency of a call for proposals with specific goals and criteria; a review committee selects the most responsive proposals for funding.) Just as at the community level, statewide planning would be a high priority for a statewide Youth Development Commission. It could also stimulate community education about the problems of high-risk youth; offer conferences on effective strategies; develop manuals, resource directories, and training programs for practitioners; and set up arrangements for monitoring and evaluation. As effective communitywide models are identified, the YDC could work with communities on replication.

Even without the formal organization of a commission, state agencies could be working together to pool their resources for serving high-risk youth. The departments of education, health, mental health, labor, and justice have many areas of overlap. Less fragmentation of services at the local level would result from better integration at the state level. As we have seen (Chapter 8), statewide voluntary groups and advocacy organizations are very important because they serve as watchdogs to ensure that programs are implemented and budgets renewed. However, few statewide advocacy groups have been identified that cross categorical lines and advocate services for the whole child.

### Precedents for the Youth Development Commission

Few states have been identified with commissions or youth development agencies that have policies, funds, and legislation enabling the crossing of categorical lines of education, social services, and health.[13] Most statewide initiatives are centered on educational policies and program development, but in several states, the initiative has started on the health and human services side. The MDC study asserted that there were four stages in the process that leads to collaborative state programs for school reform in the interest of high-risk children: (1) awareness of the problems of youth at risk; (2) action in the form of plans or policies; (3) consolidation through legislation and funding of comprehensive programs; and (4) implementation of program development, including restructuring of schools and equalization of funding. They identified 14 states that were at least at stage two in regard to school reform (efforts in five of these states are described here).[14] A number of states have Commissions on Children and Youth, but none has been identified that has the authority to integrate educational and support services. Oregon and Massachusetts have developed the most comprehensive initiatives to address the problem of fragmented services. In Wisconsin, a state with few children at risk, the governor is currently attempting to initiate a Children at Risk Program. States with programs initiated by health or human services departments are more likely to focus on direct program services in schools and in the community, such as in Illinois, New Jersey, and New York.

Oregon's governor started his administration in 1987 with a strong commitment to lowering the state's dropout rate from 25 percent to 10 percent by 1992. Two concurrent initiatives have been launched—one directly aimed at dropouts, the other at younger high-risk children. The statewide *Student Retention Initiative (SRI)* brings together resources from federal drug and alcohol programs, dropout prevention, employment and training, the Juvenile Services Commission, and Oregon General Fund dollars for a community grant program administered by the Department of Human Resources.[15] A Youth Coordinating Council with representatives appointed by the governor reviews proposals and advises on awards. SRI planning grants were awarded to 35 core groups in most of Oregon's counties. To receive support, the groups were required to demonstrate that educational, job training, juvenile court services, alcohol and drug programs, and other social agencies were going to work together. State-level SRI staff were available for technical assistance and information on models; for example, they produced a manual, "Low Cost No Cost Models for Preventing Dropout."

A Children's Agenda Office was also created in Oregon for planning services for younger children. The culmination of this community planning process has resulted in a statewide proposal for a Great Start program, including Head Start, parent education, and other services for the age group from infancy to 6 years. In addition to these efforts, an extensive Partnership Program has been implemented in 16 communities. Businesses supply mentors to school systems with a view toward keeping children in school. Also, the Oregon State Health Department funds 12 school-based clinics and has the intention of expanding these services when funds become available.

Oregon is clearly a state that is moving toward a comprehensive approach to solving the problems of high-risk youth. Many state agencies are involved in an intricate pattern that reflects the particular bureaucratic realities in that state. In the 1989 legislature, a bill has been introduced to create the Oregon Youth Services Commission that would pull all the pieces together. The governor would appoint commission members (none of whom would be state employees) as well as representative advisory committees for special projects, including Great Start, juvenile justice services, and the Student Retention Initiative. In addition to making grants available for juvenile services and the SRI, the commission and its advisory committees would be responsible for initiating new grants to counties for Great Start projects, including programs for child care, early childhood education, prenatal and health care, teen pregnancy prevention, child abuse prevention and treatment, and parent education and support. The commission would be charged with evaluating the effectiveness of the various state agencies administering youth services and reporting biennially to the governor and the legislature.

Massachusetts's governor launched the Commonwealth Futures program in 1987 as the principal strategy for dropout prevention.[16] Supported with a line item in the education budget ($1 million a year), 13 communities have been assisted to develop integrated plans for working with high-risk youth and to implement the plans through a coordinated funding process. After receiving technical assistance from state staff, participant communities submit a single application for funds from five different state sources (employment, school reform, dropout prevention, teen pregnancy, and the Commonwealth Futures state appropriation). The state agencies (employment, education, health, and the governor's staff) have to work together to respond to the applications.

The Futures strategy, passed on to communities through workshops, conferences, and on-site training, focuses on the development of interagency community teams, use of case-management and information systems, a combination of advisory boards from categorical programs, and techniques for leveraging coordinated policies and funding.[17]

Wisconsin's governor recommended funding to establish a formal Children at Risk Program.[18] This new initiative involves collaborative demonstration programs co-sponsored by the Department of Public Instruction and the Department of Health and Human Services to integrate social service and school programs designed to address the problems of at-risk children. This initiative builds on the legislated goal of reducing the annual dropout rate (from 3.5 to 2.0 percent by 1992) by adherence to 20 educational standards.[19] By statute, in Wisconsin, each school board must identify children at risk in the district, develop and implement a plan of programs and activities to serve their needs, notify each child in writing of being identified, and on request of the child or parent, enroll the child in the district's at-risk program. Each district has received a grant to implement the plan and to appoint a children-at-risk coordinator. An Education to Employment Program also has been implemented statewide with business partnerships, and state funds are used to support preschool programs and yearround academic assistance to minority students.

Illinois has pioneered the concept of pooling public and private resources at the state level. In 1983, a State of Illinois Teenage Pregnancy Prevention Initiative was launched by Governor Thompson with the creation of the Parents Too Soon (PTS) program. Funds from several state agencies were pooled to develop more than 100 diverse community-based health, educational, and social services programs targeted at high risk 10- to 19-year-olds, either teen parents or young people at risk of pregnancy. The major funding agencies are the Departments of Public Health, Public Aid, and Children and Family Services, with coordination provided by the Department of Public Health. The Departments of Education, Commerce and Community Affairs, Alcoholism and Substance Abuse, Mental Health and Developmental Disabilities, Employment Security, and Services for Crippled Children are involved at the state level in planning and coordination. A major PTS grantee, the Ounce of Prevention Fund, a statewide nonprofit agency jointly created by the Department of Children and Family Services and a private foundation (Pittway Corporation), has also stimulated program development in 40 community agencies for services to teen parents and primary pregnancy prevention, including three school-based health clinics. The Illinois experience demonstrates that it is possible to pool state agency funds and use them to develop comprehensive community-based programs.

Some state initiatives directed toward high-risk youth are centered in one agency. In New Jersey, the Department of Human Services has created the School-Based Youth Services Program to provide adolescents, especially those with problems, the opportunity to complete their education, obtain employment skills, and lead physically and mentally healthy lives.[20] This initiative has led to the development of 29 projects, at least one in every county. The concept is "one stop shopping" to consolidate existing services needed by high-risk youth "under one roof"; 16 of the centers are placed in schools and 13 nearby. The centers are open during and after school, weekends, and summers. All of the centers must provide mental health and family counseling, health and employment services. All do provide information and referral, substance abuse counseling, and recreation. Many provide family planning, child care, transportation, and a 24-hour hotline. The actual mix of services was left up to applicant communities, but each project was required to demonstrate collaboration of the schools with one or more community agencies. Community advisor groups were also obligatory. Funds ($6 million) have been placed in the Human Services budget to fund these centers (which must also demonstrate a 25 percent in-kind contribution to the budget). About half the managing agencies are schools. Medical schools and local agencies, including mental health, health departments, a Private Industrial Council, an Urban League, and a community development organization operate the rest.

New York State also has an extensive School Health Demonstration Project that funds 80 elementary, middle, and high school clinics. The State Department of Health is the lead agency, in cooperation with the Departments of Education and Social Services, but the funds all come out of the Health budget. The New York State Department of Education in conjunction with the State Department of Social Services recently developed a Community Schools Project that will fund 10 demonstration schools.[21] The project is based on the assumption that, in distressed communities, a wide array of social, medical, recreational, and other human services should be brought together to address the diverse needs of children and their families, and that this can best be accomplished through partnerships between school-based and nonschool organizations and individuals (e.g., service providers, parents, business and industry, unions, etc.). Each community school must remain open nights, weekends, and during the summer. New York State also has a Governor's Council on Children and Families charged with coordinating and planning the many diverse initiatives.

## Implications at the Federal Level

What happens in the White House and in Congress has a significant effect on state and local activities. One crucial element is money, and with the exception of education, most of the money needed for youth services flows from Washington on down. These have been lean years for local programs. Neighborhood health and family planning clinics, emergency rooms, drug treatment programs, and afterschool recreation programs are shutting down or cutting back staff and hours from lack of support. Welfare families are expected to get along with less and less subsidy relative to the cost of living. Edward Fiske depicted what happened to education during this era.: "The Reagan Administration, in its efforts to trim domestic spending, went to great lengths to disparage the notions that quality in education is a function of spending and that more Federal aid would assure better schools and a more secure nation."[22]

The Reagan administration did acknowledge the problems of high-risk youth and the interrelationship between problem behaviors. A program was launched in the mid-1980s called "Youth 2000," combining funds from the Department of Labor and the Department of Health and Human Services to promote social and economic self-sufficiency among disadvantaged youth by motivating youth to "believe in themselves." Secretary of Labor Brock asserted that "communication and coordination between agencies which serve the same segment of the population are minimal and often non-existent."[23] In 1987, 16 grants were funded jointly by these two agencies (demonstrating that co-funding is possible). Ten states received support for policy analysis and planning, workshops, and conferences on the needs of high-risk youth. Oregon's Partnership Project and Hawaii's Schools to Work Transition Centers for career and life employment training were also supported under the Youth 2000 program. A number of other grants were made by the Administration for Children, Youth and Families (DHHS) in the name of the Youth 2000 Initiative, for the prevention of substance abuse, assistance for runaways, and other high-risk youth, but these grants did not represent any special new funding. The Youth 2000 effort also stimulated (but did not fund) a number of national organizations to join the movement toward helping youth to become more economically self-sufficient. The National Alliance for Business established the Compact Project, based on the Boston Compact model (see Chapter 12) to develop school-business projects in other communities. ASPIRA, long involved with the problems of Hispanic youth, launched a Public Policy and Leadership Program to foster Latino leadership through training and internships. The National Assembly/National Collaboration for Youth, representing the major youth-serving organizations, developed the Making the Grade program, involving a National Report Card on major youth issues utilized in telecast conferences held in more than 200 cities.

The Youth 2000 Initiative never obtained enough visibility or funding to move beyond the planning stage. It relied heavily on public relations techniques and slogans to try to stimulate states and communities to measure up to goals for the year 2000 that would demonstrate reduced high-risk behavior. As of 1989, in a new administration, the Youth 2000 Initiative appears to be heading toward a phase out at the federal level. However, some states have picked up the funding for the Youth 2000 coordinators appointed during the brief period when federal grants were available.

President George Bush says he wants to be the "education president" and make this into a "kinder and gentler" nation. During his campaign he pledged to increase the Head Start Program, provide monetary awards to National Merit Schools, encourage states to support magnet schools, create a voucher system for child care, redirect family-planning funds toward adoption services, and get tough with crime. The president also proposed the creation of the YES (Youth Entering Service) to America Foundation, a public/private grant venture to stimulate youth community service. President Bush has made a number of speeches encouraging local reforms of education and promoting locally supported strategies for youth services. Few concrete proposals have been forthcoming. It may be too early to judge, but as the Bush administration enters its second year, strong presidential leadership to develop comprehensive services for high-risk children is not yet visible.

What should the federal government do to create a large-scale youth development initiative to prevent high-risk behavior? How could the government help communities and states set up and maintain comprehensive Youth Development Agencies? To specify a more rational structure for coordinated youth services, it may be useful to review the current placement of programs for prevention of high-risk behavior throughout the government (see details in Chapter 8). Delinquency prevention rests entirely in the domain of the Department of Justice. However, services to runaways and homeless youth, many of whom are considered status offenders (e.g., commit acts that are illegal only if performed by a juvenile), are administered by the Youth Bureau of the Administration for Children, Youth and Families of the Office of Human Development Services (DHHS), the same agency that administers Head Start and the Children's Bureau. Substance abuse prevention is supposed to be coordinated by the Office of Substance Abuse Prevention (OSAP) of the Alcohol, Drugs and Mental Health Administration (DHHS). However, the Department of Education is currently administering most of the government's "War on Drugs" through funds for drug prevention curricula in schools and "saying no" media campaigns. The Department of Education is responsible for specialized programs for educationally disadvantaged children, primarily through Chapter 1 funding. (Most funds for public education derive from state and local sources.) Teen pregnancy prevention has virtually no categorical support, except in terms of the services provided to all low-income women through the family-planning program administered out of the currently isolated Office of Population Affairs (DHHS). Other DHHS agencies that fund family-planning clinics, adolescent health clinics in hospitals, and school-based health clinics include the Office of Maternal and Child Health, Medicaid, and Social Services block grants. School sex education programs are not federally funded, but a minimal amount of support is being provided by the Office of Adolescent Pregnancy for abstention education. The Centers for Disease Control (CDC, part of the Public Health Service located in Atlanta) operates a Division of Adolescent and School Health that provides grants for demonstration projects and surveys which cut across prevention behaviors. CDC also has a Division on Sexually Transmitted Diseases that provides funds mostly to states for epidemiological purposes. The Department of Labor supports the major youth-training and employment initiatives.

It is clear that the major categorical youth programs are embedded in different bureaucratic structures. Even those in the Department of Health and Human Services are in separate offices, administrations, and centers. Adding up the 1988 federal expenditures presented in Chapter 8, roughly $9.2 billion were used in programs that had some prevention components geared to high-risk children aged 10 to 17.[24] Of that amount, *80 percent* was under the control of the Department of Education, and 13 percent was used for Head Start (DHHSD). As clearly evidenced, what is left for prevention of delinquency, substance abuse, and teen pregnancy is so minimal, fragmented, and uncoordinated that, as national initiatives, they are showing only marginal impacts. Although the Department of Education has the bulk of the funds that are directed toward the problems of high-risk youth, neither that agency nor any of the others currently appear to have the clout or the inclination to act as the lead agency for youth.

One approach to creating a sharper, more centralized focus on youth might be to create an independent federal agency, a *National Youth Development Administration* (NYDA) to launch a major program to ensure that all American youth would gain the skills and support they need to grow into responsible and productive adults (to make the United States competitive with other nations in its ability to produce effective workers).[25] A precedent for such an agency might be the National Aeronautics and Space Administration (NASA). NASA has its own line-item budget and is not part of any department. The primary purpose of NASA was to rapidly create a space launch and make the United States competitive with other nations in its ability to land on the moon and explore other planets. As with NASA, NYDA would be charged with the challenge of bringing together the technical expertise and the most knowledgeable practitioners to move as quickly as possible toward solutions. As with NASA, Congress would have to indicate its commitment to youths' futures by appropriating money to create the necessary structure for an effective agency. However, categorical funds from agency budgets could be pooled and transferred to NYDA to develop coordinated and comprehensive programs at the state and community levels (e.g., Chapter 1, Head Start, drug prevention and treatment, educational remediation, juvenile justice, child and adolescent health services, mental health services, adolescent family life funds). NYDA could include functions such as creating demonstration projects in communities and states, conducting research and evaluation, and providing technical assistance and training. Having a special administration of this nature would lend an urgency to this cause and give visibility to its leadership.

The concept of NYDA is presented here as a tool for sorting out how the country might respond to its youth crisis, if it really wanted to move rapidly. One could easily quibble with the notion of creating yet another bureaucratic agency to make up for the shortcomings of the multiagency confusion that already exists. One must also recognize that NASA has encountered many organizational problems that should be avoided. One reason for taking this new route, however, is that none of the other existing agencies has the capacities required to impact simultaneously on both the educational system and the support systems that will need to be part of what was described earlier as the *parallel thrust*. No existing entity is in place to lead this kind of collaborative initiative. As we have seen in Chapter 8, the Department of Education has little power to influence state and local operations and, by reputation, limited sensitivity to issues surrounding disadvantaged communities. While many of the federal youth-serving programs are located in the Department of Health and Human Services, they have low visibility within that large agency and have no relationship to the educational reform movements.

Short of designating a lead agency for a national youth development initiative, the federal government can stimulate many kinds of collaborative approaches within the current administrative framework. The Youth 2000 project at least showed that joint funding of youth-at-risk programs is possible. There are precedents for pooling federal agency funds and reorganizing programs to have greater impact; for example, the Office of Substance Abuse Prevention (OSAP) was created out of separate drug and alcohol agencies and co-funds projects with the Departments of Justice and Education. Many of OSAP's 132 community projects are focused on mental health services and counseling for economically disadvantaged high-risk youth. The major federal departments that work with youth (already mentioned) formed an ad hoc committee to oversee the implementation of the Anti-Drug Abuse Act of 1986. Increasingly, federal adminstrators at the program level are acknowledging that it makes no sense to treat ''their'' problem in isolation. For the first time, DHHS is considering as a health objective for the United States the reduction of the number of ''high-risk'' youth, based on the data presented in Chapter 7. Thus, public health officials are promoting the improvement of academic achievement and attachment to school as a strategy for improving health outcomes. The goal of collaboration could be furthered by revising grant guidelines to require the joint participation of schools and other community agencies in youth programs.

Michael Kirst and Bernard Gifford believe that more government help for children will be forthcoming in the future because ''the needs of a burgeoning capitalist economy and the needs of disadvantaged children may coincide.''[26] As they point out, because of federal budget deficits, the current fashion is to talk about low-cost programs and partnerships with business and private agencies. However, this will not pay for expanding Head Start nor will it provide the necessary services that at-risk children need. Kirst and Gifford call for the creation of a national spokesperson for children to address the problems of fragmentation, coordination, and monitoring. One approach might be for the White House to develop a children's policy and coordinate its implementation through the Domestic Policy Council in the Executive Office of the President. Kirst and Gifford would also give federal incentive grants to states and communities that integrate their children's services and use the Education Department to "broker" these services, including alliances with private groups.

Congressional leadership on youth issues is, of course, essential. During recent sessions of Congress, there has been some action on legislation that affect youth. In 1987, a Young Americans Act was introduced (but not passed).[27] This act called for the establishment of a Commission on Children, Youth and Families, which would be advised by a federal council and informed by a White House Conference on young Americans. Block grants would be made available to states to coordinate planning of services to prevent young people from "failing through the cracks" by setting up ombudsman programs to oversee children removed from their homes, in foster care and juvenile correction facilities. More recently, the expansion of Head Start and provision of child care have received a great deal of attention.

Other new initiatives have centered on the issue of youth service. As of the summer of 1989, six bills had been introduced to encourage student participation in volunteer community work. The most comprehensive legislation called for $100 million to support part-time student community service beginning in elementary school through college.[28] This bill promotes the ethic of service as an expected part of the educational experience and requires strong local community links in planning and implementing service. Youth Service America, the major nonprofit advocacy group in the youth service field, supported this legislation but recommended establishing a Trust of the United States as the administrative mechanism rather than relying on the federal and state education bureaucracies. Other bills tie the concept of higher education benefits to youth service, creating a requirement that will place a new burden on low-income youth.

And, as always, there is endless discussion about the crisis in education but few new dollars to support programs. This administration and several governors are very supportive of the concept of "choice," allowing children to cross school district lines within a state in order to attend whatever schools they select (and can gain admission to). They expect that this approach will stimulate school systems to compete for students, raise test scores, and increase the level of community support. To some observers, this appears to be a concept similar to educational vouchers, giving parents coupons to purchase their children's education wherever they want. Concern has been expressed that inadequate schools, as they lose students and funding, will not disappear; they will further deteriorate. Also, transporting children from cities to distant suburbs would create even larger barriers to parental involvement than presently exist.

Almost every major national organization that brings together highly placed officials and representatives of business has produced recommendations about initiatives to alter the course of youth-at-risk, including the National Governor's Association, the Council of Chief State School Officers, the Committee for Economic Development, the National Association of State School Boards, and many others. One of the strongest recommendations (from the Council of Chief State School Officers) calls for legislation that *guarantees* all students a high quality education. According to David Hornbeck (the council's past president), the new legislation must create an *entitlement* accorded to all children to attend a successful school as well as a system of rewards and sanctions that can be applied. This approach relies on the availability of measurable outcomes to determine whether school systems are succeeding or failing.[29]

A National Commission on Children has been appointed that includes representatives from many of these national organizations and Congress, as well as leaders from business and the media. Its mission is to develop a policy agenda "to improve the opportunities for every American child to achieve her or his full potential and to enhance the capabilities of families to care for and nurture their children." This group will report to the president and Congress in the spring of 1990.[30]

## Last Words

If the findings from the four prevention literatures have been interpreted correctly, the strategy for assisting high-risk young people can be constructed on several solid principles: the interrelatedness of problems; the need for early, sustained interventions; the importance of one-on-one intensive attention; and the importance of basic educational skills, social skills, and experiential education for gaining the necessary competencies to function in the adult world. More global concepts shared in common among successful programs focus on broad, comprehensive, communitywide approaches with a heightened focus on schools. Consensus is powerful that attention must be paid to basic school reform and reorganization, alternative ways to retain students in school, and schools as locations for non-educational programs operated by outside agencies.

The prevention strategy that emerges from this analysis is centered in schools for many reasons: educational failure appears to be a significant common marker for many behavioral problems (and it is a problem in itself). Children are located in school, at least nominally, and therefore interventions can be targeted more readily. Community agencies are being allowed to bring their services into schools, especially in needy areas. School administrators increasingly acknowledge their roles as "surrogate parents," a role they are forced to assume if they are to educate children with multiple problems and overburdened parents. Putting all these factors together, the strategy calls for the parallel implementation of school reform and support services. Based on the study of the antecedents of high-risk behaviors, this approach addresses the need for a quality education, so that children can learn, and the provision of various kinds of support—health, intensive counseling, family welfare, cultural and recreational services—so that children can take advantage of the quality education.

These common concepts lend support to the youth-at-risk initiatives that are being promulgated by state and local governments, foundations, and school systems. A number of independent appraisals of the status of high-risk youth in the nation, states, and communities have led to conclusions that are similar to the common concepts from the prevention literatures. The new wave of program grants call for programs to achieve multiple rather than single goals (i.e., dropout prevention, pregnancy prevention, and improvement in job placements).

This is one book that is not going to conclude with the statement that more research is needed before interventions can be initiated. Enough is known about the lives of disadvantaged high-risk youth to mount an intensive campaign to alter the trajectories of these children. Enough has been documented about the inability of fragmented programs to produce the necessary changes to proceed toward more comprehensive and holistic approaches. Enough is known about the inadequacies of the educational system to give the highest priority to school reform. The comprehensive multicomponent framework appears to make sense, linking educational enhancement with social supports of all kinds. Money and commitment are the bottom lines. The funds have to be located and redirected toward a giant rescue operation.[31]

All in all, prevention *practice* is probably way ahead of prevention *research,* especially if school reform efforts are included in the aggregate. An extraordinary amount of energy is being expended at the local level by teachers, counselors, health workers, and other practitioners. These are highly committed people who work for low salaries and under difficult conditions. Since we have the know-how, we should use these energies in more productive ways that will vastly improve the quality of life for young people. Clearly, further work must be undertaken to refine this framework with a view toward integrating research and practice. We can proceed with the research we have, but more focused operational and evaluation research could produce more efficient methods for working with disadvantaged children and families.

There are compelling reasons why our attention should focus on the communities where the highest risk children live. In the growing literature on youth at risk, cost-benefit arguments are usually presented as the rationale for action. The very influential *Children in Need* report of the Committee for Economic Development says it all in the subtitle: *Investment Strategies for the Educationally Disadvantaged.* The message to business is that if you don't invest now in improving the outlook for the "educational underclass" it will cost you more later. The figure cited in that report is $240 billion in lost lifetime earnings and taxes resulting from each year's class of dropouts. A recent *New York Times* headline gives further evidence of the current thinking: "Business Sees Aid to Schools As a Net Gain." There is a growing awareness of the cost-benefits derived from investing in prevention now to save remediation costs later.

Aside from the cost-benefit arguments, it would be much better for this society if it could be moved by a sense of moral obligation to ensure equal opportunity for all its people. The situation calls for a collective revulsion against the despair and alienation in inner cities and the apathy in rural areas that have become the environments for high-risk youth. Of course, disadvantaged children also live in suburban areas, on the social fringes, with less visibility than in urban areas. Any observant person must by now be aware of the plight of children in this country, and the almost impossible conditions in which they are expected to survive. The statistics presented in the earlier chapters should be understood as symbols of this critical problem.

This country and its people have a great capacity to respond to crises and to launch large-scale interventions to rescue the victims of disasters. The time for handwringing about the status of youth has passed and now communities, with support from the states and the nation, have to get down to the hard work of creating a viable system for the future.

## Notes

1. This may reflect differences in the way questions are posed, for example, "How do you feel about yourself?" in comparison with "Do you feel distressed or worried?".
2. A recent report showed that 83% of male arrestees in New York City in 1988 tested positive for cocaine.
3. There are 39,000 local governmental units in the United States; 3,041 are country governments, 19,000 municipal, and 17,000 towns. In 1980, there were 2,205 cities in the U.S. with populations over 10,000. Of these, only 169 (15%) were over 100,000, but they contained more than half of all city dwellers. Bureau of the Census, *Statistical Abstract of the United States, 1987* (Washington, D.C.: 1987), Table 445, p. 266, Table 38, p. 33.
4. The author was Director of Planning and Research at The Alan Guttmacher Institute from 1969–1978 and produced local plans for comprehensive family planning services in 10 metropolitan areas and four rural areas.
5. One local health official described the planning process as useful because it gave people "something tangible to fight about" rather than personalities.
6. In addition to reports cited previously, see Research for Better Schools (RBS), *National Reports on Young Children at Risk* (Philadelphia, undated summary of many reports). RBS also is summarizing national reports on students at risk in middle school and high school. See also AMA National Congress on Adolescent Health, *Adolescent Health: Charting a Course Through Turbulent Waters* (Chicago: American Medical Association, 1988), and other materials which form AMA's Initiative on Adolescent Health. Also D. Both and L. Guardique, eds., *Social Policies for Families: A Review of Selected Reports* (Washington, D.C.: National Academy Press, 1989).
7. See Public/Private Ventures, *A Practitioner's Guide: Strategies, Programs, and Resources for Youth Employability Development*, rev. ed. (Philadelphia: Public/Private Ventures, 1988), 64–88, for an excellent outline of the steps involved in building a coordinated delivery system for youth services.
8. The Annie E. Casey Foundation, *A Strategic Guide for the New Futures Initiative* (Prepared by the Center for the Study of Social Policy, Washington, D.C., July 1987).
9. Institute for Responsive Education, *Schools Reaching Out* (Boston: Institute for Responsive Education, 1989).
10. Study cited in "Education's Partners," *Education Week*, May 10, 1989, 3.
11. Community Service Council of Central Indiana, Inc., *A Model for Comprehensive Coordination of Youth Services in Greater Indianapolis, Vol. I* (Indianapolis, Ind.: Youth Services Project, March 1988).
12. MDC, Inc., *America's Shame, America's Hope: Twelve Million Youth at Risk* (Prepared by MDC, Inc., Chapel Hill, N.C., for the Charles Stewart Mott Foundation, 1988).
13. See E. Rodriguez, P. McQuad, and R. Rosauer, *Communities of Purpose: Promoting Collaboration Through State Actions* (Denver, Colo.: Education Commission of the States, 1988).
14. States listed as moving ahead with school reform that deals with issues related to high-risk youth: California, Connecticut, Florida, Illinois, Maryland, Massachusetts, Min-

nesota, New York, Oregon, Pennsylvania, Rhode Island, Texas, Washington, Wisconsin. MDC, Inc., *America's Shame,* p. 26.

15. State of Oregon, *Governor's Student Retention Initiative: A Report Card* (February 1989).

16. MDC, Inc., *America's Shame,* pp. 47–48.

17. Background information on Commonwealth Futures supplied by Governor's Executive Office, File No. 2540 B, 1989.

18. The amount requested in the Governor's budget for the Children at Risk Program was only $75,000 for 1990 and $150,000 for 1991, with no staff positions.

19. MDC, Inc., *America's Shame,* p. 52.

20. D. Altman, Commissioner, Department of Human Services, New Jersey School-Based Youth Services Program, flyer, undated.

21. University of the State of New York, *Current Education Department Programs Serving At-Risk Children and Youth* (Albany, N.Y.: State Education Department, May 2, 1988).

22. E. Fiske, "Lessons. Education as Investment: Creating a Buzzword to Make the Nation More Competitive," *New York Times,* April 26, 1989, B7.

23. U.S. Department of Labor, News Release, Office of Administration, USDL 86–242, 1986.

24. This estimate does not include youth employment funds or Medicaid and social services. It also does not include Department of Agriculture funds for 4-H Clubs.

25. There are no new ideas! Franklin Roosevelt created the National Youth Administration during the depression as a rescue operation for poverty-stricken youth.

26. Stanford University, *Accelerating the Education of At Risk Students,* Conference Papers, November 17–18, 1988.

27. February 4, 1987, *Congressional Record,* 100th Cong., 1st sess., 13317.

28. The bill was sponsored by Senator Kennedy (S 650). See *Streams,* a monthly publication of Youth Service America, Washington, D.C., for a running account of the development of this concept.

29. MDC, Inc., *America's Shame,* p. 37; David Hornbeck, personal communication, November 20, 1989.

30. National Commission on Children, flyer describing activities made available by Cheryl Hayes, staff director.

31. In a study of the alternative funding policies for meeting the needs of high-risk youth, estimated costs of policies range from 140 million to 20 billion dollars, depending on whether the views are "conservative" or "liberal." The authors portray the conservative approach as relying on state and local demonstration projects, by setting and enforcing behavioral standards through mechanisms such as child support and tough graduation standards. The liberal approach involves large-scale interventions such as preschool, job corps, and Women, Infants and Children (WIC) food programs. See R. Barnes, J. Jeffras, and J. Minarik, "Policies to Help Disadvantaged Children: Financing Options for the 1990s" (Unpublished report, Urban Institute, Washington, D.C., September 1988).

# Index